THEOLOGY MEET

STUDIA SOCIALIA

Published by the Faculty of Social Sciences
of the Gregorian University

1. LEONI, ALDO, *Sociologia e geografia di una Diocesi*, 1952.

2. BELTRÃO, PEDRO, S.J., *Vers une Politique de bien-être familial*, 1957.

3. PELLEGRINI, VINCENTE, S.J., *Algunos Aspectos del Mercado Comun Europeo*, 1960.

4. CARRIER, HERVÉ, S.J., *Psycho-sociologie de l'appartenance religieuse*, troisième édition, 1966; traduit en anglais, en italien, en espagnol.

5. GREMILLION, JOSEPH B., *The Catholic Movement of Employers and Managers*, 1961.

6. GARRET, THOMAS, S.J., *An Introduction to some Ethic Problems of Modern American Advertising*, 1961.

7. *L'Enciclica « Mater et Magistra »: linee generali e problemi particolari*, a cura di TH. MULDER, S.J. e HERVÉ CARRIER, S.J., 1963.

8. CARRIER, HERVÉ, S.J. - PIN, EMILE, S.J., *Sociologie du Christianisme: Bibliographie internationale; / Sociology of Christianity; International Bibliography*, 1964.

9. JARLOT, GEORGES, S.J., *Doctrine pontificale et histoire*. L'enseignement social de Léon XIII, Pie X et Benoît XV vu dans son ambiance historique, 1964.

10. *Theology Meets Progress: Human implications of development*, edited by PHILIP LAND. Authors: ZOLTÁN ALSZEGHY - GERHARD BAUER - JOSÉ DIEZ-ALEGRÍA - MAURIZIO FLICK - JOSEPH FUCHS - PETER HENRICI - TRUTZ RENDTORFF - JOSEPH SHIH - PAOLO TUFARI, 1971.

« TEXTES ET DOCUMENTS »

1. CARRIER, HERVÉ, S.J., *La Vocation: Dynamismes psycho-sociologiques*. Une enquête réalisée en collaboration, 1966.

2. BELTRÃO, PIETRO CALDERAN, S.J., *Analisi della popolazione mondiale*, 1966.

GREGORIAN UNIVERSITY PRESS - ROME 1971

THEOLOGY MEETS PROGRESS

HUMAN IMPLICATIONS OF DEVELOPMENT

Edited by

PHILIP LAND

Zoltán Alszeghy — Gerhard Bauer — José Diez-Alegría
Maurizio Flick — Josef Fuchs — Peter Henrici
Trutz Rendtorff — Joseph Shih — Paolo Tufari

GREGORIAN UNIVERSITY PRESS
ROME 1971

This book by Philip LAND, S. I. (Ed.) *Theology Meets Progress*, was edited and published with ecclesiastical approval by the Gregorian University Press in Rome, 1971.

FOREWORD

Preparations for the Second Development Decade of the United Nations have brought out still more clearly the vast dimension and gnarled complexity of the world development process. The goal of full and integral development of every man and of all peoples calls for a new level of accord among nations and for Herculean strivings to build up new economic, social and political structures for a more just and peaceful international system.

This demands fresh and deepened vision of life and work, of nation and world, of God and man. The Good News of Christ does offer this vision.

But to become incarnate today the Gospel Message must enroot itself in real-life through the disciplines of economics, politics and sociology. These are "the big three" of the social sciences through which the accelerating findings of the exact sciences—physics, chemistry, biology, astronomy—become the technology which is now applied on massive scale to all the human family, for the first time in history and at accelerating pace.

Economics, politics and sociology deal with those human motives and societal structures which pull together coherent combinations of skills and resources, plant and management, and human participation, appropriate for forging the myriad discoveries of the exact sciences into manageable economic and social units.

This troika, begets and implements today's technology and societywide planning, the applied power of science which now transforms the world, physically and culturally, through governmental bureaus, business enterprise, worker, farmer and professional associations, communications, educational and social institutes, and the rest.

In short, the social sciences offer "the flesh" for continuing the Incarnation in the modern world—and continuing the Incarnation is what "Church" is all about. The Word, in turn, offers a vision of man which transcends the flesh of technology, permitting man's liberation from the determinism of a development process which would confine and oppress.

It is therefore most heartening and hopeful that the faculties of the Gregorian University have cooperated in writing this interdisciplinary study. Although the "up there" of theology is its main concern, this volume seeks to relate the "light from above" of revelation with the "down here" of the social sciences. It focuses on a methodology for this reflection, on the how for continuing the Incarnation in contemporary realities.

To heed the call to continue Christ in today's world, freshly set forth by the Second Vatican Council, we Christians must heed the call of the poor of the world, now set forth by the Second Development Decade.

As Secretary of the Pontifical Commission Justice and Peace, I am grateful that the faculties of the Gregorian University are exploring the theological meaning of this call of Christ and the world. If we understand more clearly what we are called to do and why, we might be able to respond with that competency and commitment which world development requires.

JOSEPH GREMILLON

CONTENTS

EDITORIAL NOTE

The reader will find in this book four things treated. First, the description of a complex of phenomena which for the moment we leave loosely designated as « development ». Secondly, the interpretation we humans put upon these phenomena, thus giving rise to ideologies and utopia. Thirdly, the search for that meaning which God's Word attaches to these same phenomena. Fourthly, the need for an adequate methodology for discovering this Word of God—in the context of One and Two.

Essentially the book is this fourth thing—a methodological probe. To achieve our purpose we required and sought light from several directions. Thus results this inter-disciplinary effort, which draws upon the Gregorian University's faculties of social science, philosophy, theology and missiology, as well as upon the Protestant theological faculty of Munich. Roughly one half of the book is contextual material, the other theological reflection.

The opening article by Philip Land begins the attempt to identify the phenomena of development—economic, social, cultural and political. This leads him to the much debated question whether the basic issue is not rather that of liberation; that is, emancipation from unjust and inhibiting social and political structures. He concludes by raising on the basis of his discussion of issues certain questions for theological consideration. Perhaps, the most prominent of these is the question of liberation.

The next three contributions are concerned mainly with the interpretations men have historically given the phenomena of change and development. Peter Henrici analyses the history of the idea of progress, giving special emphasis to the seemingly radical change of attitude toward it on the part of the official Church. To understand this change of attitude, one must, in the author's view, keep in mind the varying interpretations thinkers have given the idea.

Some may be tempted to move directly to the final sections where the author explains why, following on the Second Vatican Council, the official Church has come to take a more positive attitude toward development. But this would be to miss his study of erroneous ideologies and their influence in making the Church suspect all progress.

A short period of Chinese history, 1917-1921, serves Joseph Shih to show how certain Chinese value systems of religion have been used in the one case to support traditional social institutions and in the other to promote their transformation. He ends by suggesting conclusions of a more general character for theological reflection on change.

Ideological linkages appear throughout the volume. These are finally brought together for more systematic treatment by Paolo Tufari in « The Church Between Ideology and Utopia ».

After this contextual presentation comes the theologian's turn. From him today men seek what meaning God's Word can provide for the task of development, humanisation and liberation. To discover this Word turns out to be, unfortunately, not so simple as might at first appear. Zoltan Alszeghy and Maurizio Flick explore first the difficult problem of relating to empirical fact and processes (which, perforce, must be expressed in the technical language of economics and sociology) theological data arrived at by totally different processes of thinking and through different language. The authors are drawn to observe that theological discussion of development up to the present has not always succeeded in avoiding the impression of unwarranted extrapolations. Finally, after giving particular attention to the distinction between ideology and theology they set up lines of an appropriate methodology.

Dr. Trutz Rendtorff considers the ecumenical effort of the Churches making up the World Council to produce a theology of development. His essay embraces the short but important period covered by the conference on Church and

Society, Geneva, 1966 and the General Assembly of Upsala, 1968. Noting that revolution dominated in the earlier consultation whereas the second swung back more to the line of development, the author gives theological reasons for finding the latter more promising.

José-Diez-Alegría treats revolution more systematically. He describes various types of violence and explains the possible need for « qualitative » changes of structures to rectify unjust situations. Attempting an approximative ethic he first structures his norm then tests it in the light of the New Testament and attitude of the Primitive Church.

It is, of course, recognized that different approaches to theology of development are possible and that one's choice depends partly on how one conceives the role of the theologian here. Loosely these approaches may be labeled traditional, existentialist, prophetic and pastoral.

The systematic approach explores the biblical and historical record in search of themes which appear relevant to the problem. The danger that such method become too deductive is noted by Alszeghy-Flick, who insist upon the theologian critically understanding development in its different contexts. Theologians of this approach hope, by setting theological themes in dialectical inter-action, to arrive at a satisfactory statement of God's Word about development.

Parenthetically it should be noted that this volume makes no attempt at such a statement, for this would lie beyond our scope. Still at various points the need of explaining some methodological problem gives rise to weighing the inter-action of certain biblical themes. Take one example. Does the stress some give to the Creation Mandate lead to an optimism unwarranted by the record of progress? Must not all enthusiasm for men's projects of development be judged triumphalistic in the light of the ambiguity and equivocalness of development? If this be so, should not the operative Word of God rather be *metanoia,* the conversion from egoism, greed, oppression?

Still another enthusiasm that gets chilled in the light of experience is that for planning. In a world in which we walk in so much obscurity and ignorance, how do we presume so confidently to be able to project our human future? And what will that be—a straight-line projection of present goals, structures and plans or a fundamental turning upside-down of the present? Given the unsureness of tomorrow, would it not rather be for us to take our halting steps into the darkness, moved by faith and accepting God's judgment, while leaving to the Lordship of Jesus to create the order he chooses for this world?

Ranging still more widely over the whole of revelation taken together with the history of God's People, many more relevant themes are discovered. Eschatology, the Eucharist as efficacious sign of community, the social power of the gifts of the Spirit—to mention only a few others.

If our volume stands more in the traditional approach than in the other three (still to be described) it yet distinguises itself from that by its constant challenge to theological reflection which fails to equip itself with adequate undestanding of processes and projects.

The existentialist approach puts in the foreground the role of the living Christian Community in defining development and posing questions emerging therefrom. Extremists, one recognizes, so « functionalize » the community's contribution as to make this from one epoch and one cultural context to another virtually the creation of a new theology. The Word of God becomes, in effect, the product of the experiencing community. Others, while avoiding this extreme and affirming the historic continuity of the Word of Scripture as well as the legitimacy of past theological language interpretative of the Written Word, are nevertheless convinced that theology of development cannot be reduced to simple adaptation of traditional theological themes to a new problem. Some among them go so far as to add that this approach requires an altogether new language for its communication.

The present authors recognise that the People of God, listening to His Word, have always interpreted it in the light of their human experience. The volume accordingly supports a creative confrontation between the Word of God (as discovered in Scripture and as meditated in the Community of the Faithful) and our historical experiences of change and development.

In any case, one problem remains for the existentialist.

This is what context should be chosen to guide this creative confrontation. That of Latin America? Or that of Asia or of Africa? And, therefore, whose definition of development ought to be adopted? The opening article « What is Development? », says something on this latter question. There, the alternative themes of Liberation and Development are explored. However, the verdict there delivered in favour of « development » (understood, let us be clear, as integral human development and for all men) is not shared by all, as said above. For these latter the language must be that of « Liberation ». We do not here re-open the debate. We want only to acknowledge that more space might have been devoted to this burning question and to say that its adequate exploration awaits wider and fuller intercultural exploration.

Linked to the existentialist approach is the prophetic. This school expresses strong concern that all systematic approaches end in stifling the voice of the Spirit. This may be unfair. But it must be conceded that the working of the Holy Spirit in history has implications for our subject that need to be worked out. This task received some attention in the early days after Vatican II when explorations into the « Signs of the Times » abounded. Socialization, a theme of the encyclicals, was seen to disclose the presence of God. But many other social phenomena, and movements were also recognized as bearers of God's presence. The question here is whether the presence of the Holy Spirit is discernible also in development, and if so where? Does it lie in the voices that call for liberation? If so, in what particular voices, for they don't all give forth the same sound.

Here many methodological questions arise as to who is authorized to speak and how we may discern true prophecy. Since the prophet—individual or community—is exigent in denunciation and in proclamation of the future, we need a theology of obedience to his or their prophetic voice.

Still another theological approach is the pastoral, conceived as preparing Christians for action in a world of change. In part this preparation is seen as a set of guide-lines for action. To the extent it is so understood it will draw (in part) upon the body of thematic dogma with which this volume is partly concerned. But it will also draw upon moral theology for guides to responsible action in the new and uncertain situations of a society undergoing rapid transformation.

In addition some would place here a spirituality for action in-this-world. Motivation for development also would find place here. Above all, a theology of charity suitable to inserting the love of God into the conflicting situations that arise in a world of change and impelling men to seek creative solutions in the form of more just and more humane structures. One principal fruit would be a ministry of reconciliation exercised by Christians, even while recognizing that social good, at times, will arise only from social conflict. Finally, it would nourish a new innerness suited to living in modern society.

The contribution of Josef Fuchs finds its place in this approach. According to the author, traditional moral theology did not provide much room for the positive value of human progress (development). But now—and here is his special contribution—it must be made clear that there exists not only an ethical mission to work for progress, but that in terrestrial (and inter-human) relations the will to seek progress constitutes the very criterion of ethics. Progress here must of course be understood as « human » and as embracing the whole of reality. Dr. Rendtorff also dwells at length on motivation for development. This perhaps reflects his experience within the non-Roman Catholic traditions of tendencies either to fly altogether from active engagement in the secular or to throw excessive emphasis on to theocentric spirituality and inwardness; or finally to turn service exclusively into witness and developmental sacrifice into purification to make the Church a holier witness.

Space permitting a fourth approach might be noted—that of ecclesiological reflection. For development also raises the question whether Church structures, including Church power, are helps or hindrances to development. These and many allied questions are only now beginning to be properly posed.

The bibliography, the work of Gerhard Bauer, student of theology at the Gregorian University, is a selective and systematic listing of several hundreds of titles in various languages covering all aspects of the problem of development.

ACKNOWLEDGEMENTS

To Msgr. Joseph Gremillion, Secretary of the Pontifical Commission Justice and Peace, we express our deep gratitude for his encouragement and help in this inter-disciplinary effort.

Other acknowledgments are in order. We appreciate the work of those who helped prepare the translations: Ernst Sands, Graham Dann, Sr. Mary Monica Wagner, Angel de Ojanguren.

We should like, finally, to acknowledge the very generous cooperation of the Directors of the Press of the Gregorian University, who showed us only understanding in the many publication problems that arose.

An exploratory probing into a suitable methodology for a theology of development was conducted recently by the joint committee of the Pontifical Commission Justice and Peace and the World Council of Churches for Society. Development and Peace (SODEPAX). Several authors of this present volume participated in that inter-faith and pluricultural effort. The report has just appeared under the title In Search of a Theology of Development (Papers and Comments on a Consultation on theology of development. Cartigny, 1969). A volume of bibliography, Toward a Theology of Development; An Annotated Bibliography compiled by Rev. Gerhard Bauer, accompanies it.

PHILIP LAND, s. j.

SOCIAL AND ECONOMIC PROCESSES
OF DEVELOPMENT

One principal theme of this book holds that theological reflection about development must be made with full understanding of what development really is in itself, and as experienced at a particular moment of history. Does this mean that a theologian virtually devoid of knowledge about development is altogether incapable of reflecting fruitfully on the subject? Obviously not. Substantial theological writings of this type have appeared. How this can be so we leave to others in this volume to say.

But it is just as undeniable that such writings will have their limitations. Perforce they will be large on generalities; and treat development only as a particular case somehow falling as an application within universal principles of Christian action.

In a word, the theologian who pretends to address the Word of God to the *specific* thing called development must go beyond generalities about action-in-this-world. Nor may he content himself with proceeding notionally, that is from a conception devoid of historical content and significance.

But where is he to find this content? Here the sociologists disappoint him. For these themselves are not in agreement. In the first place, there is wide disagreement about the facts of under-development and what explains them. Disagreement here is a matter of social and economical analysis. But it is also to a surprising degree cultural. And when we pass from the level of fact and analysis of processes to that of *design* of development, the cultural element becomes only more em-

1

phatic. Here one would have to come to grips with the force of culture and linguistics in the fashioning of different ideologies and utopias of development; the technologist's optimistic ideology of the inevitability of unequivocable economic progress; the Marxist's utopia of social processes centrally guided and controlled in the democratic society; the radical utopia of revolutionary change, and still others.

This essay does not pretend to untangle all these strands. It limits itself to exposition of the processes. As far as possible it leaves to others to discuss the ideological question. Nevertheless, the latter question cannot easily be separated from that of identifying processes, so we shall therefore be forced to enter into some ideological issues.

In Part I we shall discuss processes and designs (or projects) of development. Part II may be considered a short excursus, the purpose of which is to integrate into our discussion of development designs the definition provided by *Populorum Progressio*. Our Third Part focuses upon specific questions requiring further theological reflection.

Since Part I is rather complex it might be well to draw up a floor plan of it. It embraces the following eleven sections

1. *Agreement on what development is*. We begin with where we are, that is with today's growing agreement about what development means. 2. *A narrowly-economic view*. Here we turn back to see how we arrived at this point, passing through the stages of a narrowly economic understanding of development. This leads to 3. *The narrow view challenged*. Here is reviewed the challenge which forced attention to 4. *The non-economic factors in economic growth*. Since agriculture is so important for development, and change in this sector poses so many problems for moral and theological reflection, one section, 5. *Social change and agriculture*, is devoted to this question.

But all of this description of socio-economic development is within a model of gradual and cumulative but irresistible growth. The validity of such a model, at least as generalized, is in considerable measure questioned widely, especially in the developing countries themselves. We agree with this challenge.

2

Accordingly, we conclude Part I with a consideration of these challenges.

This discussion is introduced in 6. *Some economic discontinuities,* by first noting that many economists themselves believe that, so far as the developing world is concerned, *even as a matter of simple economics* a model of discontinuity and rupture is more realistic than one of gradual incremental growth. This leads us to consider in 7. *Power barriers,* certain questions of economic domination as barrier to progress, here using African experience as an illustration. In 8. *Foreign investment and Latin America,* and 9. *International trade,* other charges of power barriers are explored. This leads inevitably to 10. *The revolutionary hypothesis.* Part I closes on a note — 11. *Planning for development.*

I. AGREEMENT ON WHAT DEVELOPMENT IS

What is development — as men understand it? — as a design to be realized in the secular city — as a hope for men here in *this life*?

The word — used to describe a human design or project — is of very recent origin. It has in fact its beginnings in the post-war concern for the fate of the poorer nations. It is contemporaneous with the United Nations' shift from exclusively political concerns to greater emphasis on the challenge of poverty in the world.

Originally its accent was economic — though never purely so. And most certainly it was never so purely economic as its synonym "growth" suggests. "Growth" signifies that built-in capacity of the economic systems of the industrial countries to register regular annual increases of goods and services.

By contrast "development" was reserved to designate those fundamental changes — mostly but never exclusively economic — required to put a backward economy on to the road toward built-in, self-sustained economic growth.

As understanding of the implications of development grew, and as the Third World began to enter into the development

3

debate, pressure mounted to give the word development a far richer content than was initially contemplated.

For the humanist it will be the humanization of men in the fullest sense and in a global vision. That men will live in peace and brotherhood, with justice and respect for the rights of all. That they will share mutually the benefits of their diverse cultures. That the arts and sciences will flourish. Men, in short, must be dedicated to creating the New Man and to making his planet a home suited to full human fulfillment.

For the Christian humanist, development will mean even more than making of this world a livable place with decent human conditions, a fair sharing of riches, and freedom and opportunity for all. In a deeper sense humanisation will not be completed until the cosmos itself becomes man's, subject to his domination, stamped in his image. For, man's vocation (we have the authority of Genesis for it) embraces the transforming of this world. Genesis 9, 2-3. Man is called to be the cosmos' saviour. Through his spirit man must give form to the world and to its forces. Through himself, he must rationalize and spiritualize his world. As priest of the world, man stands at the altar of the universe to offer creation, through Jesus the Recapitulator of all things, back to God, its Creator. Through man, in Teilhard de Chardin's eloquent expression, the cosmos finds spiritual unity with the Omega.

But if we identify development with this total process of development, are we not in danger of forcing the word to carry too much weight? Are we not at least in danger of losing sight of that *economic* development which, as we noted in the introduction, was the problem that in the immediate post-war period caused men to become concerned?

The encyclical "Populorum Progressio", while rich in general reflections on progress in the larger sense just explained, focuses principally on development as it presents itself to two-thirds of humanity.

For these, development is something much more mundane and terrestrial. It is the transition from misery, want, disease, illiteracy to decent conditions of life. It is nourishing

4

food for one's children, decent clothing, protection against debilitating diseases, a roof over one's head.

Needless to say, the poor of the world share with the humanist the desire for humanisation in its still fuller sense. But priority must fall upon the material basis of human existence. In starkest terms one asks whether the world can feed its future billions. That this emphasis is not misplaced was the view of Mahatma Ghandi, who insisted that for the starving, God appears in the form of a piece of bread.

A Narrowly Economic View

Development, as the specific problem of whether the emerging nations can be freed from economic stagnation or inadequate development and hope one day to create economies capable of satisfying the ever growing demand of their bounding populations, was only posed toward the end of World War II.

The first postwar attempts to sketch a theory of development were narrowly economic. Economist reduced the problem to that of responding to needs through increased capital and higher efficiency in the use of this capital. (This economic solution was generally accompanied by a demographic solution, that of reducing the numbers to be fed.)

Development, accordingly, was measured in terms of a nation's gross national product. By this is meant the total of goods and services which a nation produces in a working year. For purpose of computing (and comparing) only priced goods get counted.

Apart from other limitations of such a measuring-stick, crude money measure tends to make the efforts of the developing nations look worse, in comparison with the riches nations' success, than they really are.

It must always be kept in mind that the South experienced an average growth rate of 4,5%. This is higher (though not on a per-head basis) than the North now, and higher than the North in its earlier decades of "take-off".

Still another inconvenience in money estimates of income occurs when comparisons are instituted on a *per capita basis*. Such tend to make the productive effort of the

5

rich North [1] (with its low birth rates) look much better than it really is in comparison with the productive effort of the South.

Finally, crude production statistics say nothing about institutional changes taking place, the effect of which will show up later on in higher production. Thus, much of the developing nation's effort may have gone into improving schools, education of farmers, into roads and transportation, into restructuring governmental bureaucracy. Failure to take into account these changes gives an inadequate accounting of the nation's full productive effort.

The Narrow View Challenged

A decade had to pass before economists themselves, along with other social scientists, began to challenge this narrowly economic definition of development. The first attack was to question whether it was necessarily true that if a nation in one year turned out more goods than the preceding year it had thereby shown economic progress. One now asked further pertinent questions about the kind and quality of what was produced.

If, for instance, the year's production only makes the the rich richer, without any improvement in the condition of the masses, in what sense is it development? Clearly, distribution needed to be included alongside production. Accordingly, it was not paradoxical to say that a society with lower national output might be more developed than one with a higher. To judge, one would first ask which of the two produced the more desirable combination of goods and services: of needed food, clothing, housing, education, sanitation, health, transport, and communication for the people as a whole. The opportunity for men to gain their living through work, and not as a charity, was also seen to pose a challenge to any simple arithmetic measurement of development. Two nations might have the same output. If the processes used in one provided more job opportunities, its

---

[1] "North" encompasses Nort America, Russia, Japan. "South" takes in Africa, Asia and Latin America. This shorthand will appear often throughout this essay.

performance surely must be recognized as superior and that, even though it used a less modern technology.

A second area of challenge came in the explanation of higher productivity. Emphasis here shifted from material resources and physical capital to *human capital,* that is, to the nation's social and cultural patrimony. One now asked more about the quality of the labor-force and less about its quantity. "Functional education" received recognition as a fundamental basis of development. National campaigns against illiteracy and education toward humanisation, toward *conscientisation,* were called for.

The third challenge lay in the area of developmental processes. Here one asked whether yearly advances in production could be counted true development if in the process of production there resulted undue human costs and deterioration in the worker. With the encyclical, *"Mater et Magistra"* it was recognized that men must be the subjects, and not the objects, of the economic system.

What troubled sociologists was the impact of technology, industrialization, and urbanization on workers whose work had previously been carried out through processes permitting more control by the individual in the intimacy of the family farm or family business and not in the depersonalizing atmosphere of the factory in urban conglomerates. Still another challenge was made to maximum economic efficiency as a unique norm of development. This came from those who were concerned about their political institutions. They argued that it was perfectly rational to be prepared to abandon an economically productive economic system in favor of one that produced a more humane, if poorer, society. The repudiation of Capitalism by youth of the West is only one manifestation of this challenge.

By the 1960s "development" had become generally equated with human and social advancement.

Non-Economic Factors in Economic Growth

If "theory of development" thus progressed through the decade of the sixties in its norms for estimating a nation's productive effort, it made progress in still other directions.

7

Most notably, in understanding the processes by which a nation's economy develops.

Analysis of undervelopment on a broader interdisciplinary front spread understanding that development could not be presented in such purely economic variables as increase of capital and higher efficiency in the use of that capital. No one, of course, was prepared to underestimate the importance of these and other economic factors.

For it remains true that economic development cannot be achieved without capital effectively invested. This capital investment takes the form of plant structures, machine equipment and servicing, and specialized services to enterprise. It includes an infrastructure of roads, harbors, transport systems, means of communications through postal service, wire and telephone. Technology in still other forms must exist to render more efficient man's work on his material resources.

With productive effort mostly centered, at first, in agriculture, incentives must be created for the farmer if he is to produce more. He must have markets organized in which to sell his surplus and to buy what he needs.

Organization of a market-system will, as light manufacturing and then industry make their appearance, become still more indispensable.

But the importance of economic factors once acknowledged, the conviction gained ground that still more important were the non-economic factors. First was what came to be known as human capital. To use effectively what little physical capital a poor nation has at its disposal it needs a host of skills: from artisans and craftsmen to mechanics and repairmen, from typists and clerks to bookkeepers and office-administrators. It needs shop foremen and plant superintendents. All this adds up to an immense educational effort.

Moreover, the work of all these skilled people has to be organized. This calls for still another scarce human factor, administrative capacity and entrepreneurship. But even where such managerial capacities are found available, their productive potential may never be activated if the social system resists change and opposes rationalized work. One single illustration may serve to show what this means. Pre-industrial societies tend to be based on personal status. This means that jobs are assigned on a basis of who one is. One does not ask who is most efficient for a particular post. An industrial society, by contrast, builds on the rational criterion of what one can do. In principle, jobs are assigned to those most capable of carrying them out.

In this light one begins to understand the description of the development process given by one of the best known leaders of the Third World, Kenneth Kaunda, President of Zambia. Speaking before the General Assembly of the World Council of Churches at Uppsala, July 1968, he said: "The process of development implies a total transformation. It involves in developing countries the shedding of traditional values, beliefs, and indeed, behaviour relative to membership of traditional organizations or socio-economic and political groups." At the same time, he added: "It involves the birth of new values and beliefs in relation to life and new institutions which give expression to new ideas and principles."

In only more sophisticated terminology the eminent Swedish authority, Gunnar Myrdal,[2] defines development as an upward movement in a nation's economic, social and political institutions. Myrdal gives us a list of factors that together constitute the social system of development. Of these three are economic; output and income; conditions of production; and levels of living. And three are non-economic: attitudes toward work and life; institutions, and national policies. Which are more important? The non-economic, he maintains, for "it is the lack of right attitudes that slows down the circular causality which leads to progress."

Social Change and Agriculture

A look at the sectors of a growing economy reveals still other areas in which the non-economic factors prove more important than the economic. Take first agriculture. All

------

[2] *Asian Drama, An Inquiry into the Poverty of Nations.* Three vol., New York (The Twentieth Century Fund) 1968, prologue, passim.

9

now agree that first priority must be given to it. The reasons for this have never been stated more succinctly than in the Beirut Report [3] and we shall avail ourselves of it.

"Since agriculture is the largest economic activity in all developing countries, its problems are central to progress. Moreover, improving social condition in the rural sector also deserve high priority. Often there is an almost complete lack of education, health facilities, rural electrification and other requirements of human living. Society generally remains stratified; most people have extremely low incomes and outside harvest-time, are grossly underemployed.
Agricultural production barely keeps pace with population increase. Inequality of income causes the consequent hardship to fall heavily upon the poorest. Sustained efforts will be needed to avoid disaster.
But backward agriculture affects the whole economy in many ways. By keeping income down, it limits purchasing power for other services and products. It provides inadequate supplies of raw materials to industry and to income earning exports. Necessary food imports diverts foreign exchange from the purchase of capital goods."

What strikes us in this brief summary of agricultural development is the amount of human and social change it entails. Above all, there is the educative effort to change farmers from tillers of the soil into farm-managers. Host of new skills must be learned. From the use of select seed and irrigation to storing and marketing the final product. But these innovations often entail abrupt departures from traditional ways of producing and tend to be strongly resisted.

Land reform is called for. But the propertied classes have widely succeeded in killing legislation destined to achieve the land redistribution, tax reforms and farm benefits which must be effected to create the necessary incentives for more efficient farming.

------

[3] *World Development, the Challenge to the Churches.* Report of the Conference on World Cooperation for Development, jointly sponsored by the World Council of Churches and the Pontifical Commission Justice and Peace, Beirut, April 1968, p. 28.

If we were to sketch similarly the process by which industry makes its first appearance and then expands, it would reveal, just as agriculture, the prime importance of the non-economic factors. In some measure we have already noted this when speaking of human capital. But the same is revealed if we consider the obstacles to development that archaic and inadequate social and political structures create. Societies, whose ruling classes are agrarian based, will not take easily to changes which they see as a threat to their very existence. Small craftsmen inevitably resist larger factory enterprises. Government burocrats may load onto business managers unwanted political appointees, and through red tape slow down the drive to efficiency. Unwise money management and unrealistic social welfare policies can bring on an inflation which may induce savers to transfer their money abroad instead of investing locally.

These are only a few of the many illustrations that might be made of our analysis up to this point. From it stands out starkly that the non-economic is more vital to economic progress than the economic. The barriers to socioeconomic development indeed appear formidable. For to repeat once again, it is essentially man that must be re-made if progress is to be achieved.

II. DISCONTINUITIES AND PROGRESS

Another feature of development is its *discontinuity*. This we shall first look at in a few of its more narrowly economic manifestations, then in the wider, and more controversial, context of certain *continuities*, especially of power, that must, it is believed, be *dis-continued* if a country is to progress.

During the post-war decade and up to the sixties neoliberal economists remained obstinately assured that what accounts for economic growth in the already developed world adequately explains the processes of economic development in the under-developed. Their development model was one of gradual increase in three or four economic factors (which were assumed already operative, if inefficiently and insufficiently.) So it was enough to add a bit more capital, encourage a steady flow of inventions and other innovations, provide for regular growth of the labor force (gradually endowed with improved professional capacity). In the literature this became known as "marginalism." On a graph it took the shape of an unbroken rectilinear curve.

Few economists today accept this over-simplified model. First, because, as already seen above, they have returned to recognize with Adam Smith and the rest of the Classical school that development is a question of upward movement in *the whole socio-cultural system*. Secondly, because economic growth itself is now recognized to be, at least in its earlier stages, not equilibrium growth along a homogenous rectilinear curve, but *discontinuous* movement. Models of change, not equilibrium patterns, are desired.

Some Economic Discontinuities

Let us consider briefly a few economic discontinuities. The first discontinuity is *sectoral*. At the lowest stages of economic growth agriculture absorbs 75% or more of the work force. (Hunting, fishing or pastoral activity fit this basic pattern.) At higher stages, manufacturing and still later industry, will move into first place, absorbing from a by now modernizing agriculture a large part of its displaced workforce. Finally, growing prosperity will manifest itself in the advance of the so-called tertiary or service industries. Another notable discontinuity is the rise and decline of particular industries. In the USA not a single leading industry of 50 years ago is still prominent.

These examples of discontinuity (there are others, socio-cultural as well as economic) will serve to introduce more generally the role of change — abrupt and discontinuous — in the process of socio-economic and cultural development. More concretely, we shall be concerned here with the role of power in *thwarting* the development processes. (Power, of course, can likewise promote development.)

Power Barriers

Widely through the South (Africa, Latin America and Asia) the conviction holds that development cannot take place until the power barriers supporting the status quo or establishment can be overthrown. Here the *creativity of discontinuity* will take the form of radical change. Until this happens the economic discourse of this essay will remain, in the eyes of the South, an idle, irrelevant exercise.

Let us see first how Africa typifies what is encountered widely throughout the South. Then we shall add what is peculiar to a Latin American view of its situation.

Widely in the South subsistence farming (as opposed to selling for a market) once provided adequately for the limited needs of a simple life within tribe or extended-family. At the same time, social system of tribe or extended-family managed to provide all, young and old, with work, security, and a place (or status) in the social structure.

Into this idyllic scene the colonial and neo-colonial powers broke, taking over the people's resources and labor force, forcing them into paths that served the coloniser's enterprises and not the people's. The masses were reduced to passive instruments in mine or plantation work for export. What forces of energy and progress did exist were thus stifled. The economy — apart from the export sector — stagnated.[4] In the process the social structure of the traditional society became undermined. It is true, of course, that subsistence farming with archaic methods, and the tribal and extended-family social system would in any case have had to give way in favour of modernisation. The single fact of the wiping out of malaria made this imperative. For with the ending of malaria, death rates fell at a vertiginous rate. Dramatic drops in deaths without any corresponding reduction of birth has produced *rates* of population growth that no developing nation can possibly cope with.

---

[4] This stagnation thesis is at least partly invalidated by the fact that the average rate of economic growth in the developing countries over the last 10 years has been 5 or 5,5%. This is higher than present growth rates in the USA and considerably higher than the growth rates of the North, in general, during its early decades of growth.

But even those parts of the colonialized world on the brink of a real break-through into vigorous exchange (or commercial) activity found themselves thwarted, for the colonialist would sanction no competition in markets it had reserved for its own home industries. The most notorious case perhaps is that of textile manufacturers. India's flourishing hand textile industry never got a chance to modernise because Great Britain wanted that country as exclusive market for the cotton goods of Manchester. [5]

But this "rational allocation of resources" was frustrated [6] by forcing resources and labor into distorting monoculture or mining enterprises that brought little social net return to the colonized people. Ports, roads, railroads, housing, towns — all were built up exclusively to serve the export sector.

Lastly, (though our list of alleged distortions could be lengthened), there is the charge that the colonial power taxed away income which, properly invested, might have laid the foundation for the education, transportation, modernisations and diversification that would have prepared for a "take-off [6]

Foreign Investment and Latin America

The preceding description of the negative role that power can play in the development process needs only moderate adaptation to become applicable to other areas of the South rather than just Africa. Take Latin America. That continent had already ousted its colonial masters at the very time in the 19th Century when the colonization of Africa was ad-

---

[5] The various dislocations forced upon budding economies are described in an abundant literature of *désarticulation*. See e. g. François Perroux *L'Economie des Jeunes Nations* Paris (PUF) 1942.

[6] It might be countered that once rapid population growth made modernisation imperative, the tribal authorities fighting to preserve an outworn social system (basis of their power) also represented a force thwarting progress. Undeniably so. But this in no way reduces the responsibility of the colonizers who could have promoted needed change but were concerned only to promote their own interests.

14

vancing. Hence its point of reference was no longer the distortions imposed by colonists upon a pristine tribal system.

But (in the Latin American view) the ousted colonizers only gave way to a new colonial class in the guise of foreign investors, supported by the power of their governments and abetted by pliant indigenous power interests content to receive a share in the continued exploitation of the continent's patrimony.

At first the new foreign investor was able to set himself up as virtual master of a nation as in the notorious case of United Fruit. Where he so succeeded, the pattern of exploitation that followed was not unlike that described above.

Where the foreign investor was not able to exploit with absolute freedom his monopoly power of exploitation, his distorting influence nevertheless remained, according to this view, a salient fact of life. The economics of several Latin American countries continued to be dangerously tied to mono-culture for export or to the mining of a metal or petroleum exclusively. Resources, including scarce abilities and managerial capacity, were then drawn off into industries which do not necessarily have significant overflow into other sectors.

To support its investments the foreign investors allied themselves with the dominant indigenous power structure. This meant the few propertied people, local business interests and the military that together constitute the top of the social pyramid, at whose base lay the masses — rural and urban — an alienated proletariat. (To give the impression that no middle class or skilled workers existed or exist would be exaggeration. But only exaggeration.)

Where the foreign investment represented a fairly high percentage of total productive assets, its power to influence national legislatures in directions favorable to its interests was obvious. This was (and continues to be) especially true where the foreign investor's own government was prepared to interfere as need arose either openly through military power or more subtly through the threat to reduce aid or to cease its purchases.

All this alleged foreign distortion of the economy and support of oppressive social and political structures was only

15

enhanced where the foreign investor's government supported the established powers — including military dictatorship — in the supposition that they assured freedom from Communism and protection of US investments and markets. One final charge is that overseas investors remand to their own country excessive profits or arbitrarily withdraw the investment itself.

It is not our task here to say to what degree all these changes can be sustained. That they are exaggerated or even badly analysed has often been the case. [7]

International Trade

International trade is confidently presumed in the North to be a powerful instrument of development. It astonishes and pains the North Atlantic to discover that the South (Latin America only more decidedly than the others) regards trade as a principal barrier to their liberation and development.

In fact the historical record shows that trade did promote development among Western nations, and in theory — a carefully formulated theory — it might achieve the same for the South. As the North in its over-simplified model saw it, 1) as economic activity rises in the industrial nations these demand more raw materials from the developing nations, thereby increasing the latter's income and capacity to import modern technology. 2) At the same time labor costs rise in the industrial nations as full employment approaches. The presumed result is to make attractive a shift in investment to the non-industrial nations where labor costs are presumed lower. This transfer of investment brings an increase in the manufacturing sector in the hitherto exclusively agricultural economy. In short, by allowing men, materials, goods and investments to flow freely according to supply and demand, world prices of labor and capital tend to become equal and the world including the South gains.

---

[7] A classic example of weak analysis and exaggeration is Claude Julien, *L'Empire American* Paris (Ed. Grasset) 1968. For an incisive demonstration of its weakness see J. M. Domenach and others in: *Esprit,* Avril 1969.

Not many economists even of the North remain confident about the automatic flow of these supposed benefits. Their reasons are several.

First, capital goes where capital already is. This is understandable; for the investor will seek a location where he can be assured of skilled labor, services, and markets.

Secondly, the long-run prospects for agriculture are not thought to be bright — despite population growth. There is the fact that it is at least questionable that growing industry brings greatly increased demand for raw materials. This is due to several things. First the technically more efficient use of raw materials which thereby reduces demand for them. Secondly their substitution by a growing number of synthetics; thirdly as income increases in the developing nations themselves, they tend to spend more, not on their own products (tea, bananas, coffee) but on industrial products, transistor radios, watches, bicycles and so forth.

The final reason why economists are not impressed by the belief in the automatic flow of benefits from trade is that it can turn out to be in the long run in the interest of a country to sacrifice short-run trade gains. Stemming the flow of imports behind a wall of production, local industries can be started up. In the short-run, admittedly, domestically produced goods will be more costly and of poorer quality than imported. But with experience, costs of labor, management and marketing can be reduced and production become competitive. Thus the "natural advantage," according to which they were destined to remain forever agricultural producers can be changed.

Nothing in these qualifications negates the case for beneficial results from foreign trade. They only warn that we must study more rigorously the conditions under which benefits can be supposed, while giving due recognition to the possible advantages of protectionism. But this is not the place to attempt a thorough-going analysis of this important topic.

One thing, however, must be added. This is that however refined trade theory be, the developing countries are persuaded that commerce under any circumstances gives them the short end of the stick. In particular they point to the so-

17

2

called deteriorating terms of trade. As they see it, the fact that over recent years agricultural prices have been falling while industrial prices were rising must somehow find its explanation in the power of the industrial nations to manipulate markets.

Precisely how world prices of coffee, cocoa, cotton, are manipulated is never explained. Economists would point to overwhelming evidence that world demand and supply, and not domination, account for these prices being where they are. This would suggest to them the need for food and raw material suppliers to recognize that they are over-producing and therefore must diversify.

Still, behind demand (as well as supply) there may be some power to influence markets. One example is the support Northern countries give their own very high-cost beet-sugar producers. Without high tariffs to artificially lift the price that imported cane can be sold at, their own beet-sugar could not be marketed. Agricultural protection, as practised by the industrial nations, constitutes one power structure with built-in injustice.

The Revolutionary Hypothesis

Perhaps enough has here been said about power structures to show why so many in the South, especially youth, believe that a new deal can come only after the stranglehold of power structures, internal and external, has been broken. We need not pretend to say to what degree these charges are demonstrated — or even demonstrable. If the internal are often more pervasive and more baneful, the external — because foreign — spark sharper resentment. Yet precise facts and analyses are hard to come by. And if the North has its myths about the South, so the South can have its myths about the North and the North's presence in the South. [8] In any case there is much to all these accusations that must

---

[8] The most eminent protagonist of the "external barrier" thesis that foreign trade and investment provide the essential explanation of under-development, Gunnar Myrdal, (*Economic Theory and Under-developed Regions*) has recently virtually repudiated this position (*Asian Drama*).

be weighed. If so, certain fundamental questions present themselves. We began by describing development in terms of a number of economic and social processes. But if prejudicial power structures lie athwart the path of development, doesn't development turn out to be a question of liberation?

Unjust structures, the South does not cease repeating, itself constitutes violence. If there is violation of human rights, dignity and aspiration, men find themselves alienated in their own land. If so, doesn't justice and a place in society for these alienated marginal men turn out to be a goal more worthy of national purpose than procuring a 6% annual growth rate of goods and services?

If so, must we not also recognize the role of social struggle in achieving justice and therefore accept class confrontation as a process made inevitable to human development? Surely it was so recognized in England and on the continent in the 19th and early 20th Centuries. Church authorities have long since ceased their unqualified opposition on doctrinal grounds to that degree of class struggle inherent to socialist labor parties of Europe, e. g. Great Britain. Countervailing power with its group antagonisms likewise may not constitute an ideal social principle. But until the ideal is both identified (and demonstrated realisable), it must be expected that the "outs" will fight their way in.

It may be supposed by some that the immediately foregoing analysis, in so far as it concerns internal re-structuring, points in the direction of revolution. Not necessarily so. There are alternatives of radical structural reform short of revolution — some within, some outside the existing legal structure. Is it naive to hope that moral and social pressure can be counted on to persuade the powerful to forego privileges and government to implement needed reforms? All this we must leave to others: to say when theoretically revolution may be justified; to tell us when a specific revolution is so justified.

But within the framework of our discussion of issue raised by the processes of development, we may conclude by mentioning briefly one inevitable dilemma. Where illiberal power and social structures constitute violence, one must suppose that the alienated masses want liberation. But suppose they fear violence, dread great social disorder, mistrust the uncertainty of the revolutionary future? Suppose, again, that the masses because of their impoverishment would vote for more economic gains, bread, shoes for their children, housing, schools, better medicine? Suppose that they would forego, however reluctantly, "liberation" if they believed that the revolution would not hasten — but even delay — the day of having these? (To make this last supposition starker, reflect on the population pressure everywhere building up). Perhaps the answer is *conscientisation* to prepare them to espouse revolution.

Planning for Development

The foregoing analysis of the process of development makes abundantly clear the need for planning. We often think of planning uniquely in terms of mathematical projections of future needs and corresponding resources. But before planners would find it useful or practical to make such projections, they would first have to create a productive economic system. Accordingly, the first priority in planning is to lay the basis for a viable economy. Since this requires a host of changes of attitudes and institutions, planners' first concern ought to be to effect these changes.

At the economic level strategic decisions, more important perhaps than matching future wants and resources, are dictated. Such as how much to invest in education, how to diversify agriculture, where and when to protect local industries, and the renegotation of agreement with (or nationalization) of foreign enterprises.

If the whole social system is badly dislocated in the ways illustrated above, it will be a matter not of giving the economy a further upward push. It will rather be a question of putting it on the right track and then getting it moving toward the people's social and economic goals.

Ideally — and very properly — planning should be directed to effecting all these changes. Were this the place to pursue the question one might demonstrate the unlikelihood that either the Establishment *or* the Revolution would produce such planning — though, obviously, for different reasons.

The problems confronting the developing nations are indeed awesome. Meanwhile the material gap between them and the rich industrial nations widens. This indeed presents a discouraging picture. There is, however, one — but only one — advantage in being behind. This is that it at least affords them the opportunity to test the fruits of the North's technology, industrialization and high consumption economies. The developing countries, in the face of the growing recognition on the part of the North of their cultural pathology and approaching degeneration, perhaps will yet save the rich by providing them with a more human design of development.

III. POPULORUM PROGRESSIO

After our brief sketch of the principal processes of socio-economic development, we are in a better position to understand what questions we want to put to the theologian. These we shall take up in Part Four. Here, in Part Three, we make a bridge by drawing together the elements of a definition of socio-economic development. For this we can do no better than follow the guidance provided in *"Populorum Progressio"*.

The encyclical first takes note that in defining development "we must have a clear vision of all the economic, social, cultural and spiritual aspects" (nr. 13). This acknowledged, development, the encyclical goes on to say, "cannot be limited to mere economic growth." On the contrary, in order to be authentic it must be integral; that is, it has to promote the good of every man and of the whole man (nr. 14). In support, the eminent Dominican authority on economic development, Père Lebret, is quoted. "We do not believe in separating the economic from the human, nor development from the civilisations in which it exists. What we hold important is man, each man and each group of men, and we even include the whole of humanity."

For this self-fulfillment every man is responsible. But, he is responsible, too, by reason of human solidarity, for the communal development of his own people (nr. 12).

21

That this human progress, this "harmonious enrichment of nature" (to use still another expression of the encyclical) is itself ordained to still further fulfillment of man goes without saying. For, in and through Christ man "is destined to a transcendental humanism" (nr. 16).

The encyclical also makes use of another, more functional way to describe development. Development is now seen as the passage from the less human to the more human. The less human is both material and moral; material, the lack of the daily necessities of life; and moral, abuses of property and power, and the exploitation of workers. The more human is described as including a number of elements. First, men must possess the necessities of life. These must be fairly shared among the people of the world. Men, too, must have equal opportunities to find work and to get ahead. They must also, as befits their dignity, have a voice in economic affairs and in the political decisions which often determine their economic future.

In all this, we should see development as liberating. But it liberates in still other ways. For as development proceeds, men abandon superstitions and their irrational subjection to the brute forces of nature. Change cannot be projected except on a basis of education. The ensuing educational effort elevates still higher the capacity of men to live as men. As affluence is achieved, or at least freedom from the all-engrossing search for daily bread, the arts and sciences can be cultivated, and civilisation promoted.

Still other elements enter into the Encyclical's synthetic definition. For development, even to be truly human, must embrace a certain spirit of poverty. The profound implications of this for theology we leave to Part Four. We must add, too, that development will mean peace; for as Pope Paul declares "the new name for peace is development." This idea has vast implications which, unfortunately, we cannot explore.

Beyond all this humanisation, development will include "acknowledgment of supreme values" and a necessary openess to the transcendental. And still further beyond there are in prospect "the gifts of faith and charity" (nr. 21) that belong to that "transcendental humanism" mentioned above (nr. 16).

One element only needs to be added. No development is truly human that centers on the self to the exclusion of one's neighbor. Therefore development must be "communal" (nr. 12). And since our neighbor is everyone on a globe that can be circled in eighty minutes, nothing short of a planetary vision will satisfy the communal dimension of development (nr. 17).

IV. THEOLOGICAL QUESTIONS

We come finally to our task of indicating certain aspects of socio economic development which need the further attention of theologians.

Material Progress

The first is the very option itself in favor of material and technical progress. That the aspiration generally exists no one can reasonably doubt. The poor of Asia, Africa and Latin America yearn for the enjoyment of the material benefits of civilisation they see enjoyed in the richer nations. Everywhere the "demonstration-effect" has been felt. The transistor and the movie have brought to the remotest corners of the globe awareness of how the better-off live. The attractiveness of this picture constitutes a compelling force for the productive effort that will produce the same for them.

That some people of the developing nations themselves question this aspiration is undeniable. That still more are troubled by some of its implications is also undeniable. But the fact of a general desire for the benefits of technology remains.

The moral justification of this urge for material and technical betterment seems unchallengeable despite the ambiguities involved. *"Gaudium et Spes"* is definitive in this respect. The battle has been won against all heresies that consign the material and bodily pleasure to a god of evil. It remains decisive that the Word of God, became man, fully man, and that in Himself He sanctifies the bodily and the material and through man its extension into the Cosmos.

Flight From the World

Where theology must still provide light is in the resolving of the conflict between a legitimate material progress and the withdrawal implicit in flight from the world — or the injunction of St. Paul to use this world as if not using it. Protagonists of development feel at times that much of present day writing on poverty and on Christ as the Suffering Servant seems virtually to exclude the aspiration to material and technical development, or at least to the abundance which is implicitly promised. If it were only a question of the inquietude that arises when we contemplate the prospect of mankind engulfed in a sea of riches and of the material comforts and pleasures that affluence brings, one could only welcome the message of the Poor Man of the Gospel. The same could be said if what were at stake were the justly indignant denunciation of that violence done the rights of the poor by the unconscionable amassing of riches in the hands of the few.[9]

But these same theological writings appear at times to question the very basis for responding to those aspirations that are legitimate. For, if in recent years fewer Catholic theologians are disposed to mount an unequivocal assault on technology, there are the many who have an abiding suspicion of economic rationality; while they are led by the manifest evils, widely associated with industrialisation and urbanisation, to see in modern society something unredeemably inhuman.

This attack is up to a point understandable enough. For, to repeat, if there be any part of progress that bears in it the sign of contradiction it is economic development and the processes that bring it about. But all this said, the theology of the "Poor Man" must be written in the light of the just insights of sociology and the prospects of man's future civilisation.

---

[9] We prescind here from other claims of Christian asceticism.

Benefits of Economic Development

Theology of the "Poor Man" must also take fuller cognizance of economic reality. Economic development, on the one hand, is clearly a good. This is so, first of all, because it produces the necessary material basis for decent human existence. It is also a good because (as mentioned earlier) it is only in affluent societies that great expansion of the arts and sciences have occurred. In societies that are poor, where man's best effort is eaten up in the sheer fight for survival, it is not easy to imagine the appearance of much art beyond simple handicrafts and primitive drawings or sculpture. This is surely not to despise the significant contribution that certain societies, poor in material means, have here made. But by and large the truth seems to remain that men have always needed the leisure and the savings that only abundance supplies in order to produce major art, and above all, science, the practical arts and inventions.

At any rate, it is beyond dispute that economic development is a necessary condition for much of what we mean by humanisation. For much of this depends on the indispensable capacity of a society to save. Without savings there cannot be schools, books or time free from work for teaching. The same is true for clinics and other social services. Without transportation and means of communication men would remain circumscribed by the confining limits of tribe or clan, and thus never be able to experience other men as like themselves and therefore brothers and not enemies.

Still another important element of humanisation is peace. Development serves peace in several ways, thus earning the dictum that development is the new name for peace. This it does insofar as development takes the form of liberation from the unjust structures that constitute a violence and a temptation to revolution. It also promotes peace in the sense that growing abundance reduces the tensions that breed strife. It would obviously be too much to say that all wars are economic. Indeed, they are not. But many are. Tribal wars are often begun as expanding population puts pressure on the arable land at a tribe's disposition. Wars among nations have had the same motivation. Inadequate markets or supplies of raw materials to maintain a fully-employed economy has sometimes motivated colonial ventures.

Economic Arts and Progress

All these above-mentioned forms of humanisation depend on the critical factor of society's capacity to save, that is to create a surplus over what is required to maintain its workforce.

This is the inexorable law of development, and the theologian who wants to help elaborate a theology of development must understand the full implications of this law of growth.

How are surpluses generated? Out of the gifts of nature, yes. But it must be said that nature has been niggardly and has yielded a surplus only when men have wedded productive arts to the crude forces of the earth.

Let us see what some of these arts are.

The first is the technology that puts tools into man's hands, thereby enormously enhancing the fruitfulness of his work on natural resources. It also provides him with energy beyond that of animal, wind, and water-wheel. Properly speaking, most of what we call capital is only such tools and power in prodigiously productive forms.

The second of the arts is the specialization of labor. Instead of each trying to produce everything for himself, men begin to concentrate on one task. As they do so, their skill in it grows. The end result for society is that the output of the collected specializations is far higher than the individual unspecialized products. This division of labor and social exchange makes its appearance in early stages of development. Later, as tools and power and specialized labor grow, the factory will make its appearance. For the factory assembles workers in a place where power and machines can be made readily available. Factory work at some stage of development becomes as inescapable as the requirement itself of proper tools, power and specialization. At later stages it turns into fractionalization of a single task through machine processes. Men at this stage perform only one small piece of a total task. Their fractionalized efforts are then reassembled into the final complete product. The assembly-line is, of course, the quintessence of this stage of industrialization.

Undeniably, the socialisation of work through highly elaborate machine processes has disquieting consequences. The moralists ask whether the whole must not be repudiated as completely de-humanizing. We are not prepared to give an answer here. Our task is only to point out that along the continuum of industrial development automation becomes an inevitable "set" of society. We cannot undo it. We must comprehend it and live with it.

The third of the arts is that of rational economic decision. This is not the same as industrial organization itself. Rational economic decision puts in its appearance as soon as a producing society confronts the problem of making the best possible use of its scarce resource, whether these be raw materials, labor-time, or available capital.

Everyone at times makes such calculations. Few are capable of the sustained effort or possess the competence that choice of best alternatives require where many "unknowns" enter into the calculation. Here, the role of the decision-maker begins to emerge as critical for society.

Since scarce labor, managerial capacity, and capital bear a price tag, a rationalizing society puts a premium on their most effective organization. Here arises still another art, that of administration. The administrator will on the basis of the preceding cost calculations, proceed to coordinate labor and capital. He will be exigent in demanding work discipline and the exact fulfillment of assigned tasks. Proved competence will be his norm of promotion. Sentiment will be sub-ordinated to the exigencies of plant and office efficiency.

Once again, it must be recognized that the art of administration exists in limited supply, especially in an underdeveloped society. It must also be recognized that with development the art of administration will become more sophisticated, acquire new tools for understanding and rationalizing the work assignment and for controlling results. Today computer control of human work understandably troubles the humanist. And yet we are hardly coming to understand this phenomenon before the portent is already present of still more sophisticated form of economic organization and administration. And at the edge of the horizon loom the awesome prospects of systems analysis. Rightly, the humanist asks how men in such a technologized society can remain subjects of the economy and not be reduced to objects.

It should here be noted in parenthesis that nothing in this analysis of rational organization implies that the capitalists or property-owner should make the decisions. If they have any implication for authority it is that authority should be vested in whoever is best capable of making the competent decision. But the question of authority in the enterprise goes beyond the scope of our present inquiry.

Economic Motivation

Similarly, there is the moral question of incentives. At least in the earlier stages of development, saving requires sacrifice of present consumption. And people are not easily disposed to let the claims of capital-formation get in the way of the costly marriage feasts that are traditional. Incentives must be given to coax them to save. No farmer, for instance, will produce more than is needed for himself and family if he cannot be assured a profit. Managerial capacity in all the forms above described is scarce and valuable. It too will ask rewards in forms that it finds satisfying.

It can be presumed that human nature in a state of original innocence would have worked purely out of altruistic motives. But humankind as presently constituted will not do so. If there is one thing we can be sure of, it is that if in egalitarian enthusiasm the rewards of the modernizing elite be reduced beyond what is tolerable, we shall have only succeeded in making our societies materially (and perhaps humanly) poorer. How men are to be moved to more altruism at the same time that working for self-interest is conceded them is a decidedly difficult question. But these questions of incentives are more moral than dogmatic. Hence may be set aside.

There are implications for dogmatic theology too.[10]   For

---

[10] The writer knows that he is on shaky ground in distinguishing between moral and dogmatic questions. He hopes he will

there is, first, the assumption that men normally act rationally and that to do so is a good thing. But isn't this too much to say in the face of the failure of the Age of Reason? Isn't there an arrogance in man's assumption that he can create his own economic miracles? Doesn't this rationality submerge the spirit and virtually exclude God from economic life?

Planning and Providence

And when rationality takes the form of planning [11] must we not ask whether man is setting up his own providence against that of God? How do we dare presume that our model of the future is how God projects our future? At any rate are we not in danger of becoming so free of dependence on God that we will implicitly assume that the future is wholly of our own making? Will we not even in our fury of planning ever-brighter futures tend to acquire a distaste for that ultimate future of the Eschaton and the transformation of all that is ours which will then be effected by other hands than our own?

Is Urbanisation Development?

Up to the present the considerations of this fourth part have borne largely on the changes that take place in the higher stages of economic development. But many find disturbing implications in the earlier, even the first stages. They are troubled over what takes place in the shift from subsistence to commercial farming.

---

be pardoned (and understood) if for his present purpose he works within this distinction. Thus, as here for the question of economic incentives, so later when he touches on international economic relations and international investment, both critically important for economic development, he will set that area aside because the questions do not appear to him to bring out manifestly "theological" i. e. dogmatic implications.

[11] It will be remembered that our earlier analysis of planning emphasized that this embraces, beyond projection of needs and resources, and the taking of strategic decisions, the *projects men make of their world.*

If the society in which change occurs is the feudal sort that may still be found in the world, its break-up can only be welcomed. For in such, the propertied few have all the privileges; the masses live like dispossessed serfs, illiterate, with virtually no protection, legal or other, of their rights.

But elsewhere primitive agrarian society has attractive features. Tribal societies, to take one instance, often produce a satisfactory living with social sharing, social security and warm family and communal ties. In the extended family (running over several generations) young and old both play their roles. The old are respected and secured. All work in the intimacy of the family circle. Life is lived close to nature and in intimate face to face relations.

The modernizing elite, with their insistence on agricultural efficiency, break critically into this social pattern. To create a marketable surplus (plantation farming may be a partial exception) better tools, then machinery must make their appearance. But with machinery, one man does the work of two or more. These must leave the family circle to seek employment elsewhere.

The young who begin life in the city find themselves in a totally new and unstructured situation. There is no social organisation to receive them. The moral protection of the rigidly controlled society they have left is not replaceable. They possess a freedom for which they have no preparation and in situations for which they have no norms of behaviour.

Apart from these moral consequences, if job anticipations fail them, they find themselves reduced to living on the margin of society in total alienation.

Much, but not all of what has been said in these last paragraphs, is applicable to change in forms of agrarian society other than tribal. We need not enter into these differences in order to accomplish our purpose which is to illustrate the general problem of change from traditional society posed by development.

That there are negative aspects is clear. Yet despite these, the sociologist in general believes that the change is constructive because modernization is needed to take care either of expanding population or expanding wants of the existing population.

Constructive because it releases the energies of the more active members of the traditional society, — those prepared to introduce innovations in farming methods but who have been held back either by tribal resistance to change or by the fact that the system of social sharing would require that all the fruit of their innovation be shared without any material advantage accruing to themselves from the extra effort.

Still another constructive feature is that the change liberates men from the unreflecting adherence to a traditional code of behavior and forces them to assume adult responsability for making their own moral choices.

Moreover the change is inevitable. The sheer pressure of population growth generally is forcing or will soon force the pace of modernisation everywhere, with its attendant destruction of traditional societies. Assuming even the most moderate population projections, it is certain that many more billions will soon be sharing our earth. Present methods of agriculture, while providing impressive results, are barely keeping up with present rates of populations growth. Clearly the modernisation effort in agriculture will have to conquer areas of the globe into which it has not yet penetrated. As in the presently industrialized nations that will inevitably mean reduction of the work-force engaged in agriculture from 75 per cent to 50 and then to 30, and in a more distant future to the under-20 or even under 10-percent experienced in several countries of western Europe.

Industry, obviously, must grow to provide alternative employment as well as to meet the other than food needs of the world's future billions. The inevitable conclusion is the break-up of traditional society and the emergence over the whole face of the earth of industrial and urban society. [12]

---

[12] Between 1920 and 1960 rural population in the South rose by a half billion. But urban growth rates were even higher, bringing city population from 68 to 320 millions. Estimates put that latter figure at 800 millions in 1980 with half in big cities. To avoid urban catastrophe, technology, since agriculture cannot

· To sum up this part of our discussion. There are favorable and unfavorable aspects to traditional society. The changes called for by modernisation inevitably strike a death-blow to such small societies. And modernisation cannot long be staved off for the reasons mentioned.

Do these changes prove disastrous? If ambiguously, do they not move in the direction that men of our times, with their own intuition into values, are taking — and must inevitably take for the reasons given. If our analysis forces us to accept this conclusion, what, we must ask, does the revealed message tell us of God's call to men in this world of rapid technological change and industrialization and urban growth?

In short, the challenge appears to be to give us a final theology of the Secular City. For it cannot have escaped readers familiar with the literature in that field how much the logic of development presented here has in common with the secularizing forces expounded · and endorsed by a Harvey Cox. It is easy enough to say what is wrong with the Secular City. The challenge is to say what is right.

Socialization

We have one final approach to the problem of development which may raise other questions for the theologian. This is socialization. Much, if not all that we have described has from the time of Pope John's encyclical, "*Mater et Magistra*", been known as socialization.

The Council, for its part, describes this as a "growing interdependence promoted chiefly by technological advances." (*Gaudium et spes*, nr. 23). This interdependence is further described as "reciprocal ties and mutual dependencies which grow and give rise to a variety of associations and organizations" (nr. 25).

In evaluating these tendencies the Council strikes a moderately optimistic note. For this socialization "consolidates and increases qualities of the human person"

---

provide jobs for the masses, must bring industrial jobs to the country-side.

(nr. 25). Furthermore, while there are undeniably many disturbances in the process, these, due certainly in great part to sinful pride and selfishness, are also explainable in part "as natural tensions of economic, political and social forms" (ibid.).

Social Conflict and Sin

Surely we are not here entitled to underestimate the extent to which sin "at a deeper layer" (ibid.) accounts for the disorders of modern society. But neither may we equate all disorder with sin — at least personal sin. Men can at times be disorderly because they have not yet known how to establish codes of behavior adapted to new and complex circumstances. In unstructured situations, even people disposed to sacrifice for the common good will fight to maintain their own little perch-hold. Many conflicts rest unresolved only because convergence of interest cannot be determined. But to find these in the tangle of highly complex and dynamic situations requires experience beyond what at times we presently possess. The same is true of justice. It is easy to condemn the endless quarrelling of pressure groups in industrial society. There may have been other times when producers felt that the "social price" of their contribution to society was reasonably assessed. In our complex economic order, with its international dimensions, no one can pretend to arrive at anything better than approximations to justice, socially-acceptable for the moment, subject to reappraisal with the changing situation of tomorrow.

One might argue that if the modern industrial, technicized city is so complex that we cannot establish norms of behavior or find justice in it, it thereby stands condemned. Admittedly, today's megalopolis does not lend itself to easy defense.

It would take us beyond our present scope to say more about this. But it must be remembered that many of the ills of the city do not stem from technology and industrialization or urban growth. They can have other roots-political, social and even personal failure. It is not wholly unreasonable to hope that with experience we can come to a better understanding of how to create more human cities. And create them we must, for they are the life of our planet.

At any rate it is our understanding that the essential problems posed — and this is our main point — are deeper than just moral questions. They are essentially theological.

Teilhard and Development

This appears more emphatically so if we reflect for a moment on Teilhard de Chardin's optimistic appraisal of socialization. [13] For the Council, socialization had certain undeniably positive manifestations; others were equivocal. Only the former clearly stemmed from man's social nature. In Teilhard's account (of processes which forty years ago he had already denominated socialization) it is not clear that the question of ambiguity need arise. The processes are generally presented as unequivocal steps forward of evolution under the guidance of the interpenetration of consciousness. The social nature of man not only discovers that certain forms of organized life are necessary or useful and therefore adopts them. It appears rather to rush forward to embrace them as being in all their reach and complexity only higher manifestations of the spirit of man. For, as surely as at an earlier stage of evolution, cells became organized into the totality of the brain, so the individual atoms of self must be organized into the totality of socialized man.

For Teilhard there can be no questioning that this totalization increases the qualities of the human person. The French Jesuit was, of course, not unaware that one could raise the challenge that totalization leads inevitably to a Communistic generation of materialism. But his own understanding of socialization was that it, on the contrary, necessarily generated Spirit.

---

[13] These ideas of Teilhard may be found especially in *Le phénomène humain,* Paris (Seuil) 1955; *L'avenir de l'homme,* Paris (Seuil) 1957 (The ideas run through many of the articles that make up that volume); *Le groupe zoologique humain,* Paris (Albin Michel) 1956. See also P. Smulders, *La vision de Teilhard de Chardin,* Paris (DDB) 1964, p. 101-172: La voie de l'humanité.

34

Here surely we have a question about anthropology of development that has yet to receive definitive treatment. What is acceptable in this Teilhardian approach to development? And if one cannot accept the whole of his thesis, is it because, at times, it seems to preclude original sin? [14] Or is it because human nature's basic impulse to socialize itself cannot be that much trusted? Or will it be because solidarity in the Teilhardian system swallows up subsidiarity, and that, not just practically, but metaphysically? If, finally, Teilhard's understanding of socialization needs re-dimensioning, what is a reasonable theological statement of the direction this should take? [15]

Long as this essay has been, it cannot be concluded without one or two final observations as to what the author has tried to do. First, readers may have at times been puzzled that dogmas, obviously pertinent to certain parts of the exposition, were not even alluded to. Here, it must be remembered that the task was to explore the realm of socio-economic development in order to bring out questions requiring further theological reflection. *It was not to supply the theological reflection itself.*

Secondly, the writer made his own distinction between moral questions and dogmatic ones. All that seemed to him to fall under the former he excluded from consideration for the reasons explained previously.

Part Four has proposed certain problems falling under "dogmatic theology". The list cannot be supposed to be exhaustive. It is probably even too much to hope that the problems raised have all been properly posed. But after all, this is only an attempt to explore in dialog a field admittedly of considerable obscurity.

---

[14] Supporters of Teilhard will be quick to point out that Christ's redemption with its saving grace is prominent enough in his works. See, e. g. Christopher Mooney, *Teilhard de Chardin and the Mystery of Christ,* New York (Harper and Row) 1964.

[15] There are, of course, other themes of the Teilhardian system that bear upon development. But since these are not rooted in the *processes* of development but rather in his cosmology, we do not enter into them.

PETER HENRICI, s. j.

FROM PROGRESS TO DEVELOPMENT:
A HISTORY OF IDEAS

Theological questions about progress arise as soon as the subject is mentioned. The idea of progress forms part of a cluster of ideas — progress, evolution, development — the meanings of which shade into one another, with no sharp distinctions. In the attitude itself of theology and church officialdom toward this complex of related ideas we have an additional and noteworthy instance of "progress" within the past hundred years. Today this set of concepts is axial in church preaching [1]; yet only a few decades ago theology and official levels of the church were so negatively disposed toward this same idea that the church was repeatedly obliged to defend itself against the charge of being in reality opposed to progress.[2] How is this reversal to be explained?

For the answer to this question we should like at this point to make a kind of preliminary study in an attempt to draw from the history of the idea of progress, first of all, its structural components and implications. Like the concepts "evolution" and "development", the idea of progress is not a purely empirical notion stemming from the analysis of facts. In the case of all these ideas, we deal with a process

---

[1] Besides the Encyclical *Populorum progressio* see *Gaudium et Spes, passim,* and the *Papal Message for the Day of Peace* (30 nov. 1969), in: *AAS* 61 (1969) 794-798.

[2] Denzinger-Schönmetzer, n. 1875; 2912 f; 3463; 3465; see also n. 2980; 3028; and (31st ed.) 2094 f.

to be understood as a *whole* and as supplemented by a *value index*. To qualify as progress, the phenomena must be interpreted through the a priori categories "process" (i. e., a linear nexus of successive changes), "wholeness" and "value"; and it is a likely presumption that in the case of progress we are dealing not so much with a fact as with a way of viewing facts. The history of the idea will show what validity there is in this presumption, providing at the same time more particularized information regarding the a priori structures of the idea of progress, their presuppositions and eventual shifts. A theology of human progress must have continually in view these structural components of the idea that are derived from its history.

The history of the idea of progress will then answer the further question as to the necessity of using the structures of the idea of "progress" to interpret historical phenomena and how this explanation is related to traditional Christian thought. KARL LÖWITH's interpretation [3] that the idea of progress is the outcome of the secularization of Christian doctrine on providence and of salvation history, is well known and widely acclaimed. This thesis, to be sure, is itself ambivalent, even if it proved to be well-founded; a process of secularization can be evaluated either from the viewpoint of its Christian origin or from that of its anti-Christian end. In any case, it must be made clear whether Löwith's secularization thesis is in principle correct and whether the eventual shifts in the structures of the idea of progress entailed also some disarray in its relationship to Christianity.

As has already been said, all these clarifications will come from the history of the idea of progress itself, as we attempt to delineate this history in its broad contours and articulations, so that the components of the idea may be brought to light and become the subject of reflection. Naturally, we cannot here be concerned with reproducing this multi-layered history in faithful historical detail (the greater part of it remains to be explored for the first time) but some main lines of development can be derived from materials that have already been studied several times [4] and described with suffi-

---

[3] *Meaning in history,* Chicago 1949.
[4] See our bibliography at the end of the article.

cient certitude to warrant their use as at least working hypotheses; more than that, indeed, this entire collection of essays does not propose to offer.

I. The prehistory and the presuppositions of the idea of progress

I. - Even a cursory acquaintance with classical antiquity forces recognition of a fundamental truth which appears to confirm the thesis of Karl Löwith. The idea of progress, in any authentic form, had no place in the intellectual milieu of the ancient world. The Greeks lived in the closed circle of the πόλις within a κόσμος likewise circular; the notion of progress, on the contrary, assumes as its inevitable, if inadequate, representation, the "schema" of the straight line, along which, by advance or retrogression things "progress" linearly. Even in euclidean geometry, this linear concept was, in fact, a geometric construct, not a "given". Nature followed a circular pattern: over-arching a round earth were the heavenly spheres; their motion, their progression (κίνησις) in its highest and most characteristic form was depicted as cyclic — and this not only for the wheeling constellations whence all things proceed; there were also the cyclic relationships in biological nature: seed-tree and birth-death, and the cyclical recurrence of the ages.

The circularity which characterized the ancient Greeks' understanding of nature influenced also, via their concept of time, the understanding of history. For us today time is *the* linear, irreversible "given", because we measure it by our lifespan. But the Greeks measured time by the orbiting of the stars. In only one instance, with Aristotle, does the difficulty arise that "numerus motus secundum prius et posterius" presupposes an infinite numbering (and so probably "linear") soul [5]; but this objection had no consequences on a philosophical, and even less on a life-view level.

Where historical reflection advanced beyond the circle of the polis and mere chronological inventories (ἱστορία)

_____

[5] Phys. Δ 14; 223 a 21 ff.

39

toward a real understanding of history, it was conditioned by a cyclic notion of the course of events: only what is cyclically recurrent is intelligible and partakes of the eternal verity and "universality" that characterize scientific data. As a consequence history became a series of circular movements, interpreted for the most part tragically, as records of decadence. Thus, in Plato's model account of political history, justice as a political principle is supplanted by inordinate ambition, craving for glory, luxury, effeminacy, which in their turn give rise to the opposition of ordinary citizens, demagoguery and tyranny. A circular process in the sublunary sphere where it cannot resonate the eternal harmony of the circling courses of the stars, inevitably becomes a cycle of decadence. Ancient man was homesick for an irretrievable Golden Age; the proclamation by the court poets of Augustus of his new dawning future, faithful though it was to the cyclic time scheme, was all too easy to unmask as hollow flattery.

But this poetic use of the cyclical world concept seems to limit decidedly its definite value in the history of ideas. Is it not a relic of mythical times which could serve the enlightened and secularized society of later antiquity, at best, merely as rhetorical ornament? Did not a valid concept of progress enter the ancient world along with the secularization of myth — a concept of progress toward decadence at least? We think not. The Greek secularization of myth came by way of science (the דָּבָר) not by way of history (λόγος). The subject matter of Greek science, precisely as such, remains cyclic, inasmuch as it is the science of the constants (the "universal") in nature. Even today, the cyclical aspect is still basically valid for the data of the natural sciences; it is essential for experiment in these fields that the phenomena recur. The exception to this rule that evolutionary theory represents remains to be discussed. Nevertheless, in terms of technological application or broadened and deepened knowledge of its own subject matter, science can progress. In both kinds of progress the parameter is man, through either his doing (technology) or his knowing. In reality an awareness of these two types of progress is marginally found in later antiquity also; but it is noteworthy that both were not

40

applied to science as theoretical logos, they were operative on the practical level in ethico-political theory.

The *word* "progress" (προκοπή) was in the Stoic vocabulary and meant advancement in virtue, i. e., toward "perfection". To be sure, man lives within the invariable circles of cosmos and polis, but he can endeavor to live an ever more perfect inner life: progressing from ἀφροσύνη to σοφία from κακία to ἀρετή, from κακοδαιμονία to εὐδαιμονία. This progression, treated in the Περὶ προκοπῆς of EPICURUS and in PLUTARCH'S "De profectibus in virtute", remains intentional, however, and strictly limited to the individual. Human nature as such does not progress, much less the human race, which for the Stoic always represents consummate perfection already achieved. Indeed, on-going progress, stimulated by a nature basically good, sound instruction, the help of friends, and, above all, by one's own will power is rather the mark of the still imperfect man; the wise man makes no further advance. This point of view is share by PHILO OF ALEXANDRIA, who nevertheless contributes to the Stoic concept two judaeo-religious amendments: God is the real Author of human progress and this progress itself is primarily the reward of askesis, the struggle against sin and the world. This originally Stoic conception of progress has persisted throughout the entire Christian tradition as a key principle of ascetical theology. The theology of progress, however, is not concerned with this inner personal advancement, but with the outward and collective progress of all mankind.

It would seem likely that such a concept of progress could be found in the Epicurean LUCRETIUS. In the second and fifth books of his "De rerum natura" he traces civilization back to a series of consecutive improvements which man himself was able to accomplish[6]. Yet also for LUCRETIUS — and precisely for him — progress is merely an episode, doomed to swift oblivion, in the essential chaos of an atomistic universe. "Eadem sunt omnia semper"[7] and "ex nihilo nihil fit" enunciate the unbelief in progress which constitutes the fundamental tenet in the philosophical creed of this alleged

---

[6] *De rerum natura*, V, 1448-1457.
[7] ibid. III, 945.

earliest prophet of progress. He thereby gives expression in other terms to the same basic conviction as in the cyclic conception of being.

II. - Linear thinking, then, was lacking in the graeco-roman period, but it emerges as the foundation of the hebraeo-christian world concept. It is neither necessary nor possible to deal here with the relationship of the biblical world-view in its multiple strata to the idea of progress; a specialist will do this in an independent monograph. For our purpose only one point in this connection has to be established: The excoriation by the prophets of political and nature divinities in favor of the *one* Lord of history Yahweh first opened a path for the entrance of the idea of progress. When, for instance, the recurrent canaanite fertility festivals are reinterpreted as commemorations of historical events, or when, as in *Genesis* 9, there is promised, along with the "Never-Again" of the deluge, an ordered sequence of the seasons, a radical change in the mode of understanding time and existence is to be noted. When events are presented as unique and incapable of repetition and, in addition, no longer as retrogressive, then a time period (sufficiently large, notwithstanding the regular rotations of nature) is forced into an irreversible, ordered linearity in which also an idea of progress can be discerned. And it was within the context of this biblical conception of time and existence that the earliest theologies of progress began to take shape. Two apposite examples must suffice here.

IRENÄUS OF LYON develops the idea of "Economy" as signifying the progressive realization of salvation — progressive on pedagogical grounds. "All that is made necessarily has a beginning, an intermediate stage and a maturity."[8] God stooped to this law of development and little by little instructed His people as he led them "through things of small consequence to that which is of highest importance, through counterfeits to truth, through temporal to eternal realities, through fleshly to spiritual, through earthly to heavenly."[9]

In CLEMENT OF ALEXANDRIA this law of "Economy" ap-

---

[8] *Adv. Haer.* IV, 11, 2; PG VII, 1002 A.
[9] ibid. IV, 14, 3; PG VII, 1012 A.

pears in a still more explicit form as a law of being for every created thing. "Every creature developed itself and goes on developing itself toward its own ever greater improvement (προκόπτει εἰς τὸ αὐτοῦ ἄμεινον)". [10] Accordingly, even eternal life is to be conceived of as perpetual progress. But progress is particularly manifest in salvation history, which advances from paganism to the Mosaic Law, from the Law to the Gospel, from simple faith in the Gospel to the γνῶσις of the τέλειος ἀνήρ. In this gnostic doctrine (which, mutatis mutandis, we find again in the joachimite Doctrine of the Three Kingdoms and in Hegelian philosophy), we first encounter the tendency to project, on the basis of past advances in salvation history, a future progress still to be accomplished.

Yet another essential component of the idea of progress can be inferred from these two first examples of a theology of progress: the concept of generations set off and grouped as whole. Only thus was it possible for their particular destines to be summed up, in order to apply what the Stoics said of the progress of the individual to a theory on the "Education of the Human Race." [11] Probably this point of view, which, in fact, we find again in a more developed form in the German Idealists, stems from the doctrine of Christ as Head in Whom all things and all men are comprised.

Salvation economy, however, as progressive realization of salvation does not necessarily imply continuous human progress. AUGUSTINE's theology of history witnesses to this. For him also salvation history unfolds in successive steps and is absolutely irreversible, because every stage of development is marked by a new salvific event, a definitive intervention of God in history. But by the same token there is no human progress within each stage leading on to the next; what does take place is rather a process of decline, for, as a consequence of original sin, life on earth necessarily entails deterioration:

> The consequence of the bad use of free will is this chain of disaster which leads the human race, depraved from its inception, radically corrupt, as it were, by a

---

[10] *Stromata* VI, 17 (152, 3); PG IX, 348 C.
[11] We allude to the title of LESSING's famous essay, of which we shall treat hereafter, p. 62.

succession of linked miseries, to the endless doom of a
second death, except only for those who by God's grace,
are delivered from it.[12]

Salvation itself consists not in progress, but, on the contrary, as the final clause of the text just quoted shows,
in being released from this life, as with Plato and the Stoics.
It is true that in our twilight era between Easter and parousia,
salvation is worked out through the wayfaring of the Church
through time — and time thereby acquires a positive meaning.
"Tempora ... inaniter currerent, nisi in eis Dominus Jesus
praedicaretur." [13]   But this positive meaning, precisely as
such, maintains an absolute transcendence in regard to
history; likewise transcendent is the growth of God's Kingdom,
(which constitutes the very content of the present stage of
salvation economy) and it is not to be equated with earthly
progress as a coordinate.

To convert this transcendental salvation economy into
a program of historical progress, requires that the expansion
of the Kingdom of God be made immanent in history. This
was realized not so much in the medieval doctrine of the
Three Kingdoms, which remained an essentially eschatological
theory, as in the baroque revision of Augustine's theology
of history by BOSSUET. His "Discours sur l'histoire universelle" is based upon the equation of the history of the Kingdom
of God with the historico-political history of the People of
Israel and of the Catholic Church. The role of divine providence is set forth in empirically historical terms in the
development of both the above-mentioned institutions, which
themselves, in turn, serve as fulcrum and parameter of progress for secular history. Questionable as this caricature of
salvation history may be as the expression of a christian
theology of providence (as a mirror for princes, it is perhaps
excusable), still it is necessary to point out that BOSSUET
project no *ideology* of progress, since he recognizes no advance
as initiated by man; every instance of progress is of divine
origin. His thought consistently remains strictly theological.

---

[12] *De Civitate Dei*, XII, 14; PL XLI, 386.
[13] *Tract. in Jo.* IX, 6; PL XXXV, 1461.

A little later, G. B. Vico likewise undertook to present a rationalized theology of history in his "Scienza Nuova." In this work divine providence manifests itself first, as with the ancients, in an ordered cyclic flow of historical epochs; then, and predominantly, in the typically christian sense of a transformation (thanks to salvation history) whereby the decadence which marked the end of the ancient world becomes a "ricorso," with rich implications for progress: The barbarism with which our history began has returned, but now there comes along with it the right of appeal to the superior court of Christianity; so that in reality this new beginning is better and more blessed. The fatalistic rotation of the circle is thus opened toward an optimistic spiral.

III. - With the consideration of these two theologies of providence we may conclude the prehistory of the idea of progress. What we have seen thus far is indeed only prehistory; neither the motion which characterizes all that is imperfect, nor salvation economy inserted into history from above evinces the distinctive characteristic of a valid idea of progress, i. e., on-going growth or movement toward the More and the Better *here below*. Yet, though admittedly the structural elements and the hypotheses thus far presented will not permit us to construct an authentic idea of progress, they do, with increasing clarity, establish limits beyond which the idea is not to be found.

These boundary signs we now summarize briefly, with reference to the theological problems of development, which constitute the principal theme of this volume.

1. The idea of progress is not an indispensable idea. There have been cultures — therefore they can exist also today — to which this idea is foreign. Cultures which may show, from the standpoint of Western culture, a certain discernible "progress", have, at least in the sense of their own cultural convictions, a cyclic (and so in the last analysis static) orientation. In this first boundary sign there is implied one of the main difficulties for the development required by the actual world situation; the difficulty, namely, that development may encounter individual cultures to which

the idea of progress is totally foreign and which, therefore, will resist the efforts made for their "development" because the whole concept is fundamentally incomprehensible to them. Would aid for development then entail the disruption of the deepest cultural convictions of one of these cultures?

2. The judaeo-christian world view with its linear concept of salvation history appears *de facto* to have opened the way first for the realization of a true idea of progress. It would seem then that such idea is possible *de facto* only within the context of a judaeo-christian orientation. In terms of the problem of aid for development this means:

a) that the christian mission will *ipso facto* prepare the ground in a given culture for the implanting of the idea of progress;

b) that, inversely, the implanting of the idea of progress in a given culture area also constitutes a pre-christianization of that culture, in that it is thereby made more receptive to the idea of a divine economy of salvation.

3. Though the judaeo-christian world-view may appear to be a presupposition in the formation of the idea of progress, nonetheless this idea cannot be regarded as merely the secularized end-product of a process initiated by Christian thought. The linearity of salvation history is not the linearity of "progress" working upward from below. Frequently it appears to be exactly the opposite; when, for example, divine intervention is seen as a highpoint following and elicited by decadence. The idea of progress in the 18th and 19th centuries is, as we shall see, in every way peculiar to this period and not rooted in theology; it is not surprising that it lent it self soon and often to conflict with Christianity. Furthermore, LÖWITH himself, in his "Meaning in History," sees fit to designate philosophy of history, not the idea of progress as such, as the product of the secularization of Christian theology.

II. The history of the idea of progress from the 17th to the 19th century

The *history*, in the true sense, of the idea of progress develops from the 17th to the 19th century in three broad currents of thought. The first, which may be called scientific-technological, or better, mechanistic, begins with FRANCIS BACON and leads to the Positivism of AUGUSTE COMTE. This historical orientation shaped the visage of 18th century France and received monumental expression in the "Encyclo-pédie." The second, or Rationalist, movement found a good home in the history of German philosophy from LESSING to HEGEL. It led to the "realized" or "returned to its feet" Rationalism of Marxist historical materialism. In the third, or evolutionary current, human progress is viewed as the extension and consummation of biological evolution. The names of HERBERT SPENCER and TEILHARD DE CHARDIN are associated with this orientation, which through ENGELS was likewise absorbed by Marxist thought in the form of dialectical materialism. Finally, to the history of the idea of progress belongs also the 20th century critique of it; this will be treated below in our third section.

I. - At the head and source of this entire historical development stands in lone eminence the figure of FRANCIS BACON, Lord Chancellor of England, who aptly characterized himself as an ideologist of the new age.[14] His prodigious "Instauratio Magna Scientiarum," as everyone knows, remained a torso and by no means effected the revolution in scientific method that was originally claimed for it. But it was precisely the practical infeasibility of this new understanding of science that revealed with particular clarity its ideological assumptions. If, from antiquity through medieval times to humanism, pure knowing ($\Theta\epsilon\omega\rho\iota\alpha$) was man's highest goal and knowledge therefore its own end, now for the first time the worth and even the validity of knowledge were assessed in terms of its practical utility. Not that Bacon would have defended

---

[14] "Ego enim buccinator tantum, pugnam non ineo" (*De augm.* IV, 1; ed. cit. I, p. 579).

a vulgar utilitarianism. Indeed, in his view, the weighty implications of science for future progress are the guarantee of its truth: "Truth therefore and utility are here the very same things: and works themselves are of greater value as pledges of truth than as contributing to the comforts of life." [15] Purely theoretical systems of knowledge belong to that distorted world of images ("idola"), which is proper to human knowing and thinking; where genuine progress is found, we may be sure that the learning whereby it was achieved has encountered truth in the real nature of things. "For what is founded on nature grows and increases; while what is founded on opinion varies but increases not." [16] Progress, however, in its full sense, that is, as signifying ongoing development, is to be found only within the compass of technology. Technological advances represent the only actual possessions held in common by all men; they condition all other changes that take place in the world and verify the mastery of man over nature — his supreme earthly goal. Even in the centuries that followed no one asserted more unequivocally or more uncompromisingly than Bacon that technological progress has to be the alpha and omega of man's comprehension of the world and of himself. "That which can be made by man" now overtakes and even overmasters "that which is" in the purview of the philosopher. Thus a turning point in man's understanding of the world was reached, which could at least equal in importance KANT's Copernican revolution.

It is true that with Bacon the world of technological progress remained an unrealized forecast . His new Organon proved incapable of furthering the progress it announced; for Bacon's natural science continued to be merely natural history, his methodology one of discovery, not of "invention" — that is, the planned construction of something new, not simply the discovery of what has always been there. Moreover, the construction proper to "invention" presupposes accurate knowledge of the primary data as well as awareness of the laws according to which nature is constructed. It was the concept of "mathesis universalis" which GALILEO GALILEI in-

---

[15] *Novum Organum* I, 124; ed. cit. IV, p. 110.
[16] ibid. I, 74; ed. cit. IV, p. 74.

troduced into natural science that first made possible the elaboration of a real methodology of "invention" with its fruitful implications for progress. The philosophical work of DESCARTES and LEIBNIZ depended, each in its own way, upon such a methodology. We need not interest ourselves here in the differences that exist between Descartes' "Regulae" and Leibniz's "Ars Combinatoria," nor in their real or supposed contribution to the progress of science and technology. Much more decisive for the history of the idea of progress is the fact that philosophy and science (still largely undifferentiated) are now for the first time clearly defined as *methodical* knowledge. In late antiquity and in the middle ages science was seen as the assimilation of traditional learning (as the great Commentaries show); later on it was defined by the systematic re-ordering and supplementing of the learning of the past. But from the 17th century onward, science is characterized by *method*, i. e., as a *way* of arriving at truth. While contemplative knowledge, the *theoria* of the ancients, circled around the Given, modern science goes forward to new findings which it invents by constructing them and then submits them to verificaion. The understanding of mathematics also (and particularly this understanding) was affected by its being selected as a norm of the new scientific method: the pythagorean type of mathematics as insight into the essence of things is now replaced by a science of the laws of construction.

Along with the conversion to method goes a transformation in the understanding of that which is termed "nature". "Nature" comes to be seen no longer as a given "Whole", which is to be gradually and systematically investigated, without the possibility, however, of penetration to its ultimate depths; rather, nature now represents something unalterable and irreducible, which can receive different formations, which underlies them as their base and remains itself unchanged throughout. Philosophy and theology are dependent upon an exact knowledge of this unalterable minimum in order to "understand" the transformations of nature; that is, in order to be able to construct them theoretically. The instrument for the knowledge of nature so understood is no longer the *intellect* endeavoring to penentrate to the innermost essence, but discursive *reason* which seeks in all things that which is the same in all; the "general" notions replace the platonic aristotelic "universal" concepts.

In this connection also, the traditional philosophical statement about the unity of mankind, already noted as an indispensable component element of the idea of progress, takes on a new sense, which has no metaphysical implications. It simply means the uniformity and equality of human reason throughout all ages and, therefore, the possibility of transmitting from one subject to another accurately definable, non-arcane information, without detriment to content. This opens the way to teamwork (which Bacon already projected programmatically in his *New Atlantis*), to accumulation of knowledge, and therefore to cumulative expertise in construction from generation to generation. It is this capacity for accumulating knowledge that differentiates human reason from animal instinct, says PASCAL [17]; and from this follows by natural necessity constant scientific progress.

The 17th century "conversion to methodology" implies, then, the idea of progress not only because it starts from and tends toward technological propress, but also because of its unexpressed philosophical assumption. It thereby lays a foundation for an *ideology* of progress which reaches beyond technological advances to all areas of life. It is noteworthy that this first becomes evident in a context which has not the slightest connection with technology: the *Querelle des Anciens et des Modernes* in the field of literary criticism. What was for most champions of the "moderns" a question merely of aesthetic judgment, the Cartesian BERNARD DE FONTENELLE (who was to deliver the official memorial address for Leibniz), in his "Digression sur les Anciens et les Modernes" (1688), wished to demonstrate as necessarily true by philosophical arguments; namely, the superiority of the new over the ancient poets. From the immutability of nature and human reason follows the impossibility of decadence; therefore those born later will have, on the average, no more limited intellectual capacity than their forebears. Consequently, they can and must on the one hand avoid the faults of

---

[17] *Préface pour le Traité du vide,* ed. cit. p. 533.

earlier poets and on the other draw on the useful knowledge acquired by them. Their work will therefore be inevitably more perfect than that of earlier poets; i. e., they will have "fewer defects in just as many excellences." [18] "The spirit that has reached full developments is made up, as it were, of all the spirits of earlier centuries; it is, indeed, one and the same spirit which has been in process of formation during the whole time." [19]

The *Querelle* now led — on the part of these same spokesmen for the "Moderns" — to the insight that a pattern of cumulative progress does not admit of being simply transferred from the domain of natural science and technology to other areas of cultural creation. The universal sameness of human nature is a minimal constant; human nature impresses itself on different ages by differing customs and a different "spirit" in evervarying ways. Along with the linear, fundamentally unlimited perfectibility of *reason* in natural science-technology, account must be taken, then, of the perfection of the *spirit* of each epoch, ever different and ever to be defined anew. Thus reflection on progress in terms of the future was given (in the very moment it began to be an historical force) a balancing complement and counterpoise in an historical understanding no less "modern" — the recognition, namely, of the relativity of the past.

II. - Yet it was the overwhelming evidence from that relativistic point of view that awakened mid-eighteenth century Europe to an awareness that real and general progress had taken place. VOLTAIRE may serve as chief witness to this. In his philosophy of history he sought to understand the ever-shifting diversity in spirit and customs among nations and from age to age; but he was so strongly convinced that the "siècle de Louis XIV" represented unparalleled achievement that to him all of the past seems an inevitably imperfect prelude to this real history. Consequently, his "philosophy of history" (the name comes from Voltaire) is a philosophy of human torpor rather than of human progress. But how is it that the age of Voltaire can claim normative

---

[18] *Oeuvres,* ed. cit. IV, p. 184.
[19] ibid. IV, p. 189.

status? Along with the uprooting of antiquity as criterion, a process which had been going on for two centuries, two additional reasons may be considered decisive. There is, first, the evidence of technological and cultural advances during the decades immediately preceding that have raised the level of civilized living. They have made life so much pleasanter and more worthy of man, that there is no longer any interest in looking for a Golden Age in old primeval times.[20] The Golden Age is to be found in the present or, at any rate, in the immediate future. The passing of the age, therefore, portends augmented value, not decline. The second, and deeper, reason for the normative status of the "siècle de Louis XIV" lies in the equation of the refinements of civilized living with rational living, an equivalence which became all the more obvious after Descartes had replaced in the sphere of practical judgments the all-too-demanding "rationality" by the more accommodating "reasonableness". But now, since reason, that is to say, the reasonable, must and actually will overcome (and here for the first time the proverbial optimism of the Enlightenment comes into play), progress toward the more civilized is inevitable for it is a progress toward the more reasonable. No external norm is required to certify progress as authentic; it is its own norm. Progress purely for the sake of progress is not an absurdity; it is an exigency of reason.

Such exigency motivated two rationalist productions, which are the hallmark of the second half of the 18th century. The French *Encyclopedia,* which appeared in 35 volumes between 1751 and 1765, is wholly committed to the cause of progress, not merely for the purpose of recording it, but intending, in so doing, to promote it. This intent DIDEROT formulates in the prospectus given in his article "Encyclopédie":

> The purpose of an encyclopedia is to bring together items of knowledge scattered over the face of the earth, to explain such knowledge systematically for the benefit of our contemporaries and pass it on to those who will come after us; so that the work of past ages may not be

---

[20] Se *"Le Mondain,"* ed. cit. p. 203-204: "Il leur manquait l'industrie et l'aisance: Est-ce vertu? C'était pure ignorance."

without fruit for the ages that succeed; that our descendants may be the happier in being better informed, and that we may not die without meriting well of the human race.

Furthermore, as the title ("A Dictionary based on Reason of the Arts, Sciences, and Trades") and the prominent plate volumes of the Encyclopedia show, the editors have in view primarily technological progress; the commanding position of this practical aspect, especially gratifying to the bourgeosie, was far more responsible for the ideological impact of the Encyclopedia than its philosophical articles.

During the same years which saw the publication of the Encyclopedia, a radical change was taking place in another quarter — in the field of *political economy,* now slowly achieving status as a science. Over against the populationism of the mercantilists, QUESNAY and the physiocrats were conscious of the dangers implicit in the demographic pressure for shared material prosperity. But since reason demanded the extension of material well-being, political economy must endeavor to understand the laws involved in the increase of production, which has to keep ahead of population expansion. That classical political economy does actually rest upon such an ideological premise is brought out with particular clarity by TURGOT, a contributor to the Encyclopedia. At the beginning of his career, even before abandoning his clerical status, Turgot drew up several schemas for a history of human progress, one of which was presented at the Sorbonne in 1750 as a formal academic address and gained wide renown. The basic postulate of this philosophy of history is the unlimited perfectibility of man, on the grounds of the infinitely varied range of human possibilities, as they appear, not only in historical retrospect, but also in the multiplicity of contemporary cultures, wherein we can view historical development synoptically, as it were. Within this wide and varied range, something new is, necessarily, always being produced, and these new productions, in being preserved and passed on, either orally or in writing, form an accumulation and thus make for progress. Corresponding to this breadth and diversity are the differing lines along which progress occurs; always normative among these is the progress of reason in science, for science conditions technological advances, and ethics and politics also must aspire to become scientific disciplines. Turgot touches also upon the phenomenon of the acceleration of progress, which is a function of the linearity of scientific technological progress. So far his thought on progress is solidly rationalistic; a new element in it, however, is the fact that the *moving force* of progress is no longer sought in reason but in the *appetites* clamoring for gratification; thus, even « unenlightened » ages and cultures (they in particular) become carriers of progress, while a hyper-rationalistic culture stagnates, as the example of China shows. Progress itself becomes a blind force which aids reason in non-rational ways toward a breakthrough, while it is self-interest that gives rise to the common good.

This paradox, first expressed in DE MANDEVILLE's celebrated and ill-famed "Fable of the Bees" (1714), became the fundamental law of classical economic analysis, where it plays the part of a secularized providence. ADAM SMITH, for example, devotes Books II and III of his "Inquiry into the Nature and into the Causes of the Wealth of Nations" (1776) to the analysis of economic progress. Allow competition free play, and the market will regulate itself automatically; the expectation of interest revenue will encourage thrift—that is, for the purpose of investment—and continuous progress will result, not subject to crises nor necessitating change in economic structures. The extent to which this belief in progress was Smith's hypothesis and not the finding of his analysis becomes apparent with his successors MALTHUS and RICARDO, who prove much more pessimistic than their teacher. In addition, signs of approaching economic crises will controvert the doctrine of uninterrupted economic progress.

III. - But the difficulty which would be brought up against the theories, so filled with faith in progress, of the physiocrats and of liberalism, lay deeper; it concerned the contradiction inherent in a theory which saw in progress, on the one hand, reason infallibly winning through, and on the other, an allegedly permanent social inequality as the moving force of progress. Such a position was at variance not only with humanitarian sentiments, but, above all, with the nature of reason itself, supposedly the same everywhere and in every-one, and therefore plainly calling for universal equalization. This is why ROUSSEAU, using the same parameter as Turgot and the encyclopedists—he also a contributor to the Encyclo-pedia—came to completely different conclusions and require-ments. In the same year as the young Turgot set forth his philosophy of history, so optimistic of progress, Rousseau gave his negative answer to the prize question set by the Academy of Dijon: "Whether flourishing Sciences and Technology have contributed to Moral Improvement," This reply and the "Essay on the Origin of Inequality among Mankind" which followed, may have been seriously meant or, as DIDEROT would have it, may represent merely philosophical finger exercises in paradox. In either case, there is without question a strong caesura to be noted here in the history of thought on progress. For Rousseau places in question not progress itself, but the assumption that it is to be identified with economic and cul-tural advances. And if such identification is disallowed, then the status of the "progressive" present as normative goes as well; and also the obligation of accepting into the bargain the glaring defects in the existing political and social order, merely because these make economic and cultural progress possible. There is an open prospect that reason calls for a politico-social order consonant with the principle of equality. As an ideal, this social order demanded by reason must be sought either in a mythical past — the Golden Age moves back to its ac-customed place — or it must be set up as a program for the future. In the "Contrat Social" both these perspectives are combined and in "Emile", published in the same year, Rousseau goes even further: He draws the picture of a new, perfect mankind, reared and educated in accordance with reason. Progress assumes a dimension which embraces man-kind as a whole, changing from a normative reality to an ideal, impossible to realize, at least for the present.

This new dimension of the idea of progress we find in the schematic outlines for a communistic political system of MORELLY (1753, 1755) and MABLY (1778) and especially in the thought of Turgot's friend and biographer CONDORCET. His "Esquisse d'un Tableau historique des Progrès de l'Esprit hu-main" is the first attempt to raise the theory of progress to the level of a scientific discipline, which Condorcet defines as follows:

> If we only observe and understand the general facts and the unvarying laws which the development of our human faculties reveals to us concerning that which is common to all the different members of the human race, the resultant knowledge is given the name metaphysics. But when we consider the effects of such development on individuals who exist at the same time in a given space and study these effects from generation to generation, then we are presented with a tableau of the progress of the human spirit. This progress is subject to the same general laws that are observed in the development of the faculties of each individual, because it is the consequence of this development considered with reference lo a large number of persons joined together in society [21].

This scientific recognition of progress as subject to law was needed by Condorcet to enable him to execute his main intent: the prediction of future progress in the tenth and last "Tableau." Rational prognosis shall replace prophecy. Therewith Condorcet's interest shifts increasingly from economic and intellectual to social and political progress. The axis for every instance of progress is, as with Turgot, the progress of reason in the field of scientific knowledge. In the past this was impeded by unsatisfactory economic conditions, which fostered superstition and despotism. Until the ninth epoch—the period between Descartes and the revolution—Condorcet's presentation coincides in its main lines with Voltaire's philosophy of history. But at that point victorious reason is to make possible the construction of a new politico-social order (Rousseau is called in as chief witness to this); [22] since in a world in which all material wants are fully satisfied and life expectancy it steadily increasing, equality will prevail among peoples and also within individual nations — at least to a relative extent because full equality would bring

---

[21] ed. cit. p. 2-3.

[22] In order to construct this new social order, Condorcet made the first attempt to introduce mathematics (statistics and probability calculus) into the social sciences.

56

the economic process to a standstill. The basic tenet of the science of progress continues to be the unlimited perfectibility of man and the irreversibility of progress. As long as no cosmic disaster intervenes, the further progress of man is assured.

From Condorcet a straight line now leads to the great designers of the future social order, SAINT-SIMON and AUGUSTE COMTE. For both, Condorcet is their unique precursor.[23] Both reflect upon the experience of the revolution which had indeed shown that progress is possible also in the politico-social domain, but had proved incapable of giving durable form to such progress by the short-lived revolutionary and post-revolutionary Constitutions. The task now, therefore, was to find the principle for an order that would be stable and still answer the requirements of progress. Unlike the Liberals, who favored the idea of permanent, and hence controlled, revolution as the key, Saint-Simon and Comte strove for an established social order. They could not, like the traditionalists, base it theocratically, since for them, as heirs of the 18th century and the revolution, the absence of God was taken for granted. The ordering principle must consequently be sought in the nature of society itself, insofar as it is ruled by the law of progress; here again progress itself becomes an ultimate norm, although in a new way, because now a scientifically exact understanding of progress is required.

Up to this point SAINT-SIMON and his dissident secretary are in full accord, but now their paths separate. Deeply impressed by the revolution and its intellectual prehistory, Saint-Simon distinguishes between "critical" and "organic" periods. The former contribute to progress in a negative way only, by eliminating antiquated principles and prejudices — an explication which suits the predominantly negative idea of progress in the first half of the 18th century. But so as to be able to understand and project for the organic period, which

---

[23] See Frank E. Manuel, *The New World of Henri Saint-Simon,* Cambridge Mass. (Harvard) 1956, p. 75; E. Littré, *Auguste Comte et la philosophie positive,* Paris ²1864, p. 70. — For what follows, we are largely indebted to: Henri Gouhier, *La jeunesse d'Auguste Comte et la formation du positivisme.* III: Auguste Comte et Saint-Simon, Paris (Vrin) 1941.

has obtained since the end of the revolution, Saint-Simon reverts to political economy (after an unsuccessful attempt to place progress in physiological categories). The ultimate criterion for the new ethic, which will characterize this (and every other) organic period, will be economic progress. Whatever increases industrial production is good — that is, growing socialization ("association") and especially the new "spirit" which is henceforth to stimulate economico-social relations. Saint-Simon himself, especially in his later years, spoke of this new spirit with its pregnant significance for progress, in religious terms; finally, with his posthumous disciples, his doctrine was completely reinterpreted as a new religion, which, being a religion of progress, was to represent the perfection of all religions, "the criterion of which is progress." [24]

In the meantime, while the theory of progress according to Saint-Simon is turning into religion, AUGUSTE COMTE, following his mathematical bent, was designing what was probably the most succinct and compelling *scientific* construction of a theory of progress. Comte would have politico-social progress be both demonstrable and calculable, through its incorporation in an encompassing body of a theory of sciences. He distinguishes, firstly, between pure and applied science and requires accordingly a theory of political science as presupposition and base for practical politics. This science is then — secondly — placed, as sociology (with "morals" later superimposed) at the apex of a hierarchical ordering of all the sciences. But all knowledge — thirdly — yields to the dynamic law of development, which governs the progress from the theological through the metaphysical to the positive, essentially scientific, stage where the earlier causal explanation of phenomena is replaced by the simple recognition of uniform laws. Applied retrospectively, this Law of the Three Stages makes it possible to infer the progress of the sciences and the social order by an inductive process from the relativity of their transient situations, without having to accept progress from the start (as does Condorcet) as an all-conquering absolute. Looking ahead (and this is the decisive point) this Law allows the assessment that and how sociology, as the

---

[24] *Doctrine de Saint-Simon,* ed. cit. p. 33.

highest and the ultimate science, shall reach presently the positive stage, so that a precise account of the social dynamic is possible and also of society's progress at any given time in the future.

In later years Comte too developed a new religion of the "grand-Être" — which is nothing but the sum of all mankind that has grown up to "existence commune" and therefore to progress. Three paths led Comte to this new religion: the need of supplying the practitioners of his science with a missionary calling, since they were to replace the decadent clergy as "pouvoir spirituel"; discovery of the role of feeling and its importance for human beings; and, above all, the desire of a synthesis which no single science of itself could provide. Accordingly, the positivist religion of Auguste Comte is to be sharply distinguished from the religion of the Saint-Simonists, in which progress is transformed into a mystique, while the religion of Comte ministers to scientific progress. For both, however, progress is the supreme absolute.

Once again the discourse on progress, religion, and the absolute is joined by another of Comte's contemporaries, PROUDHON; however, in this case, not to bind them together, but to put them forcibly asunder. Faith in progress, for Proudhon, is inescapable:

> We all believe indefatigably in progress, just as we believe in Liberty and in Justice. On this point, theologians and philosophers, theory and practice, rich man and proletarians, all, are substantially in agreement. That harsh dictum: humanity is ever the same — as foolish, worthless, and wicked as it on its first day, strikes us as blasphemy.[25]

This unavoidable idea of progress Proudhon takes advantage of in an initial phase to eradicate the absolute: Everything is in ferment; over and over again the revolution is obliged to disavow the old ways; it cannot reverse history, but it can accelerate it or guide its course. In its ultimate form, Proudhon's philosophy eliminates fatalism in all its forms from the idea of progress. Movement is indeed necessary,

---

[25] *De la Justice ...*, ed. cit. III, p. 511.

but it depends on freedom whether this movement advances toward the realization of justice or whether because of hesitancy to believe in such realization, or lacking the necessary force for a new adaptation to reality, it eddies about an idolatrous or religious *ideal*. If the latter is the case, we are no longer dealing with progress, but with decadence, of which religion is one of the most conspicuous symptoms. Progress comes to pass automatically, for man is free and strives after righteousness; it is decadence that requires an explanation. Yet more decadence than progress is found in the history of mankind; even the usual theories of progress "hope for progress rather than believe in it" [26]; for progress certainly cannot happen through fate; it has to be won by freedom. "Actually, Proudhon lost sight entirely of the idea of progress, without being aware that in the end he has given it up. He makes further use of it only to have the advantage of its revolutionary impact on the proletariat." [27]

IV. - Among the fatalists of progress against whom Proudhon draws his sword, HEGEL holds first place,[28] and in Proudhon's theory of the ideal one finds echoes of KANT, for which Proudhon was probably indebted to his friend TISSOT, Kant's translator. The Saint-Simonists also knew Hegel at second-hand, and Auguste Comte had studied Kant's outline for a philosophy of history.[29] Inversely, Kant, Herder, and Hegel were influenced by the French theorists on progress, mainly Voltaire and Rousseau. Therefore, our survey, oriented thus far principally to French thought on the history of the idea of progress must be supplemented by a brief periscopic view of German speculation on this subject. Brevity is justified in that German thought on progress became influential historically only with the Hegelian school. It is true that the philosophy of progress seems to have more depth in the German classical thinkers than in their French contemporaries; but its efficacy was far more limited. This sterility on

---

[26] ibid. IV, p.

[27] Georges Gurwitch, *Proudhon. Sa vie, son oeuvre, avec un exposé de sa philosophie*, Paris (PUF) 1965, p. 31.

[28] See *De la Justice ...*, ed. cit. III, p. 513.

[29] E. Littré, op. cit. (note 23), p. 52; 155-158.

the level of practical politics, for which left-wing Hegelians were always reproaching classical German thought, may have been connected, on the one hand, with the decentralization of German principalities and cultural centers, which simply did not permit the forces of social criticism to build up the revolutionary impetus that we find in Paris. On the other hand, German speculation, even in the period of the Enlightenment was strongly influenced by scholastic philosophy and protestant theology, and received therefrom a pronounced metaphysical impress. The question of progress was, accordingly, approached from the standpoint of theology and the nature of man and history, not "from the bottom," that is, from the presuppositions and realizations of technological progress. Consequently, progress was sought first and foremost in the realm of morality, because there (and there only) does man draw nearer to his true perfection. Soon, however, biological evolution also claimed attention; but this too for German thinkers signified more than pure contemporary concurrence: spirit and βίος were inter-related by a special kind of elective affinity. Archetypally, their reciprocity has been asserted in Leibniz's "Monadology," which ends with the harmony between the realm of nature and the realm of grace (or morality).

In the same Monadology, there are two other features of German thought on progress to be noticed; namely, the category of *development* and that of *wholeness*. The idea of "progress," basically static with the French, is, generally speaking, replaced by the Germans with the idea of "development," or a change in the same thing. Leibniz's monads are continually developing; each of them *is* nothing else but the particular law of such a continuing development sequence. Each, however, despite all changes remains itself; that is, it really "develops itself," because it is conceived of as strictly a *whole* and not as a "sum-total," merely, of its successive states. Comte's "Grand-Être" was never more than a mere "ensemble": The unity or union of human beings growing toward community was not thematic with him. The German problematic, on the contrary, is attached precisely to this wholeness of the social structure, even where (as with Herder) it is to come about solely by means of the physiological *con-*

61

tinuity of the chain of generations and the equally continuous chain of cultural tradition.

With these prefatory remarks we can now sketch briefly the various theories of progress held by individual thinkers, and so establish chronologically a gradual transition from the more metaphysical to the more materialistic idea of development. The first work to be mentioned in this connection, LESSING's "Education of the Human Race" represents an attempt to harmonize theology with belief in the general and inevitable progress of human reason. Faith in progress is gained by establishing a parallel between the history of the education of the human race and that of the individual man, which passes from instinctual responses and fear morality to morality for its own sake. As for the past, revelation is supposed to have fostered this development of reason in the individual, inasmuch as it provided for reason the "facit," so to speak, "which the arithmetic teacher gives beforehand to his pupils, so that they may find the correct result more easily themselves thereafter." [30] From now on, "the divine education" (or "eternal providence" or "nature") will be called upon to guarantee the progress of the human race, because it will work toward this goal as persistently as in the case of the education of the individual. Revelation and providence, therefore, are to serve the progress of reason, which thereby is tacitly elevated to the status of absolute criterion.

With KANT a rupture occurs in this normative functioning of progress, in accordance with the fundamental dualism of his system. The categorical imperative alone is absolute norm. Totally inapposite as a goal for progress, it is, in its pure rationality, a sort of eternal "now". Progress, however, takes place in the effort of rational beings to assimilate the moral law—in other words, to be holy—and, what is more such progress has to be conceived as unending; indeed, it is on this ground that the immortality of the soul is postulated. So much for Kant the metaphysician; for the problematic of earthly progress here being considered, his metaphysical do-

---

[30] *op. cit.* § 76. — Most of the texts of the German philosophers, we have to cite here, may be found in: K. Rossmann, *Deutsche Geschichtsphilosophie von Lessing bis Jaspers,* Bremen (Schünemann) 1959.

trine has no direct contribution to make. Yet, the observance of the kantian moral law has to be at least *possible* in the terrestrial-empirical world—and no less in the world of history than in the world of nature. Therefore, it must be assumed that history aims at a "natural end" (and, therefore, that it makes continuous progress); this end could only be an historico-social situation in conformity with the moral law; that is, "an internally—and for this purpose also externally— perfect political constitution" [31] and an international order that will guarantee "everlasting peace."

And now Kant, the philosopher of the "fertile bathos of experience", unrolls the chart for a universal history that would have to show how self-interest and wars *must* in the end lead man "naturally" to the best political constitution and to a cosmopolitan outlook—in which connection "must" is to be interpreted "obliged by duty" and not in the sense of utopian expectations.[32] The paradoxical mechanism of evil that necessarily produces good, which we have already met with in economic liberalism, is here applied (in a manner worth pondering today) to socio-political progress. In being moored thus in the natural malevolence of man, Kant's optimistic view of progress takes on an undertone of sobering realism, which is lacking in the schemas of his contemporaries, near and more distant. It acquires also a theological overlay in that the doctrine of "radical evil", i. e., of original sin, is the cardinal tenet of Kant's philosophy of religion.

HERDER likewise develops his theory of progress against a theological background, but in polemic with Lessing and with Kant. He rejects Lessing's notion of an education of the human race (the genus), as "averroistic", and likewise Kant's tenet that the goal of progress is not in the happiness of the individual, but in the best possible political constitution. The root of this controversy is in Herder's radical rejection of the Enlightenment's conception of reason. Against Voltaire, he asserts that civilization and "enlightenment" are to be found in all periods, and that every culture has its own "maximum" in which it attains its ultimate goal. This cultural pluralism,

---

[31] *Idee zu einer allgemeinen Geschichte*, 8th proposition, ed. cit. VIII, p. 27.

[32] *Erneuerte Frage*, § 9 note, ed. cit. VII, p. 92.

which does not allow practical reason to serve as the only parameter of progress, results from the fact that, while it is the essential characteristic of "humanity" not to be confined to the compulsion of instinct, every culture is permanently conditioned by its milieu. Therefore, humanity arises always and only in a multiplicity of cultures. The unity of this pluralistic self-development is preserved by reason of each phase of development being embedded in a "tradition" which men of other cultures and cultural epochs assimilate by cultural formation ("Bildung"). Thanks to this chain of civilizing tradition—and only through such continuity—mankind is made a whole. Herder speaks of this chain of succession in theological terms as "voice of God"; but the schema of wholeness through continuity was borrowed from physiology, specifically, from the *evolution* of man from the lower animals, which is treated at length in the first four books of Herder's "Ideas". Hence, the history of civilization is only a secondary phase—a "second Genesis"—in the history of mankind.

In HEGEL's philosophy of history, the source of many, if not all later currents, Herder's viewpoint is finally merged with Kantian thought in an autonomous union. On the one hand, Hegel with Herder rejects the immutable reason of the Enlightenment, and seeks wholeness in the continuity of progress itself; but this continuity is seen by Hegel in a plenary dimension: it is an absolute which develops *itself,* unfolding its own virtualities. "Development" and not "progress" is the watchword of this philosophy of spirit, which sees history as *mind becoming itself*; and which, in expressing this idea, chooses, revealingly enough, the image of the shoot becoming a tree. The meaning of this historical process is immanent to it; it need not be sought in a transcendent goal.

As to its content, Hegel understands this process as "progress in the idea of freedom"—that is, progress toward a socio-political order which makes true morality possible; i. e., free action in the highest sense. Here for once there is agreement in principle between Hegel and Kant; but Hegel lacks Kant's unlimited, open, cosmopolitan perspective. Living at a later time and of petit-bourgeois outlook, he favored the perfect social order already realized in principle in the "civil

64

society" and in the Prussian State. But the decisive difference in relation to Kant lies in Kant's interpretation of socio-political progress as a (statistical) product of empirical social forces, whereas Hegel sees it as the willed manifestation of the world-spirit moving toward its own reality, namely, freedom.

The metaphysical overlay which makes Hegel's whole philosophy seem to be a metaphysic of development, ought not, nevertheless, obscure the fundamental insight that his philosophy deals primarily with society evolving toward a concretized political freedom. Everything else is subordinated to this central theme: logis is its interior framework, philosophy of nature a gateway to it, and philosophy of religion its indispensable capstone; because it is "one of the follies of modern times" to desire "a revolution without a reformation." [33] So understood—and on the evidence of his first drafts and lectures, we must so understand Hegel's thought—the step from Hegel to Marx is shorter than Marx himself realized.

It was for KARL MARX, then, to undertake the search for the *actual laws* governing this society which is evolving into a social order of practical freedom. The moving force of this progress cannot reside, as Hegel supposed, in the idea; the political barrenness of "German ideology", i. e., of the Hegelian left, sufficiently demonstrated that ideas alone do not bring about social change. The required thrust will lie, therefore, in the structure of society itself. The characteristic features of this structure are the division and nexus between the material means of production, the conditions of production and ideology; of these, the means of production, not the ideas, is the determining feature. Change in a society structured in this way is provided by the possible and necessary antagonism between the means of production and the social conditions of production and, from a deeper point of view, by the actual technological progress on the level of means of production. This last is for Marx a given which he appears to regard as foreordained. He does not consider the question whether, conceivably, future progress might place the definitive truth of the Marxian social system in doubt. Basically, he is interested only in discovering laws of movement for the

---

[33] *Enzyklopädie der philosophischen Wissenschaften,* § 552.

5

immediate next step of social development which would lift the working masses out of their misery.

History as we know it, did not, in fact, follow Marx's law; none the less, Marxism in its various forms is at the present time probably the most powerful intellectual force. And this ascendancy has been won by the very thing Marx rejected: the moving force of ideas. Thanks to his apparently exact scientific analysis of historical factors, he arrived at a supremely victorious ideology of progress, which was able to assert itself against economical and social development that was following a different course. It was especially the eschatological pathos inherent in Marxism that molded its ideology. The dialectic of history was supposed to lead to a perfect classless society, but in face of the realities of historical development this objective had to be set always farther into the eschatological future; still it did not degenerate into a utopian dream. It remained the realizable goal of a realizable, inexorable, but probably unending historical process. Because, in this sense, the classless society was to be actually "the end of history", all of history has to be understood, in reverse, as continuous progress toward this final goal. Thus, in contradiction of its original orientation, Marxism acquires the characteristics of a (structurally bourgeois) ideology of progress.

Marx himself did not express the compulsion he found in the historical process in terms of the idea of progress.[34] In the preface and epilog of "Kapital" he compares it rather to the law of biological evolution—and this will suggest to Engels the program of his philosophy. ENGELS expanded Marx's historical materialism to dialectical materialism, according to which one and the same law of dialectic was to govern both evolution in nature and the progress of history; thus (in an entirely different sense than with Marx), the progress of history becomes "scientifically" necessary.

V. - At this point, where speculation in German philosophy of history intersects with the idea of *evolution*, we shall have to consider, however briefly, the history of this idea, which

[34] The term "progress" is entirely lacking in the indices of the MEGA-edition of Marx's works.

belongs primarily to natural science, and show its effects on the problematic of progress. This is not the place to clarify in detail the quite obscure origins of evolution theory. Certainly, it does not derive directly either from the palaeontological classification of species or from the speculation on development in German philosophy of history. Hegel, for instance, does indeed suppose an idealistic development of the whole of nature, but not precisely as "an actual external production" of one species from another.[35] Evolution comes into question only where the hierarchical gradation and chronological ordering of the species is explained by *continuity of generation*. And the decisive (though negative) impulse to this kind of explanation could have come from geology, since it was through a geologist, CHARLES LYELL (1830), that the catastrophic theory was replaced by the theory of continuity. The 19th century historical outlook also could have facilitated the introduction of the idea of evolution, because it permitted even biological phenomena to be conceived of "historically", in as much as their *modifications* were causally *linked*. In response to palaeontological findings and also to the general enthusiasm for progress in this period, the linked modifications were interpreted as a *steady upward movement*, from which was inferred a basic law of finite being, operative far beyond the limits of biology, and valid also for the future.

In this generalized form we find the idea of evolution especially in HERBERT SPENCER, from whom toward the end of the 19th century strong philosophical influence was transmitted, particularly to French circles. Even before DARWIN [36], Spencer developed a general theory of evolution, which defined it as transition "from an indefinite incoherent homogeneity to a definite coherent heterogeneity," [37] and made the law thus

---

[35] *Enzyklopädie*, § 249.

[36] E. Halévy notes: "H. Spencer commence à employer avec précision le mot *évolution* dans son essai intitulé *Genesis of science*, juillet 1854. (V. *Essays*, I, pp. 185, 227). Mais c'est seulement en 1857 (*Progress, its law and causes*, avril 1857; *Transcendental physiology*, octobre 1857) que sa théorie se trouve constituée, en tant qu'elle définit l'évolution par le passage de l'homogène à l'hétérogène. En octobre 1859, Darwin publie son *Origin of Species*, où le mot évolution n'est pas employé." (in: A. Lalande, *Vocabulaire*, [6]1951, p. 313).

[37] *First principles*, ch. 17.

enunciated the fundamental law of every kind of progress: "the development of the earth, the development of life on earth, the development of society, forms of government, trade, commerce, language, literature, science, art." This panevolutionism of Spencer, A. LALANDE will censure as an illegitimate extrapolation from the biological to the intellectual sphere; in the intellectual-moral realm progress signifies increasing assimilation rather than differentiation. TEILHARD DE CHARDIN, who had made contact with Spencerian ideas through BERGSON [38] and also, presumably, in connection with the whole environment of his studies, assumed likewise in his "integral evolutionism" a uniform law for biological evolution and for the progress of civilization—the evolution of the "noosphere". But this progress is no longer viewed as *parallel* with biological evolution; it is the real (and necessary) *continuation* of it, and thus the basic law is transposed to a higher plane. Indeed, this law of "Convergent-Complexity," understood as higher organization through interiorization, transcended the insights of Spencer and Lalande. It seems, in general, to have had originally a psychologico-spiritual orientation, which Teilhard refers to in somewhat Cartesian style as "conscience" and "reflexion", just as he deduces the irreversibility of evolution from the noosphere. Biological evolution, then, is a mere presupposition of Evolution in the full meaning of this term —the progress of humanity, an inference which favors Teilhard's radical deduction that only a teleological view of evolution can explain it effectively. Teilhard's theory of progress therefore becomes eschatological, but not, (like Marxism) in substitution of an unattainable immanent end of history, but because, once the Omega Point is beheld (and this faith promises with absolute certitude) all past happenings will, from that vantage point, be ultimately illumined.

VI. - With regard to this theory of progress, which is probably the most comprehensive of all and the most optimistic of the future, and which has been, understandably, received with enthusiasm, the question arises whether it should be

---

[38] At the end of his *L'Évolution créatrice* (Paris [14]1913, p. 393-399) Bergson discusses and criticizes the doctrine of Spencer, to whose influence he had been exposed during his studies.

classified in intellectual history as an offshoot of the 19th century or as a harbinger of the 21st. For, in actual fact, the idea of progress as a scientific concept fell into disrepute in the first half of the 20th century and was subjected to severe criticism. As popular ideology, of course, it continued to live on as a groundswell, and very recently it joyfully celebrated its "second spring." Meanwhile, a new world problem presented itself, and while it has nothing to do with ideology, it lends new reality to the idea of progress; it is the problem of (under)development. But before we turn to this latest problematic, we must summarize the results of our inquiry thus far.

1. Amid all the disguises, shifts, and transformations of the idea of progress which its history has shown us, a persistent continuity is to be noted, which seems to take a specific direction. The point of departure for the entire history of the idea was the *step toward a new mentality* taken by BACON and DESCARTES, which marked the beginning of modern philosophy. The whole history of thought on progress takes place within this new world concept and it seems to represent a necessary presupposition for serious discussion of progress and also for its realization. The ensign-bearer for the theory of progress is first and foremost "homo technicus," for whom there is no problem of ultimates, only the necessity, always recurring, of finding a new (technological) solution for every new problem.

2. As the history of the idea of progress proceeds, there is entwined within it a progressive and apparently unavoidable change of the content — and consequently the parameter also — of this idea. Interest shifts from culturo-technological progress to economic, to social, to politico-moral progress, so that its idea embraces ever wider and deeper areas of human life. Consequently, there was a change in defining what ultimately constitutes progress. Regarded first as an amassing of external economic and cultural goods, progress was sought finally in the transformation of organic structures.

3. Along the same lines, there is a change to be noted also in the conception of progress as necessary and with this an

inversion of the (prevailing) orientation: with the desirability of progress as point of departure, the actual (but chiefly negative) realization of it is first found in the past; then progress becomes a norm, is compulsory for the future as a duty or as an absolute; and finally, by virtue of a general law, is predicted as necesarily occurring henceforth. Therewith, progress increasingly assumes a religious dimension, either with the value of absolute norm or as an eschatological reward. At the same time it keeps drifting further away from being an idea founded in reason or fact and becomes ideological.

4. In the light of these conclusions, as our last point, the question of the relationship of the idea of progress to the Christian religion can and must be discussed. The definitive status of the idea of progress toward the end of its history as an ideology with a religious thrust accounts, at any rate, for the distrust of it on the part of theology and ecclesiastical officialdom. Christianity can neither settle for becoming substituted in the future by a religion of progress, nor can it allow itself to be miscast as guarantor of progress by guaranteeing socio-political order. Yet the question still remains whether the idea of progress in its earlier (and, perhaps, in its future) historical configuration, was just as incompatible with Christianity and whether the inner dynamic of its history had necessarily to ring it to a terminal form inimical to Christianity.

a) With regard to the first question, it is certain, at all events, that "homo technicus," as leading standard-bearer for progress theory, does not represent specifically either a non-Christian or a positively anti-Christian figure. Bacon, Galilei, and Descartes wished to be good Christians, personally at any rate, not to mention Pascal. There is a well-founded opinion that holds that the Christian desacralization of the world and the Christian valuation of manual labor (as opposed to the one-sided emphasis of *theoria* in ancient philosophy) were determining preconditions for the rise of "homo technicus." Yet it should not be overlooked that the theorists on progress were oriented from the beginning to a prospective view of the world that ran directly counter to the theological focus on the ancient truths of tradition [39]; so that unavoidable tensions and misunderstandings ensued. The cultural values that were set up first as parameter for progress, also lay so very far outside the traditional Christian value system that, on the one hand, the spontaneously defensive attitude in ecclesiastical circles toward theories of progress is understandable. On the other hand, the so-called Christian centuries appeared to the champions of progress as expressly alien to progress — rampant with superstition, despotism, social injustice, which religious Christianity appeared to sanction. From this opinion it was a short step to the conclusion that progress must carry on without and in opposition to Christianity — a conviction that contributed a handy new argument, at least, to Voltaire's campaign against the church, to the militant anti-clericalism of the 18th and 19th centuries, and to the programmed atheism of the Hegelian left. Moreover, the impending clash between progress theory in all its forms and Christianity was hastened to such an extent by historical circumstances that it would be almost impossible to decide whether such collision had its roots in the very essence of either of the two doctrines.

b) A similar answer might be given to our second question, whether the hostility to Christianity which actually characterized the idea of progress in the final stage reached in the 19th century, was a natural outgrowth of an intrinsic and compulsory dynamic. We have seen how much the theories of Saint-Simon, Auguste Comte, and Karl Marx were determined, not by an inner logic of the idea of progress, but by existing politico-social conditions which they sought to alleviate theoretically and practically with the aid of this idea. That Saint-Simonism and Comte in the end developed a new post-Christian religion is mainly attributable to their finding themselves in a society where *de facto* "God" (meaning Christianity) was "absent." The circumstances of Marxism's explicit warfare against all religion were somewhat

---

[39] One may note, that in the "Querelle" (see here above p. 50-51) the predilection for the "anciens" went with that for the pseudo-traditionalist jansenistic theology. The anti-religious progressivism of the French XVIIIth century was in fact largely a reaction against jansenism.

different. The battle here was not so much against Christianity in itself as against its value as symbol of an unprogressive (and closed to progress) social order. The fact that Marxism, as time went on, took on an eschatological (and therefore religious) dimension can be traced, as we have seen, to a compulsion inherent in the system and its historical destiny, and not to rivalry with Christianity.

5. Everything we have seen so far can be summarized once more in connection with the question whether LöwiTH's secularization thesis can be accepted. At first, the thesis looks attractive and several indications seem to speak for it. Doubtless, Bossuet's "Discours" furnished a pattern for Voltaire and Turgot and the calvinist republic of Geneva for Rousseau, to say nothing of Saint-Simon's and Comte's Christian mimicry. Certainly, notable structural similarities are found between the progress of reason making its way in and through the irrational, and the image of divine providence as developed in the Christian theology of history. But, on the other hand, we have seen how the first appearance of the idea of progress and each new advance in its history could be explained in every instance by specific causes and conditions; and how for the most part this history took place in an intellectual milieu, from which Christianity was *de facto* already absent. The German thinkers are the only exception; particularly Hegel, who, indeed, made secularization (that is, the attempt to make Christianity an idea) the program of his philosophy. We should like to hazard a guess that Löwith's secularization thesis was obtained by an extrapolation from the consideration of Hegelian philosophy (its native soil). But such an extrapolation is possible only if the ideas are highly formalized and one may question whether this is permissible at all in the case of an idea as historically conditioned as the idea of progress. In our opinion, from the conjunction of progress theory and non-Christianity that actually occurred, there cannot be inferred either a "post hoc," so that the idea of progress would appear as specifically "post-Christian," or a "propter hoc" of non-Christianity as preliminary condition for theorizing on progress, or an "in vicem" of progress as ersatz Christianity. It remains for Christian

theologians to meditate upon a full and unadulterated Christianity and to make it viable in the world we have with us, which is now permanently stamped *de facto* with the concept of progress — a concept which (again *de facto*) originated outside and in some degree in opposition to Christianity. The final section of our inquiry may specify further the nature of this theological task.

III. THE ACTUAL SITUATION.

A comprehensive study of the history of the idea of progress since the close of the 19th century is still a desideratum. This is probably not to be ascribed only to the difficulties involved in any contemporary history of an idea, but also to the fact that the idea of progress appears to have undergone no further change in contemporary times. Consequently, it was rather a question of writing a history of the *ideology* of progress, i. e., a contemporary history of its diffusion and the acceptance as well as the opposition it met with. This is, of course, not tne appropriate place for such an inquiry. We can only cite a couple of symptomatic instances which will indicate this history in a fragmentary way and so provide background for the new problem which suddenly appeared after the second world war and which seems to be opening an entirely new phase in the history of the idea of progress.

I. - The first thing to be noted is a growing scepticism from the end of the 19th century regarding the idea of progress, prompted not so much by disappointed expectations as on the grounds of theoretical difficulties. In the area of historical science, RANKE and JACOB BURCKHARDT raised doubts about the constructions relating to progress and universal history; the relevance of historical change, in which is involved the very foundation of the idea of progress, was obscured by KIERKEGAARD and his theological imitators through their existential interpretation of history; and lately it has been rejected by structuralism also. Moreover, the cyclic concept of history has in recent decades been revived, most influentially by OSWALD SPENGLER's doctrine on decline, which provided an opportune world-outlook for the years following the first world war.

In the field of the social sciences, the idea of progress was exposed by GEORGES SOREL (1908), from a Marxist standpoint, as a bourgeois, anti-revolutionary invention; thirty years later GEORGES FRIEDMANN verified empirically the failure of socialist efforts on behalf of progress, and after another interval of twenty years, ERNST BLOCH called attention to the fundamental ambivalence in the idea of progress. A step forward in the economico-technological substructure can be the cause of a step backward in the superstructure. And the most difficult task of all is to integrate the different aspects of progress in the different cultural milieus in terms of the global progress of mankind. We can only *hope* that the various manifestations of progress will merge as one eschatological-overall-"human" progress. Progress for Bloch is not a fact or a program; it is a hope.

In making these distinctions, Bloch is calling into question, not scientifico-technological progress, but the parameter of progress. His position in this regard may be considered paradigmatic for the present-day stand on the idea of progress. No one would attempt to deny the progress in technology, science, and economics, so clearly evident today on almost all fronts. "Science fiction" is both the expression of and the stimulus for unlimited expectations, which are directed beyond accomplishments already realized to progress still to come. The division into "conservatives" and "progressives" which was established for practical purposes by Council journalism even in the sphere of theology elevated the abetting and the opposing of progress, respectively, to the level of a universal value standard. In fact, belief in progress is probably the only operative "ecumenical" credo of modern man that embraces both East and West. Yet, at work beneath all this enthusiasm for progress, like a groundswell, is a widespread cultural anxiety which, with E. MOUNIER, we may term the "petite peur du XXe siècle" or with K. LÖWITH, the "Verhängnis des Fortschritts." [40] If, until recently, this anxiety

---

[40] in: *Die Philosophie und die Frage nach dem Fortschritt,* ed. H. Kuhn - F. Wiedmann, München (Pustet) 1964, p. 15-29.

was over possible reverses — economic crises and an atomic war — it is now anxiety over the (biological) consequences of progress itself: pollution of the "environment", cancer-inducing products, genetic manipulation. The quarantining of the astronauts was only an exceptionally bizarre symbol with worldwide resonance of this covert fear of progress. The average citizen of our progressive world of today knows, although he may be unwilling to admit it, that technology, science, and economics, do not yield ultimately valid parameters of progress.

The protests of "youth" against contemporary social progress and its alienating structures are challenging these traditional parameters openly and caustically. Where the protest is expressed by a simple "opting out" of the established social order, as in the case of the hippies, it probably signifies an "opting out" also of the idea of progress. But where the protest becomes theoretical (MARCUSE) and practical (the student revolts) denial of the existing order, it represents a metamorphosis of the idea of progress which looks not unlike the transformation it underwent in the second half of the 18th century. Where this whole intellectual movement will eventually lead cannot yet be foreseen — and prediction becomes even less likely in view of the fact that the protesters themselves seem unable to express their dissatisfaction with contemporary social progress in any but negative terms.

II. - This uncomfortable tension regarding social progress, together with the insight that further progress is absolutely essential, was given a whole new dimension by the sudden appearance about twenty years ago of a new problem. The revolutionary new phenomenon is the converging movement of peoples and cultures in the new world of global communication. World trade and economic interconnections are drawing the five continents together more and more into one single economic area. Intercontinental mobility and intellectual interchange through mass media create the prospect of the emergence of a unified world culture. The cultures, and even more, the specific problems of peoples in faraway places are communicated by press, radio, film, television, to the most distant corners of the earth, indeed into private family living rooms; and thus our planet is being transformed increasingly into a "global village." Apart from the quite small enclaves which either isolate themselves or are assimilated, there are no longer any cultural groups that are closed off from one another; and inversely, because of this global interconnection and exchange, the distinctions between individual peoples and cultural traditions are becoming evident and — again via mass media — generally recognized. The idea of progress thus acquires for the first time a strictly empirical, if negatively defined, content, in so far as the scale of gradation from "advanced" to "underdeveloped" economic and social structures can be accurately measured; hence the idea of progress is freed from the necessity of concern about a projected parameter to be sought in the past or even in the future.

Yet, in this assembling of new data, the 18th and 19th century idea of progress, with the historical orientation it then acquired, was still operating as a norm, and this in a three-fold way:

1. The criterion for determining a condition of underdevelopment is furnished by that same economico-cultural parameter that was found to be the chief parameter in the 18th century. Consequently, the problem of aid to development appears to be a typically western, or more specifically, a post-voltairian problem. A traditional African society would doubtlessly not consider itself underdeveloped, even though it lacked nearly all civilized refinements and conveniences. And it is in fact more highly developed in some respects than most of the so-called "advanced" societies. However, such an evaluation offers no appeal today, even to the African himself, because he finds himself incorporated *de facto* in an all-embracing socio-economic complex in which his particular way of life *must* appear "underdeveloped", culturally and technologically. Today he is no longer in a position to say: It is better (and more "progressive") for me to go on planting manioc with a spade and so preserve my integrated human and religious view of the world, than to accomodate myself to the dynamic of world progress.

2. Indeed, the discovery of different culturo-economic levels soon led to the insight — first of all in the so-called

76

development countries themselves — that this is not the only, or the most decisive, perhaps, (though it may be the most conspicuous) inequity. The difference in socio-political standards and, in any case, the disparity in the area of education are to be taken far more seriously. These inequities — again in the context of today's coalescing world — expose the peoples of the Third World to oppressive structures and deprive them of real possibilities of self-expression. This explains the insistent cries for real political independence and self-determination that have been heard from all sides since the second world war, and also the more subdued demands for worldwide education and training missions. Here also western-style training, i. e., scientifico-technological, and political organizations in effect in the Western world, i. e., democratic, were extrapolated as parameters for non-Western cultures. Behind the extrapolations, however, is reason's demand for a realized equality of all men — the demand that accounts for the decisive shift in the idea of progress in the second half of the 18th century. This call for equality in its present worldwide dimension has lost the abstractness that was still connected with it in the 18th century, for it is now a very concrete insistence that (materially vast) bases and preconditions be created for the genuine equality of all the citizens of the world. Furthermore, from this worldwide viewpoint, equality can never mean uniformity. Fundamentally and chiefly it must signify an equal right to that which is proper to each individual and to every nation and the recognition that this which is proper and of equal value in every instance gives rise to equivalent rights; i. e., in terms of structure, it claims a solidarity by federation, which is perhaps the closest approximation to a socio-political translation of Christian brotherhood.

3. The demand for equality is acknowledged as a realistic demand only because there is a concomitant awareness that we have at our disposal, in principle, the means to eliminate the existing difference of level. Underdevelopment as a fact is an appeal to "homo technicus" to promote progress; so that here the problem becomes again and in the widest sense a technological problem. What is needed is to find an

operative technique — and no one doubts the possibility in principle of finding it — that can make progress toward equality on a world scale feasible. It is this prospect of technological breakthrough that gives positive significance to technological progress in the West and its apparently senseless peak-points — space flights, for example. For a technology of world progress becomes a possibility only in a world of technological progress. A definitive parameter of the multi-faceted technological progress which can be achieved today or in the future is not so much the actual or potential results as the question whether such accomplishments really contribute to that dynamic of progress which seems to be indispensable for the redress of underdevelopment.

4. In summary, the structural elements of the idea of progress so far ascertained are: identification of an existing difference of level, demand for its redress, on the grounds of an acknowledged right to equality, possibility of such redress through a technology of progress — and here we find ourselves, for the first time, dealing with progress in the sense of an *imperative*. Progress shall occur because life worthy of a human being, in other words, effective equality for all, has to be made possible. In this context the idea of progress is no longer historically conditioned, nor is it any longer eschatologico-utopian; it is a *moral* concept; its proper milieu is the *future*, that is to say, the very next step which *can* be taken, and therefore *has to* be taken.

Here then is the place where theology and church officialdom could and should make peace with the idea of progress. For despite all the layers of ideological overlay which has accrued to it by reason of its history, we are now dealing with an imperative, devoid in principle of ideological connection because it is determined by a situation with negative factual value; this imperative Christian morality cannot, on principle, ignore. A *theology of human progress* will above all have to consider this imperative on the moral-theological plane and from this standpoint take up the underlying dogmatic question as to the connection this (in the first instance humanitarian) imperative has with the coming of the Kingdom of God, and also what should be said concerning the

78

relationship of human progress to salvation history. In such theological debates there cannot and there need not be question of adding an ideological groundwork to the imperative of progress. It is far more a question of evaluating the idea of progress according to criteria of Christian discernment. And, in our opinion, a knowledge of the structural components of this idea, as these are revealed by its history, can shed light on this task. One example (but a pivotal one) might illustrate this point conclusively. We have seen how the quest for progress in a really valid sense began in the culturo-technological sphere, shifted definitively to the socio-political, and ended finally in the moral realm, and how this shift brought with it a transition from a cumulative to a transformative concept of progress. But transformation on a socio-political level signifies at the peak, "revolution," and revolution can represent genuine progress only in the measure that it is the expression and realization of a *conversion* on the moral level. Kant's ingenious construction of politico-moral progress was defective in so far as it opposed to a static human depravity an equally static practical reason. Thus the whole movement of progress towards a political system ordered to morality had to be ascribed paradoxically to the mechanical operation of depravity. If, on the other hand, we assume, with the Christian message, that man is neither incorrigibly depraved nor confirmed in virtue, that he is rather called perpetually to conversion, then speculation on progress takes on a new perspective. The decisive question of a theology of progress, as to what meaning earthly progress has in view of the Messianic proclamation: "The kingdom of God is close at hand" might be answered perhaps with another question: What then of the proclamation which immediately follows and is not to be separated from the first: "Repent and believe the Good News"? (Mk. 1. 15). What can and what must it signify for the future of our human world? A theology of progress might see as its task the examining of the claims and consequences which flow from the initial christian act, conversion, in their socio-political and indeed cosmopolitan implications.

BIBLIOGRAPHY

A. *Studies on the History of the Idea of Progress* (in chronological order):

Ferdinand Brunetière, *La formation de l'idée de progrès au XVIIIe siècle*, in: *Etudes critiques de la littérature française*, 6e série, Paris (Hachette) 1893.

N. K. Mikhailovski, *Qu'est-ce que le progrès? Examen des idées de M. Herbert Spencer*, 1897.

Gaston Milhaud, *Le positivisme et le progrès de l'esprit*, Paris 1902.

J. Delavaille, *Essai sur l'histoire de l'idée de progrès jusqu'à la fin du XVIIIe siècle*, Paris (Alcan) 1910.

John B. Bury, *The Idea of Progress. An Inquiry into its Origin and Growth*, London 1920; New York (Macmillan) ²1932.

P. Mouy, *L'idée de progrès dans la philosophie de Renouvier*, Paris 1927.

E. Dupréel, *Deux essais sur le progrès*, Bruxelles (Lamertin) 1928.

Carl L. Becker, *The Heavenly City of the XVIIIth Century Philosophers*, New Haven, 1932.

J. G. Frazer, *Condorcet on the Progress of Human Mind* (Zakaroff Lectures), 1933.

René Hubert, *Essai sur l'histoire de l'idée de progrès*, in: *Revue d'histoire de la philosophie et d'histoire générale de la civilisation* 2 (1934) 289-305; 3 (1935) 1-32.

Henri Gouhier, *Programme pour une étude historique du prépositivisme*, in: *La jeunesse d'Auguste Comte et la formation du positivisme*, Paris (Vrin) 1936, II, p. 5-62.

Kurt Breysig, *Gestaltungen des Entwicklungsgedankens*, Berlin (de Gruyter) 1941.

H. Linn Edsall, *The Idea of History and Progress in Fontenelle and Voltaire*, in: *Studies by the Members of the French Department of Yale University*, New Haven 1941, p. 163-184.

P. Menzer, *Kants Lehre der Entwicklung in der Natur und Geschichte*, Berlin 1941.

Robert C. K. Ensor, *Some Reflections on Herbert Spencer's Doctrine that Progress is Differentiation*, 1946.

Ch. Frankel, *The Faith of Reason*. The Idea of Progress in the French Enlightenment, Oxford, 1948.

Karl Löwith, *Meaning in History*. The Theological Implications of the Philosophy of History, Chicago (Univ. of Chicago) 1949.

L'Encyclopédie et le progrès des sciences et des techniques, ed. S. Delorme - R. Taton, Paris (Centre international de synthèse) 1952.

Wolfgang Zorn, *Zur Geschichte des Wortes und Begriffes "Fortschritt"*, in: *Saeculum* 4 (1953) 340-345.

Alberto Cento, *Condorcet et l'idea di progresso*, Firenze, 1956.

W. M. Simon, *History for Utopia: Saint-Simon and the Idea of Progress*, in: *Journal of the History of Ideas* 17 (1956) 311-331.

A. L. Harris, *Stuart Mill's Theory of Progress*, in: *Ethics* 66 (1956).

N. Petruzellis, art. *Progresso*, in: *Enciclopedia Filosofica*, Firenze (Sansoni) 1957, III, col. 1656-1658.

H. Maus, art. *Fortschritt*, in: *Die Religion in Geschichte und Gegenwart*, Tübingen (Mohr) ³1958, II, col. 1006-1008.

H. Franchini, *Il progresso: Storia di un'idea*, Milano 1960.

Michelangelo Ghio, *L'idea di progresso nell'Illuminismo francese e tedesco* (Studi e ricerche di storia della filosofia, 49), Torino (Filosofia) 1962.

Michelangelo Ghio, *L'idea di progresso in Lessing*, in: *Filosofia* 14 (1963) 90-98.

Gianni M. Pozzo, *La storia e il progresso nell'Illuminismo francese*, Padova (CEDAM) 1964.

Jean-François Faure-Soulet, *Economie politique et progrès au "Siècle des Lumières"* (Thèse pour le doctorat ès sciences économiques, Dijon), Paris (Gauthier-Villars) 1964.

Hans Robert Jauss, *Ursprung und Bedeutung der Fortschrittsidee in der "Querelle des Anciens et des Modernes,"* in: *Die Philosophie und die Frage nach dem Fortschritt*, ed. H. Kuhn - F. Wiedmann, München (Pustet) 1964, p. 51-72.

Charles Frankel, art. *Progress, the Idea of*, in: *Encyclopedia of Philosophy*, New York-London (Macmillan) 1967, VI, col. 483-487.

Ludwig Edelstein, *The Idea of Progress in Classical Antiquity*, Baltimore (Hopkins) 1967.

B. *Classical Works from XVIIth to XIXth Century:*

Francis Bacon of Verulam, *Two Books of the Proficience and Advancement of Learning, divine and human* (1605), in: *Works*, ed. Spedding-Ellis-Heath, reprint Stuttgart (Fromann) 1963, III, p. 259-491.

—, *De dignitate et augmentis scientiarum* (1621), ed. cit. I, p. 423-837.

—, *Novum Organum sive indicia vera de interpretatione naturae*, (1620), ed. cit. I, p. 119-365; ed. Th. Fowler, Oxford 1878; ed. F. H. Anderson, New York 1960.

—, *New Atlantis* (1627), ed. cit. III, p. 125-166; ed. A. B. Gough, 1915.

Blaise Pascal, *Préface pour le Traité du vide* (1647), in: *Oeuvres,* ed. La Pléiade, Paris (Gallimard) 1954, p. 529-535.

Bernard de Fontenelle, *Digression sur les Anciens et les Modernes* (1688), in: *Oeuvres,* Paris 1766, IV, p. 169-198; ed. R. Shackleton, Oxford 1955.

Voltaire, *Le Mondain* (1736), in: *Mélanges,* ed. La Pléiade, Paris (Gallimard) 1961, p. 203-206.

—, *Essai sur l'Histoire générale et sur les moeurs et l'esprit des nations, depuis Charlemagne jusqu'a nos jours.* Genève 1756; ed. R. Pomeau, Paris (Garnier) 1963.

Jean Jacques Rousseau, *Discours sur les sciences et les arts* (1749), in: *Oeuvres complètes,* ed. La Pléiade, Paris (Gallimard) 1964, III, p. 1-30.

—, *Discours sur l'origine et les fondements de l'inégalité parmi les hommes,* ed. cit. III, p. 109-223.

Turgot, *Tableau philosophique des progrès successifs de l'esprit humain,* in: *Oeuvres,* ed. G. Schelle, Paris 1913, I, p. 214-235.

—, *Plan de deux Discours sur l'histoire universelle* (1751), ed. cit. I, p. 275-323.

—, *Discours sur les avantages que l'établissement du Christianisme a procuré au genre humain,* ed. cit. I, p. 194-214.

Encyclopédie ou Dictionnaire raisonné des Sciences, des Arts et des Métiers, Paris 1751-1772; especially:
Jean Lerond d'Alembert, *Discours préliminaire,* I, p. I-XLV.
Denis Diderot, art. *Encyclopédie,* V, p. 635-648.

—, art. *Philosophie,* XII, p. 511-515.

Morelly, *Naufrage des isles flottantes* ou *Basiliade du célèbre Pilpay.* Poème héroïque, Messine 1753.

—, *Code de la nature* ou *Le véritable esprit de ses lois de tout temps négligé et méconnu* (1755), ed. V. P. Volguine, Paris 1953.

Sébastien Mercier, *L'An 2440* ou *Rêve s'il en fut jamais,* Amsterdam 1770.

Gabriel Bonnot de Mably, *De la législation* ou *Principes des lois,* Paris 1778.

Buffon, *Les Epoques de la Nature.* Septième et dernière époque, lorsque la puissance de l'homme a secondé celle de la nature (1778), in: *Oeuvres,* ed. J. Piveteau, Paris (PUF) 1954, p. 184-196.

Condorcet, *Esquisse d'un tableau historique des progrès de l'esprit humain,* Paris, An III (1794); ed. O. H. Prior, Paris (Boivin) 1933.

Cabanis, *Lettre sur un passage de la Décade philosophique et en général sur la Perfectibilité de l'esprit humain* (1799), in: *Oeuvres,* ed. C. Lehec - J. Cazeneuve, Paris (PUF) II, p. 512-519.

Doctrine de Saint-Simon. Exposition, Première année 1829, ed. C. Bouglé - E. Halévy, Paris (Rivière) 1924.
Auguste Comte, *Cours de philosophie positive*, 51e-60e Leçon. Paris (Bachelier) 1842.
—, *Système de politique positive*, III. Dynamique sociale (Théorie du progrès), Paris 1851-1854.
Pierre Joseph Proudhon, *Philosophie du progrès* (1853), ed. Th. Ruyssen - J.-L. Puech, Paris (Rivière) 1946.
—, *De la Justice dans la Révolution et dans l'Eglise*, vol. I-IV, ed. C. Bouglé - J.-L. Puech, Paris (Rivière) 1930-1935.
Johann Gottfried Herder, *Auch eine Philosophie der Geschichte der Menschheit* (1774); Frankfurt (Suhrkamp) 1967.
—, *Ideen zur Philosophie der Geschichte der Menschheit* (1784-1791); Darmstadt (Melzer) 1966.
Gotthold Ephraim Lessing, *Die Erziehung des Menschengeschlechts* (1777-1790), in: *Schriften*, ed. K. Lachmann, Leipzig ³1913, XIII, p. 413-436.
Immanuel Kant, *Idee zu einer allgemeinen Geschichte in weltbürgerlicher Absicht* (1784), in: *Gesammelte Schriften*, ed. Deutsche Akademie der Wissenschaften, Berlin 1903, VIII, p. 15-32.
—, *Erneuerte Frage: Ob das menschliche Geschlecht im beständigen Fortschreiten zum Besseren sei?* (1798) (Der Streit der Faklutäten, II), ed. cit. VII, p. 79-92.
Herbert Spencer, *Progress: its Law and its Cause*, in: *Essays. Scientific, Political and Speculative*, London 1858.
—, *First principles*. A System of Philosophy, London 1862.

TRUTZ RENDTORFF

CHRISTIAN FOUNDATION OF WORLDLY COMMITMENT

I. DIMENSION OF A THEOLOGY OF DEVELOPMENT

Christianity has entered the era of its incorporation in world history. The momentous consequences resulting from this process have only within the past decade begun to be consciously perceived by Christianity and, particularly, in any comprehensive sense, by the churches. For generations, fundamental changes in the modern world affecting all areas of life appeared to Christianity in the guise presented by the churches; that is, predominantly as crisis and threat. Preservation of Christian belief and of its churchly manifestations vis-a-vis the great competing forces of world structure in political, scientific, and cultural realms decisively influenced the kind of instruction given by the church during this period. Even where such world changes were accepted as challenge, response to which called for a reformation and transformation of Christian belief, this happened mainly for interested motives, i. e., to give renewed value to Christian belief as such. Under these circumstances, change in the modern world, and the problems it involved for Christian belief, are seen as questions put to Christianity from outside, as it were, and forcing a Christian reaction; that is, a turning outward "from the church to the world." But here a really basic change begins to manifest itself. The interrogations of the "world" are revealed in growing measure as authentic Christian questions. The historical interdependence existing between human, social, and political

85

problems and religious problems is being recognized as a presupposition for a theological understanding of reality. The confrontation of "church and world" is being eased increasingly by serious and deep meditation on their prior relationship an exercise which tends to break up the stereotypes of theological and churchly conceptions and patterns of action.

The concrete basis for this process whereby Christianity is becoming known in the dimension of its incorporation in world history is a new, worldwide Christian praxis, involving an acknowledged commitment to the unqualified solidarity of Christianity with the life problems of the modern world. By reason of its own dynamic and its inherent testimony (Evidenz), this praxis, which clearly differs from the traditional forms of church procedure and theological thought, necessitates the transcending of hitherto accepted theological formulations and churchly self concepts. It requires that theology blaze new paths for Christian praxis and conceptualize them. It is in this context that we must look for the role of a theology of development. The new historical technique of formulating questions or themes responsive to these demands can be illustrated from a threefold aspect:

a) The dominant themes of the general Christian awareness of the present are no longer specifically churchly in the sense that they could be adequately defined from the viewpoint of a particular church or creed. They are of an ecumenical nature. For this reason, the great ecumenical Conferences serve as definitive *loci* for the orientation of Christian thought. These Conferences reflect the diversity and conflict of viewpoints among the churches and in theological convictions. Yet it was precisely the World Conference at Geneva in 1966 and the Plenary Assembly at Uppsala in 1968 that made it impressively clear that superimposed upon this diversity is an underlying thrust toward unity. The mutuality of the two Conferences is evident in their common desire to come to grips effectively and unreservedly with the human, social, and practical problems of today's world. Thus the ecumenical movement takes on a significance that goes beyond union of the churches and the idea of Christian unity.

b) The dominant themes of the general Christian awareness are no longer specifically churchly in the sense that the special identity of the Christian church is the first consideration. The main interest is directed rather to world development in all its aspects. More and more the churches are seeing themselves as part of a Christian process which thematically and institutionally leads far beyond the boundaries of the established churches and the theological overtures they have hitherto made toward mutual understanding. In this connection, a communication from the Fourth Plenary Assembly of the Ecumenical Council of Churches in Uppsala in 1968 contains the statement that we Christians bear witness to "the unity that is ours in Christ when we all, each in his own sphere, make common cause with men of different races, classes and age groups, or of different religious and political convictions." [1] The report continues: "The scientific discoveries and the revolutionary movements of our time offer to mankind new possibilities and risks." The task thus implied is stated as follows: "Therefore we accept our mandate as trustees of the universe when we take care of, develop, and share its bounty with one another." [2] The problematic of development with its complex economic, cultural, and institutional aspects has become exceptionally viable for very concrete frames of reference of a new Christian orientation. Both organized and non-institutional Christianity have begun to be involved actively, materially, and spiritually in this area—a step which the theoretical or merely nominal discussion of the global responsibility of the Christian has overlooked. A comprehensive analysis of church practice and church structure at the present time would reveal to how great an extent the churches are already actively interested in a range of themes that in the past have been cloaked by their traditional self-concept. This explains why the impact of this process on Christian orientation is being discussed everywhere today. It also explains why there is real pressure for a new theological orientation that would provide theological formulations suited to the altered frame of reference for Christian action.

---

[1] *Uppsala Report 1968. Official Report of the Fourth Plenary Assembly of the Ecumenical Council of Churches,* Geneva, 1968, p. 1.
[2] op. cit.

c) These themes of global responsibility are being accepted by the churches in growing measure as properly belonging to them; no longer does the question of Christian or church identity enjoy that unquestioned primacy of former times. An irreversible process has been set in motion. No one can seriously assert today that in the name of Christian or theological integrity the churches must retrace the steps they have taken toward that dimension of Christianity which incorporates it in world history. In the nineteenth century and until far into the twentieth, steps in the direction of world responsibility which led beyond the set pattern of the churchly self-concept, could be taken only by non-institutional Christianity or by individual groups within the church, who thereby exposed themselves to suspicion of heresy. Today it is maintained that it would be heretical for the church to seek to disclaim such areas of concern. Consequently, the Christian situation has reached a stage where it is impossible to regard the turning-to-the world by the church as a turning to something outside; rather, this turning-to-the-world goes hand-in-hand with a radical change and a renewal in the understanding of Christian belief and theology. The change is most strikingly evident perhaps in the current understanding of mission, as it was formulated by the second section of the Plenary Assembly at Uppsala. There among other things it was said that: "In a world in which the whole of mankind strives to realize their common humanity, and in which all share proportionately hope and despair, the Christian church must identify itself with the community of all men if it desires to fulfill its mission of service and witness and administer responsibly the goods at its disposal." [3]

II. INCENTIVES TO A THEOLOGY OF DEVELOPMENT

The incentives to a theology of development have without question issued from the great Ecumenical Conferences in Geneva (1966) and in Uppsala (1968) already referred to. [4]

---

[3] op. cit., Report of Section II; "Renovation of Mission," p. 35.
[4] No mention will be made here of other Conferences and Consultations, as in Beirut and Zagorsk, where questions of de-

Not only have these Conferences served as a representative forum for giving public expression to what the Christian attitude should be in that which concerns the Christian's world responsibility; but they have given to the Christian churches themselves a compelling theoretical and practical impetus. And with respect to the importance of a theology of development, there is clearly discernible between these two conferences a line of descent showing that questions of development represent the most comprehensive viewpoint for theological orientation also. As its main contribution, the Geneva Conference gave the Christian world a rousing program for a "theology of revolution." [5] The Plenary Assembly at Uppsala which had to analyze the results of the Geneva Conference and formulate the response of the churches to them, manifests by comparison a decided retreat from the revolution problem in favor of the problem of development, as being long-range, more significant, and richer in practical implications. Section III, the theme of which was Economic and Social World Development, continued directly on the course set by the work at Geneva. With Jan M. Lochman, the chairman of Section III, we could say "that the topic of this section could serve as a test case for the Fourth Plenary Assembly." It was asserted further "that this Plenary Assembly itself would be both sectarian and heretical in the exact and original sense of these words if it did not devote itself wholeheartedly and with full attention to the concerns of worldwide development." Furthermore, the theme of this section was characterized as "a central ecumenical question of our time." [6] Actually, this section continued the work of the Geneva Conference, the first section of which dealt with the topic "Economic Development — a Worldwide View."

While the development problematic in all its ramifications dominated the substantive discussions of the Geneva

---

velopment and revolution were pursued further. The contribution of the Roman Catholic Church to the development question can also remain unnoticed.

[5] For the theology of revolution, cf. Trutz Rendtorff und Heinz E. Tödt. *Theologie der Revolution,* Frankfurt/M., ³1969.

[6] *Uppsala Report,* Introduction to the schema of the report of Section III: "Economic and Social World Development," p. 39.

Conference, still questions related to revolution occupied the foreground in the form of theological and ethical repartee and in the impression given the public. At the same time, however, it was quite evident that the question of revolution represented only an abridged and politically explosive facet of the highly complex problem of development. It was precisely the massive difficulties with which the churches and Christian thinkers saw themselves faced in connection with the worldwide problem of development that misled them to the point of allowing their practical and theological focus to center on the idea of revolution. This concept appeared likely to respond more immediately to the extraordinary pressure which world problems were placing on everyone who seriously addressed himself to them. The catchword "revolution" symbolizes a discontinuity, as it were, between the deadweight of the past and hope for the future. The dynamic of practical measures could be most readily set in motion by a concept of action which claimed for itself a revolutionary character. Nevertheless, the actual involvement of the churches and Christians in these questions has proved that a stable focus, and practical action as well, can be claimed much easier under the categories of development than under those of revolution. As early as in the report of Section I of the Geneva Conference we find this challenging passage: "We know that God has set no limits to what can be achieved in and by the men of our time, if only they understand their problems rightly; and He wills that they show themselves obedient to the requirements of their situation." [7]

The connection of the two Conferences can be just as clearly established in the relationship of the section in each which dealt with international situations. Here the political problem of peace is seen to be an integral and permanent part of the whole development problem. At Uppsala, the chairman of Section IV, the theme of which was "Toward Justice and Peace in International Affairs," affirmed: "Peace is more than and other than the absence of war and a state

---

[7] *Appeal to the Churches of the World. Documents of the World Conference for Church and Society*, Report of Section I: "Economic Development — A Worldwide View," sect. 10, p. 112.

of armistice; but it is also more than and other than the mere maintenance of the status quo in the distribution of power among the nations. If we wish to unite peace and justice, we must think of peace not as a static but as a dynamic concept, as a process or way of living together, not as a cessation of movement achieved once and for all." [8] The indissoluble interdependence of economic, social, and cultural development and politico-institutional changes, as well as the stability and openendedness of the development process corroborate ever more strongly the insight that the problematic of development, not that of revolution, provides the basis for a far-reaching ecumenical and theological idea of the future. In view of this, it is not fortuitous that in the relationship between the two Conferences a shift of emphasis can be noted from the "theology of revolution" to a prospective "theology of development." At Geneva, on occasion, both aspects were already being mentioned in conjunction. [9] Yet the point still to be proved is, to what extent a "theology of development" can offset satisfactorily those advantages in a "theology of revolution" that are warranted and necessary.

The concept "Entwicklung" can be regarded as an alternative to the opposition between revolution and evolution. It is, of course, connected semantically not with the notion of "evolution," but with the English term "development." This concept denotes something more and something other than social change, which is effected according to general, inevitable, and, so to speak, anonymous laws. It is also more rational and more comprehensive than the idea of revolution. For the concept of development implies the impetus to projection, to planning, and to positive reflection and consciously ratified change. It is no less dynamic than the concept of revolution, nor less political. But it is more complex, because "development" includes consideration of the interdependence and the participation of all productive forces. In this context, on ethical, human, and theological grounds, certain tendentious procedures have to be encou-

---

[8] *Uppsala Report,* Introduction to the schema of Section IV: "Toward Justice and Peace in International Affairs," p. 60.

[9] E. g., in the address by Vitaly Borovoi at the Geneva Study Conference, in *Appeal to the Churches of the World,* p. 24.

raged, the validation of which is provided by the phenomenology of development processes. Scientific analysis and practical motivation to action pertain in equal measure to the rational core of the idea of development. To be sure, one still cannot claim that the theoretical consideration of the concept of development is widely popular in ecumenical discussions, to say nothing of a theological evaluation of the problems connected with it.

Even at best there is still question merely of *incentives* to a theology of development. In Uppsala, the report of Section III made only the following reference to it: "It was recognized that a search for a theology of development is urgently needed. This section could not begin to address itself adequately to this question and the first paragraph contains only a reference to it as a need.[10] It is asserted in this allusion that for the first time in history "the unity of mankind comes into view as an actual prospect."[11] The theological formulations connected therewith are still generalizations. The fact that its theological orientations "could not be adequately discussed"[12] was a problem even at the Geneva Study Conference. It is precisely in view of the new questions with which ecumenical Christianity finds itself not only confronted but with which it is increasingly identifying itself, that the theological lacuna becomes noticeable. Still this deficiency should not occasion great surprise. In regard to theology, it is characteristic of the ecumenical situation that there is on the one hand a large accumulation of traditional theological insights which can become viable only after a troublesome effort; on the other hand, a great store of new ethical and human problems have been taken on for which there are as yet no established theological frames of reference.[13] There are

---

[10] *Uppsala Report*, Minutes of the discussion of the schema of Section III, p. 44.

[11] Ibid.

[12] *Appeal to the Churches of the World*, Report of Work group B: "Theological Problems in Social Ethic," sect. 38, p. 258

[13] See on this whole question, "Bericht über das Echo der Weltkonferenz für Kirche und Gesellschaft von 1966," presented by Paul Abrecht to the Plenary Assembly in Uppsala; published in *Kirche zwischen Gott und Welt*, Suppl. 9/10, *ökumenischen Rundschau*, Stuttgart, 1969, p. 166ff.

voices in plenty calling it an idle academic exercise to ask for a theology to aid in the solution of practical problems, whose factual aspects seem perfectly evident. "If Christians cannot go to the place where men are experiencing their problems without holding long discussions about the weighty reasons for them beforehand, they should leave them alone." [14] Frequently enough, objection has been raised against theological superstructures. But there is an unmistakable need to unite the very complex problems of development and the theological labors of ecumenism. [15] Yet this gives rise to serious methodological difficulties. It is generally agreed that theology has its own distinctive contour, both in the techniques it employs and also because, as biblical theology, it deals with Christian tradition by interpretation and commentary. Up to the present time theologies and theologians who did not hold to the accepted norms of theological thought could take practically no part in ecumenical discussions. On the other hand, it is also recognized that theology does concern itself with non-theological disciplines and fields of knowledge. This function of theology, which is recognized in the traditional schema of "Church and World", also contributes to the trend of "toward the world." Yet the new and unparalleled character of the present situation consists precisely in the fact that the church and Christians in general have deliberately accepted as their own, problems and experiences that do not derive from traditional Christianity and do not belong even to a particular sphere outside it. For this reason the development problem urgently requires a theology of development, a new theological effort demanding that theology find a way of expressing the radical change in the Christian self-concept. Following is a presentation of the theological consequences of the fact that Christianity has entered the era of its incorporation in world history.

---

[14] Theodore A. Gill, "Die grosse Konvergenz," in *Kirche zwischen Gott und Welt,* p. 91.

[15] This is the sense of a report presented by Max Kohnstamm to the Plenary Assembly in Uppsala for the Committee on Fellowship, Development, and Freedom of the Roman Catholic Church and the Ecumenical Council of Churches. (*Uppsala Report,* p. 366f.)

III. Structural Elements of a Theology of Development

At the present stage of our discussion it would be a mistake to treat of a theology of development as thought we were giving a lecture on dogma or fabricating an uninhibited theological dream, concocted from some principles taken from traditional formulations and some theological ideas operative at the present. Rather, the discussion of the possibility of a theology of development must be geared to conditions which will allow it to come into existence and then become matter for further church as well as ecumenical discussions. For methodology this means that the first step toward a theology of development is to examine such conditions as are already present. We shall consider next some of the relevant factors in this connection which derive from the actual development problematic itself.

We begin with a point that has already been referred to several times: the real, factual, established, and growing engagement of the Christian churches in the whole development field. The very heart of the development problematic can be identified with the radical and mandatory "involvement" of the churches and Christians in the contemporary social order. The term "involvement" corresponds to the German phrase "Christen in Gesellschaft verstricht," as it was used in a retrospective reference to the Geneva Conference.[16] This kind of participation in the development process and its activities signifies that development of economic, social, and cultural conditions necessarily includes change and development in church and Christian life. This essential connection between social development and ecclesiastical change is therefore to be considered the first structural element of a theology of development.

But problems of development have a broader relation to theology because they extend beyond the limits of the established churches, especially where these limits represent "inheritances" from an earlier period of the church, and because they constitute in tangible form the common and

---

[16] Cf. also Hermann Ringeling, *Christen im technischen und socialen Umbruch unserer Zeit,* in: *Ökumenische Rundschau,* 1967, p. 9ff.

worldwide Christian project. In assisting development, Christians both give and receive; they experience being both challengers and challenged. So the development process is seen in its entirety as a new form of Christian unity in the world. It is no exaggeration to say that in all probability ecumenism has begun to take shape as a specific, independent, Christian reality only because of the worldwide development problematic, as it has made itself felt everywhere in the past decade. A theology of development which takes these two factors into account can therefore only be an ecumenical theology.

No one would deny that the intricate, diverse, and widely ramified problems of development exceed the competence of the churches. These can take only their allotted portion of the tasks involved. An exclusively ecclesiastical work of development would be either presumptuous or naive. On the contrary, there is in this matter urgent necessity for co-operation with all social, national, and international agencies who are interested in the work of development. The imperative need of co-operation makes it mandatory that agreement as to the purport and aim of development be set in a context which is intelligible and accessible to all concerned. The humanistic base and the objectives of the work of development must therefore serve as frames of reference also for its fuller theological interpretation. The implication of this element of co-operation for a theology of development is that it cannot be simply annexed to existing church dogma and teaching. This factor necessitates a new and so to speak super-churchly concept of theology.

The substantial emphasis of the development problem is unquestionably on the problems of economic, technological, and scientific development; yet at the same time it is admitted even now that the development problematic has a much greater complexity and embraces all spheres of life. This holds good especially for the cultural dimension, for the reason and to the extent that the work of development requires a prodigious amount of education and instruction, without which it would be folly to expect real and enduring assistance. Almost more important still is the inseparable connection between the problem of development and the problem of peace. This link with the peace problem and its ethical as well as institutional aspects is the most impressive example of the complexity of development problems. This element of complexity implies that a theology of development cannot be designed simply as a special theology for a particular area of church activity and Christian responsibility. On the contrary, one is obliged to say that for practical reasons a theology of development must necessarily be a theology of the world. Consequently, unlike traditional theology, it cannot be bound by a static ontology, but must be developed from ethical principles which give involvement in the development problem its specifically humanistic character.

Finally, as has already been noted, for those who devote themselves to it, the development problematic constitutes a motivation for a process of renewal. Its strong impact on church structure and Christian consciences is now recognized at least in general. But this aspect of renewal should not be understood in the sense of a stirring up of fervor. Rather it calls attention to the broad frontiers of the world's capacity for development. It requires that we view all questions of development reasonably and soberly within the framework of human and churchly potentiality and that the responses to the need for change be introduced gradually. With this factor of renewal as a point of departure, a theology of development must be made applicable to real situations and be thought through in terms of a firmly established reciprocal relationship with changes that are factually-based, possible, and feasible.

These factors which would have to be taken into account in constructing a theology of development show clearly that such a theology cannot be pre-empted by a particular theological school; it can only (for its own good) evolve methodologically and in content through ongoing co-operation with other theological systems.

In addition to the above-mentioned factors in the construction of a theology of development, there are particular and distinctive problems of orientation, a few of which will be mentioned here and briefly discussed. Participation in the development process involves for the churches unprecedented problems in the matter of research. Running through all the documents and reports on the subject like a scarlet thread is the motif that a responsible and controlled participation in the development process is possible only on the basis of a sound understanding of and a relevant body of information concerning the complicated interconnections which have to be taken into account. Doling out money and collecting it is really not enough. At this point we face a touchy problem. For there is absolutely no concrete issue relating to the development problematic in which the church or Christian groups are involved for which a broad range of scientific literature does not already exist and for which there is not a great store of pertinent international experience. The danger of a hopeless dilettantism has been mentioned with sufficient frequency by critics of an ecumenical involvement in the development problematic. On the other hand, such investigations lose their value if they lead us to specialize in development research. It is precisely in the process of specialization that general accessibility is lost for those who wish to participate in carrying out and furthering the program of development. The problem of the relationship between theological orientation and scientific research is today in no field so beset with hazards as in the field of development. For this reason the churches are faced with a twofold difficulty. The must themselves make progress toward acquiring a soundly based understanding of the complex problem of development research; yet it is on the churches that also devolves the onerous task of shaping opinion and of exercising a guiding influence on the community in general and on Christians who have to share with the churches this task and responsibility. At the present time the task has assumed a unique form by reason of the clash between the traditional pulpit themes of the church and the vast amount of research which global responsibility necessitates. The question is whether the kind of subjects for inquiry now considered appropriate to the "household" of the church can be broadened in the church's own good time, or whether it must very soon reckon with the fact that the tasks imposed by the new orientation of the church and of Christianity can be performed effectively only by a simultaneous sacrifice of other theme repertories. This theme conflict makes unavoidable the question:

What Christian and theological value assessment can be assigned to the actual tasks in the service of development and the research connected with them? In other words, how legitimately can they be taken into the household of Christian belief? Again and again one can observe in modern history of Christianity that relevant and current questions and orientations have pushed aside or modified the claims of tradition. The whole story is found only in theological textbooks. But we have here a particularly striking instance because once the churches really and energetically address themselves to the tasks of development as a manifestation of Christian love, the expansion in new directions and in research this will necessitate appears to be almost unlimited. The hermeneutic problem which will ensue therefrom for a theology of development takes on stunning proportions.

The second problem of theological orientation, the pertinence and methodological importance of which is already clear from our discussion, arises from the question how those aspects of man's present and future, which still await theological definition, are related to the great historical dimension of the theology of development, inasmuch as they assume both a well-defined and a challenging form in the problem of development. The theology of revolution has already been accused of investing empirical political events with a quasi-revelatory character. On the other hand, it is asserted that: "Theological reflection on development would be superficial and oversimplified if it appealed to scriptural sources as evidence, or if it limited itself to only one aspect of the total viewpoint of the scriptures." [17] There is the closest possible connection, therefore, between the theological view of development and a theological understanding of the history of Christianity. The latter cannot be determined exclusively by the visible life of the church and her preaching. In this connection, M. M. Thomas, president of the Geneva Study Conference, observed "that the churches have played no small part in creating the spiritual climate which is causing the revolutions of our time. They have done this directly through preaching and instruc-

---

[17] Richard Dickinson, *Richtschnur und Waage. Die Kirchen und die sozialökonomische Entwicklung*, Geneva, 1968, p. 40.

tion and indirectly through the cultural values which have flowed from this preaching and instruction. Consequently, if the church is defined not merely as an institution but in terms of its far-reaching influence, then we would have every right to say that wherever the church as institution has remained aloof, the mission of the church has created fertile soil for the type of human attitudes which have called forth the signs and omens of God's kingdom as represented by the revolutions of our time." The comment continues with the observation that in present-day political and economic developments can be seen a "part of the enduring action of the life-giving Christ, in whom man reaches his true measure of manhood." [18] A theology of development is necessarily, therefore, a distinctive form of a theology of history; yet it may not on this account be construed exclusively in terms of dogma or scripture, since it relates to the present day in too perceptive and encompassing a manner for the preservative techniques of such an historical discipline.

A further orientation problem for development has to do with its vision of the future. The concept of development, so comprehensive and so important for theology will materialize only when it is understood that more is involved than a sharing of material goods. Development of the possibilities for human living is included—a task which calls puon man's full capacity for discernment, a task of which the proportions bid fair to transcend the limits of world structure in its present form. As might be expected, it was at the Geneva Study Conference that the following observation was made concerning the possibilities of science and technology: "We see no basis for the assumption that man's capacity for knowledge should not in principle be equal to the discovery and understanding of natural phenomena to an unlimited extent." [19] To be compared with this are other interpretations of the manysided concept of development that are in full agreement with the tradition-inspired reminder of the sinfulness of mankind, that

---

[18] M. M. Thomas, *Fragen zu Leben und Arbeit der Kirche in einer revolutionären Welt,* in: *Kirche zwischen Gott und Welt,* p. 117.

[19] *Appeal to the Churches of the World,* Report of Workgroup B, sect. 8, p. 250.

with a certain anthropological skepticism prefer to view even
the possibility of development only in the sense of a correction
of human wickedness and the preservation of due order in
human affairs. The problem of human progress invites a
theology of development to a fresh approach, not indeed in a
spirit of naive optimism, but in response to the pressures necessarily created by human progress, which have a way of
forcing man to manufacture new possibilities for the human
race with his scientific and technological abilities. The tendency of this viewpoint is to understand the problem of man's
sinfulness, not ontologically, but in terms of ever recurring
failures in the process of development. Without a firm con-
fidence that progress in world development is really possible,
it could scarcely be expected that the human energies needed
today on a global scale would be released and properly directed.

In summary, these problems of orientation can be presented in the form of a question: How can the theological potential of the Christian churches be assimilated to the already
accepted development prom—as a productive or restricti-
ve element? For the attentive reader of this discussion, this
question does not admit of a pat answer. The voices of those
who would like to assign to theology a preponderant critical
and admonitory role carry impressive weight. But those who
approve the development theme as a central theological theme
and are seeking to make this come about have the stronger
arguments on their side. For every phenomenology of the
present world situation comes down to the primary question
of survival. Above all, however, one must acknowledge that
to an ever-increasing extent general and public Christian conviction is supporting a productive theological awareness of
development. In this regard, Christian piety is beginning to
come to life and acquire renewed vigor. Criteria of what is
true or false theology can no longer be taken only from traditional dogmatic doctrine on revelation. Rather, such standards
must be regulated by what is immediately evident to an alert
Christian awareness. But now the question arises: In what
sense can a theology of development be called "theology?"

IV. The Task of Theology

What has "theology" to offer the development problem? Surely, not solutions for all the aspects of the development problem. Richard Dickinson says in his ecumenical discussion of the development problem, still the most detailed work on the subject: "What development needs is a correlation of analyses and interpretations, which could supply a basis for intelligent action." [20] The worldwide scope of the development problem requires the formation of comprehensive and fundamental concepts from the most disparate viewpoints to provide a certain perspicuity and systematic ordering for the many-sided practical problems. Only in such terms can one speak at all of a "theology of development." Three areas of work at once suggest themselves as sources of the answer to the question: In what sense may one in this context speak of "theology?"

a) A theological perspective appears necessary to development in order to motivate Christians by appropriate and clear formulations to commit themselves to this work. At appropriate points during the great ecumenical Conferences theology was charged again and again to quicken its momentum toward participation in great world projects and to Christianize them. "Theology" appears, then, as the integrating starting point of a new task of Christian preaching and education.

b) The task of theology can be represented as the redefining of Christian tradition. The "application of the basic tenets of Christian belief according to the articles of faith to the world of today in its global relationships" [21] seems to call for a basis which would be supplied by theology. Upon this basis the church can validate her continuity with her own tradition and simultaneously interpret anew the intent of this tradition. Various possibilities which here come to mind Dickinson has already identified and described: "The varying interpretations among Christians make it impossi-

---

[20] Dickinson, loc. cit.

[21] Minutes of the first meeting of the Board of the Evangelical Churches of Germany for Service to Development by the Church.

101

ble to speak of *the* Christian theology of development." [22] In fact, it is appropriate to the work of a theology of development to signalize the plurality of theologies, since theological pluralism is the mark of a living Christianity. While, in historico-hermeneutic discussions of theology, there is a prevailing impression that the various theologies counterbalance one another, practice-oriented efforts in the area of the development problematic make it clear to how great an extent the rivalry and juxtaposition of theological orientations determine the outcome, necessarily so, perhaps.

c) A further task of theology is that of integration. Divergent secular viewpoints, economic, political, social and cultural, as well as disparate ideological, ethical, and religious convictions pose the difficult scientific problem of their integration. Integration can be effected by theology only if theology is removed, through some form of counteraction, from the direct impact of the existential situation and endeavors to obtain an overview of the complex field of development from a distance which still does not entail disengagement. It is the very thrust toward the demands of praxis which animates the development problem with a kind of superficial verve that calls for a higher level of theory than would normally be required of theology in the area of ecumenism. Although a theology of development cannot and must not be expected to produce deeper practical, economic, and sociological insights than those provided from other sources, it may not on that account be excused from keeping in view the development of proposals for such practical application. On similar grounds, the work of a theology of development cannot be thought of as only involving concern that the church maintain its identity or as making sure that the church undertakes a specific Christian task and then assuming responsibility for the manner in which the task is performed. This question has greater urgency today in view of the awakened Christian conscience. The task of integration consists further in shaping a Christian understanding of man, the world, and history in a frame of reference in which a dynamic understanding of

---

[22] Dickinson, p. 41.

102

reality will actualize the world's potentialities and possibilities of development.

Since these considerations have reference chiefly to the methodological problems of a theology of development, it would be inappropriate to provide here in a few broad strokes an outline of the content of such a theology. As a final word, however, this much can be said: that since the real necessity of a theology of development can no longer be successfully contested, such a task, i. e., the determination of its content must be accompanied by a reassessment of theology vis-a-vis ecumenism. The theology of development should be connected with a theory of development. It is intimately related therefore to a theory of contemporary Christianity which has passed beyond its exclusively churchly phase. The theology of development must in any case be multidimensional; that is, it must evolve as contemporary theology in general has done on its scientific side. It may be that the development problematic offers the first opportunity to the churches and to piety of perceiving theology in terms of scientific research rather than as threat and crisis. Today the churches and Christian belief are beginning to identify with the life problems of mankind, but practical awareness of these problems without critical scholarship would open no vistas on the future of mankind.

ZOLTAN ALSZEGHY, s. j. - MAURIZIO FLICK, s. j.

THEOLOGY OF DEVELOPMENT:
A QUESTION OF METHOD

I. DEVELOPMENT: EXISTENCE AND PROBLEMS

In the field of technology, development *is a fact of imme-diate experience.* The humanisation of the material world and man's control over his own destiny change the daily pattern of life of one and all. Alongside technological development, there is a series of changes in the economic, cultural and po-litical fields which inclines one to think that the conditions of human existence, as known from history, are progressively being changed, both qualitatively and quantitatively.

In addition to this *objective* fact, there is what could be called a *subjective* fact, in as much as it deals with the col-lective consciousness of man. Public opinion, challenged by technological, sociological, political, and cultural development, reacts to it and judges it.

The key judgment is, generally, a *positive* one. It recog-nises in the actual phase of the transformation of humanity the progressive realisation of a value. Humanity, improving material and cultural conditions of life, and overcoming the alienation of person from nature, is constructing a new col-lective Ego, based on a synthesis between individuality and sociality. Past history is now seen as a slow climb towards this value. Disasters are interpreted either as isolated regres-sive events or rather as preconditions for further strides for-ward. Thus people are optimistic about the future. Man's utopias and dreams become anticipations of a future which is

105

mysteriously hidden, already taking place, and irresistibly transforming itself into the present. Often this optimism provokes a moral imperative of involvement so that progress may be achieved more quickly and universally, and be spread to areas which up to now have been less developed.

Most of the main current ideologies, such as those of Hegel and Marx, are inspired by some form of evolutionary optimism. The appeal of the "hope principle" of Bloch, or the cosmic vision of Teilhard, is evidence of this widespread way of thinking today. It is also shown by the fact that present human change is being called "progress" more or less spontaneously. It is true that the word can mean the gradual fulfilment of any situation and that it is possible to speak of the progress of an epidemic or famine. Yet the current meaning of the word "progress" is the change from a neutral or satisfactory state of affairs to a better one; in other words, a constant improvement of man and the world.[1] But even clearer is the a priori optimism in the terminology of "development." Development in fact means a movement towards a goal, in which the original value becomes reaffirmed in deeper, purer and more explicit terms. This movement is seen as due to a principle inherent in the being that is developing, which is growing towards its complete fulfilment. Iron does not "develop" when it rusts or when it is used for the making of an instrument, but a seed does "develop" in an ear of corn. Hence to call the present transformation of human conditions "development," supposes that man changes himself, becoming more of a man.[2]

The positive appreciation of present transformation is more or less accepted by all. There is no sizeable opinion which thinks possible, or even desirable, the return of humanity to the state before technological development. But if optimism is unlimited in places where human needs have up to now been frustrated, one observes at the same time, a certain bewilderment and "crisis of hope" in those areas

---

[1] On the notion of progress see below, *Systematic Bibliography*, sect. III, n. 1.

[2] On the notion of development see below, *Systematic Bibliography*, sect. III, n. 3.

where development has achieved notable success.[3] Man's instinctive impulses will be more than satisfied with certain things and will not go beyond an upper limit. The increase in foodstuffs, clothing, hygiene, education etc. at a certain point ceases to have any meaning, because it no longer improves human conditions, but simply exists as a result of the artificial stimulation of needs. Thus it is not immediately evident that the indefinite and continuous growth of the "affluent society" fulfils a value for man. What will happen, for example, when material production becomes so automated as to satisfy all vital needs, while the time for the work required is reduced to a minimum? Isn't it possible that the advanced industrial society is approaching a stage in which the continuation of progress will require a radical overthrowing of the present management and organisation of progress?[4] Such diverse symptoms as world-wide revolution, hedonistic escape etc. seem to indicate that there is awaking in the collective consciousness a certain diffidence towards the value or possibility of those goals which technology offers man, and towards the institutions that it has created as well.

Now this collection of objective and subjective facts inevitably raises a *question mark in theology*. The first encounter between problems of development and the science of faith is dealt with at the *ethical level*. The christian is asked to fully commit himself to further development and to question what institutions are proper to contemporary society. Which choices require the faith of the individual christian and which of the christian community? This question cannot be answered adequately without further reflection. In theology every *imperative* is based on an *indicative*. Therefore, the taking of any position (whether individual or collective) as regards progress, implies an opinion about the relationship between that salvation offered by Christ and that offered by humanity—fully developed in accordance with

---

[3] For an analysis of this crisis, see A. Edmaier, *Horizonte der Hoffnung*, Regensburg 1968, p. 11-33.

[4] H. Marcuse, *One-Dimensional Man. Studies in the Ideology of Advanced Industrial Society*, Boston 1964; A. Böhm, *Lebensstandard, wozu*? Osnabrück 1961.

the aims of technological and cultural progress. Is the eschatological kingdom promised by Christ, identical to, connected with, independent of, or completely opposed to development? Has eternal life, already possessed by those reborn through Christ and in the Holy Spirit, any value as regards temporal development? In a nutshell: what is the relationship between hope as a christian characteristic, and hope which leads man along the path of technological and cultural development?

II. The problem in more detail

Questions such as these, especially since the last war, are attracting the attention of theologians more and more. In the past they used to make unconnected, and often contradictory, judgments on *progress,* treating it as only a side issue. [5]

In the conflict of those ideologies which promised a re-ordering of the world, christianity was forced to reflect on its own attitude towards this ideal.

Originally the main problem was the search for a "theology of temporal reality." One asked up to what point one could say that temporal reality (i. e. material well-being, culture, correct ethical behaviour etc.) was not simply a means, occasionally useful in the order of supernatural value, but had a value in itself, constituting an end (even if only secondary) of action based on charity. [6]

Although the posing of the problem in these terms was often too abstract and generalised, the theology of temporal values did provoke positive research. Until now, this formed the basis of theological reflection on the relationship of christianity to the present development of man. In the

---

[5] See M. Seckler, *Der Fortschrittsgedanke in der Theologie,* in: *Theologie im Wandel,* München 1967, p. 41-67.

[6] The classical work on this subject is G. Thils, *Théologie des réalités terrestres,* I, Bruges 1946. For the typical polarization of the literature, see B. Besret, *Deux chapitres d'histoire du vocabulaire religieux contemporain en France: Incarnation et Eschatologie (1935-1955),* Paris 1964.

field of biblical scholarship we find, in addition to the exegesis of a few relevant texts [7] and articles on biblical themes connected with the problem of temporal value,[8] some serious attempts at synthesis.[9] In the field of historical research there are some particularly interesting studies which synthesize the ideas of certain great thinkers of the past as regards temporal reality.[10].

The attempt to acquire a complete picture of temporal values poses the problem of a "theology of history." Originally the question was asked whether, according to faith, the series of events which formed communities and human institutions had any "meaning." Did they, in fact, tend to a definite end, was this end simply transcendent (the preparation of the "heavenly Jerusalem,") or was it immanent as well (a determined state of society and humanity to be fulfilled in time)? [11]

---

[7] G. Hierzenberger, *Weltbewertung bei Paulus nach 1 Kor. 7, 29-31,* Düsseldorf 1967; N. Lohfink, *Technik und Tod nach Kohelet,* in: *Strukturen christlicher Existenz,* Würzburg 1968, p. 27-35.

[8] A. Gelin, *Le pauvres de Yahvé,* Paris 1954; J. M. Gonzalez-Ruiz, *Pobreza evangélica y promoción cristiana,* Barcelona 1966; F. Gryglewitz, *La valeur morale du travail dans la terminologie grecque de la Bible,* in: *Biblica* 37 (1956) 314-337; S. Légasse, *La révélation aux Népioi,* in: *Revue Biblique* 67 (1960) 321-348.

[9] J. Levie, *Les valeurs humaines dans la théologie de S. Paul,* in: *Biblica* 10 (1959) 800-814; and especially R. Völkl, *Christ und Welt nach dem Neuen Testament,* Würzburg 1961.

[10] We may cite, for example, Z. Alszeghy, *Ein Verteidiger der Welt predigt Weltverachtung,* in: *Geist und Leben* 35 (1962) 197-207; P. Delhaye, *S. Augustin et les valeurs humaines,* in: *Mélanges de Science Religieuse* 13 (1955) 121-131; H. Dittburner, *A Theology of Temporal Realities. Explanation of St. Jerome,* Roma 1966; J. Gribomont, *Le renoncement au monde dans l'idéal ascétique de S. Basile,* in: *Irénikon* 31 (1958) 282-307, 460-475; R. Schlette, *Die Nichtigkeit der Welt. Der philosophische Horizont des Hugo von St. Viktor,* München 1961. R. Bultot has made an analysis of various medieval authors with regard to this viewpoint; for critical response to his work, see L. J. Bataillon-J. P. Jossua, *Le mépris du monde. De l'intérêt d'une discussion actuelle,* in: *Revue des Sciences Philosophiques et Théologiques* 51 (1967) 23-38; see also Z. Alszeghy, *Fuite du monde,* in: *Dict. de Spiritualité,* V, 1575-1605.

[11] See our bibliographical review: *Teologia della storia,* in: *Gregorianum* 35 (1954) 256-298, and that compiled by C. J. Geffré,

More recently it has been seen that "temporal reality" and human history can only be adequately understood in a *"synthetic vision of the world."* This world was designed by God with its own structure, relative autonomy, and need of development; a world in which the supernatural isn't an extrinsic element, but the crowning goal to which all creation tends from the very beginning. This approach had already been mapped out in the many works of Teilhard de Chardin [12], and led, especially during the 1960's, to the elaboration of the so-called *"theology of the world."* [13]

The reawakening of lay theological interest and the greater understanding of the role of the *"laity"* in the Church, produced a notable series of theological ideas having an even closer connection with the theology of development. Given that temporal involvement is one of the hallmarks of the lay vocation, this theology, right from the beginning, paid a great deal of attention to effort to improve man's condition. In so doing it prescinded from whatever value good intentions might add to the effort. [14] Connected with the *"theology of the laity"* is the theological research on the meaning, dignity and nature of *work.* [15]

Théologie de l'histoire, in: *Revue des Sciences Philosophiques et Théologiques* 47 (1963) 130-135.

[12] See R. Gibellini, *La discussione su Teilhard de Chardin,* Brescia 1968.

[13] We may cite as representative examples J. B. Metz, *Zur Theologie der Welt,* Mainz 1968, and the studies by E. Schillebeeckx, collected in: *Theologische Peilingen* III: *Wereld en Kerk,* Bilthoven 1965.

[14] After Y. Congar, *Jalons pour une théologie du laïcat,* Paris 1954, and G. Philips, *Le rôle du laïcat dans l'Eglise,* Tournai 1954, mention should be made of P. Brugnoli, *La spiritualità dei laici,* Brescia 1963; P. Brugnoli, *La missione dei laici nel mondo di oggi,* Brescia 1966; M. Flick, *Santità laicale nell'impegno temporale,* in: *Spiritualità dei laici,* Roma 1966, p. 106-131; and the bibliographical studies of B. D. Dupuy, *Recherches récentes sur le rôle du laïcat dans l'Eglise. Bibliographie organisée,* in: *Vie Spirituelle* 105 (1961) 408-420; *Laici in Ecclesia. An Ecumenical Bibliography on the Role of the Laity in the Life and Mission of the Church,* Genève 1961; *Les laïcs face à leurs responsabilités,* Léopoldville 1964.

[15] See, for example, M. D. Chenu, *Pour une théologie du Travail,* Paris 1955; H. Rondet, *Eléments pour une théologie du tra-*

After the Council, *the problem of "secularisation,"* originally to be found only in protestant theology, gave new
stimuli to catholic thought also, due to the theological appreciation of human development. [16]

The influence of this debate on the theology of development can be seen in new approaches to various practical
aspects of human existence, (e. g. peace, [17] revolution, [18] and
in the recent need for a *"political theology."* [19])

One of the more positive aspects of these writings is
their strictly theological outlook. Their solutions do not
intend to be mere philosophical conclusions confirmed by
Revelation. Rather they claim as their source the mystery
of Christ. This characteristic, influenced to a certain extent by
protestant theology, is to be seen in the structuring of the problem in terms of *"christian hope."* [20]

---

vail, in: *Nouvelle Revue Théologique* 77 (1955) 27-48, 123-143; K.
Truhlar, *Labor christianus. Initiatio in theologiam spiritualem
systematicam de labore,* Roma 1961.

[16] From the extensive literature on secularism (see *La foi chrétienne et l'Eglise face au monde en voie de sécularisation,* in:
Nouvelle Revue Théologique 90 (1968) 307-334) we will mention
the important article of K. Rahner, *Réflexions théologiques sur
le problème de la sécularisation,* in: *La théologie du renouveau,*
Paris 1968, II, p. 257-280.

[17] The classic work is that of J. Comblin, *Théologie de la
paix,* Paris 1963; see also K. Rahner, *Der Friede Gottes und der
Friede der Welt,* in: *W. Bec - R. Schmid, Der Streit um den
Frieden,* München 1967, p. 64-85.

[18] We may refer to the excellent bibliography of J. Ramos-
Regidor, *Sviluppo dei popoli e rivoluzione,* in: *Aggiornamenti sociali* 19 (1968) 495-518, 575-602; see also E. Feil-R. Weth, *Diskussion zur Theologie der Revolution,* Mainz-München 1969.

[19] J. B. Metz, *Les rapports entre l'Eglise et le monde à la lumière d'une théologie politique,* in: *La théologie du renouveau,*
Paris 1968, II, p. 33-48; id., *Church's Social Function in the Light
of "Political Theology"* in: *Concilium* 6, 4, p. 3-11; E. Schillebeeckx,
The Magisterium and the World of Politics, in: *Concilium* 6, 4,
p. 12-21.

[20] See J. Moltmann, *Theologie der Hoffnung,* München 1964;
G. Sauter, *Zukunft und Verheissung,* Zürich 1965; W. D. Marsch
(ed.), *Diskussion über die Theologie der Hoffnung,* München 1967;
K. Rahner, *Marxistische Utopie und die christliche Zukunft des
Menschen,* in: *Schriften zur Theologie,* VI, Einsiedeln 1965, p.
77-88; id., *Fragment aus einer theologischen Besinnung auf den*

Another positive aspect in this orientation is that it gives ever more consideration to the living reality of human existence. No longer does it speak in merely abstract terms; it attempts a theological position based on that *technological and cultural* development being achieved by man today.[21]

One of the fruits of this theological work is that the *magisterium of the Church* has been able to establish certain norms regarding the relation of christianity to development. These are found in the second Vatican Council (especially in the "Pastoral Constitution of the Church in the Modern World") and in certain papal writings (notably the two encyclicals of John XXIII: "Mater et Magistra" and "Pacem in Terris," and that of Paul VI: "Populorum Progressio.") This teaching of the magisterium gave rise to commentaries which effected considerable doctrinal deepening. [22]

III. THE NEED FOR REFLECTION ON METHOD

The theology of development has produced an abundant, well-documented body of writing. From the publishing point of view, this is one of the most prolific fields in theology. In the face of this mass of often excellent publications, it might look as though nothing remains to be said on theology of human development. It might further appear that

---

Begriff der Zukunft, in: *Schriften zur Theologie,* VIII, Einsiedeln 1968, p. 555-560; id., *Zur Theologie der Hoffnung,* ib., p. 561-579; id., *Über die theologische Problematik der "Neuen Erde",* ib., p. 580-592.

[21] We shall cite in chronological sequence three important and indicative studies: Ch. Duquoc, *L'Eglise et le progrès,* Paris 1964; A. Z. Serrand, *Evolution technique et théologies,* Paris 1965; J. Alfaro, *Hacia una teología del progreso humano,* Barcelona 1969.

[22] See in *Archivum Historiae Pontificiae* the bibliographies of P. Aratò on *Mater et Magistra*: 1 (1963) 652-656; 2 (1964) 525-527; 3 (1965) 536-538; 4 (1966) 566; 5 (1967 593-594; 6 (1968) 670-671; 7 (1969) 722; on *Pacem in terris*: 2 (1964) 527-532; 3 (1965) 538-539; 4 (1966) 566-567; 5 (1967) 594; 6 (1968) 670-671; 7 (1969) 722; on *Gaudium et spes*: 3 (1965) 560; 4 (1966) 594-595; 5 (1967) 623-628; 6 (1968) 689-692; 7 (1969) 734-735; on *Populorum progressio*: 6 (1968) 698-700; 7 (1969) 741.

there is nothing left to do but treat in depth particular questions and to construct a complete synthesis.

In fact, research done up to now (as in the case of other sciences) has only demonstrated a further need. In order to have a valid theology of progress one needs to tackle the question of *method, a question still not fully resolved.* Up to a certain point it has been dealt with, yet it can be perfected by means of further reflection.

The problem of method is one of the most important in dogma today. But it is particularly delicate in the case of the theology of development. In fact, every dogmatic reflection requires a twofold investigation. Taking the Church's preaching as its basis, it seeks an understanding of it, travelling like an alternating current between two poles—the revealed word on the one hand, and the theoretical and practical problems of the present moment on the other. [23] Thus dogmatic theology interprets the christian message in the light of revelation (its norm), [24] while at the same time trying to comprehend it in such a way that theology becomes "the yeast, or as it were, the soul" of contemporary sociocultural environment. [25] This method results from that juxtaposition, inevitably present, between "divine revelation" and "the changeable situations of this world." [26] However, the synthesis of these two points of reference, always difficult, is particularly so in the case of the theology of progress.

The concrete methodological problem becomes more apparent when one examines two basic criticisms made of present theology of development.

The first criticism is levelled by those theologians most concerned to give biblical data its proper importance in every theological investigation. [27] They argue that the object of

---

[23] For a study of this concept of dogmatic method, we may refer to the small volume of W. Kasper, *Die Methode der Dogmatik,* München 1967, with whom we are in substantial agreement.

[24] *Dei verbum,* 24.

[25] *Gaudium et spes,* 40, 58, 66.

[26] *Optatam totius* 16.

[27] An extreme form of this criticism appears in the spirited observations by some non-catholic theologians regarding *Gaudium et spes;* see, for example, H. Roux, *Note marginale sur le fonde-*

8

theology of development is a reality about which God has
not spoken, and about which we cannot therefore make judgements if we are to remain faithful to the Word of God.
In fact the word of God in its biblical form, and in its later
interpretation, has no experience of the phenomenon of progress as it is understood in the world today. Indeed, it goes
against all principles of hermeneutics to expect to find in a
biblical text an interpretation of a reality outside the cultural
horizon in which the text was conceived. The transition
from the word of God to dogmatic assertions about present
progress could only be made if the bible had known an experience, which, proportionate to the world of its time, corresponded to our present experience of creating a world
with the forces of science and technology. To say, for example, that the activities of an oriental potentate in building
palaces and planting vineyards are comparable to those of a
technician commissioned to improve the hygienic conditions
of a developing country, is quite as untrue as it is to conclude with Cohelet that they are both a waste of time. [28] The
two creations, in fact, are essentially different in their finality and inherent values. Nor is it possible to derive from the
bible dogmatic assertions on present development by means
of a "theology of conclusions." This is because there does
not exist a "middle term" to pass from biblical concepts to
the present experience of progress. It is also because such
a procedure would stray from the Word of God to reality
foreign to it. It would be no less atheological than the reasoning of the medieval scholastics concerning the possibility
of the Word assuming a non-human nature. [29] Thus biblical
(as well as patristic and medieval) ideas on the flight from
the world (whether for or against), cannot be used without
further methodological refinement, if we are to resolve the
problem of a theology of development. Catholic theology is

ment théologique de "Gaudium et spes", in: L'Eglise dans le monde de ce temps, III, Paris 1967, p. 109-122; N. Struve, Quelques
réflexions d'un orthodoxe, ib., p. 123-129.
[28] Qoh. 2: 11.
[29] On the limits of reasoning in materia theologica, see our
Lo sviluppo del dogma cattolico, Brescia 1967, p. 30-42.

aware of this epistemological problem [30] and must study it further.

Toward this deepening of insight, one must take into account another criticism, diametrically opposed to the first. Those who are involved in the Church's social work, directors and promoters of the Church's mission in the area of poverty, justice, the development of the Third World, etc., consider the work done inadequate, not because it is insufficiently biblical, but because it is too far removed from the problems of the present moment. They feel that the much needed theology of development which will give credibility to the christian message and spur christian action in the world, does not yet exist. [31] When one sees the intellectual hunger and corresponding dissatisfaction of theological students, faced with the present state of theology of development, it is difficult to suppose this criticism without foundation. We must, however, leave aside these general criticisms, and center our attention now on the needs of the Church's life to which our theology of development still fails to correspond.

Men of action seek what we could call an *ideology*, in the best sense of the word. As Houtart aptly describes it: " An ideology is a system of opinions, founded on a complex of agreed values, which determines at a particular period of time the attitudes and behaviour of man, as he confronts the goals hoped for from the progress of society by the social group or the individual. " [32] An ideology, so defined, might be considered not as pure science, but rather as science *applied* to concrete situations and to the aspirations inherent

---

[30] See the remarks of J. Comblin, Théologie de la paix, II, Paris 1963, p. 9-10, 167-172; for the papal encyclicals in particular, see G. Jarlot, *Doctrine pontificale et histoire*, Roma 1964.

[31] See, for instance, J. Gremillon, *The Church in the World Today-Challenge to Theology*, in: *Vatican II. An Interfaith Appraisal*, Notre Dame-London, 1966, p. 521-544; F. Houtart, *Suggestions for Doctrinal Development*, ib., p. 545-552; id., *L'Eglise face au dévelopment dans le Tiers-Monde*, in: *La théologie du renouveau*, Paris 1968, II, p. 133-154; F. Hourtart-F. Hambye, *The Socio-Political Implications of Vatican II*, in: *Concilium* 6, 4, p. 46-51.

[32] *Concilium* 6, 4, p. 46.

in a community: a sort of "objective spirit", without which community action can have neither unity nor dynamic thrust. Thus, ideology is not science. It creates "dynamic imperatives" with regard to what one should do in a particular situation, whilst science determines the principles upon which such calls to action are based. [33] Moreover, an ideology is always provisional and must change according to the fluctuating temporal situation, whilst science looks for statements of unchangeable value. An ideology supposes the acceptance of an axiological approach, whereas a scientific statement remains true whether anybody recognises it or not. An ideology gathers all that is geared to action, whereas science has for its term of reference whatever belongs to exact knowledge of the object under study.

This second line of criticism of present theology of development also brings us to the question of methodology. Can theology, of its nature a science, serve ideologies? How can one create a theology which while remaining the science of the Word of God, serves also to direct christian action in the world?

IV. Contingent data in the theology of development

The "Pastoral Constitution on the Church in the Modern World", a document which can be considered a typical product of today's theology of development, points out that it is dealing with two series of data. On the one hand it is expounding "the doctrine of the Church in regard to man, the world in which he lives, and his relationship to it". But in addition to these "doctrinal principles" it considers the "changing circumstances which are intrinsically connected with the above reality." [34] *The image of the condition of man in the modern world* belongs essentially to the theology of development. In fact the two documents of the magisterium which have given a definite stimulus to the

---

[33] Our distinction between *imperatives* and *principles* follows the sense of K. Rahner's suggestion, in: *Das Dynamische in der Kirche*, Freiburg ²1960, p. 14-37.

[34] *Gaudium et spes* 1, note 1; cfr. also ibid. n. 91.

theology of development, the constitution " Gaudium et Spes ", and the encyclical " Populorum Progressio ", both begin with an analysis of the phenomenon of present progress resulting from man's achievements and his aspirations. [35]

Naturally every theology is constructed on unique and unrepeatable events which do not spring from the nature of things, but are the fruit of a free decision of the saving God, and of man, who either accepts or rejects his divine vocation. Without these events *salvation history* would not exist.

But such events, which did not necessarily take place, once they did occur determined in a definite manner the way along which man would travel towards his salvation. One has only to think of Original Sin and the Redemptive Incarnation, for example. But the facts upon which a theology of development must be constructed are " contingent elements ", in the special sense of being "a great variety of situations and forms of civilisation " and " continuously evolving subjective reality " [37], without, however, changing the fundamental structure of salvation history.

Moreover the facts considered by other branches of theology are revealed by the World of God, and because of (and supposing this), they have a certitude which is greater than all the guarantees that a human science can give. However, the knowledge of the contingent element in the theology of development is the fruit of psychological, sociological, biological etc. research, which the theologian must use in his own reflection, without the validity of such analysis being guaranteed by specifically theological method.

These "contingent data" are quite complex. Doctors psychologists and sociologists, each describe in their own way different aspects of colonisation, industrialisation, urbanisation etc. As they observe, the same facts produce a variety of results, which influence in different, and sometimes opposite ways, human development. Not infrequently a partial aspect of development promotes, up to a certain

---

[35] *Gaudium et spes* 4-10 ("The situation of men in the modern world;") *Populorum progressio*, 6-11 ("The data of the problem.")

[36] *Gaudium et spes*, 1, note 1.

[37] *Gaudium et spes*, 91.

point, total development, but going further, impedes, or even destroys it. Certain provisions that are necessary for a major increase in industrial production can be harmful to the well-being of the working man; a far-reaching system of social security may diminish personal initiative; a one-sided specialisation in science can be useful for technology, yet injure humanistic and artistic culture.

For the theologian to understand the christian vocation towards such phenomena, he must study each of these aspects by means of exact and highly specialised research methods. Obviously this is not possible. Hence if he wishes to avoid the charge of dilettantism (one of the main criticisms levelled against the theology of progress by specialists in human planning, and not without reason), he should avail himself of the information provided by those competent in particular fields, knowing that, as a theologian, he will not be expected to judge their validity.

We believe that the only way to avoid confusion of method is to separate, if possible, what we know from faith from what we know through psychological, sociological, and other analysis of the present condition of humanity. The pattern according to which theology of development will make its assertions ought to be this: where humanity has such needs and opportunities as are described, the mystery of Christ demands a certain individual or collective behaviour and implies a certain help to imitation of this action.

The expression " in the case where " demonstrates the hypothetical nature of the " contingent data » with regard to theological speculation. The understanding in theology of the needs and possibilities of development have a function comparable to that which empirical data and scientific theories have for philosophy of nature. The philosopher must know and use these data, given their validity, in order to seek ultimate explanations Similarly the theologian takes as his starting point the expert's description of present reality in order to discover its relationship to the christian message.

This approach makes possible the elaboration of theologically certain propositions based on data, valid indeed in other realms of knowledge, but incapable of imposing

118

that consent which is proper to theology. In fact, the assertions which determine the relationship between a contingent situation and the mystery of Christ are independent of the reality of such situations. Even if the analysis of the contingent situation were false, it still remains that if it had been true it would have imposed certain exigencies and have received definite stimuli from the mystery of Christ. The theology of development, so proceeding, will be able to deal with continuously changing data, drawing from it assertions which rightly claim enduring value. The result of the confrontation with the word of God remains valid, even when the contingent term has already undergone change.

Naturally the above-described logical scheme will never be applied in this abstract way. Separation of the two noetic fields was necessary in order to distinguish the various levels of assent. But it is more than evident that the theologian working on development does not try to form his judgements on the conditions of a utopian society. The search for a relationship between the mystery of Christ and a socio-cultural situation supposes a certitude in one's acceptance of both as realities. The pre-theological persuasions of the theologian give existential meaning (and hence also an affective tension) to his thought processes. Precisely because of this, theology of development cannot be reduced to a mere academic exercise about the Word of God, but belongs to the obedience of faith, by which the human situation is submitted to the judgement of the word of God.

V. SPECIFICALLY THEOLOGICAL DATA.

The normal task of theology of development, therefore, is to relate the description of present human conditions to the christian message.

But what do we mean by the " christian message ", in contrast to the phenomenon of present development?

Those who understand the christian message to mean a set of logically ordered propositions (biblical quotations, assertions from biblical and patristic theology, theses of speculative theology etc.), encounter an enormous difficulty

119

because, these propositions either do not refer to the concrete situation of man in the world or else refer to a world considerably different from ours. Thus, apart from a few universal propositions, (e. g. the absolute dependence of all creatures on God), the rest, in themselves, cannot answer the questions posed by theology of progress.

It would simply be a deformation of the object of faith to reduce it to a collection of propositions. Studies in development of dogma show that faith is not just contact with propositions; but, by means of more or less explicit or virtual affirmations, *understanding of the very reality* to which the single propositions refer. As the often-quoted text of St. Thomas has it "actus credentis non terminatur ad ennuntiabile, sed ad rem."[38]

We do not, however, intend to conclude thereby that the term to be compared with the development phenomenon is the reality of Christ himself, who gives Himself to us as word, food, grace and the awaited eschatological presence. Such a statement would just skirt the problem, for reality can be data for a scientific operation only insofar as it is known. We are further aware that believers do not generally have a clear and distinct reflective experience of the gift of Christ they possess, such as to become noetic data of scientific operations. Still, there does exist a *knowledge of revealed reality* which, while not experience, still goes beyond single partial propositions in the sense that the mind of the believer, working from single propositions as its basis, constructs *an objective image of the revealed reality*.

The "objective image" *isn't a concept that is specifically theological*. A man who has never taken part in a polar expedition can still know about arctic regions. Nor is this simply a collection of phrases that he has learnt, but it is an "image" (not just an imaginative one, but strictly mental), built up on pieces of information, perhaps some even forgotten, in which similar personal experiences play a part (e. g. the experience of cold, of snow etc.), as also judgements of a universal nature.

---

[38] *S. Th.*, 2-2, q. 1, a. 2, ad 2.

120

Such objective images exist also with regard to the messages of different religions. Scholars of comparative religion, are making a serious attempt to familiarise themselves with the morphology of individual religions in order to understand the structure and organic unity of various beliefs, so that they can compare one religion with another. It will be even easier to obtain an objective image of the world vision of a particular religion for those living in a community where a particular religion is professed and transmitted by means of symbols, gestures, and collective experience.

The believing christian is particularly capable of gaining this objective image of his faith, since he is *aided by grace,* which gives him an interior con-naturalness with the content of the message he accepts through faith. Not infrequently, dogmatic development (e. g. in Mariology), is achieved in this way. [39] The objective image which constitutes the specifically theological data for the theology of development is revealed progressively through *salvation history.* The theology of development has gathered together in the last ten years the contributions offered by various branches of catholic dogma in order to build up this image. " Gaudium et Spes " in its first three chapters has synthesized the results. It treats of the creation of the human person in the image of God, the corruption introduced by sin, the meaning of death for the christian, the value of the paschal mystery as related to human action, and the relation between material progress and development of the kingdom of God in its present and eschatological stages. [40] However, we must not think that this list of " Gaudium et Spes " is exhaustive. Other documents of the magisterium [41] have underlined, for example, the importance of christian love in shaping man's vocation in the construction of the world.

---

[39] See our *Lo sviluppo del dogma cattolico,* Brescia 1967, p. 42-66.

[40] For a development of these principles we refer to Z. Alszeghy, *La chiesa e la vocazione dell'uomo,* in: *La chiesa nel mondo contemporaneo,* Torino 1966, p. 419-452; and M. Flick, *L'attività umana nell'universo,* ib., p. 481-632.

[41] *Populorum progressio* n. 44, 66; *Profession of faith,* of Paul VI, AAS. 60: 1968: 443-444.

The objective image which the christian message gives of man's relation to the universe is thus sufficiently *rich in content*. However, in the theological reflection which attempts to give this image expression, divergent elements enter and rest in unresolved tension. We must keep in mind the structural complexity of these if we are to avoid oversimplification of the past. [42]

Vatican II has pointed out a way to understand this structural complexity. It determines the value of human action in the light of the plan of God the Creator who wants to realise His Image in the world as a sign of His greatness. [43] This approach represents a return to the category of " divine exemplarism ", familiar enough in patristic and medieval [44] thought but neglected in post-tridentine theology.

The main insights of exemplarism are contained in the following three propositions:

1) Each being has a value of its own in that it participates in the divine goodness from which it takes its meaning.

2) This participation is communicated to all beings, and they exist precisely in so far as they participate in this divine image.

3) The various orders of beings participate in the divinity in a way that is qualitatively different.

The perfection of an inanimate being, while a perfection indeed, never approaches the value of a human being, however much it increases. Irrational life never attains the natural perfection of a person; while the life of a person in his natural perfection remains qualitatively inferior to the value of a person reborn in Christ and possessing the participated life of the Trinity and hence " sonship in the Son. "

The various phenomena of development, therefore, should be interpreted in the light of the *Divine Plan*. God

---

[42] This complexity is emphasized in *Apostolicam actuositatem* 7.

[43] e. g. *Gaudium et spes*, 34.

[44] Cfr. our *Fondamenti di un'antropologia teologica*, Firenze 1970: n. 96-106.

wishes to imprint on this world an image of His goodness to which each creature with his own qualitatively different perfection must tend. Every creature is destined to attain the whole Christ, who is the ultimate end of creation as He is the perfect image of the Father. It follows from this that when one judges a phenomenon of development one should consider all its repercussions in various layers of the universe on " cristogenesi ".

If theological appreciation is to be in any way realistic, one should take into consideration the *concrete way* in which humanity is to be inserted into the *whole Christ*. Man, as known from revelation, is marked by sin and redeemed in the death and resurrection of Christ. These truths are not just " historical data " that once took place. They are " historical factors " that have changed human reality for ever. Accordingly, the theological data to which the phenomenon of development must always be referred, embraces the mystery of sin operative in the world, the mystery of the *Cross* in which all the redeemed must participate, and the mystery of eschatological participation in the glory of the risen Christ.

The presence of sin in the world does not mean only the possibility that progress can sometimes deviate or be hindered. As a result of sin, " concupiscence " operates also in redeemed man.[45] This is a force, which, where not overcome by charity, makes man take as his supreme norm of life his own individual, material, and temporal satisfaction. It is man's deeply rooted experience, frequently instanced in the bible, that power, riches and self-love, can give concupiscence an uncontrollable force. It follows that not every development conducive to man's well-being constitutes definite value. The reason is that there is always the danger that it may harm man's supernatural development in Christ

---

[45] On the theological notion of "concupiscence", frequently bereft of its true meaning, see K. Rahner, *Zum theologischen Begriff der Konkupiszenz,* in: *Schriften zur Theologie,* I, Einsiedeln 1954, p. 377-414; B. Stoeckle, *Erbsündige Begierlichkeit. Weitere Erwägungen zu ihrer theologischen und anthropologischen Gestalt,* in: *Münchner Theologische Zeitschrift* 14 (1963) 225-242.

by standing in the way of his readiness to accept transcendent values.

Just as the struggle against the power of sin is a constant and inescapable dimension of christian life, so also is the sharing in the Cross of Christ — a participation which grows towards the sharing in His glory. The recognition of the cross as a value for man on his journey towards glory is a fundamental element of christian preaching. [46] Hence, a theology of development which fails to discover " beatitude " [47] in suffering and privation of material goods, and which denies that from a certain point of view the poor of Yaweh, the sick, the afflicted, and the persecuted are right in being content with their lot [48], ceases to be christian.

In final analysis, *christian hope* has as its goal the " absolute future "; in other words, full participation in the life of the Trinity, a good greater than any human achievement and beyond man's wildest dreams, and one only to be enjoyed in the future life. [49] The christian involved in the common effort to construct a better world on earth should always remember that no matter what results he may achieve, they will still only prefigure those better things which will come one day as God's gift. Any earthly hope that precludes further expectations for the people of God, negates true christian hope. [50]

From this description of the specifically theological data of a " theology of development " springs an important *methodological conclusion*. Theology of development does not constitute a *new theological discipline*. Rather it is a new aspect of theological research which the various branches of theology must take into account. [51] True, there are new branches of theology added to already existing disciplines, either because they developed hitherto little studied biblical themes (e. g. theology of preaching); or because they gather-

---

[46] Cfr. Mk. 8: 34; Mt. 16: 24-27; Lk. 9: 23-26; 2 Cor. 4: 8.
[47] Mt. 5: 3-12.
[48] Col. 1: 24; 1 Pt. 4: 14; Jas. 1: 2.
[49] 1 Cor. 23: 9.
[50] Cfr. Heb. 4: 9; 11: 13-16.
[51] See J. B. Metz, *Zur Theologie der Welt,* Mainz 1968, p. 106-107.

ed theological insights under a hitherto insufficiently considered aspect, (e. g. the theology of the laity). The theology of development is not like these. It has not opened a new seam in the revealed deposit of fait, nor does it have to group particular propositions and refer them to a hitherto ignored goal. Its novelty consists in profitably relating *all parts of theology* to a problem which the world imposes in the christian. Practically all fundamental dogmas can and should find a place within this perspective of theology of development by making them face the questions that the phenomenon of modern progress puts to christian conscience.

VI. Contingent data confronted with theological data

The theology of development does not simply gather " contingent data " and " theological data ", but is *achieved by bringing them face to face.* Paradoxically, the theologian in this way discovers what faith can legitimately hold as God's thought on the subject, even though He has not expressly spoken about it. [52]

The technique of confronting the two data, according to the Council's terminology [53], is " discerning the signs of the times. "

The Council calls " signs of the times " " the world in which we live, its expectations and aspirations, its often dramatic characteristics ", [54] that is the " events, searchings and aspirations, " in which the people of God " take part today together with the rest of mankind. " [55] " Signs of the times, " is often understood, as in Mt 16.4, to mean a starting point adequate to discovery of the needs of salvation in a particular situation. Clearly the Council did not use the expression in this sense. The " characteristics of the modern world " do not reveal definite teachings but do

---

[52] A. Z. Serrand, *Evolution technique et théologies,* Paris 1965, p. 11.

[53] M. D. Chenu, *Les signes des temps,* in: *L'Eglise dans le monde de ce temps,* Tours 1967, p. 97-116.

[54] *Gaudium et spes,* 4.

[55] *Gaudium et spes,* 11.

raise some useful questions. Thus, the christian, according to the Council, should not just "discern the signs of the times," but also "interpret them in the light of the gospel." [56] In other words, he must "evaluate those values held in great esteem today and lead them to their divine source." [57] Hence, the fact that men have certain aspirations is not sufficient reason for embracing them indiscriminately. In fact, even the christian in his concrete situation "finds himself divided." [58] On the one hand, he "believes himself led by the Spirit of the Lord, who fills the universe" [59]; on the other, "if man looks into his heart he finds himself also inclined to evil," [60] "and discovers that he is, by himself, incapable of overcoming its attacks." [61]

The signs of the times result from these two opposed forces. "These values, in fact, in that they proceed from the ingenuity given to man by God, are in themselves excellent, but due to the corruption of man, become not infrequently distorted in their correct tendencies, and therefore require purification." [62] The christian attitude towards the signs of the times consists, therefore, in neither unconditional consent or dissent, but in the discernment by which he tries to distinguish "what are the true signs of the presence and plan of God." [63]

A confrontation of this kind should be quite possible. The christian message certainly does not contain the solution to all the questions raised by present development as regards the relationship between causes and effects in the world. Specific questions of technology, sociology, politics, science etc. must be resolved, whilst at the same time respecting their autonomy. [64] But the christian message is destined for men of all times and situations. Thus in it we must find answers to the questions which the phenomenon of

---

56 *Gaudium et spes*, 4.
57 *Gaudium et spes*, 11.
58 *Gaudium et spes*, 13.
59 *Gaudium et spes*, 11.
60 *Gaudium et spes*, 13.
61 *Gaudium et spes*, 13.
62 *Gaudium et spes*, 11.
63 *Gaudium et spes*, 11.
64 *Gaudium et spes*, 36.

today's progress poses for christians as christians, i. e. as ordained to the whole Christ. [65]

Naturally this *does not mean that it will be easy* to form clear judgements as to how the community or individual should respond to the challenge to faith in present circumstances. The data to be related (as seen), are *extremely complex*. Then the relationship between immanent and transcendent values is ambivalent, having both a positive and a negative side. Sometimes holding to the spiritual treasures of the "kingdom of heaven" exacts a renunciation of inferior goods. At other times, a participation in the kingdom consistent with victory over sin, adherence to the Cross and faithfulness to eschatological hope, requires christian commitment to development and search for peace and justice. At the same time, this participation cannot be divorced from opposition to the world in so far as dominated by sin. [67]

The demands made on the christian, clearly, are not the same in every situation. Sometimes it will be necessary to emphasize christian construction of the world; on other occasions, christian pilgrimage through the world. Furthermore, "the gifts of the Spirit are different; He calls some to give witness to the heavenly life. By desiring it one hopes to keep it alive among men. Others are called to dedicate themselves to the service of man in this life, and so prepare through their ministry the raw material, as it were, for the kingdom of heaven." [68] In addition, the relating of the two sets of data is often achieved by a sort of global intuition enlightened by faith, the gifts of the Holy Spirit and the charism of discernment. [69]

But science can neither produce such an intuition nor content itself with such. Its task is to produce systematic judgments, which, by means of certain techniques may be

---

[65] On the definitive reason for this virtuality of the christian messge, cfr. *Gaudium et spes,* 10.

[66] Mt. 5: 29-30.

[67] *Gaudium et spes,* 38.

[68] *Gaudium et spes,* 38.

[69] On this existential and charismatic knowledge see the observations of K. Rahner, *Das Dynamische in der Kirche,* Freiburg ²1960.

verified in the community in which the judgments are arrived at. Consequently, the theology of development *prepares* (*as well as probes*) any global intuition by means of a series of propositions. On the other hand, no human affirmation can, of itself, express all the aspects of a global intuition. Therefore, the theology of progress will always proceed through affirmations which must be sharpened and limited by contrary assertions. This style, (which appears also in documents of the magisterium discussing theology of progress), does not necessarily result from fear of involvement. Its origin is rather the necessity of expressing in a dialectic manner the tension existing between various complementary aspects of concrete reality. [70]

Perhaps there is one judgment only that can be expressed without resort to antithesis. Practically speaking, a general and absolute proposition is always *in need of correction*. Hence, the Church's voice is raised mostly as a *constructive criticism* of one-sided programmes and syntheses which tend to transform a partial truth into an absolute and universal principle. [71]

VII. THE FRAILTY OF THE THEOLOGY OF DEVELOPMENT

The antithetical affirmation of the *possibility* on the one hand and the extreme *complexity* on the other of the comparison between contingent and theological data, shapes the peculiar fragility of theological judgment on the phenomena of social, economic and cultural development.

---

[70] From these observations follows the necessity of that "christian sobriety" regarding the various forms of progress, of which K. Rahner speaks (*Experiment Mensch. Theologisches zur Selbstmanipulation des Menschen,* in: *Die Frage nach dem Menschen* (Festschrift Max Müller), Freiburg 1966, p. 45-69). See also J. B. Lotz, *Möglichkeiten und Grenzen der Manipulierbarkeit des Menschen,* in: *Zivilisation und menschliche Zukunft,* Würzburg 1966, p. 123-151.

[71] This conclusion confirms the comments of E. Schillebeeckx on the predominantly negative character of the theology of progress; see *The Magisterium and the World of Politics,* in: *Concilium* 6, 4, p. 12-21, especially 20.

Elsewhere we have placed the precariousness of the union with Christ in the category of "historicalness." [72] Christian reality, which has not yet achieved eschatological perfection, is placed within the horizon of hope. In other words, it remains always subject to perfection, and thus exposed to dangers of turning in on itself, of deviating from its path, and even of complete defeat.. This is also the state of theological doctrines. These likewise are immersed in history, and so are capable always of more perfect encounter with truth. But similarly, they can be obscured and, within certain limits, vitiated by error. [73]

This is verified in a singular way in the theology of development, mainly on account of the difficulty of comparing complex data, which are in a continuous state of change, with the permanently valid and objective image of the relationship between christian and universe.

This particular frailty of theology of development would be reduced to a matter of degree with respect to other branches of theology if one could apply to the mental operations peculiar to this theology the division between hypothesis (the existence of a particular development) and thesis (that such development is properly related to the revealed image of man in the world). This distinction, while valid as an abstract epistemological model, is not valid as a division of the various phases in the development of thought.

Not only is the theologian persuaded from the beginning that his understanding of the contingent data is valid, but also in the phenomenological image of contingent data there is an implicit appeal to the taking of theological positions. Pre-theological data do not, in fact, consist only of strictly verifiable propositions (e. g. statistical data, laws expressed mathematically); but imply also an explanation of the structures, causes and effects of the data. This explanation already contains the elements of a judgment. It is, for instance,

---

[72] *Fondamenti di un'antropologia teologica,* Firenze 1970, n. 812-817.

[73] See our *Lo sviluppo del dogma cattolico,* Brescia 1967, p. 128-134; also *Quid reflexio ad historiam salutis a theologia catholica exigat,* in: *Acta Congressus Internationalis de theologia Concilii Vaticani II,* Roma 1968, p. 444-454.

impossible, or at least unprofitable, to make purely abstract considerations about slavery. When a modern thinker speaks of slavery, he implicitly remembers how slaves were captured, treated, reacted to their plight, and how one could change the system (or could have), etc. Abstract reasoning on the legitimacy of slavery has been displaced, not by other reasoning, but by images such as that of "Uncle Tom's Cabin," which persuaded public opinion that such reasoning had no factual justification; nobody would know how to judge an abstract notion if we had no experience of its concrete realisation.

Perhaps two examples will serve to illustrate the frailty characteristic of propositions of theology of development.

The first is the biblical judgment on Israel's monarchy. At a certain period in Israel's history, the vague and sporadic unity achieved by the Judges fell under the pressure of Philistine power and ceased to serve the needs of national existence. Now the ensuing political structures are given contradictory judgments by the bible. On the one hand 1 Samuel 8 presents the introduction of a monarchical system as displeasing to God; on the other, 2 Samuel 7 gives the impression that the stable centralisation of power is in conformity with God's wishes. We know that both judgments have had steady repercussions in the religious and national consiousness of Israel and find expression in parallel series of texts. (We prescind from difficult questions of historical and textual criticism). [74]

Transferring the case to the level of general principles, we ask whether it is possible for the same phenomenon of political development to be the object of two opposing yet theologically valid points of view. In fact the two books of Samuel show that it is possible and why. A judgment of value, intuitive, charismatic and global, is made about a concrete historical fact. Consequently, it can disapprove these concrete phenomenon while yet considering the motives for

---

[74] For a perspective on these problems, see H. J. Kraus, *Die Königsherrschaft Gottes im Alten Testament*, Tübingen 1951; E. Kutsch, *Die Dynastie von Gottes Gnaden*, in: *Zeitschrift für Theologie und Kirche* 58 (1961) 137-153; and the articles of H. Seebass, in: *Zeitschrift für die alttestamentliche Wissenschaft* 77 (1965) 286-296; 78 (1966) 148-179; 79 (1967) 155-171.

which men in a certain case want to effect it (1 Sm. 8: 7: "they have not rejected you but Me from being king over them.") But at the same time the bible approves because this event is lived out in faith in God's covenant. In fact, neither the judgment which condemns the enthronement of a king at a particular time, nor the approving judgment in another context, say anything about monarchy in abstract. To quote one or other series of texts as a norm for choosing a form of government here is quite erroneous.

This explains why the Church also can shift its judgments with regard to facts of political, social, and cultural development, and not thereby necessarily fall under the charge of inconsistency or intellectual dishonesty. A phenomenon of development may in fact be associated with false theories and therefore be integral to a system opposed to the kingdom of God and the true well-being of man. In this case the christian in the light of the gospel must refuse any part in it. At another time, the same phenomenon, separated from the previous context, can appear indifferent or even as serving the needs of the moment. "Hence it can happen that a practical event or encounter, which yesterday is considered inopportune or fruitless, can be quite the opposite today or tomorrow." [75]

Another historical example, illustrative of the "frailty" of theological judgment on the fittingness of a particular christian behaviour in the world is the *Church's position on the crusades*. Today no one would accept as valid the call to war for the re-establishment of christian sovereignity over Palestine. Yet this summons was taken as expression of God's will for two centuries by practically the entire christian West and with the enthusiastic approval of the bishops. The change is explained by looking at the motives with which it was taught that the crusades corresponded to exigencies of christian life. Behind these motives lay a *set of principles*, which today would not be accepted without distinctions (e. g. the theocratic compenetration of the kingdom of God with the christian kingdom; the honour of God and of the Holy places to be defended by armed force; the licit killing and plundering of infidels opposing christian rule, etc.). There was also a *set of facts*,

---

[75] *Pacem in terris*, 85.

131

which no longer exist (e. g. the hard lot of the christians in Palestine; the opinion that a military victory could change the situation in a definitive way, etc.) [76]

The example of the crusades can serve as areas affecting christian action in the world. The judging of contingent facts necessarily implies acceptance of a set of general principles and particular facts, unchallenged—and therefore not reflectively conscious—convictions.

Theological judgment on what behaviour requires in a determined historical situation can, using its own means, guarantee only propositions of the following type: if the implicitly accepted principles are valid, and if the facts implicitly taken for granted are true, then the christian must behave in such and such a way. It is enough that one discovers, for whatever reason, that some principle or fact is questionable or patently false for theological statements on christian action in the world (though remaining hypothetically true) to cease to be valid norms for action in concrete situations.

A similar change of judgment is at issue when the theologian discovers other principles or facts of which he was hitherto unaware (at least partially), or of which he had not seen the relation to problems of concrete reality. This can depend on a better understanding of the christian message which progressively deepens in the Church, or on progress in philosophy. Thus, for instance, a more exact appreciation of the dignity of the human person, of the fundamental equality of all men etc. progressively brought catholic theology to condemn salvery, serfdom, religious bigotry etc., and not to oppose the "declaration of human rights." [77]

For the same reasons *modern theology of development* should be aware of its particular frailty.

For it is tempted, as theology in the past, to judge ambi-

---

[76] Cfr. for such implications, e. g., the discourse of Urban II at the Council of Clermont (*Mansi* 20: 824-827), or Innocent III's exhortation on the crusade (*Mansi* 22: 956-960).

[77] See the brief exposition of such reversals in Ch. Duquoc, *L'Eglise et le progrès*, Paris 1964; texts from the magisterium that alternately encourage and discourage progress have been collected by M. Seckler, *Der Fortschrittsgedanke in der Theologie*, in: *Theologie im Wandel*, München 1967, p. 41, note 2.

guous behaviour in the light of motives which at most animate it without being inseparable therefrom. For instance, lack of interest in "lifting up" the Third World is condemned as always the product of egoism. But in fact it can also result from misgivings about imposing procedures for improving the condition of man borrowed from Euro-american life, which only alienate people from their own culture without replacing it with anything better.

The danger of error is even greater if one uses the presuppositions implicit in today's common vision of "development." It is generally supposed that progress is a uniform process which has advanced from the discovery of the first stone instruments, through the spaceship age, towards always more desirable goals. It thus presumes that human history has a unity and that technological progress always improves man. But there have been many thinkers who emphatically denied the existence of a uniform ascending movement in history; They held, on the contrary, that each civilisation pursues a path of development, which concludes inevitably in complete failure. They denied any identity between progress towards the perfection of man and progress in technological mastery of the world. For them the evolution of history, as we know it, cannot be traced graphically by an ascending straight line, but rathed by a curve which slopes away from the peak reached earlier by antiquity. Such opinions have been held by historians and philosophers of considerable note. [78] Nor are we dealing with pessimistic exaggerations, for many who denounce the affluent society of today unconsciously repeat oversimplified fragments of these theories.

The theologian, adhering to the means his science puts at his disposal, is absolutely incapable of judging these controversies. Moreover, it is an illusion to think that he can use as presupposition for his theological reflection that which "modern science" says about present-day development of man. The sciences, precisely because living sciences, do not lead to undebatable and definitive axioms. The opinions that the

---

[78] See, for example, A. J. Toynbee, *A Study of History* (Abridgement by D. S. Somervell), London 1960; K. Jaspers, *Vom Ursprung und Ziel der Geschichte*, Zürich 1949.

133

theologian utilises (eg. on the problems of Southern Italy) is not "what science says," but rather that which the theologian finds in the works of recognised scholars, which after ten years will be in considerable part judged out of date.

This does not mean that the theologian should not make use of the prevailing opinions of today on socio-economic situations. If he were not to do so he would be deprived of all means of communication. But he must realise that his conclusions, even if theologically unquestionable, will always remain hypotheses and have validity only insofar as the pre-theological ideas, more or less consciously implied in them, are valid.

The frailty distinctive of theology of development may be greater or lesser depending on the ecclesiastical grounding of judgments about the relationship between contingent data and the image revealed of the christian in the world. When a theological statement regarding progress is the work of one theologian only, the danger of imperfection or error is considerable. When such a statement receives general assent of the people of God, its value is greater and better proportioned to the depth of the Church's acceptance of it, as she takes it, in fact, as a norm of her own action. For example, the interest aroused in the whole Church by the appeal to resolve the problem of world hunger guarantees the value of the motives behind this call to action.

A reaction accompanied by signs of deep supernatural life can increase even more the value of a speculative judgment. For example, the charismatic flourishing of theological life (that accompanied increase in aid provided to the sick and pilgrims in the christian past) gives greater assurance that the christian ideal embraces also a collective interest for the suffering. The intervention of the magisterium will give to the assertions of the theology of progress a special weight.

The value of the Church's magisterium for theology of development becomes determinate if we avoid two opposed misunderstandings.

Not enough importance is shown the magisterium by those who fail to see that the hierarchy's position on the phenomenon of progress is of such great doctrinal value that (unless there exist clear reasons to the contrary) its probability can become a practical certainty. In fact, given the hierarchy's need of passing judgment on man's present situation in the exercise of its pastoral mission (of pointing out to christians of all ages individual and social practical attitudes corresponding to their faith), we must acknowledge the special assistance of the Holy Spirit in arriving at these judgments.

Others, on the other hand, *exaggerate the function of the magisterium* in theology of development when they exclude every possibility of error in hierarchical pronouncements regarding present day questions. In fact, the object of the infallible magisterium is that which is contained either explicitly or implicitly in Revelation. Infallibility extends further to those facts, which although they cannot be deduced from Revelation, should none the less be recognised by the Church because they constitute the necessary presuppositions for the infallible preservation of the deposit of faith (i. e. "dogmatic facts," as, for instance, the legitimacy of an ecumenical council, etc.).

Now, the correct evaluation of christian action in a determined historical situation bears a resemblance to the judgment of dogmatic facts, while at the same time differing from it. The resemblance exists because, just as the recognition of dogmatic facts is necessary for the infallible preaching of the gospel, so the correct appreciation of the concrete situation is necessary for the pastoral care of the people of God. Thus both judgments have the special assistance of the Holy Spirit.

Yet while the determination of dogmatic facts is necessary for the mission of teaching truth, the theological appreciation of the value of contingent facts corresponds to the need to discover appropriate behaviour patterns. The Church cannot err in the first field, but can in the second. The Church can, in fact, maintain intact the whole of revealed truth, and yet be mistaken over particulars, in its evaluation of present day needs. If the Church were to teach today, for example, that the evils resulting from suppressing rural civilisation outweighed the advantages of urbanisation, it would probably be committing an error—but such an error would not mar the purity of the message of faith.

Correct judgments on the function of the magisterium in the theology of development are thus based on the nature of

135

the charism the magisterium enjoys in this field. Its charism is a help for the pastors of the Church in the exercise of their office, a help similar to "the grace of status" in other vocations. It is, however, not the same as a Revelation, since it does not introduce new elements into human reflection and does not reach that guaranteed assistance proper to the Church as definitive interpreter of revealed truth.

The teaching of the magisterium on theology of development is not therefore exempt from the "frailty" characterising this theology.

The above observations certainly do not deny that eclesiastical authority can, and sometimes should, give practical ruling on social or political action binding in conscience. These prescriptions, however, do not belong specifically to the theology of development, but correspond to the need for communitarian action in the Church, whose life inevitably unfolds in the present process of human development. [79]

VIII. Ideology and the theology of development

We conclude our reflections on the specific method of the theology of development by indicating the *functions of such a theology as related to the ideology which meets the desires* of men of action. It seems to us that there is a threefold function, consisting in the *preparation, constructive criticism*, and *integration* of the ideology.

Above all *theology prepares the ideology* of development. In fact in constructing the objective image of the situation of the christian in the universe, it draws from Scripture and Tradition conceptual models and reflective patterns according to which the believer can see development as responding to *existing* and existential needs of his faith. We give just two examples.

---

[79] On the difficulty of faith, see K. Rahner, *Grenzen der Amtskirche*, in: *Schriften zur Theologie*, VI, Einsiedeln 1965, p. 499-520; id., *Zur theologischen Problematik einer "Pastoralkonstitution"*, in: *Schriften zur Theologie*, VIII, Einsiedeln 1967, p. 613-636; id., *Réflexions théologiques sur le probléme de la sécularisation*, in: *La théologie du renouveau*, Paris 1968, II, p. 257-279.

We think that the most important of these thought patterns is *love of one's neighbour,* essential to christian life, which must manifest itself in works of mercy.

Scripture lists a series of these works [80], proclaims the necessity of practising them [81], specifies that one's practise must not be influenced by individual prejudices [82], explains this exigency in terms of the internal drive for divine sonship [83] and condition for divine pardon [84]. The theology of development finds that in the present circumstances of society the best way to feed the hungry, clothe the naked etc., is to become involved in development, promoting and guiding it so that it does not become an end in itself but is efficaciously placed at the service of man.

Another of these typical models is man's vocation to play the role of God's image on earth [85]. The theme of "image" in the New Testament and in christian theology has been developed mostly in its vertical dimension. Man participates in the unique perfect image, that is Christ; in that, like Christ, he lives perfectly his life of Sonship accepting and carrying out the will of the Father. The theology of development here places in greater evidence what had indirectly been recognised by classical theology. [86] Man is more in harmony with the divine exemplar when, working in a horizontal dimension as well, he completes creation; and this progressively and without limit as he subjects himself and the forces of nature to the order of a more human existence on earth.

The second function of theology, when confronted with the ideology of development, consists in *constructive criticism.* A criticism that would tend to suppress ideology would deprive the Church's action of vitality and unity. But constructive criticism deepens the validity of ideology, assuring it christian authenticity.

---

[80] e. g., Mt. 25: 31-46.
[81] 1 Jn. 3: 17-18.
[82] Eph. 6: 9; 2: 1-4.
[83] Mt. 5: 45.
[84] Mt Jas. 18: 33.
[85] Gn. 1: 26-30.
[86] *S. Th.* 2-2, q. 66, a. 1.

In the history of christian thought we find one clear example of constructive criticism levelled by theology against an ideology (one contrary to what is sought today). We refer to the ideology of "flight from the world." In a christianity where temporal structures were penetrated by spiritual and the latter were menaced by the threat of absorption into the former, it was necessary to accent those aspects of the christian message which emphasized the transcendence of the christian life with respect to terrestrial reality. In this way the ideology of the "contempt of the world" was developed. The one-sided preaching of this ideology was on occasions pushed so far as to present the existing institutional structures of the world as evil and the product of the devil. The anti-manichean war waged by theology did not diminish the force of ascetic movements. Instead it reinforced them and gave them a more lasting efficacy by securing their orthodoxy. The franciscan spirit of poverty, for instance, far from being hindered was aided by the joyous contemplation of the goodness and beauty of creation.

In the same way, that ideology which assembles reasons justifying commitment to temporal development can only gain from a theological criticism which completes it where it is silent; reinforces its appeals by placing them within the total context of faith; and *preserves* it from a distortion which might tend to reduce christianity to activities limited to achieving worldly happiness. In this way, theology animates ideology by motives of faith. It also prepares further developments so that when it becomes necessary in the future to accentuate another aspect of Revelation, christians there will be open to the call of that time, instead of remaining confined to the problems of the last century.

One way of criticising theologically ideology of development is to confront the appeals and exigencies of modern ideology with the christian past. This confrontation is to some extent similar to the method that discerned the "signs of the times" in the light of the gospel. By returning to the past one encounters ideas, behaviour patterns and institutions which, having already been judged to some extent in the context of faith, are valid criteria for judging other phenomena. To use a classical expression, we can speak of the "norma normata normans" of the present life. This does not mean at all that christians must act today as they did in the past. But it does imply that they cannot act as though the Church and its life of yesterday had somehow apostatised from the gospel. When a historical period has produced such great holiness, when it has been heralded by the whole Church for a sufficiently long time as authentically responding to the christian vocation, when it has been approved and defended by the hierarchical Church, then this phenomenon is a "sign of the past", ratified as authentically christian. It may be that there were in the past deviations from the spirit of the gospel even in the Church. But it is not possible that the saints of the past were inspired by totally erroneous ideals, or that the Church approved behaviour completely alien to the christian spirit. One might think, for example, that the monastic ideal does not conform to the needs of the present, that the Imitation of Christ is out of date, that the preaching of the faith to pagans is not really a pressing need at the moment. But if one were to condemn such an ideal, book, or behaviour as contrary to the gospel, he would thereby only find himself condemned by Church norms of the past.

But if it is discovered that a particular ideology corresponds — in present conditions — to an appeal of spiritualities ratified in the past with Church approval; or it even appears that one or other of these spiritualities cannot be properly appreciated unless one is prepared to accept attitudes postulated by the ideology in question, then such recognition will constitute a favourable criterion for judging the evangelical worth of this ideology.

In most cases, however, there does not exist a clear opposition or harmony between a present ideology and a past Christian spirituality. But one does recognize a complementarity with a series of partial overlaps, positive or negative. By weighing up these overlaps one gains a better understanding of the ideology itself, avoids unfortunate expressions, and rediscovers authentic christian structures.

Theology's constructive criticism of ideology of development by means of a confrontation with the past is still only in its first stages. Too often either modern ideology is simply written off as a deviation from a christian spirituality preached and lived for centuries in the Church; or (more frequently) the entire past is dismissed because it fails to respond to the call of today. Some theologians, impressed by the values to be found in the patience and recognition preached by Christianity in the past, have tended to dismiss the Church's present social teachings. While others, convinced of the need to change institutions that had turned into obstacles, were prompted to deny all value to the obedience extolled in the past.

The theologian, avoiding oversimplification of development, will note, for instance, that today's call to love of the world is not opposed to the biblical prohibitions to love the world. This is because " the love " that prompts one to acquire values by making them serve one's self-interest is far different from " the love " prepared to sacrifice itself to promote a value judged good. The former was rejected in the past in the name of the gospel.[87] The latter is supported today—also in the name of the gospel.[88].

The theologian will note, too, that the absence of a call to self-involvement in technological progress in the Church's past teaching does not imply a condemnation of the modern call to promote development. It can be explained by the fact that until recent times isolated individuals or even Church communities could not effectively do much to improve living conditions. Today this impossibility is eliminated by technological progress and democratic structures which give every individual at least a modest share of power.

Finally it will be possible to establish that attitudes once accepted as consonant with the gospel of the Church could not have been recognised as such if commitment to technological and sociological development were not recognised as christian today. If, for example, it was once justifiable for " knights " to defend the poor and oppressed by force of arms it is also right for people of today to be involved in the development of depressed areas. And if at

---

[87] 1 Jn. 2: 15; Jas. 4: 4.
[88] Jn. 3: 16; Eph. 5: 25-33.

one time it was right to devise strategies to defeat the "enemies of the cross", then industrial or educational planning must not be judged foreign to the christian spirit.[89]

In the third place, the function of theology as regards ideology is also to systematically integrate the great themes of development in the synthesis of faith.

One dimension of this integration is concerned with human action. Man's activity, subordinate to God's creative *concursus,* collaborates in building the world. Seen this way, human development can be classed under the biblical theme of "edification." We should note, however, that whereas the bible speaks of edification as related to the supernatural life, the theology of development extends it to include the substratum of grace.

A second aspect of theological integration concerns results of human work, that is the development that ensues. In the structured scheme of exemplarism, progress — technological, sociological and cultural — appears as the incarnation of a divine value, but at a lower level than that corresponding to participation in the divine life. By comparing the result of human development with the supernatural life, progress is a likeness to divine perfection, imperfect and less specific when compared to participation in the life of the Trinity. On the other hand, earthly progress helps to bring about salvation, in providing the raw material to be animated by grace. We should not forget, however, that as a result of sin earthly progress can also diminish the impulse and desire for this gift of Christ.

Keeping in mind these two dimensions, we could define earthly development as an imperfect incarnation of the divine exemplar, ordained to answer more perfect participation in it; promoted by human action, in struggle with sin, under the sign of the cross. In this way development is also vitally integrated into the fundamental law of christian existence, which is the love for God, the source of christian love of all creatures. He who loves God, in fact, wishes that the reflection of the divine splendour be imprinted on

---

[89] In this connection the ritual in the Roman Pontifical *"De benedictione novi militis"* should be interesting.

the universe, and thus desires to become an instrument of creation and re-creation through Christ. The love of God does not simply mean rejoicing in the fullness of the divine beauty (" hallowed be Thy name "). It means entering into that dynamic love by which God loves Himself, and by Himself, loves all creation (to love God is also to desire " Thy Kingdom come, Thy will be done " — at all levels of creation).

By means of theological integration, the objective phenomenon of development and the subjective desire for progress become inserted into the structure of faith, and receive a new dimension.

Earthly development is recognised as a divine value in virtue, not of any extrinsically-added consecration, but of its " secular " reality. Nevertheless, the value of development does not appear as the central value of christian existence. It would be an ideal state of affairs if christians were perfectly developed in every sense of the word (physiologically, psychically, culturally etc.) Yet if one had to choose, the living faith of a primitive would be closer to God than any refined culture not animated by charity.

With this observation we reach to heart of the problem of the christian ideology of development. Ideology must give the stimulus to action. Can catholic theology inspire an enthusiasm for technological and cultural development? For those who dedicate themselves, under the impulse of grace, enthusiastically to fulfil the will of God, the answer is yes. For such, the promotion of progress will appear as a concrete application of their fundamental option. But in the case of those who remain indifferent to the call of God's love, the answer is no. But to ask from theology efficacious motivations also for those not " polarized " towards God would be to ask the impossible. For theology is the science of faith. In fact, history shows that mass religious enthusiasm, which is not penetrated very deeply by a christian spirit, is frequently just a dressing-up of baser instincts. One only has to think of the cruelties committed against the enemies of the faith.

We have listed the functions that theology enacts towards ideology in preparing, criticising and integrating it.

The relationship between theology and ideology can, however, be inverted. Under certain conditions ideology becomes a criterion of the validity of theology.

By this we do not intend to approve a certain way of justifying all calls to progress with the affirmation that otherwise " modern man " will never embrace christianity. A pragmatism of this sort turns the order of values upside down. No doctrine is " offered " to induce people to accept the Church externally. The aim of the ecclesiastical institution is to have the gospel of grace accepted and lived out. The theologian's task is not to cover any and every wail with a veneer of christianity.[90] but to seek an understanding of the word of God even when it foresees that its refusal to be embarrassed by the gospel [91] attracts the hatred of " this world ".[92]

There is, however, one way in which an ideology can provide itself a christian auto-justification, not indeed at the level of popular success, but at that of authentic christian life. According to the gospel one is to distinguish false from true prophets by their fruits.[93] Accordingly, an ideology can be judged authentically christian if it produces fruits of christian life. If today's ideology, which spurs men to commitment to earthly development, were to become a spirituality in which men might intensify their theological life, manifested in a commitment prompting them to sacrifice their own interests for the individual and collective interests of others; and if this involvement, far from alienating from prayer life, makes easier (perhaps in new forms) union with the living Christ and joyously accepted immersion in the paschal mystery of cross and resurrection, then the present ideology of development will itself become the " norma normata normans " of theology. A theology incapable of explaining, establishing and promoting, an ideology experienced in life, would be a theology perhaps true, but abstract and hopelessly irrelevant.

---

[90] Ez. 13: 10.
[91] Rom. 1: 16.
[92] Jn. 15: 18-19.
[93] Mt. 7: 16.

143

JOSEF FUCHS, s. j.

MORAL ASPECTS
OF HUMAN PROGRESS

When the moral theologian in a series of theological lectures [1] speaks of human progress, he must confine himself to a theme in moral theology which he can presume has not already been appropriated by the dogmatic theologian. For it is a fact that in contemporary theology the dogmatic and moral theologian deals with themes like this one in more or less the same way. In order to avoid overlapping we shall deal with the theology of human progress under an aspect which traditionally belongs quite clearly to the field of moral theology.

The description in Section I of some traditional difficulties in the way of an adequate moral theological evaluation of human progress is followed by Section II in which progress is shown as a mandate and consequently a moral duty of man. Then in Section III come considerations of the 'moral standardization' of human progress, and in Section IV the relation is recognized between a valid appraisal of progress and a dynamic understanding of the moral philosophy. A comprehensive reflection on the religious-ethical character of human progress forms the conclusion in Section V.

---

[1] One of a series of lectures of an interdisciplinary course on the theology of human progress given at the Pontifical Gregorian University, Rome, January, 1969.

145

I. DIFFICULTIES CONFRONTING A MORAL THEOLOGICAL EVALUATION OF HUMAN PROGRESS

The fact must not be overlooked that traditional moral theology has experienced difficulty in ascribing sufficient value to human progress in the sense of the active development and evolution of man and his world. It has regarded this active development primarily as of very relative and purely secular value in contrast to the absolute and non-secular value of the moral, the religious and the supernatural. One is conscious here of a tension that obstructed a moral evaluation of the development of man and universe—whose worth was always qualified as purely natural, purely secular, purely immanent; the word 'purely' is significant. Nevertheless the continuing development of the human world was understood as an objective manifestation of the greatness of the Creator and, accordingly, as the glorification of God. One was correspondingly aware of the possibility that man was capable of a subjective understanding of the development of creation as the glorification of the Creator. Yet the active development of man and his world appears simply as the setting in which man can exercise religious-ethical motives. Thus progress may bear an *indirect* relationship to morality and religiosity; but an interior and direct relationship to absolute values is not apparent.

In this view the supernatural above all appears as that value, in opposition to the merely secular, which man must realize as the absolute. The reality of grace may be understood as this 'supernatural' of sole importance—be it only very narrowly regarded as an 'it' or rather as the personal relationship between God calling to salvation and man accepting this call. Against this unique value of the supernatural the value of human progress in this world—as being only secular—is extraordinarily relative. Should one in the development of the world, and by means of it, make a supernatural gain, the earthly progress appears of indifferent value as against the supernatural.

One often speaks instead of the value of the supernatural, of the value of the moral, which is regarded as the absolute value in contrast to the relative human values. However this

146

absolute value of the moral is not perceived in the active development of man himself and of his world, but rather in the moral method followed in archieving progress. Progress itself is only of value in the realm of the secular—of science, of technology, of biological-psychological life, of the material etc. Progress itself dose not bear an intimate and direct relationship to the moral value which man in his progress at any rate achieves. Progress does not appear as a moral task; but as being able to provide the material for a man who acts properly to achieve moral worth, to live a virtuous and supernaturally worthy life.

Another definition, which basically means the same thing, states that the sole absolute and lasting value is fulfillment of the will of God. Instead of 'will of God' we should perhaps say 'moral order'. This will of God, the moral order, is somehow regarded as a static gift and obligation. It is to be observed in the continuing development of the human world; but progress itself remains in an indifferent position, in so far as it is without intrinsic relationship to the will of God.

It will scarcely be denied that the tension between the 'really true' values and the merely secular values has been widely regarded more or less in the way described here—if this is perhaps a somewhat one-sided description. And certainly in this view the active progress of man and his world belongs among the purely secular, purely immanent, purely relative values. Perhaps without undue exaggeration the position could be stated as follows: there were two mutually competitive relationships of man—his horizontal relationship to his fellow-men and to the world on one side and his vertical relationship to the absolute on the other. But both relationships were largely regarded as *categorical* relationships, which exist alongside each other and because of this can and must enter into competition with each other. From this it is also clear that the higher will win the day over the less high—that the latter, because it is in competition with the other, becomes relative and indifferent.

II. Progress as a Mandate for Man

The difficulties which in the past often stood in the way of an adequate moral evaluation of human progress, arose primarily because the horizontal and vertical relationships of man were regarded as categorical and thus as being in competition. However, the vertical relationship of man to the Absolute is in fact to be understood as a primarily transcendental one when considered in connection with the horizontal relationship man-world. As such it does not enter into competition with the categorical relationship of man to the age he lives in and to the world, but exists and is achieved precisely *in* the realization of the horizontal reality of mankind. If one can speak of a possible rivalry, it is not between the horizontal secularity of man and the vertical relationship with God of man as a totality, as a person, but between worship and meditation on the one hand and 'worldly' efficacy on the other. But worship and meditation do not form the real and transcendental relationship of man to God; they belong rather to his categorical and horizontal self-realization. Both, that is the categorical self-realization in worship and meditation as well as the categorical 'worldly' efficacy, are means of self-realization in which and through which the transcendental relationship to God can be achieved. The 'absolute' and 'supernatural' worth is not actually to be sought in the categorical acts of worship and meditation, but in that relationship to the Absolute, to God, to Christ, which lives and operates in categorical acts—worldly reality as well as worship and meditation.

In the categorical view what does the creation of this world require with regard to the world itself? Just this one thing; that man and his world—and this as the world of mankind—should *be*; we can put it like this—that man should be *human*, i. e. a person in this world. But this means that man as a person should develop the World; the world, that is, of men and, in their service, the rest of the world, developing himself thereby. But that implies progress, progressive humanization of the man-world reality, i. e. of mankind and his world. In the fulfilment of this mandate of creation and by means of it man realizes himself as a person in the vertical

148

direction; he does this, finally, not in the categorical but in the transcendental sense.

This reflection obviously implies a precise concept of the so-called natural moral law according to which, it must be unequivocally recognized that man's duty lies in being man, in being himself. This natural law does not consist merely in a collection of demands or orders to be accepted—but rather in the demand to accept oneself as a mandate from the Creator. The concept of the natural moral law as produced as it were above and beyond the creation of mankind (and his world) to which it is in some way 'added', in the sense of a collection of principles or demands, would be basically voluntaristic and thus the direct opposite to natural law. Man is supposed to be a man, a man among men, a man of this world, a worldly man; such is—in a horizontal categorical respect— the content of the natural law. What this means in concrete terms it is up to man, i. e. humanity, to find out for himself; that belongs to the essence of the natural moral law as the law of the nature of man.[2] Should this 'nature of man' be more closely defined, we must take into consideration that man is a *personal* and *historical* being.

The fact that man—as the image of God (*Gen.* 1)—is a *person* means not merely that he can accept, preserve, contemplate mankind, the world of man and himself as a given reality, but rather that he should grasp it, have control over it, shape it, develop it, increasingly and in a more active fashion stamp it with his own nature—in other words increasingly 'humanize' it. Man and his world are not simply actuality, but

---

[2] This is also true of the Church's knowledge of the natural law—even of the official Church, which does not arrive at a knowledge of the natural law via some private revelation, but by human effort. Where particular truths of the natural law appear in Revelation, a second source of knowledge of these truths is thereby provided. Naturally, the evaluation of this source demands exact exegesis. Here we will not tackle the difficult question of the theological value of the norms of the natural law, historically formulated in the Church—be it among the faithful, the theologians, or the Magisterium. Clearly, for a knowledge of the natural law as treated above, the norms of the natural law which have developed in the ecclesial community based on Revelation and moral perception must be considered according to their theological value.

149

also potentiality; given reality and possible development are a single actuality and are in the charge of man as created person-in-world. As person-in-world, man has make an ever fresh attempt to discover in what way man's conduct, the formation of human society and the control and 'utilization' of the reality of the world in the service of mankind can be truly human, can measure up to the dignity of man as a person in this reality. In other words; what kind of progress can be called 'human' progress in the true sense of the word? In so far as he discovers this correctly, he arrives at a knowledge of the natural law.

Personal man is at the same time an *historical* being. That does not mean simply that he lives in a time sequence and can thus look back on the past and perhaps also have a presentiment of the future. It means primarily that by reason of his self-understanding and experience of the past and present he both can and must plan the future as a truly human future. Is not all moral knowledge, even the knowledge of the situation-conscience, really an active plan of a possible, perhaps the only possible (or so it is understood) truly human realization of a given reality; and, in so far as this realization has not yet been achieved, a plan for the responsibly formed future of man, a plan for his advance—as person-in-world— into the future? As beings in history we cannot adopt a static attitude; we have to be incessantly making plans for the future —the next moment, the next day, the coming years, the future of humanity following on after us. So we must always attend, as our most specific duty, to the development of our own persons, of the human world around us and of the world in the service of mankind. The carrying into effect of such plans, i. e. of the knowledge gained in consequence of certain behaviour as to what at any given time is to be done from the human point of view, deals with experiences which in their turn can make fresh reflection, knowledge and planning possible and necessary. As an historical being man must be unceasingly concerned about the future, he must think about progress, and so—what in fact is the same thing—his concern for 'the knowledge of natural law' has no definitive end.

Natural law—in the sense of natural moral law—cannot thus be regarded as a static quantity and reality. It cannot be preserved in a book as a collection of precepts and commands. Neither can it be read from facts of nature as though God had woven it into them; for all that can be read from the facts of nature are physical data and laws, not moral regulations and commands. The natural moral law is rather to be understood in a dynamic sense; as the ever new and still to be solved problem of being a person of this world. This, however implies development and progress. Many branches of knowledge of the natural law concerned with human behaviour and conduct will show themselves to be—at any rate substantially—lasting and do not require repeated calling into question. But there are also areas of knowledge where solutions—arrived at by us humans and held as good and right—are open to doubt. Most important of all, completely new questions are constantly arising particularly at a time when man's probing into the facts of nature and their changing character make it possible for him as a result of experience to regard previous answers to questions, which may have been well-intentioned, as in fact basically 'in-human' and therefore incorrect.

Development of oneself, one's environment and the world always implies probing into the given facts, conquering the bounds of nature's given reality, in other words *artificium* in relation to *natura* understood as the given facts of nature. The invasion of nature, thus understood, the conquering of its limitations, the *artificium*, is an essential part of being human, of humanizing nature's realities, of the transformation of nature into human culture, of the fulfilment of the mandate to be a person in this world: indeed, the *artificium* pertains to man's nature, if one understands nature, not merely in the sense of actuated given reality, but as personal human existence in its totality. Certainly not every arbitrary invasion, not every arbitrary *artificium* is human culture. The invasion, the *artificium* must be of such an order as to be worthy of man—as a person in nature and the world—and as to create human values—'human' understood in the fullest sense of the word—and not 'un-values'. But whether certain invasions, *artificia*,—are to be judged as—in the best sense—'human' or as basically 'un-human', we will often discern correctly in our first 'draft', i. e. at the first attempt at a moral judgement;

but it can also happen that experience leads us sooner or later to revise this draft, our moral pronouncement.

When we regard the natural moral law in its dynamic sense, in other words as the mandate to live as a person of this world, it becomes apparent that this achievement always demands some use of force—taking this word in its widest sense. We have to tear away the secrets and potentialities from this world entrusted to us, have to free it from its fixity and pure reality, have to impose on it our reason and our will. The same holds good of the shaping of human society and humanity. For our task is not simply to protect the given realities—neither the realities of human ignorance or indolence, nor the realities of social order created or evolved in good or ill will; the goal of human society is not its ever existing condition and order, but its ever improving formation —the common good in the best and fullest sense of the word. The fulfillment of this mandate involves a struggle in various ways against much and many—thus the use in some form or other of force. And must we not in order to live in the sense of 'people of this world' constantly force ourselves to rid our minds of ideas, knowledge, customs, which have become too dear to us? The 'fight' for truth and for a better shaping of life and the world has not only to be waged with others but with ourselves. That which is given, has become, has been formed by us, is also that which in some way has to be overcome because it is to be continued.

III. The 'Moral Standardization' of Human Progress

The idea has already been repeatedly expressed that not every type of progress, certainly not every probing into facts 'in the name of progress' is morally justifiable—since it is not 'human' in the fullest sense of the word. But one could well ask: if 'being a person of this world'—in other words progress—constitutes, according to natural law, the task of man in this world, then isn't progress itself the real moral norm of man, so that there is no need to search for moral norms for progress—the development of the 'man in world'? The question is perfectly justifiable. But before we turn expressly to this question let it be said that progress which is effected in opposition to a real moral order is in reality no progress.

If the question is concerned with whether the unjustifiable and accordingly immoral could exist in the realm of development of the man-world reality, a twofold reply is indicated. (a) It would be unjustifiable and thus immoral if man wished to be indifferent to the development of the mankind-world reality, not to concern himself with it. For this would mean that man was not accepting and fulfilling his mandate to be 'a person in the world.' (b) It would be unjustifiable and immoral if man wished to pursue a course of development which was basically only alleged progress. This because man is committed to progress. Here the following should clearly be stated: progress must always be 'human,' may never be 'inhuman.' Yet it is a question of the development of the man-world reality. Whoever speaks of progress, of the progress and development of the world in its material aspect, in other words of technical progress, must ultimately mean the progress of man, of human society. The wold has no meaning except in its relation to mankind; it only possesses meaning as a world of men. Thus 'inhuman' progress is not in the true and full sense progress; and therefore it is immoral. On the other hand this means that it is immoral to remain indifferent to—true—progress, not to concern oneself with it.

The danger of man serving the cause of spurious development, and thus basically non-development, instead of true progress lies in the concupiscent egoism of man 'of the Fall.' This man can be so fascinated by the possibility of a merely 'partial' and therefore 'inhuman progress' that he disregards mankind to achieve, for example, purely technical progress. The will to progress must withstand the attempt to exclude man and to overlook the question of whether a particular 'development' is worthy of man and will be of service to him.

The second of the principles mentioned for the morality of human progress poses the question of whether we can establish more concrete principles to indicate more closely just what man desirous of progress must heed, what he may aspire to and what not, what means cannot be employed to achieve a progress worthy of man, what calculated dangers and consequences he may not take on himself and more in this vein. In short, have knowledge of moral principles which—apart from the basic requirement that man must concern himself with progress and indeed with 'human' progress in the full sense—in some way regulate the active progress of the man-world reality and confine it within certain bounds? Obviously this question is identical with the general question concerning the possibility of moral principles for human conduct in general.

This means repeating the thesis often expressed to-day, that there are very few moral principles which make purely a *priori*—in the strictest sense of the term, and in this sense metaphysical—assertions concerning man's moral conduct as such. They relate primarily to man's personal, responsible, social and historical nature which, as in all human behaviour, demands consideration in the realization of his mandate and desire for progress. These general moral principles are of considerable importance and have their consequences in all human conduct, but alone they scarcely produce concrete guide-lines for human behavious and human progress. More concrete guide-lines presuppose experience and knowledge of concrete reality and its possible method of realization—together with the consequences. This experience of and information about the man-world reality which is constantly changing because of its achievements and experience—experience of the past, present and the immediate future—lead us continually to raise afresh the question of the true humanity and worth in human terms of our action and progress.

Some considerable problems follow from this, which—at least as problems—must be looked at. Can it be perhaps that in some areas of human action and behaviour several truly human solutions are possible—not merely as a result of erroneous judgement and assessment, but in truth and objectively? Is it perhaps conceivable that, in different cultures by reason of a different context and a partly different scale of values, slightly differing norms of behaviour develop and indeed—justifiably in this context—must develop? Can we perhaps say that an ideal of human conduct which presupposes a certain level of culture and a certain scale of values at a certain time in history cannot be regarded as the optimum in behaviour when this culture level is not reached and the corresponding scale of values not comprehended? Take, for instance, many of our present-day pronouncements on the correct social relationship between man and woman— whether in Europe or America: were not these still regarded at the turn of the century as to some extent neither judicious nor acceptable? And on the other hand are not the pronouncements of the Apostle Paul on this relationship (e. g. the subordinate position of woman in society) to some extent unacceptable to us and therefore of no account?

There can be no doubt that man can know, or by working can arrive at more concrete principles and guide-lines for the way to his—truly human—progress. Yet new experiences and reflection on these can never put man once and for all in complete possession of all guide-lines and principles, down to the smallest detail, with no further need for change. For man seeking progress must continue to look for and discover certain principles concerning the humanity of his progress, in other words moral principles.

Anyone wanting to achieve progress must plan the future. It is often not possible to assess in advance with complete certainty the consequences for the future of certain projects, whether in the field of social work, hygiene, economics, space-research etc. Here imperatives [3] must be laid down of which one cannot say with certainty that they are the right ones, i. e. that they will prove in the long run to be worthy of man and therefore morally justifiable. Man committed and bound to progress can and must, if he wants to comply with his existence as a 'being of progress', have the will to adopt courageous and at the same time intelligently worked out imperatives. Experience and foresight, a look at the goal, means and possible consequences allow one to arrive at a sufficiently safe judgement as to whether the attempt at a step forward, and thus a necessity, is humanly-morally

---

[3] Cf. K. Rahner, 'Prinzipien und Imperative' in: *Das Dynamische in der Kirche,* Freiburg i. Br. 1958, p. 14-37.

defensible. While the combination of courage and intelligence in the drawing up of imperatives does not permit man to shrink back from the risk attached to taking a step forward in the not completely discernible future, it leads him to take care to see that the attempted step proves to be true human progress. A complete rationalization of the assent to or rejection of an imperative or even the superiority of one imperative over another is often not feasible. The better someone knows the totality of the reality implied in the imperative and the deeper and more genuine his human image, the more fit he will be for an imperative of true human progress.

The Church, too, will constantly find herself in the situation either of setting herself concrete imperatives—e. g. in the encyclical laid down or in the process of being laid down by certain persons or groups. In this field she will more often give pastoral guidance than magisterial teaching. Since such imperatives often presuppose a high level of knowledge in various profane sciences, it would be better for the official Church to be cautious on these questions [4]—in so far as they lie outside her field of operation. Politics, sociology, technology, biology and much besides are, however, not the field of competence of the Church—even if these fields are as open to those who make up the Church as to other men. Indeed in so far as the Church and the true believing Christian have a view of mankind—a view which in faith and under the dynamics of faith has become freed and is truly *human*—and correspondingly an understanding of the 'humanity' of imperatives, they are called to have a voice in judging the imperatives governing human progress. [5]

---

[4] Cf. K. Rahner, 'Theologische Reflexionen zum Problem der Säkularisation', in:*Schriften zur Theologie,* VIII, 637-66.

[5] K. Rahner speaks of a 'moral instinct of faith' ('moralischen Glaubensinstinkt'). E. Schillebeecks interprets in a similar way the words of the Constitution *Gaudium et Spes* (No. 46), that we recognize what we ought to do 'in the light of the gospel and of human experience'. See K. Rahner, 'Zum Problem der genetische Manipulation ', in: *Schriften zur Theologie,* VIII, 303 f, and E. Schillebeeckx, "The Magisterium and the World of Politics" in: *Concilium* (4) June 1968, 16f.

IV. PROGRESS AND THE DYNAMIC UNDERSTANDING
OF MORALITY

A proper understanding and moral evaluation of progress depends in no small measure upon a proper understanding of moral concepts and principles. At the same time it is of decisive importance whether one is dealing with a mainly static or a truly dynamic interpretation. Only by overcoming a one-sided, static way of thinking, by the ability to think dynamically in the moral field, can one find the way to a moral understanding of human progress. Here I would like —by way of example—to set out the significance of the dynamic interpretation of certain moral principles for the understanding of human progress. This will be followed by a short reflection on the relationship of progress and force.

1. The so-called principle of totality means, in traditional moral theology, that the part stands at the service of the whole and may therefore be sacrificed in its service—at least in so far as this whole represents a unity of being and not merely a working unity. This principle has often been understood in a onesided, static way. Thus it is said that part of the whole may be sacrificed in order to keep the whole in being or in health and strength, or to restore it to this condition by averting a present injury or an imminent danger. A dynamic conception of the same principle would assert that a part may be sacrificed in order to bring about the development of the whole beyond its static givenness, in order to achieve the development of its latent possibilities. And this is progress.

Some examples may illustrate this point. Moral theology never put any difficulties in a doctor's way when it was a question of removing an inflamed appendix. The diseased part could be removed in order to save the organism as a whole from the danger that threatened it and so to preserve it in its given state. On the other hand, if it was a question of removing a healthy appendix which did not threaten the condition of the entire organism either directly or indirectly, then objections were raised. Even reference to the anticipatory elimination of an eventual future danger which could

157

perhaps—above all in special circumstances, for example, the absence of medical help—prove fatal, even this was not sufficient. It was not admitted that this kind of medical removal of a part (the appendix) could be justified as treatment required by the organism as a whole, and therefore as a step forward.

A number of theoreticians and practitioners have now changed their view. For instance, an operation for aesthetic purposes—on the face of it an interference and to that extent a 'sacrifice'—does not serve the preservation or restoration to health of the whole, but signifies an 'improvement' of the whole beyond its given state. Accordingly, objections were raised to such an operation on the basis of a solely 'static' understanding of the principle of totality. If, on the other hand, a person was suffering psychologically from his disfigurement, then intervention was allowed in order to free him from his psychological illness, that is, in the interest of the health of the whole. But why should not an intervention for the 'improvement' of the whole, for appropriate reasons, i. e. for the sake of progress, be justified as rational and, therefore, moral? In that case the principle of totality would, of course, be understood dynamically, not statically. At the present time, and in the near future, new possibilities seem to be opening up. Our aim increasingly is to influence and control the biological reality and structure of mankind. May one or may one not make use of these possibilities which, by and large, are intended to promote the qualitative improvement of man rather than preserve him in his existing state and cure him of his ills? That will depend largely upon the question of the conditions for realizing these possibilities and the long-term risks of such interference. The basic question, however, is whether the principle of totality is to be understood only in a static sense—preservation and healing of the whole—or also dynamically. A progressively deepening understanding of this principle, and the conception of human morality (natural law) expounded above, justify its dynamic understanding and application in the service of progress, rightly understood.

There is a principle of law and morality that in doubtful cases favours the fortunate party in possession: *in dubio, melior est condicio possidentis*; when in doubt, the legal presumption favours the actual possessor. The principle that legal certainty must be guaranteed in the community tends in the same direction. Both have led, and easily do lead, people to be inclined to look for law and justice—and consequently 'the will of God'—on the side of the actual order of things. But this betrays static thinking. Basically, however, it is a question neither of the existing order as such, nor of some other order, but of the just order which has continually to be sought for, planned and put into effect. Alongside the principles of legal certainty and the preferment of the actual possessor there must stand this other, more dynamic principle, namely that our real task is always to seek the better order of things. Only by reference to this other, dynamic principle can both the aforesaid principles be properly understood. Conversely, dynamism would turn to revolution and disorder if it did not have regard to the importance of legal presumption and legal certainty. The desire for progress, which seeks always to create a better and more just order, is only truly human, and progressive in the real sense, if the static elements of legal presumption and legal certainty are properly regarded. On the other hand, regard for legal presumption and certainty becomes anti-progressive and thus 'inhuman' if it overlooks the necessary drive towards an even better order.

As the re-orientation from a static to a more dynamic way of thinking proceeds, it affects, for example, the evaluation of revolution. [6] Towards the end of the last and the beginning of the present century, both in the writings of theologians and in the documents of the Church, there prevailed the thesis, illustrating a static way of thinking, that revolution, as a violent overthrow of a given order, was a violation of law, contrary to justice, and therefore immoral. Only if, later on, the new order brought about by the revolution could not be reversed without great disadvantage to the common good, did it thereby become legitimate. This thesis

---

[5] Cf. R. Hauser, *Autorität und Macht*. Die staatliche Autorität in der neuen protestantischen und in der katholischen Gesellschaftslehre, Heidelberg 1949.

has now changed. If the common good can retrospectively legitimize the new order, then this is tantamount to admitting that it is not the actual existence as such of a particular order that gives it legitimacy, but the more dynamic requirement of the common good. But in that case the possibility cannot be excluded that an actually existing order might prove unjust from the point of view of the common good, and that its preservation would therefore depend on unjust force. This means, however, that the enforced introduction of a new order will not necessarily be legitimized only in retrospect, but also on occasion in advance—though naturally only as a last resort and on condition of a tolerable relationship beween the ills of revolution and its anticipated success. Pius XII made this teaching his own in his letter of 8 March 1937 to the Mexican bishops. [7]

The example cited in itself explains how in many other questions also the right way, that is the way of (true) progress, is to be found not by a one-sided, static assessment of the actual state of affairs, but by a dynamic outlook on the more correct and better solution. Without this dynamic outlook neither the mastery of situations of social injustice nor the decolonization of peoples capable of free self-determination would be possible, so long as a one-sided, static view insisted on the—formal—rights of the existing order. To say this is not to say what kind of means may be applied for the alteration of the actual situation in given circumstances.

That the rights of the dynamic will to progress, as against static rigidity, can also be of importance in the Church is understood today even by those who do not wish to speak of this question or are actually afraid of it. The fact of a hierarchical authority established in the Church by Christ does not necessarily stand in opposition to the dynamic will to progress in the ecclesiastical community. For the Church, as a human society, despite the hierarchical authority established within it, is not exempted from the laws of social life, above all the law of the primacy of the common good. A brief example can be given. If in the field of positive law there

---

[7] Denz.-Schönm., *Enchiridion,* 3775 s.

exists *Epikeia,* as the virtue of a superior sense of justice,[8] then this virtue also has its importance in the ecclesiastical community and in relation to the order established by its hierarchical authority. To be sure, it is easier for *epikeia* to permit or require a responsible action which does not correspond to the letter of ecclesiastical order in the private than the public sphere. But an action based on *epikeia* is not fundamentally excluded in the public field either. If one follows up this line of thought consistently, then pressure and action on behalf of an alteration of the established order cannot, basically, be absolutely and in every case unjust. Firm action to replace the good by the better for the sake of progress, motivated by a correct understanding of the common good, must also have a place in the Church. The Spirit of the Lord, and the understanding of reality in this Spirit, are not absolutely reserved to Church authority. Of course, great delicacy and a high gift of discrimination will be needed to establish the right relation between willing and respectful readiness to obey on the one hand, and on the other, zeal in the service of progress on behalf of the people of God. When the matter is looked at in this way, it is as true of *epikeia* as of the will to progress that it can only be properly put into practice by a person of true competence, great sense of responsibility, and humble readiness to serve.

Moral theology is accustomed to distinguish between negative commands, i. e. prohibitions, and affirmative commands, i. e. precepts. So far as prohibitions are concerned, they are not only always valid, but have to be respected on every occasion. Precepts, on the other hand, are, it is true, always valid but do not have to be carried out on every occasion: *praecepta negativa valent semper et pro semper, praecepta affirmativa valent semper sed non pro semper.* The meaning is clear. A prohibition may not be disregarded but an action cannot always be commanded. One does not constantly have to smile at one's neighbour, give alms to all the poor without distinction, and renounce every justified action that might possibly cause annoyance to someone else. Let us now consider the meaning of that part of the principle that reads:

---

[8] Thomas Aquinas, *S. Theol.* II-II 120, 2 ad 1.

praecepta affirmativa valent semper sed non pro semper. It expresses the precept that one must put into practice the values involved in these commands, but that this putting into practice has to be co-ordinated with the realization of other values, that is to say that the best combination of values must be discovered and put into effect. The values whose realization is under discussion are in the first place only relative values, *bona physica,* not absolute values, *bona moralia.* To smile at one's neighbour, to give alms, to avoid distressing one's neighbour—these are human values, but only relative values. To put them into practice is *often* appropriate or necessary, but not *always*—the latter applies only to absolute values, *bona moralia.* Thus the principle we are discussing really means this: there is an absolute moral duty, to put into practice *in the best possible manner* the values indicated in affirmative commands, that is to say with regard to other equally necessary values. This expresses the basic precept of human morality. In this world we have an (absolute) duty to make the best possible effort towards the realization of (relative) values. What this 'best possible' is, what the best possible realization of the man-would reality can be, today and tomorrow, this mankind has to find out for itself. But this search for the best possible concrete solution itself forms part of the absolute moral precept, to make the best that is possible out of the man-world reality. The principle, *praecepta affirmativa valent semper sed non pro semper,* is therefore to be understood dynamically, and means in the last analysis that man, in building the man-world reality, is bound constantly to build for the betterment of the world, that is, to progress.

2. There are other moral principles to be examined for their dynamic meaning and corresponding relationship to human progress. What follows, however, comprises an enquiry into another link between progress and the dynamic interpretation of morality—the relationship between progress on the one hand, and power and force on the other. For the realization of the best that is possible, i. e. progress, in the last analysis permits of no *quieta non movere* but requires the application of power and force. Progress has continually to

be extracted anew from static given reality, and this comes about by the dynamic of power and force legitimized by progress.

Nature only yields its secrets, its latent powers and laws, its as yet unexplored and unrealized possibilities, if man with his mind and will and the powers they control wrenches them loose by power and force, to make them his own. Progress, however, requires man to confront in all kinds of ways, with power and force, not only nature, which is not free, but also free humanity itself. To be sure, progress can only be genuine human progress, if it is attained by an exercise of power and force that is *humanly justified*.

Even the *upbringing* of children is, in a sense, an exercise of power. Children are not simply left to themselves but are given into the superior power of adults. They may not and cannot develop in unfettered freedom but come, under the 'power-ful' influence of adults and only thus, to human development—in knowledge, ability, conviction and right conduct. The actual or intended influence of *social groups* on the opinions and behaviour of many individuals is a true exercise of power, without which the progress of humanity would be impossible. The direction of the community by the *state*, its deliverance from individualistic thinking and behaviour, its guidance along lines of cooperation for public order and the common good, the systematic cultivation of a necessary public opinion (without suppression of the right to legitimate information) are in the same way, exercises in power aimed at achieving the best that is possible. But such power becomes compulsion if, culpably or not, individuals do not fit into the right and necessary order, and even set themselves against it. Or if, following the egoism embodied in the preservation of the *status quo*, they oppose necessary social reforms. Or if, on the other hand from the same egoism, they work for upheaval and disorder, which prevent *real* progress. The state, too, stands at the service of the best that is possible by way of progress, and it cannot give this service without the exercise of power and force (cf. *Rom.* 13: 1-7.) [9]

---

[9] The problem of violence versus non-violence demands careful treatment. In the present situation violence is usually understood

There also exists, of course, an objectively unjust, and at the same time in many ways subjectively egoistic, exercise of power and force, which gives itself out as acting in the

---

in the narrow sense as an attack on a person's life and limb. This is so despite the fact that there are many other forms of violence against persons which can be even more damaging to individuals or groups or society as a whole than an attack on life and limb (cf. 1. above).

Quite often today non-violence is proposed as an absolute (human or Christian) imperative, and the use of force (above all in the sense of an attack on life and limb) as an absolute prohibition. Apart from the fact that this does not accord with traditional Christian teaching (cf. the doctrines of justified self-defence, of 'just war' and justifiable death penalty), there seems here to be an inaccurate idea of the related concepts of 'absolute' and 'relative' values in the moral field. Love and justice are moral, that is, *absolute* values (*bona moralia*) which, as such, may never be violated. The use of force involves an action that violates a *relative* human value, and accordingly inflicts a *malum physicum*. Even the preservation or the taking of life are not, in themselves, an absolute value or an absolute evil, else it would not be permissible in any circumstances to kill or allow to die—and this is contrary to all tradition. Only a correct assessment of advantage, an assessment of the various values and evils implicit in an action (abstract or concrete) makes it possible to establish an absolute. In practice, moral theology has always applied this principle, for example to the question of what relevant values justify the killing of a man (e. g. capital punishment). This does not only apply to an action with a double effect, that is, the case in which the relative human evil, e. g. injury or death, is brought about freely and consciously, without this evil being the motive of the action.

The Sermon on the Mount does not teach non-violence as an absolute imperative; but rather, it teaches the absolute imperatives of love and justice. As these in certain circumstances, taking into account the balance of the implied (relative) values and evils, may require the renunciation of force, the *readiness* for such renunciation is necessarily implied in the absolute value of love and justice. But concrete ways of behaving which the Sermon on the Mount prescribes, are to be understood rather as 'ethical models', as is shown not only by the hyperbolic style of expression but also by the behaviour of Christ (for example, his *self-defence* before the court).

If it is said that non-violence is more in accord with the gospel than the use of violence, that is in a certain sense true, but should not be wrongly understood. For the gospel does not absolutely exclude the use of force in the world of the Fall. The absolute command of love may even require the use of force. Of

164

service of progress. Such progress is 'in-human' and therefore only an apparent progress, in fact it is a lack of progress. Where objectives are aimed at or methods applied (for ends just in themselves) with power and force which is unworthy of humanity and therefore 'in-human', there progress does not really exist. Slavery—whatever the 'lofty' objectives in view—can in our society only be seen as an instance of the unjust use of force. Equally, the enforced maintenance, by whatever means, of a *status quo* where social equality is inadequate is, objectively, an unjust exercise of power and force. It can be classified as lack of (human) progress, even though it may allow for partial progress. The manipulation of public opinion by false information or by the unlawful prevention of a free flow of information, the non-safeguarding of personal rights, the enforcement of objectives by the dictatorial exercise of power—none of these serve progress in a way appropriate to human dignity, and they therefore do not contribute to a truly 'human' progress. It may be that in special circumstances, and for a temporary period, this kind of use of power and force is the only way to realize the good of necessary progress. A correct judgement on this presupposes a high level of knowledge of the issues, a deep understanding of the dignity of the human person, and great consciousness of responsibility.

A use of power and force that is unjustified, because it does not really serve the cause of 'human' progress, cannot

---

course, force is then not an ideal but the best that is possible. For where it is a symptom of the Fall, i. e. of the sin that has entered into this world, there it has to be reckoned as something that, in the field of the possible (the calculation of advantage), must in this sinful world increasingly be made superfluous. But so long as this possibility does not actually exist, the use of force remains a possible expression of love and justice as an absolute precept.

It would therefore be wrong to say that the 'just' use of force was nothing but the application of the principle that 'the end justifies the means'. Something could also be said about this principle. The following must suffice here: In this principle 'means' signifies a *malum absolutum* (*morale*). If the use of force were absolutely, i. e. morally, bad, it would obviously never qualify as a justifiable means in the fallen world. But it is precisely this assertion that has been questioned above.

be in the interests of man's duty and will to progress—that is a tautology. There remains the question of how the justified use of power and force is to be more precisely understood. A few comments are offered here. Certainly, not all justified exercises of power and force on behalf of progress stand as signs of the sin that has entered into this world, and their justification or necessity therefore makes visible the real condition of the fallen man-world reality. All who do not subscribe, as far as they are able, to the best possible progressive realization of man, his society and his world, or who actually resist it out of personal egoism or the blindness that springs from the fundamental egoism of fallen man, act sinfully in so far as they do this. On the other hand, power and force used in the service of real progress are not in themselves sinful, but are a defence against objectively unjust and perhaps also subjectively egoistical and sinful behaviour, and in any case a defence against 'the sins of the world', and their consequences. But if the use of force can be justified, its relation to the sinful condition of the world should not be overlooked. From this follows that we are always bound so to change the world's condition that the application of force, which is a sign of the world's sinfulness, will become increasingly unnecessary.

V. The religious and moral character of human progress

We began by examining the problems which caused moral theology to arrive only with difficulty at a correct moral and religious assessment of human progress. Seen as a purely natural, purely secular, purely immanent value, progress seems to be in competition with the absolute values of morality, religion and the supernatural. So far we have tried to indicate the place of human progress in the moral field. In conclusion, we shall briefly investigate the moral and religious character of human progress by means of a summing up and a theological continuation of the foregoing observations. This leads to an evaluation substantially different from that conditioned by the difficulties mentioned above.

It is interesting to note that people have been more ready to regard as morally valuable the healing of the sick, for example, or the support of the needy, than human progress in the sense of the active development of the man-world reality . And yet both these activities are 'moral' in *the same sense*. In themselves, it is true, they are only *relative* values. But their proper and meaningful realization is part of man's moral and therefore *absolute* duty. Progress is not merely a physical possibility, and not merely a morally unobjectionable exercise, but a moral duty. That should be plain enough from the preceding exposition.

The turning to the world expressed in the will to progress is, 'since the Fall', in permanent danger of running away into a secret or open egoism. The Son of God made man has brought to this world the new man of the kingdom of God, in whom the Spirit conquers egoism. Despite the 'Fall', the world has once and for all been taken up by God, through the sending of his Son. The positive application to the reality of man and his world and their development, that is progress, does not simply belong to the task of creation but also to the expression of God's will and the commission entrusted to men in the sending to them of His Son. God's turning to the world in the incarnation and self-giving of his Son carries with it the task of accepting and bringing progressively to development God's creation, that is, man and his world. This is part of the realization of God's incarnation in this world.

At the same time the development of reality that is man and his world, in other words progress, is not to be seen as something that has nothing to do with the supernatural and with grace. For the bond of supernatural, grace-given life between the Father and those who are taken up into the divine community of love, does not exist in isolation from man in the world, but is indeed man's true life. This true life of community of grace with the Father is fulfilled in and through the immanent formation of the reality of the world. But this forward-moving world-formation is already something more than itself, more than a purely immanent, intra-worldly happening.

It has already been pointed out that one can make the immanence of world-formation, and of progress, into an absolute and thus misunderstand it, that one can be hypnotized by the immanent possibilities and take to egoistical sham-progress, that is, 'inhumanity', instead of to (human) progress. Grace, faith and love make fallen man open to real progress. Thus grace, faith and love enter into progress and it becomes itself a sign of grace working for faith and love in the world. We are not raising the question of how this takes place in Christians and non-Christians, in just men and in sinners. But if true progress is only possible if the man under grace constantly detaches himself and, by power and force others also, from egoism, then the active realization and development of the man-world reality that is to say progress, is always signed with the cross. A will to progress that is absolutely opposed to this sign ultimately makes for inhuman progress, non-progress. It does not make way for the power of Christ transforming man through grace. It resists that immanent formation of the world in and through which the mission of the incarnate Son is to be completed. But where progress takes place under the influence of grace, and under the sign of the cross, there it is able to bring about the true formation of 'man-in-the-world' as this is intended by our creation and salvation [10]. At the same time the continuing immanent formation of the world leads to an increase in

---

[10] Thus a free renunciation, for example voluntary poverty, does not contradict the commandment of human progress, For a free renunciation, as witnessing hope in the transforming power of grace upon the destructive egoism of fallen man, has the prophetic mission in the world of warning men against the danger of an in-human 'progress', and pointing to the principle of all progress which is that it has to be the progress of *man*, of *humanity*. Renunciation and poverty do not constitute a value *as such* and indeed would have to be considered as obstacles to progress if fallen man did not continually feel and experience his own egoism and were unable to hope for its overcoming—a process which only the Christian can understand as 'fall' and 'redemption' by grace. If man is to progress in the world, two things are needed, depending on the individual's vocation—active participation in the world, and renunciation of the world. Only thus will it be possible for man's progress to be truly 'human'.

human freedom, in so far as the world, in its continuing formation, offers less resistance to the realization of the 'new life' of the Christian as he lives it in the midst of the world.

In this way true progress becomes the expression and sign of the eschatological salvation that is already present and is also drawing ever closer to us.

JOSE DIEZ-ALEGRIA, s. j.

A CHRISTIAN VIEW OF PROGRESS THROUGH VIOLENCE

I. INTRODUCTORY OVERVIEW OF PROBLEM

The subject of this chapter is a difficult one. Even the terminology creates problems. For, how are we to understand the word "violence"? And what do we mean by "progress"? Since the latter is analysed elsewhere in this volume we can here set aside that problem except to indicate at once in what sense we use the word.

Progress surely must have a humanist interpretation. It must be understood as a forward movement in the growing humanisation of man and his environment. Environment embraces both society and its structures (cultural, political, juridical, economic and others) and the natural world as modified and modifiable through work and technology.

Humanisation, unless we are prepared to reduce the idea to empty formality, brings us to the question of how we are to understand man himself (philosophy or Weltanschauung.). Upon this answer (it may be a theological one) depends the categories one uses in defining progress (or retrogression) in humanisation. The same holds good for determining which environmental changes are humanising and which are dehumanising.

Instead of here proposing our own theory about man we content ourselves with appropriating the concept which Pope John XXIII gave us in his encyclical *Pacem in Terris*: man is an intelligent and free person, subject of rights and duties

171

which are universal, inviolable and inalienable. [1] Man is also essentially social, so that the destiny to which he is called can be achieved only if men assume joint responsibility for it. This will demand, in the words of the encyclical that "the living of men together be ordered, and thus mutual rights and duties be recognized and made operative. This in turn requires that all contribute generously to the creation of proper human conditions such as will render effective and constantly enrich these rights and duties." Hence "it is not enough to respect in each human being the right to means of livelihood. Each must also work according to his capacity to ensure that all men will have at their disposal an adequacy of such means." [2]

The pastoral constitution, *Gaudium et Spes,* speaks in similar vein. "Hence, the social order and its development must always work to the benefit of the human person if the disposition of affairs is to be subordinate to the personal realm and not contrariwise, as the Lord indicated when He said that the Sabbath was made for man and not man for the Sabbath (M.k. 2, 27). This social order must always improve. It must be founded on truth and justice and be animated by love. In freedom it should advance daily toward a more perfect human equilibrium. (Cfr. *Pacem in Terris* A.A.S. 55, 1963. 266). But these goals will not be realized without fundamental changes in attitudes and in social structures ". [3]

Widespread changes in society will have to take place. Here is the heart of the matter. But if this be true, it must be said that the undoubtedly spectacular technical and economic advance of one part of mankind, with society generally being scarcerly changed, is ambiguous from the viewpoint of authentic human progress. One part of humanity is enjoying prodigious growth. But is this growth along the path of human progress and jointly with the rest of humanity? We are not about to launch here into a puritanical criticism of technology and modern society. We want only to pose our

---

[1] Encyclical *Pacem in terris.* (A.A.S. 55, 1963, 259).
[2] Ibidem 264-265.
[3] Constitution *Gaudium et Spes,* n. 26 c.

problem: if we are to assure human progress of society and man (of all men and every man, in the apt phrase of *Populorum Progressio*) [4] profound changes of social structures will be needed. But — and here we come to the problem of this chapter — can such deep-going transformations be brought about without resort to violence?

This bring us to the problem that constitutes the scope of this chapter. We are first forced to ask what is violence? and in what do violence and non-violence consist? Next, is violence when put into relationship with human progress in itself something positive? or something negative? If the latter, is it radically negative or only relatively negative and, therefore, also relatively positive? To put it in other terms, granting that violence can not be a constitutive of human progress, can it in certain circumstances open the way to this progress (the progress itself putting an end to the violence?)

And to shift now to the ethical viewpoint, can violence be accepted? What sort of violence? by what means? and in what circumstances? Finally, what does christian theology say about violence? Is there any precise theological datum? If so, does this coincide with the ethical datum of « moral law », knowable by human reason without explicit revelation? Or, may it be so that there is with respect to violence contradiction between ethics and the Gospel? If not, is it possible to find contradiction between ethics and reality, and indeed an insoluble one? If this be so, are we forced to question radically social ethics itself? or to reduce it to pure situational ethics?

Let us raise still a further question. Conscience has serious hesitancies when it comes to violence. If therefore it is impossible to resolve the questions of violence, are we then forced into the situation of renouncing also the progress which, ex hypothesi cannot be had without violent forcing of structural change? (The implication being that human history is the negation of a humanist progress for which is substituted scientific and technological development.)

---

[4] Encyclical *Populorum Progressio,* n. 42. Cfr. ibidem n. 14 and n. 47: "It is concerned with building a world where every man, without exception of race, religion, nationality, could live a fully human life."

Quite clearly the problems we here pose are as grave as they are real. If we seek here to advance some distance toward the solution of these problems, we do so under no illusion that we can make more than a modest contribution. That contribution will be to explore paths for future study. Our starting point is christian theology. We ask whether there is a theological doctrine on violence, what its relation to the ethical is as well as its relationship to reality.

II. Violence and its Forms

Violence may be thought of as one force opposing another (or opposing a static resistance) and imposing itself. So conceived, violence belongs to the essential dynamics of reality. This does not imply either a rigorously dialectic conception of reality or a process of idea-reality, such as Hegel's. But it does require recognition that reality — biological, anthropological and social — has elements of contradiction and moves, to a considerable extent, through dialectical processes. So understood, violence plays a necessary role in the elaboration of any possible human progress.

But when considering the relation between violence and progress we understand violence in a more restricted sense that is not easy to grasp.

Violence can be taken to refer to the military violence employed in armed warfare with lethal weapons. The reflections we are about to undertake will be based on this meaning. But first we must confront a difficulty. Is it legitimate to restrict violence to armed struggle with lethal weapons? Are we justified in confining our attention to such without examining first the structural violence which oppresses men and kills them through starvation? Can we prescind from the inhuman conditions of famine and disease, of subjugation and the oppression of every liberty, to which unjust social and economic structures have reduced people? Clearly not; and, therefore, we must bring into our considerations this as well as still other types of violence.

Four types must be kept in mind. The first is *structural violence*. This is precisely that violence effected by

174

those unjust social, economic and cultural structures mentioned above. The second violence may be called *revolution of structures*. By this we understand the violence involved in moving from one set of structures to another when this requires, not a simple evolution of an internal dynamism, but rupture from past structures to be effected by the latter's suppression.

Our third type of violence bears, somewhat paradoxically, the name of *active non-violence*. The paradox vanishes when we examine the reality, for here we encounter the exercise of non-armed displays of active opposition to the Establishment. It embraces public denunciations, mass demonstrations, the occupation of public buildings, boycotts and strikes, civil disobedience and still others. So long as this *strategy of forcing* the Establishment does not go to the lengths of armed conflict, it is designated as non-violent even though it may become extremely forceful.

The fourth type is that *armed violence* already described. But neither is this a univocal concept, for there are different kinds. There is that exercised by one state against another at the international level (*war* or *international armed action for defence*) or against the state's own citizens (*armed coactive repression*). In this latter case there are sub-types — that exercised by a legitimately constituted state pursuing the common good and that exercised by an unjustly constituted power, thus constituting a bastion of violence. A third sub-type is the resort by citizens to arms against the power of the state or of society (*armed revolutionary violence.*).

Of all the types of violence thus enumerated, two do not concern us (that of war or of international armed defence). In the forefront of consideration will be the following two: active non-violence and armed revolutionary violence. But we shall have to keep our eye on the other three: structural violence, revolution of structures, and armed coactive repression exercised by the state.

III. Revolution Of Structures and Progress

The question we begin with is whether the achievement of human progress for all men may not require in some instances, at least in the present world situation a revolution of structures.

But human progress? Are the social processes of our day moving toward the humanisation of life for all in freedom and solidarity? Some answer no; but this does not disturb them since they regard such humanisation as a Utopia impossible to realize. Others give an affirmative reply. These see in the technological advances of the developed capitalist world a dynamic force leading humanity on toward true progress. These beneficent structures must be defended at all cost — including that of armed violence. By the same token, revolution of structures, since opposed to progress as defined, will not be tolerated. It will be the task of counter-revolutionaries, where necessary and with whatever subtle methods are available, to oppose these. Not unlike the capitalist counter-revolutionary is the communist, who, maintaining that the communist world is unequivocally on the road to human progress, enforces a violent structural conservatism.

Finally, a third group takes the position that we are not yet on the road to true progress, and in addition that this progress is hindered by manifold forms of structural violence. This obstacle can only be overcome by a revolution of structures.

The existence of structural violence in many countries of the Third World is undeniable. Take Latin America. From the episcopal conference of Latin America we have this attestation:

> "Latin America seems to be living under the tragic sign of underdevelopment, which not only takes from our brothers the enjoyment of material goods, but their very human realisation of such. In spite of present efforts, there are together hunger and misery, infirmities on a grand scale, and infant mortality, illiteracy and marginality, deep inequalities of income and tensions between the social classes, outbreaks of violence and rare

participation by the people in pursuit of the public good." [5]

Of this description of the situation, the bishops make the following social analysis:

"Possibly it has not been sufficiently stated that the efforts carried out have not been able, in general, to assure the respect for and the realisation of justice in all the sectors of the respective national communities." "We cannot ignore the phenomenon of this somewhat universal frustration of legitimate aspirations which creates the climate of collective distress in which we are already living. The lack of socio-cultural integration, in most of our countries has given rise to the super-imposing of cultures. Economically, systems are being developed which provide opportunity only for those sectors with high buying power."

Finally, in the same vein, they add:

"This lack of adaptation to the characteristics and potentials of our population causes, in its turn, a frequent political instability and the entrenchment of purely formal institutions. To all this must be added the lack of solidarity, which brings about, on the individual and social level, the commission of real sins, incarnated in the unjust structures that characterise the situation in Latin-America". [6]

But this structural violence is not independent — historically, or by geographical propinquity — from the economic and political structures of the powerful developed countries. The evidence for this cannot be ignored. (These same countries experience elements of structural violence affecting their own citizens: the zones of misery — running as high as twenty percent of the population — zones that

[5] Message from the Second General Conference of Latin-American Bishops (Medellin, August 26 - September 6, 1968) to the peoples of Latin-America. See: CELAM, *La Iglesia en la actual transformación de América Latina a la luz del Concilio, II,* Conclusiones; Buenos Aires (Ed. Bonum) 1968; p. 32.

[6] Conclusiones, I, Justice, I, Action. See: op. cit., pp. 51-52.

177

result from structural deformation and are therefore a violence.)

Of a different type are the structural violences found in communist countries. But if we confine our attention to the structural violence suffered by the Third World, it must be said that this derives more support from the structures of capitalist than of communist countries.

Clearly it will not be easy to persuade the privileged to accept revolutions of structures. First, it is not easy, given the complexity of the phenomenon, to confront them with unimpeachable demonstrations of the existence of this violence. Besides, it is not easy to conduct operations favouring a revolution of structures where so many interests, conscious or unconscious, individual or collective, are at stake, and where irrational prejudices exercise so considerable an influence.

Now if the need for profound structural changes on a world scale is accepted (and I accept it) the need for a revolution of structures must be equally admitted. For, obviously, if the present structures represent structural violence and an obstacle to entering on the road toward true progress, it cannot be supposed that the dynamism of these structures is capable of shifting direction and winding up beneficent. Therefore, the young of Latin America, who maintain that such revolution is necessary cannot be supposed to be lacking in either intelligence or goodwill.

But how is a revolution of structures possible today? And what relation is there between acceptance of structural revolution and acceptance of revolutionary armed violence?

IV. REVOLUTION, VIOLENCE AND NON-VIOLENCE

The question here is whether armed revolutionary violence can produce structural changes which will put humanity as a whole, (or in part), on the road to true human progress; or may it not be that of its very nature it is incapable of achieving this goal? Alternatively one may ask whether structural revolution can ever be achieved without armed revolutionary violence, for instance active non-violence?

178

To these questions the answer may be an absolute — always or never, or a relative — sometimes yes, sometimes no, according to circumstances.

Keeping in mind these alternative possibilities we can pose the following line-up of questions: To achieve a revolution of structures oriented toward human progress is revolutionary armed violence indispensable? or indispensable in some situations, in others not? Is it possibly never indispensable because there are always other means — active non-violence? Finally, is it possible that it must always be excluded because of its very nature it cannot produce this kind of structural revolution?

Since the correlative to armed revolutionary violence is active non-violence, we must raise certain questions about the latter with respect to the achievement of human progress. Where structural violence exists and must be overcome, is active non-violence, however, the one and only method and therefore indispensable? Or is it indispensable in some situations, but in others impossible? Is it never indispensable because *armed violence* is always to be supposed possible? And to add just one more question here, is it possible that active non-violence is *never* a possible means (from a tactical viewpoint) because armed coercive repression by states founded on structural violence (abetted by beneficiaries and supporters) renders non-violence futile?

To these alternative ways of stating the range of possibilities it is, in our view, impossible to give answers that can pretend to be rigorously scientific and unquestionable guides to action. On the contrary, because we are dealing with the realm of the possible, we are forced to exclude absolutes. Accordingly we cannot exclude possible situations in which active non-violence would be possible and effective, but others in which it would be ineffective and perhaps also virtually impossible. The same can be said about revolutionary armed violence.

If the desired revolution of structures is not further specified as being conducive or not to bringing about human progress, then the range of possibilities just enumerated might be a matter of agreement. But, if the specification is that of structural transformation *that ushers in true human*

179

progress, then the range of possibilities will have to be narrowed. For, some exponents of non-violence maintain that even where armed revolutionary violence might have some chance of success, it cannot be countenanced because, far from producing structural transformation conducive to human progress, it inescapably results only in new forms of *structural violence* (not necessarily, however, worse than those the revolution aimed to do away with.)

Several observations are here in order. There is something to the supposition that armed revolutionary violence would, because of its very violence, give rise to defects in the subsequent revolutionary structures, especially in the inaugural period. But it would be unfair to expect a revolution of structures to be carried out whithout any attendant ill effects. Besides, neither may active non-violence be supposed capable of working the same transformations without some negative aspects of its own. Nor can it be supposed that a revolution of structures, brought about by whatever sort of strategy, will be able to consolidate itself in the state born of the revolution (suppose that supporters of the unjust structures violently oppose change) without some resort to coercion, the latter, admittedly, entailing the risk of unjust repression.

Presumably, revolutionary forces seeking human progress will avoid these dangers, especially those of the transition period. Finally, given the relativity and imperfection of *all* human achievement, we are entitled to maintain the possibility of a successful revolution of structures oriented toward true human progress. It would, moreover, be quite arbitrary to suppose that a strategy of non-violence will infallibly achieve structural transformation that ushers in human progress and that a strategy of armed revolutionary violence, on the contrary, can never accomplish this.

The *factual* analysis we have been pursuing in these last few paragraphs brings us to the conclusion that, speaking empirically , we cannot rule out various possibilities. Four at least are implicit to our analysis. First, revolution of structures is possible through active non-violence but impossible through armed revolutionary violence. The second possibility is the exact opposite, that is, such revolution is

180

possible through armed revolutionary forces but not through active non-violence. Third case: both are equal possibilities. Fourth possibility: the present situation precludes the possibility of achieving a revolution of structures by either strategy because each lacks adequate means.

To decide in the concrete among these it will not be enough to investigate the situations scientifically without giving attention to political realities. Here there is need of a political sense which balances many factors: first, an analysis of the situation that covers all aspects, economic, social, and psycho-sociological; secondly an appreciation that the political decision to be made here, given the situation, cannot be executed without some degree of risk-taking and the necessity of introducing into the judgment an element of intuition. For after all, what revolution could ever present itself as called for by rigorous scientific demonstration? (On the other hand, to repeat, neither can science rigorously demonstrate the impossibility of revolutionary success — in reality it is not its job to tell us whether revolution is possible, how it should be conducted, or whether it will finally triumph.)

There will always have to be a human judgment, born of an intimate sense of the totality of the situation. Accordingly it cannot, as we have said, be excluded that men of goodwill, seekers after justice and lovers of their neighbour, would come to judge, first, that for overcoming the structural violence they live in there must be a revolution of structures; and secondly that this entails recourse to armed revolutionary violence as the only road concretely open. If this political judgment cannot be excluded on any empirical or factual analysis, neither can it be excluded on philosophical or theological grounds.

But if it is not possible *a priori* and absolutely to exclude armed violence in the situation described (another way for saying that such action is possible — and even necessary in the sense that this strategy alone will be effective) a critical problem of conscience poses itself. Does ethics or a christian perspective permit this armed revolutionary violence which political and social analysis of the situation may call for?

V. Certain Methodological considerations

The need of deepening our understanding of the concept of moral law (its gnoseological and normative structures) is recognized more every day.

Moral law, unlike positive legislation, ought not be thought of as a code, for its propositions are not codifiable. Natural moral law (not, of course, natural in the strictest sense of the word) is not a closed system of behaviour norms, reducible to concrete, statically-determined "propositions" applicable to all times and places, as if they were a code written once and for all, requiring only casuistic interpretation.

Its gnoseological and normative structure is very different. *Principles* much more than *propositions* (typified by the articles of a juridical code) are its content. Nor are these principles purely formal, or reducible to conceptualizations that may be completely neutral to whatever material content may be made to fit under the abstract notion. Such procedure could result in the purely formal principle of "doing justice" being called on to force compliance with programmes of justice derived from arbitrary will or based on the blind mechanism of social forces.

Ethical principles, then, are neither purely formal nor statically concrete as "propositions." Rather they are value-indicators that serve us to choose morally among values. As such, they are inevitably open to the conditioning from an always evolving complex of historical, social and anthropological conditions. They may, perhaps, be thought of as vectors in a field of choice, like that, for instance, of material content (or acts) of justice. Hence, far from being purely formal, such principles (for example, those of respect for the person or of solidarity) are determinants in the field of values at stake and imperative. But how specifically to respect the persons or express solidarity are not things that can be codified for all times and places in a series of propositions which neatly categorize all possible ways of doing the one or the other.

Still, these principles of ethics, precisely because value-indicators, must be translated into some form of norm or of propositions which realise concretely in life the values in-

182

dicated. There is first the possibility of *limit-propositions* with a prevalently negative character, i. e. stating things that absolutely must not be done. These may well express quite concretely and specifically lines of behaviour imperative for all times and places. But such will certainly be rare.

More generally, they will be *propositions relative in character* because of the element of historical time or socio-geographical situation. Such propositions, integrative and applicative of ethical principle and human reality concretized essentially in the historical and the social, is the work of the human spirit, of moral conscience, seeking ever to provide living content in human history and fellowship to that spark of wisdom which is moral law.

Moreover, the knowability of such "propositions" is not independent of certain "options" of human conscience. These, however, are not arbitrary, but rather represent an answer to a call coming from reality and from the real meaning of existence on the one side; and on the other, from the internal light which is the moral wisdom of the "principle."

Such ethical propositions, derived from the interior light of moral wisdom projected onto reality and the inner meaning of existence, are quite different from Cartesian deductions, elicited from contemplation of necessities encountered in a purely platonic order of ideas. For some it may be discomforting to learn that so little of the moral order is deduceable and so much contains the risk of personal responsibility for moral decision. But risk is involved in man's vocation both as person and as moral being.

What we have been saying is, if we are not mistaken, quite in agreement with an important reference to natural law in the decrees of the Second Vatican Council. The Pastoral Constitution, *Gaudium et Spes* (no. 16) says:

"In the depths of his conscience, man detects a law which he does not impose upon himself, but which holds him to obedience. Always summoning him to love good and avoid evil, the voice of conscience can when necessary speak to his heart more specifically: do this, shun that. For man has in his heart a law written by God. To obey it is the very dignity of man; according to it he will be judged. Conscience is the most secret core and sanctuary of a man.

183

There he is alone with God, whose voice echoes in his depths. In a wonderful manner conscience reveals that law which is fulfilled by love of God and neighbour. In fidelity to conscience, christians are joined with the rest of men in the search for truth, and for the genuine solution to the numerous problems which arise in the life of individuals and from social relationships. Hence the more that a correct conscience holds sway, the more persons and groups turn aside from blind choice and strive to be guided by objective norms of morality. Conscience frequently errs from invincible ignorance without losing its dignity. The same cannot be said of a man who cares but little for truth and goodness, or of a conscience which by degrees grows practically sightless as a result of habitual sin."

The application of these few paragraphs on natural law ethics to our problem is clear enough. From an ethical viewpoint, we cannot pretend to arrive at a set of timelessly valid propositions about revolutionary violence. What must be done is to initiate, in the light of our principles, serious inquiry that would provide those required options of conscience. Quite often, from its nature such reflection must be carried out collectively.

To pretend to define, once and for all, in a static proposition that armed violence is intrinsically evil seems surely to result from an error in method, from a false conception of the gnoseological and normative structure of the so-called natural law.

But if it is true that natural law, is a matter of principles much more than of propositions, this will be still truer of the law of the Gospels. To freeze evangelical law in a code to be applied casuistically is totally contrary to the nature of this source of morality. However rigorous the moral law of christians be, it is not an ethical legalism. How forcefully Paul demonstrates this in his letter to the Romans. For St. Paul the fullness of the law is to be found in the love of one's neighbour (Rom. 13, 8-10). But love, far from being a matter of propositions, is a dynamic principle. Is this not the sense of the following from Augustine:

"Diversity of intention causes diversity of acts. Dealing with an action materially identical, if we judge it from

184

intention, in one case we find it worthy of love, in another worthy of condemnation; in one case it must be praised, in the other, detested. Such is the vigour of charity; consider that charity alone is the criterion for judgement, that it alone serves to evaluate men's actions." [7]

Turning from the first type of action to a second, Augustine continues:

"This we have said in dealing with materially identical actions. Dealing, then, with materially opposite actions, we are faced with a man, furious because of charity, and another who is mellow because of evil. A father slaps his child and a pimp fondles it. If you compare the two things, slaps and caresses, who would not prefer the caresses and shy away from the slaps? If you observe these people, here charity hurts, evil soothes. Look what we want to impress: that what men do cannot be valued, except starting from charity. ... There is imposed on you, then, once and for all, a short rule: Love and do whatever you wish: If you are silent, be silent for love's sake, if you shout for love: if you punish, punish for love; if you pardon, pardon for love: have within you the root of love; from this root only good can come."

The consequence of interpreting evangelical law as one of propositions has alternatively unavoidable implications. First is to suppose that christians ought to abstain from political activity so as to avoid contamination (an implication that neither Tertullien or Origin were able to avoid.) [8] The second is to radically separate religion from the political arena, thus reducing religious life to the inter subjectivity of private relationships. This is the road that christians, more or less consciously, took from the "Enlightenment" (Aufklärung) as J. B. Metz has suggested. [9] We must agree with him that this attitude constitutes a serious aber-

---

[7] S. Augustine, *Tract. in Ep. Jo. VII*, 7-8; PL XXXV, 2033.

[8] See: V. Kesich, *Empire-Church Relations and the Third Temptation*, in: *Studia Patristica*, IV (Texte u. Untersuch. z Gesch. d. altchrist. Liter., 79) Berlin, 1961, pp. 465-471.

[9] Johann Baptist Metz, *Les rapports entre l'Église et le monde à la lumière d'une théologie politique*, in: *La Théologie du renouveau*, Montreal-Paris, 1968, II pp. 33-47.

ration, for it results in christians, when they do intervene
in public life, doing so in an amoral manner or supporting
a morality of public relations not reducable to that of the
Gospels. Reinhold Niebuhr explained this clearly back in 1932:

"Whenever religious idealism brings forth its purest fruits
and places the strongest check upon selfish desire it results
in policies which, from the political perspective, are quite
impossible. There is, in other words, no possibility of harmo-
nising the two strategies designed to bring the strongest
inner and the most effective social restraint upon egoistic
impulse. It would therefore seem better to accept a frank
dualism in morals than to attempt a harmony between the
two methods which threaters the effectiveness of both. Such
a dualism would have two aspects. It would make a distinction between the moral judgements applied to the self and
to others; and it would distinguish between what we expect
of individuals and of groups ... The distinction between individual and group morality is a sharper and more perplexing
one. The moral obtuseness of human collectiveness makes
a morality of pure disinterestedness impossible. There is
not enough imagination in any social group to render it
amenable to the influence of pure love ... The selfishness of
human communities must be regarded as an inevitability.
Where it is inordinate it can be checked only by competing
assertions of interest; and these can be effective only if
coercive methods are added to moral and rational persuasion.
Moral factors may qualify, but they will not eliminate, the
resulting social contest and conflict. Moral goodwill may
seek to relate the peculiar interests of the group to the ideal
of a total and final harmony of all life. It may thereby qualify
the self-assertion of the privileged, and support the interests
of the disinherited, but it will never be so impartial as to
persuade any group to subject its interests completely to
an inclusive social ideal. The spirit of love may preserve
a certain degree of appreciation for the common weaknesses
and common aspirations which bind men together above the
areas of social conflict. But again it cannot prevent the
conflict. It may avail itself of instruments of restraint and
coercion, through which a measure of trust in the moral
capacities of an opponent may be expressed and the expansion

rather than contraction of those capacities is encouraged. But it cannot hide the moral distrust expressed by the very use of the instruments of coercion. To some degree the conflict between the purest individual morality and an adequate political policy must therefore remain." [10]

To judge fairly Niebuhr's viewpoint, a distinction should be introduced between public morality (which political power imposes coercively) and complete social morality (norms inspiring the social activity of men where acting individually or collectively and motivated by moral ideal). Niebuhr is right in saying that we cannot organize social and political life as if a large dose of egoism were not there present, in fact.. The corresponding social order (including its necessary element of coercion) is an order conformable to a sinful society, although not of a society incapable of moral progress. It is one that reckons on the egoism of social groups. It is not possible to establish a juridical obligation of the moral ideal of perfection. In its political organization society does not stand on the utopian supposition that social groups will operate in conformity with the ideal of moral perfection.

What, however, cannot be accepted is the reduction of public social morality to a system of balances between egoisms and radical refusal of solidarity (with the only check to these being a moral "goodwill" which would in final analysis be pharisaic in its pretence of accepting at one and the same time a radically anti-social egoism together with "the ideal of a total and final harmony of all life.")

We must add that the proposal of a double morality, one for relations between individuals and another for group action in society, is self-contradictory because personal action is necessarily conditioned by social structures and group relations. If this be true, one cannot accept the morality of balance of egoisms in social life and still hope that one's personal (individual) life will be founded on a morality of love. This view is endorses by Erik Wolf. Speaking of the juridical

---

[10] Reinhold Niebuhr, *Moral man and immoral society, A Study in Ethics and Politics*. New York, 1960, pp. 270-273 (st ed. 1932). For further literature on the same problem, see: Theo Westow, *The Argument about Pacifism. A Critical Survey of Studies in English*, in: *Concilium*, (engl.) May 1966, pp. 56-63.

order of political society he rightly rejects on the basis of the Incarnation and Redemption of Jesus Christ any complete separation of the human from the divine order of justice. [11] No more, to speak of present day catholic theology, does a moral law knoweable without explicit revelation permit moral dualism. [12]

In the considerations which we are now about to make, we shall start from the conception of moral and evangelical law, which we have just explained. We have established that we shall ground our inquiry on both an ethic of

---

[11] See: Erik Wolf, *Rechtsgedanke und biblische Weisung,* Tübingen 1948; idem, *Die menschliche Rechtsordnung,* in: *Die Autorität der Bibel heute,* Zürich-Frankfurt a. M. 1952, pp. 317-336.

[12] Here today's theology follows the lead given by St. Paul, who maintained that even men not subject to the Mosaic law equivalently carry out in their conscience the works of the law, (tó èrgon toû nómou - Rom. 2, 15). This law, however, which is revealed in the depths of conscience, is not a purely natural law. For all men are influenced by grace — even those who do not know the Gospel, or who have not come to an explicit recognition of God. The Second Vatican Council on this asserts "Divine Providence does not deny the necessary aids to salvation to those who (without fault) have not come to an express recognition of God, yet nevertheless strive, with the help of divine grace, to live a decent life." (*Lumen Gentium* 16).
Christ's mediation through his incarnation and redemption enters into the drama of each man's conscience — even of those who have not known the scriptures. So that the voice of human conscience is never that of unredeemed light of reason (*lumen naturale*). It is always a call from God to *redeemed man,* a solicitation of grace, a happening in salvation history. Consequently, there is always a point of contact between the inner voice of conscience (present even without ever having been exposed to biblical revelation) and that moral light which comes from revelation, especially that made in Christ Jesus. The latter provides those experiencing the revelation (and disposed in authentic faith to make it their own) with enrichment of what they already hold through the voice of conscience. But that light of conscience in itself, it must firmly be maintained, is never to be thought of as in any way oriented away from or radically divergent from the revealed word on moral life. In a word, it does not represent a different ethic. In the text quoted above from Second Vatican Council there is the affirmation that conscience, common to all men "in a wonderful way reveals that law which is fulfilled by love of God and neighbour."

natural law and a christian perspective. In either case,
we do not look for static *propositions* but for more dynamic
principles. In elucidating these principles, which are to guide
the struggle against violence as well as eventual use of violence to combat violence, far from pretending to achieve
definitive results, we are trying to remove ourselves increasingly from blind arbitrariness and to adjust ourselves to the
norms of objective morality. [13]

VI. Ethics and Theology Look at Armed Violence

If we seek without prejudice to discover in the New
Testament orientations about violence and armed violence
in particular, we come up against a certain tension between
two apparently antithetic lines of thought.

Regarding violence in general (not necessarily armed violence) there is clearly in the four gospels one line of thought
which is violent in mood: the violent proclamation of the
truth, even to death; violence in adoption of attitudes which
may cause dissension, undeterred by fear of making trouble;
violent rupture with friends and relations (compared sym-
bolically to armed violence).

Let us cite a few texts:

"I tell you, my friends, do not fear those who kill the
body, and after that have no more they can do" (Lk. 12, 4).

"Do you think that I have come to give peace on earth?
No, I tell you, but rather division; for henceforth in one
house there will be divided father against son and son against
father; mother against daughter and daughter against mother,
mother-in-law against daughter-in-law and daughter-in-law
against mother-in-law" (Lk. 12, 51-53).

"If anyone comes to me and does not hate his own
father and mother and wife and children and brothers and
sisters, yes, and even his own life, he cannot be my disciple"
(Lk. 14, 26).

---

[13] Cfr. *Gaudium et Spes*, n. 16: "the more that a correct
conscience holds sway, the more persons and groups turn aside
from blind choice and strive to be guided by objective norms
of morality."

189

" So therefore, whoever of you does not renounce all that he has cannot be my disciple" (Lk. 14, 33).

"Do not think that I have come to bring peace on earth; I have not come to bring peace but a sword. For I have come to set a man against his father, and a daughter against her mother and a daughter-in-law against her mother-in-law; and a man's foes will be those of his own household" (Mt. 10, 34-36).

"And they came to Jerusalem. And he entered the temple and began to drive out those who sold and those who bought in the temple, and he overturned the tables of the money-changers and the seats of those who sold pigeons" (Mk. 11, 15).

"And making a whip of cords, he drove them all, with the sheep and oxen, out of the temple; and he poured out the coins of the money-lenders and overturned their tables" (Jn. 2, 15). Clearly we have here a line of thought, which, while not directed in any obvious way to armed violence, calls for an active "contestation" that is inflexible, truly violent, and productive of definite action.

But alongside this, there appears another line of thought orientated decidedly towards meekness, "non-resistance" to evil, patient acceptance of injustices done to one's self, returning good for evil, loving one's enemies.

Let us recall some texts indicative of this line of thought:

"You have heard that it was said to the men of old, 'You shall not kill; and whoever kills shall be liable to judgment.' But I say to you that every one who is angry with his brother shall be liable to judgment; whoever insults his brother shall be liable to the council, and whoever says 'You fool!,' shall be liable to the hell of fire. So if you are offering your gift at the altar, and there remember that your brother has something against you, leave your gift there before the altar and go; first be reconciled to your brother, and then come and offer your gift. (Mt. 5, 21-24).

"You have heard that it was said, 'An eye for an eye and a tooth for a tooth.' But I say to you, Do not resists one who is evil. But if anyone strikes you on the right cheek, turn to him the other also; and if anyone would sue you and take your coat, let him have your cloak as well; and if anyone forces you to go one mile, go with him two miles.

190

Give to him who begs from you, and do not refuse him who would borrow from you.

"You have heard that it was said, 'You shall love your neighbour and hate your enemy.' But I say to you, Love your enemies and pray for those who persecute you, so that you may be sons of your Father who is in heaven; for he makes his sun rise on the evil and on the good, and sends rain on the just and the unjust. For if you love those who love you, what reward have you? Do not even the tax collectors do the same? And if you salute only your brethren, what more are you doing than others? Do not even the Gentiles do the same? You, therefore, must be perfect, as your heavenly Father is perfect" (Mt. 5, 38-48).

"See that none of you repays evil for evil, but always seek to do good to one another and to all" (1 Thess. 5, 15).

"Repay no one evil for evil, but take thought for what is noble in the sight of all. If possible, so far as it depends upon you, live peaceably with all. Beloved, never avenge yourselves, but leave it to the wrath of God; for it is written, 'Vengeance is mine, I will repay, says the Lord.' No, 'if your enemy is hungry, feed him; if he is thirsty, give him to drink; for by so doing you will heap burning coals upon his head.' Do not be overcome by evil, but overcome evil with good." (Rom 12, 17-21.)

The dialectic character of this double series of texts from the New Testament is now a confirmation that the evangelical norms represent *principles of orientation* and not *propositions* statically defined, requiring only casuistic application.

To infer from the one set of texts, that of meekness, the requirement of passivity and conformity in the face of social injustice, or of collaboration (by act or omission) in the injustices suffered by others would be to betray that demand of protest in the name of freedom and those struggles for human rights so clearly called for in the alternative series of texts.

Clearly the two must be co-ordinated. Such is accomplished by that love which, extending even to one's enemies, is the highest principle of moral behaviour — much higher than those of contestation and meekness, both of which it illuminates and integrates. This christian love of neighbour, open even to enemies is the great sign of the Gospel and makes Sons of God of those who accept such love. It demands at once both meekness, preparedness to pardon and love of enemies and oppressors, and that standing up against injustice we throw all our energies into the struggle against oppression of the innocent and the weak. Hence we read in St. Paul, (Rom. 12, 18): "if possible, as far as things depend on you, live peaceably with all." But in Matthew's gospel (10, 34) this word of Our Lord, "I have not come to bring peace (to the world), but a sword."

Another text which serves as an important guide and rightly understood gives us on the basis of christian love the synthesis of force and meekness, of resistance with capacity for patient suffering is the following from the first letter of St. Peter:

"Servants, be submissive to your masters with all respect, not only to the kind and gentle but also to the overbearing. For one is approved, if, mindful of God, he endures pain while suffering unjustly. For what credit is it, if when you do wrong and are beaten for it, you take it patiently? But if when you do right and suffer for it you take it patiently, you have God's approval. For to this you have been called, because Christ also suffered for you leaving you an example that you should follow in his steps" (1 Pet. 2, 18-21).

Later in the same epistle Peter returns to this theme.

"Let all of you, have unity of spirit, sympathy, love of the brethren, a tender heart and a humble mind. Do not return evil for evil or reviling for reviling; but on the contrary bless, for to this you have been called, that you may obtain a blessing. For *'He that would love life and see good days, let him keep his tongue from speaking guile; let him turn away from evil and do right; let him seek peace and pursue it. For the eyes of the Lord are upon the righteous, and his ears are open to their prayer. But the face of the Lord is against those who do evil!* Now who is there to harm you if are zealous for what is right? But even if you do suffer for righteousness' sake, you will be blessed. Have no fear of them, nor be troubled, but in your hearts reverence Christ as Lord. Always be prepared to make a defence to anyone

192

who calls you to account for the hope that is in you, yet do it with gentleness and reverence; and keep your conscience clear, so that, when you are abused, those who revile your good behaviour in Christ may be put to shame. For it is better to suffer for doing right, if that should be God's will, than for doing wrong" (I Pet. 3, 8-17).

The heart of these texts is this: Love demands that we meet our responsibilities regarding social justice in a spirit of meekness, yet with unrelenting force, sacrifice and eventual suffering for justice's sake. What is at issue is always that dynamic interdependence of christian charity and social justice. St. Paul expresses it this way: "Pay all of them their dues, taxes to whom taxes are due, revenue to whom revenue is due, respect to whom respect is due, honour to whom honour is due. Owe nothing to anyone, except to love one another; for he who loves his neighbour has fulfilled the law. The commandments, *'You shall not commit adultery, You shall not kill, You shall not steal, You shall not covet"* and any other commandment, are summed up in this sentence "You shall love your neighbour as yourself." Love does no wrong to a neighbour; therefore love is the fulfilling of the law" (Rom. 13, 7-10).

From the texts so far studied, we may conclude that the spirit of christianity is opposed to both the "spirit of violence" (violence based on the desire for vengeance, on hatred of one's enemy as a person, on grudge, on contempt of persons suffering violence) and the "spirit of conformity" to injustice. If there is an anti-evangelical violence, there is equally an anti-evangelical cowardice, which has nothing to do with the meekness we are exhorted to . The Apocalypse (21, 8) rejects cowards along with renegades, the depraved, murderers, fornicators, sorcerers, idolaters, and all other "false men."

Taking together these two evangelical ideas of violent opposition to evil (prescinding from whether it must be armed violence) and of evangelical meekness, there is no doubt that "active non-violence", carried out with courage and with personal risk (eventually even risk of one's life) constitutes the attitude at which the gospel ethic most naturally aims. Clearly such an attitude must be counted as

193

superior or "privileged", for it is a remarkable attestation to the kingdom of God, as it is also an eschatological witness. It calls, too, for a charismatic action, the lack of which in the historically existent church indicates a grave deficiency of evangelical life in the christian community.

Nevertheless there remains to be solved the problem of which pole we should be pulled to in the dialectic of violence and non-violence when it is a question of the use of arms in struggling against evil? Does the christianity of the New Testament absolutely condemn armed violence? Does it declare all use of arms incompatible with the profession of christian faith? Some christians tend to say yes to these two questions, or at least to the second. In support they appeal to early christian tradition.

But did early christianity take a rigorously defined position on this? Here we must recall our methodological explanation of the difference between an ethic of "principles" and of "propositions". For it may be the case that some supporters of non-violence seek to translate into an ethic of "propositions" what is true (and ought to be maintained) on the level of an ethic of "principles". Before deciding whether this is so or not, we must carry our analysis a bit further.

In Matthew's gospel we encounter a text in which Christ opposes the use of arms:

"And one of those who were with Jesus stretched out his hand and drew his sword, and struck the slave of the high priest, and cut off his ear. Then Jesus said to him, 'Put your sword back into its place; for all who take the sword will perish by the sword. Do you think that I cannot appeal to my Father, and he will at once send me more than twelve legions of angels? But how then should the scriptures be fulfilled, that it must be so?" (Mt. 26, 51-53).

This text is not sufficient, it would appear, to demonstrate that Christ condemns absolutely all armed defence — in whatever circumstances. Christ here refers to very special circumstances: that of his passion, in which Scripture must be fulfilled according to the will of the Father, and such excludes the use of arms to defend Christ. But from this we cannot conclude directly to the absolute condemnation of all use of arms in any circumstances. The statement of

Jesus, "He who lives by the sword shall die by the sword," is a serious warning, an admonition to "be on your guard" to men who must face the consequences of using arms, and a call to renounce the use of arms. However, it is not the same as a *proposition* which declares absolutely, always and in every case all use of arms evil. (Christ himself taught his disciples that they ought not to be afraid of the possibility of dying as a result of violence: "do not fear those who kill the body and after that have no more they can do", Lk. 12, 4.) [14]

Nor can appeal to the decalogue precept "You shall not kill" (Ex. 20, 13; Deut. 5, 17), a establish proposition forbidding absolutely, in whatever circumstances, the lethal use of arms. Exodus and Deuteronomy exclude such an interpretation. Classical scholastic theology, which interpreted the precepts of the decalogue more as "propositions" than "principles", had recourse to the expedient of saying that the absolute form of the precept was a stylistic simplification and that in fact there had to be supplied a series of implicit conditions (or exceptional cases). This gave place to a casuistry, on occasions far from convincing. It seems much more correct to understand the precept of the decalogue (as Erik Wolf does) as a principle. The command "You shall not kill" thus stated absolutely as a *proposition* could not be true. But understood as a *principle* it is always true. It is also significant here that one can sin against the *principle* "You shall not kill" by other means than that of putting to death in a material or biological way. Thus, one kills by inflicting an oppression which turns life into an endless dying. And it does not seem excluded that one could materially

[14] The fact that the apostles did carry arms (two swords, as Luke attests: 22, 38), without Jesus being scandalised, is a sufficient indication to us that Jesus' position was not exactly that of the more extreme proponents of non-violence. In Luke's account, Jesus tells the apostles (obviously in a metaphorical way) "Let him who has a purse take it, and likewise a bag. And let him who has no sword sell his mantle and buy one" (Lk. 22, 36). The apostles reply ingenuously: Look, Lord, here are two swords. Jesus answers: "It is enough." The implicit reproach here is not for having two swords, but for the lack of intelligence shown in taking Christ's statement in a material sense.

195

kill another person, without betraying the "principle" of respect for life ("You shall not kill"): e. g. to save an innocent victim. Some weight for this point of view is gained from the text quoted above from the Sermon on the Mount, in Mathew's version (5, 21-24). There Jesus explains how we are to move beyond the traditional interpretation of the precept "You shall not kill." His improved version is not that of transforming an (implicitly) conditional proposition into an absolute one, but that of extending the interpretation of the command "You shall not kill" to embrace that much higher principle of absolute respect for the person of one's neighbour seen as a brother. Not only must one not kill; one must not even insult one's neighbour (excluded are not only such great insults as calling him "apostate" but even such milder ones as terming him a "fool"). Nor may one be in enmity with his brother.

This improvement on the understanding of "You shall not kill" not by way of casuistic qualification of a *proposition* but by way of extending the dynamism of a *principle* finds confirmation in St. John's first letter. We cite some suggestive passages:

"For this is the message which you have heard from the beginning, that we should love one another, and not be like Cain who murdered his brother. And why did he murder his brother? Because his own deeds wre evil and his brother's were righteous" (3, 11-12). "We know that we have passed out of death into life, because we love the brethren. He who does not love remains in death. Any one who hates his brother is a murderer, and you know that no murderer has eternal life abiding in him. By this we know love, that he laid down his life for us; and we ought to lay down our lives for the brethren. But if anyone has the world's goods and sees his brother in need, yet closes his heart against him, how does God's love abide in him? Little children, let us not love in word or speech but in deed and in truth." (3, 14-18).

The New Testament does not condemn unequivocally the use of armed force in defence of justice in the temporal order, but admits it insofar as it does not damage the order of creation worked out in history under the providence of

196

God. St. Paul indicates this with sufficient clarity in his letter to the Romans (13, 4): [Authority] "is the instrument of God for your good; but if you do wrong, be afraid because he does not bear the sword in vain; he is God's instrument for punishing with justice the wrongdoer".

But a problem still remains: Given that the use of armed force in defence of justice might not be excluded in every case, would the use of arms *by christians* be always and in whatever circumstances reproachable?

From the New Testament it cannot be said such is absolutely incompatible with the profession of christianity. In apostolic times, we meet with the attitude of Peter who, about the year 43, baptised the centurion Cornelius without making any problem about his military status (Acts 10, 48). Paul, during his first mission (between 45 and 49) received the proconsul Sergius Paulus into the church (Acts 13, 12). (And, as we have seen in a text from the letter to the Romans, written in the winter of 57-58, Paul was well aware of the armed coercion exercised by a proconsul in the course of his duties). [15]

The New Testament records for us an analogous moral problem of the first christians, which may shed some light on our own question. The problem was that of swearing (by God). The resolution of the problem is implicitly the same one of distinguishing between principle and proposition.

"But I say to you", Jesus says, "do not swear at all ... let your words be yes or no. Anything more comes from the evil one." (Mt. 5, 34-37).

---

[15] Luke, in his narration of the preaching of John the Baptist, refers (3, 14) to the fact that, among the crowds who gathered to be baptised, there were soldiers also. "The soldiers also asked him, 'And we, what shall we do?', and he said to them, 'Rob no one by violence or by false accusation, and be content with your wages.'" It is worth noticing that the Baptist does not require the soldiers to give up their profession. It is true, however, that here we are not dealing with the christian status. But it would not have been easy for Luke to have saved this episode of the soldiers in his narrative, if the apostolic Church had considered the use of arms completely incompatible with christianity.

We find the same prescription in the letter of St. James (5, 12-13) ("Do not swear by heaven or earth, nor use any other oath. Let your yes be yes; your no, no"). Nevertheless, Peter (Acts 3, 30) and Hebrews (6, 16) seems to permit swearing by God. Paul appears to do the same when, writing to the Corinthians, and in a context which is clearly that of the norm "Let your yes be yes, your no be no", nontheless confirms his assertion of sincerity by swearing in the name of the fidelity of God (2 Cor. I. 18). This can only mean that the norm "do not swear" is not a proposition forbidding unconditionally the taking of an oath. Its sense is that the christian ought to live in that sincerity of language (yes, yes; no, no) that would make oaths superfluous. But the general prevalence of insincerity may force one to confirm his testimony by oath. In doing so, the christian's basic attitude is that of avoiding oaths and seeking the simplicity of the plain 'yes', which receives its force from the openness of a life without guile. But he has to live out this simplicity and sincerity in a world in which simplicity and sincerity do not reign with indisputable authority. So, although opposed in principle to the use of oaths, he will not deny himself such a recourse to oaths when the concrete circumstances demand it.

The preceding analysis of primitive christianity's treatment of the question of swearing permits us, since it so parallels our question of violence, to draw our conclusion in a few words. The christian is an active supporter of non-violence; his spirit is opposed to armed violence. But, this does not mean necessarily that occasionally he cannot use arms for justice's sake in opposition to unjust violence. When called to do so, the christian's spirit will remain opposed to armed violence, as it is also opposed to all forms of unjust violence.

The analysis just made of the New Testament on this seems irrefutable. We must now consider the christians who wrote between 170 and 313 for they pose a new problem.

It cannot be denied that the early church, from Athenagoras (writing around 177) to Arnobius and Lactantius (writing between 304 and 313), tended to interpret the opposition between the christian spirit and any type of armed violence in absolute terms. [16]   In this sense one could quote Athenagoras, Tertullian, Minucius Felix, Hippolytus. Origen, Cyprian, Arnobius and Lactantius.   In the same sense are the Canons of Hippolytus (probably mid-fourth century) and the *Testamentum Domini* (second half of the fifth century) both dependent on Apostolic Tradition by Hippolytus, edited around 215.

Nevertheless, it should not be thought that this position was held as an absolute proposition.   For one thing, these authors do not deny the legitimacy of a moderate use of armed force by the State.   Abstention, then, from arms *by christians* would be considered a special case deriving from their christian perspective.

Still, even this restriction was not unconditional for christians.   It had the character rather of a "value-indicator", the positive application of which required further unfolding with all its consequences.

In fact, even in the second century the christian community found itself in a certain ambivalence on the question of armed service by christians.   In the decade 170-180, the philosopher Celsus accused the christians of refusing military service.   But in 173, we find a legion (the XII legion, called Fulminata Melitensis), in which christians are quite numerous. About the year 200, Clement of Alexandria declared that the soldier who became a christian could continue being a soldier but would have to obey Christ as his Chief.

As far as the first half of the second century goes there is more uncertainty.   Toland H. Baiton believes that christians

---

[16] I have relied on the following works.   As required, they will be subsequently noted without full citation.   Roland H. Baiton, *The early Church and war,* in: *The Harvard Theological Review,* 39 (1946), 189-212. Hans Frhr. v. Campenhausen, *Der Kriegsdienst der Christen in der Kirche des Altertums,* in: *Tradition u. Leben, Kräfte der Kirchengeschichte,* Tübingen, 1960, pp. 203-215. H. Leclercq, *Militarisme,* in: *Dict. d'Archéologie Chrétienne,* t. 11 col. 1108-1191 (especially for martyrdoms of conscientious objectors and soldiers, and soldiers' epitaphs). Jacques Fontaine, *Les Chrétiens et le service militaire dans l'Antiquité,* in: *Concilium* (french) 15 Sept. 1965, pp. 95-105. Cfr. René Laurentin, *Développement et salut,* Paris, 1969, pp. 195-196. Berthold Altaner, *Patrologie,* Freiburg i. B. ⁷1966.

abstained from military service. He says: "From the end of the New Testament period to the decade 170-180, there is no evidence whatever of christians in the army. The subject of military service obviously was not at that time controverted. The reason may be either that participation was assumed or that abstention was taken for granted. The latter is the more probably." [17] But if we start from the conversion of the Centurion Cornelius, (and others like him) through the ministry of Peter (Acts 10, 7; 24. 44-48), and the conversion of the proconsul Sergius Paulus through Paul and Barnabas (Acts 12, 6-12) — both in the decade 40-50 — it does not seem probable that in the period Baiton refers to the absence of christians from the armed forces could be taken as a certainty. In any case, it cannot be said, as Campenhausen said, that before the year 175 there probably had not been a single christian soldier. [18] It is absolutely certain that during Peter and Paul's lifetime there were christian soldiers in military service. A certain pluralism of views continues to persist among christians until the fourth century. We have the authentic acts of Maximilian (12 March 295), compelled to enter armed service because the son of a veteran, and his refusal to be a soldier, because he considered military service incompatible with the christian way of life. But at the same time Maximilain was quite aware that there were christian soldiers acting as guards under Diocletian, Maximian, Constantius and Galerius, yet he refrains from judging them.

In the second half of the fourth century, when the possibility of a christian exercising military service (and command) was beyond discussion, St. Basil the Great still manifests the christian's aversion to any form of bloodshed when he asks that those whose hands are not free from blood abstain from communion for three years. [19]

To sum up, the primitive church established armed non-violence (and respect for life) as a firmly held principle. But there was at the same time a tendency to transform this

---

[17] R. H. Bainton, loc. cit., pp. 190-191.
[18] H. F. v. Campenhausen, loc. cit., p. 206.
[19] St. Basil, *Ep. Cl.* II, 188, 13 (P. G. 32, 682). Cfr. Bainton cit., p. 209; Campenhausen, loc. cit., p. 213.

directive principle into a rigid and unconditional *proposition*. Inevitably, complications (never resolved) arose. A directive principle remains sound. Instead of killing their enemies, christians are bound to confess Christ, to witness to the truth. What was found in Justin [20] in the middle of the second century is to be found in quite different historical circumstances at the end of the fourth century. Thus John Chrysostom says "I am used to suffering persecution and not to persecuting; to being oppressed rather than oppressing." [21]

It seems clear, after all we have said, that the spirit of christianity is both violent and non-violent. Violent, because of its readiness for a "structural revolution" and quite active attitudes (very strong, in that sense very "violent") of contestation and denunciation of unjustice through the means of "active non-violence." And, at the same time, the spirit of christianity is "non-violent," because of its "principle" of contestation and denunciation of unjustice through the means of "active non-violence." And, at the same time, the spirit of christianity is "non-violent," because of its "principle" of opposition to "armed violence."

But christian non-violence is a "principle," which cannot be translated straightaway into a "proposition," which states rigidly and unconditionally that all armed action is intrinsically evil, or at least intrinsically incompatible with christian life, with communion with Christ.

The "spirit of violence" is foreign to christianity. But all use of armed violence, in cases of extreme necessity and in defence of fundamental rights, must not be confused straightaway with the "spirit of violence."

The reason for the "spirit of violence" being incompatible with christianity is that the basic, essential and determining attitude of a genuine christian is love of one's neighbour, including one's enemy.

It is really difficult, if in fact we love our neighbour, even our enemy, to use armed violence against a man who is recognisable as a neighbour. But it cannot be said *a priori* to be impossible. The complexity of the historical and social

---

[20] See: Bainton, loc. cit., pp. 196; Campenhausen, loc. cit., p. 205 .
[21] St. John Chrysostom, *In Sanctum Phocam*, n. 2 (P.G. 50, 701).

situation (a situation of "sin") here comes into play, as do the ambiguity of the concept and the reality of violence in the world. Is it possible that a person, at a given moment, by refusing to use armed violence (to a given degree) must be contributing in an inexorable way (given his personal conditions and situation) to forms of unjust violence (structural or even armed) for which he makes himself jointly responsible? In this case, without betraying love of neighbour, he could agree to armed violence.

So, then, if we agree to the possibility of licit use of armed force in defence of justice, it would be absolutely inadmissible to say that the oppressed peoples do not ever have this possibility whose most fundamental rights are trampled upon in an evident and prolonged manner.

A text from the Pastoral Constitution, Gaudium et Spes, of the Vatican Council II, is interesting in this respect:

"It is therefore obvious that the political community and public authority are based on human nature and hence belong to an order of things divinely foreordained. At the same time the choice of government and the method of selecting leaders is left to the free will of citizens.

It also follows that political authority, whether in the community as such or in institutions representing the state, must always be exercised within the limits of morality and on behalf of the dynamically conceived common good, according to a juridical order enjoying legal status. When such is the case, citizens are conscience-bound to obey (cfr. Rom. 13, 5). This fact clearly reveals the responsibility, dignity, and importance of those who govern.

Where public authority oversteps its competence and appresses the people, these should nevertheless obey to the extent that the objective common good demands. Still it is lawful for them to defend their own rights and those of their fellow citizens against any abuse of this authority, provided that in so doing they observe the limits imposed by natural law and the gospel." [22]

Armed revolutionary violence could only be justified when, all other possibilities having failed, it is entered into

---

[22] Constitution *Gaudium et Spes*, n. 74 s-e.

in a spirit of non-violence — so, minimally and directed to ending institutional violence. This implies also that there must be some reasonable hope of attaining by this means to a just social order. Ventures in violence that serve only to launch people onto desperate enterprises which result only in reproducing new forms of the institutional violence they set out to destroy are condemned by moral sense.

For the rest, it is one thing to admit the possibility of a licit armed defence on the part of the oppressed against injustice, and another to argue for unlimited use of force, efficiency being the only criterion. The legitimacy of defensive action in the one case does not make licit any and all sorts of action. The need of defence and its legitimacy does not make everything permissible.

A correct ethic, and much more a genuine christianity, exclude absolutely the spirit of violence, accompanied by manifestations of hatred toward people, contempt for the dignity of the person (even enemy and culpable) the passion for revenge and sadism, the unjust repression of a neighbour and direct, intentional killing of the innocent, although attempted as an efficacious means to an end good in itself. Likewise excluded are certain methods of psychological warfare such as terrorism in the strict sense of the word.

But even where the end sought in armed action is just, the concrete execution of such raises questions. For, by its internal dialectic it can unleash a spirit of violence and lead to actions inadmissible from either an ethical or a christian viewpoint. We may not separate consideration of means from that of ends and so be led to judge ethically actions (means) taken without giving attention to the objective sought.

In this connection, one may not simply weigh up the violence of a just revolution (suppose our case of long-endured institutional violence maintained by force) against the violence of a "counter-revolution" which is set up in opposition to the revolution, but is, ex hypothesi, unjust. But by the same token, neither can ends (to take the opposite case) be separated from means as if the justice of the end (or the injustice to be opposed) justifies everything, with efficacy the unique norm. This goes for revolutionary action as well as for public force exercised by the State.

There is a dialectical play between end and means. If one truly operates in a spirit (dialectic) of justice, this will be reflected in action. But if in the carrying out of action one were to become emprisoned by the spirit of violence, (or rather obsessed by efficiency leading to extremes that unleash the dialectic of violence), the resulting existential situation will inexorably end up by influencing one on the plane of finality. That is, the finalistic impulse itself will end up by losing its character of being "in the spirit of justice."

There are quite practical consequences of what may here appear very abstract considerations. In stating them we shall not attempt to work out a complex casuistry, but will focus on certain basic principles of orientation which should never be lost sight of or sacrificed to emotional impulse in a moment of desperate protest against injustice. In doing so we must also bear in mind that given the complexity of situations, we shall have to allow for a certain margin of approximation in the concrete application of our value judgements.

Our question is this: is it possible to undertake armed revolutionary violence without losing the dialectical equilibrium between end and means and without falling into that unjust violent action which unchains the dialectic of violence? The possibility, it must be acknowledged, is rather slim: there is great danger that armed revolutionary violence will end in an unjustifiable, however comprehensible, dialectic (or spirit) of violence.

And here we may not permit a passionate love of justice for the oppressed to deprive us of that clear sightedness which springs also from a sincere love of justice (a love of neighbour which goes out in the first place to the oppressed poor).

We have, then, finally, two results. First, that the possibility of an armed revolutionary violence appropriate to the achieving of a structural revolution in the service of true human progress can not be excluded arbitrarily or a priori. Secondly, that such a possibility is in the concrete highly doubtful.

204

The doubtfulness of licit armed action forces us to investigate all the possibilities of active non-violence. And where, because of the unpreparedness of people, it seems impossible to have now a truly efficacious non-armed violence (nor even an armed revolutionary action which promises sufficient success in overcoming injustice and « institutional violence »), one will have patiently to undertake the work of awakening consciences, of providing social and political education, of cultural promotion. This education, it should be said by way of parenthesis, must not be allowed to fall into the hands of interest-serving, privileged minorities.

But for active non-violence to be taken seriously as an alternative, it must be that kind of "violent" non-violence we spoke of earlier: uncompromising and dynamic, embracing even the willingness to lay down one's life in the cause. For christians the model is Christ, crucified and risen, exemplar, in giving Himself, of that freedom of love that rises above egoism to fight for justice.

But realism forces us to recognise that, at least, at the wider (or macro) level of social and political life, the possibilities of achieving active non-violence are themselves questionable. Here it is evident that romantic solutions of individualistic and anarchic moralism or prophecy are unsatisfactory. For there exists the evident danger that a supposedly active non-violence would in practice remain dormant in a utopia or in that individualistic and anarchic romanticism which in a desire to "keep one's hands clean" ends up only by tightening the yoke imposed by the unjust system's institutional violence.

This frank reflection brings me to ask why it is that the movement of active non-violence fails to manifest with sufficient clarity and actuality that efficacy and historical relevance which many men of good will (especially youth) are looking for in their commitment to "revolution of structures" capable of orienting the march of men toward a truly human progress?

The answer seems to me to be the following. The number of believers in active non-violence engaged seriously in the cause for justice (the fight against structural violence) is really very small. It would be quite a different thing if masses of men, indeed whole cities, were mobilized for a non-violent action that was at the same time truly energetic.

It would be a grave error on the part of christians to reject armed revolutionary action because of its violence without engaging themselves at the same time in a fight for justice, lived out with all its consequences for each according to his particular circumstances.

I believe also that it would be a grave historical sin against the "signs of the times" to close one's eyes against the institutional violence of the world we live in. For christians, this sin is treason against the Gospel. For, faithfulness to the Gospel commits us to the search for those institutional conditions in which human progress becomes possible and is achieved. It seems certain that with this we are pledged to carry on with all men of goodwill a "revolution of structures" at the national and international level. If possible without armed violence.

JOSEPH SHIH, s. j.

RELIGION AGAINST DEVELOPMENT:
THE CASE OF CHINA

   This paper deals with one case of development. It proposes to discuss some aspects that call for theological consideration. The subject chosen for this purpose is China. The reason for such a preference is twofold. On the one hand, China's development has been impressive. As Doad Bernett puts it, only yesterday she was "a pawn in international affairs," today she has become "an important power with growing influence on the world stage."[1] On the other hand, her development has been ill-fated. The number of her refugees living abroad bears witness to this. Thus, with both her achievement and tragedy not only does China show the longings and frustrations of her own people. She illustrates also the hope and despair of many other developing nations. Hers indeed is a typical case.

   To state the Chinese case we recur to her history. China launched into development largely as a result of her confrontation with the West. Unlike Japan, whose reaction to a similar situation was quick and successful, China failed to respond in time. I agree with the authors of *East Asia: The Modern Transformation*, that the major determinants of China's failure "lay within the Chinese society, not outside it."[2] Later, Chinese society disintegrated under the sustained

---

[1] A. Doad Barnett, *China after Mao*, Princeton 1967, p. 9.
[2] John K. Fairbank, Edwin O. Reischauer, Albert M. Graig, *East Asia: The Modern Transformation*, Boston 1965, p. 314.

impact of Western industrialism. This at once paved the way for China's modernization and prepared troubles for her future.

With such a perspective I divide the present study into three parts. The first indicates the burden of the past. That is the thought and institution of traditional China in so far as they impeded development. Because of the definite scope and specific aim of this paper I must limit myself to expounding only the traditional religion of China. I see in it at once a mirror that reflected the Chinese society, and a rule that controlled its formation and transformation.

The second part describes the impact of the West. The effect of that impact was twofold. On the one hand, it destroyed Chinese society by sapping its economic basis, upsetting its social order, and confounding its moral standard. On the other hand, it delivered the Chinese from the burden of their past, giving them perhaps for the first time in their history a real opportunity for development. And they seized it most determinedly. Bearing in mind the particular purpose of this paper, I shall consider rather the negative aspect of their venture. I shall take into account not so much their effort to build up a new nation as their determination in casting off the inheritance of the past. In doing so I only follow the example of those leaders of the May Fourth Movement (1919) who considered Chinese development to be above all liberation from Confucianist thought and institutions.

In this paper the term May Fourth Movement is used in a broader sense. It covers the period from 1917 to 1921, and is characterized by a series of demonstrations and strikes. The Movement broke out as a protest against the Chinese government's humiliating policy toward Japan. But soon it was led to become a vast modernization movement. In the third part of this paper, I shall define the problems of development. I shall do so through examining this May Fourth Movement. The reason for such a procedure shall be explained later. For the moment I only indicate the three points I shall single out. These are: the crisis of the traditional morals, the crisis of the traditional religion, and the search for an ideology.

208

Finally I shall elaborate these three points to provide some food for the reflection of theologians, for it is from them that we expect "theological consideration of the problems of development."

I. THE BURDEN OF THE PAST

Two events highlighted recent history of China: the fall of the Ch'ing, or Manchu, dynasty in 1911 and the establishment of the Communist regime in 1949. The forty years that passed between the two dates were plagued with civil wars and foreign invasions. Consequently no spectacular progress could be expected. Yet it was during that period that the Chinese nation was called into existence. And along with the rise of the nation, nationalism also arose. We shall see in the latter part of this paper the importance of nascent nationalism for China's development. But let us first consider the "universalism" which characterized imperial China.[3]

What I call universalism refers to a doctrine known technically as the Yin Yang and Five Agents theory. The uninitiated mass call it, however, simply Confucianism. It is a doctrine resulting from the amalgamation of early Taoism and Confucianism. It originated after the break-down of the Chou order in the third century B. C. It is that doctrine that explained the title "emperor" arrogated to the ruler of the Ch'in (221-206 B. C.) and legitimated the rise of the Han dynasty (206 B. C. - 220 A. D.) Under the same dynasty, it took up the garment of Confucianism and was proclaimed the official teaching of the court. Ever since, generations of literati, who sought to become mandarins, studied Confucianism with this bias. No wonder, then, that despite the repeated denunciation of individual scholars, the Yin Yang and Five Agents theory did not cease dominating the Chinese world until the definite abolition of the imperial government. Such being its influence, we can not hope to understand the thought and institution of traditional China without an adequate knowledge of it.

---

[3] The word is coined by J. J. M. de Groot, *Universalismus*, Berlin, 1918.

I have treated the formation of the Yin Yang and Five Agents school in an article "the notions of God in the ancient Chinese religion." [4] I have discussed its esoteric language in another one "the ancient chinese cosmogony." [5] Here I shall examine rather its consequences in politics and morals. Incidently I shall indicate the impediment it constituted for development.

The Yin Yang and Five Agents theory modified Chinese politics in two points: first in its interpretation of the Mandate of Heaven and secondly in its definition of sovereignty. As to the first point, the doctrine of the Mandate of Heaven was propounded originally by the Duke of Chou. He was a brother of King Wu, who founded the Chou dynasty. As he developed it, the doctrine had a propagandist purport. Indeed, the Chou dynasty had been preceded by Shang. The Shang kings used to claim the exclusive right to rule. They based their pretension on the ground that they were descended from the ancient sage kings. Chou Hsin, the last monarch of that dynasty, is said to have pronounced the sentence: *"Wu-fu! Huo sheng pu-yu T'ien-ming tsai!"* These words admit two possible interpretations. James Legge has translated them as: "Oh! Is not my life secured by the decree of Heaven!" [6] One could also understand them in the following way: "Oh! Don't I have in my person the Mandate of Heaven!" But, whichever might be the right version, one thing seems to be certain. Chou Hsin claimed that his destiny was independent from his conduct. He based his right to rule on the virtue he had inherited by birth. The Duke of Chou contradicted this presumption with the famous declaration *"huang-T'ien wu-ch'in!"* namely "August Heaven has no kin!" [7] Thereby he meant that Heaven was not bound to any particular house. Heaven gave His Mandate to the house that pleased Him through the good deeds of its members and took it away from the same house whenever it had ceased to please Him. Since the Shang kings had displeased Heaven by their misrule, Hea-

    [4] *Numen* 16 (1969), pp. 99-138.
    [5] *Studia Missionalia*, Roma 1970, pp. 111-130.
    [6] James Legge (tr.), *The Chinese Classics*, Hong-kong, 1961, vol. 3, p. 272.
    [7] *Ibid.*, p. 490.

ven had taken away His Mandate from them and had given it over to the Chou house.

It is obvious that the Duke believed in Heaven as a Supreme God who was absolutely free in His dealings with men but was not insensible to their doings. Such a concept of God prevails indeed in the Confucian Classics.[8] But during Ch'in Han dynasties the Chinese religion underwent an important change. Under the influence of the Yin Yang and Five Agents theory Heaven came to be coupled with the earth. It became one of the two principles of creation. Being one of the two creating principles, Heaven was no longer the one Supreme God. He was replaced in that capacity by T'ai-i, or the Pole-star, to whom the Han suburban sacrifice dedicated the following verses:

> Dressed in variegated silk
> A thousand boys and girls
> Danced in eight ranks
> To delight God T'ai-i [9]

As revealed by the Pole-star, T'ai-i resided above the heavenly vault. It was supposed that He had acted before the separation of Heaven and earth but was indifferent to the actual evolution of the world. Thus, under the new religious conception, neither Heaven nor T'ai-i interfered in the affairs of human society. If the Chinese still spoke of the Mandate of Heaven they meant then something else.

Indeed, Tsou Yen, (about 305-240 B. C.), the principal exponent of the Yin Yang and Five Agents theory, taught that events in the human world were influenced by the rotation of the Five Agents, which are: Water, Wood, Metal, Fire, and Earth. Each agent took its turn in dominating over all the others. As to the order of succession, he said that "each agent was followed by the one that defeated it." Accordingly, "Wood was followed by Metal, Metal by Fire, and Fire by Water." [10] Each time that one agent came to pre-

---

[8] Tien Tchen-kang, *L'idée de Dieu dans les huit premiers classiques chinois*, Fribourg, 1942.

[9] Pan Ku, *Han Shu* (History of Han dynasty), ch. 22, f. 19.

[10] Cited according Fung Yu-lang's *Chung kuo che-hsüeh-shih*

vail it called up a new dynasty that was to rule by the special virtue of the agent, or in other words, by the Mandate of the corresponding God-on-High.

Thus, according to one dynastic legend, Kao-tzu, the founder of Han dynasty, once dreamed of killing a great snake. On that occasion he was informed by a spirit that the snake was the son of the White God-on-High and that he who had killed it, was the son of the Red God-on-High. [11] In another dynastic legend, the same kao-tzu is said to have been the son of the Black God-on-High to whom he erected the Northern Sacred Palace. [12] The contradictory stories show that the Han emperors hesitated about the virtue by which they had obtained the Mandate to rule, but it does not contradict the fact that they accepted the new interpretation of the Mandate of Heaven.

Besides the new interpretation of the Mandate of Heaven, a new concept of sovereignty was also introduced. Earlier, a ruler was to be a sage. His role consisted in ruling by means of his virtue. Thus Confucius stated: "He who exercises government by means of his virtue, may be compared to the north polar star, which keeps its place and all the stars turn towards it." [13] But, then, virtue was understood to be above all benevolence, for it was believed that by being benevolent to his people a ruler manifested the bounty of Heaven, in Whose name he ruled. The Yin Yang and Five Agents school taught instead that a ruler should be a saint, who should "assist the transforming and nourishing powers of Heaven and Earth," and "with Heaven and Earth form a triad." [14] In other words, earlier a ruler was a king (*wang*). He was the chief of a cultural group. He ruled over a known area of the world. Later a ruler became an emperor (*huang-ti*). He was the mediator between Heaven and Earth. He dominated the whole Creation. It was indeed under the in-

---

hsin-pien (Revised edition of the history of the Chinese philosophy, Peking, 1963), p. 452.

[11] Burton Watson (tr.), *Records of the Grand Historian of China,* New York, 1961, vol. 1, p. 80.

[12] *Ibid.,* vol. 2, p. 31.

[13] *The Chinese Classics,* vol. 1, p. 145.

[14] *Ibid.,* p. 416.

212

fluence of such a conception that the founder of Ch'in dynasty substituted the title emperor for the earlier one, king. [15]

The moral code of imperial China consisted of the so-called *san-kang liu-chi*, namely the three major and six minor relationships. The former referred to the relations that existed between 1° ruler and subject, 2° father and son, and 3° husband and wife. The latter indicated one's relations with 1° his father's brother, 2° his elder and younger brothers, 3° his kinsmen, 4° his mother's brother, 5° his teachers and elders and 6° his friends. [16] It is evident that these major and minor relationships represented the hierarchy of the traditional society in China. They defined at once the duties of the individuals in it. Hence we conclude that as far as the contents are concerned, Chinese morals did not derive from any divine revelation but resulted from an existing social order. Thus we confirm a thesis of Francisco Suarez, according to which it is not the divine law but human nature, namely man with his many sided relationships, that constituted the immediate norm of morality. The Yin Yang and Five Agents theory, as a theological restatement of a religious tradition, exercised therefore no influence on the content of Chinese morals. If we speak of its moral implications we mean simply that it gave sanction to the moral code and that in doing so it added to it some particular qualities. We shall determine these qualities by examining the way the sanction was applied.

A basic tenet of the Yin Yang and Five Agents school is stated under the motto, *T'ien-jen ho-i*, which means literally "perfect correspondence between what happens in Nature and what happens to men." [17] The statement was at once indicative and imperative. In the one and the other sense it served to sanction the existing social order. But the way it

---

[15] Derk Bodde, *China's First Unifier: A Study of the Ch'in Dynasty as Seen in the Life of Li Ssu* (280?-208 B. C.), Leiden 1938, pp. 124-132.

[16] Tjan Tjoe Som (tr.), *Po Hu T'ung: The Comprehensive discussions in the White Tiger Hall,* Leiden, 1949, pp. 559-564.

[17] This theory was made known principally through the writings of Tung Chung-shu. Cfr. Kang Woo, *Les Trois Théories politiques du Tch'ouen Ts'ieou interprétées par Tong Tchong-chou d'après les principes de l'école de King-yang,* Paris, 1932.

operated varied in the two cases. Indeed, as an imperative statement, the motto signified that what happened in Nature must be followed also in human society. Since heavens are high and the earth is low the relation between Heaven and Earth was taken as a prototype for the relation between superior and inferior, such as between ruler and subject, father and son, and husband and wife. Thus the *Book of Changes* states:

> As Heaven is high and Earth is low
> *Ch'ien* is placed in a high position
> And *Kun* is placed in a low position:
> This illustrates how superior and inferior
> Must keep each his proper position. [18]

It is not necessary to multiply similar quotations. What is important is to seize their significance. By proposing Heaven and Earth as a prototype of human society, they instilled actually the belief that the three major and six minor relationships in the traditional society of China conformed indeed to the law of Nature. Thus they sanctioned the existing moral code by ratifying its principal precepts.

As an indicative statement, the same motto took on another meaning. It stated that whatever happened to human society had its repercussions in Nature. Thus, when in a society the three major and six minor relationships were well kept, Nature, too, found itself in harmony. Consequently everything prospered. The following passage, which explains the hexagram *chia-jen* or "People of the household"' conveys undoubtedly such a persuasion:

> In *chia-jen* the woman has her right place within, and the man his right place outside. The correctness of position of man and woman is the great principle of Heaven and Earth. In *chia-jen* we have the idea of an authoritative ruler, that is, parental authority. When the father is father, the son, son; when the elder brother is elder brother and the younger brother is younger brother; when husband is husband and wife is wife: then the way

---

[18] Wilhelm-Baynes (tr.), *The I Ching, or Book of Changes,* New York, 1952, vol. 1, p. 301.

of the family is correct. When it is correct, all under Heaven will be established. [19]

On the contrary, when the right relationship in a given society was disturbed, particularly, when the offender was the monarch himself, Nature, too, was brought to a crisis. Thus it was said of him:

> The feelings of a monarch have their repercussions in the heavens above. When he exaggerates in chastising his people there will be much whirl-wind. When he abuses in issuing wrong edicts there will be many locusts. When he kills innocents the country will be devastated. When he does not moderate his prescription it will rain excessively.[20]

There is no point in questioning the objective truth of these statements. What interests us is their purport which was to assure retribution for offences against the established order. It was another way in which the Yin Yang and Five Agents school sanctioned the moral code of imperial China.

The effect of this operation was twofold. On the one hand, by giving sanction to the Confucian moral code the Yin Yang and Five Agents theory demonstrated its relevancy to the Confucianist society. Consequently it was made a part of Confucian thought and institution. On the other hand, in receiving this sanction the Confucianist moral code was endowed at once with a religious character; so that what had resulted from a transient social order and had been recognized as a tradition of early sage kings became finally the way of Heaven and Earth. It assumed thus a "speciem aeternitatis."

No one would overlook the fact that all these constituted serious impediments to China's development. The definition of sovereignty based on the cosmogonic function of the emperor was responsible for the difficulties China had in

---

[19] *Ibid.*, vol. 2, p. 2. 5.
[20] Cfr. Francis L. K. Hsu, *Religion, Science and Human Crisis, A Study of China in Transition and its implications for the West.* London, (Routledge & Kegan), 1952.

her relations with modern nation states. The rigid comparison between human behaviour and natural phenomena caused further confusion between an existing moral code and the abiding natural law, thus inhibiting the Chinese from undertaking necessary reform. But the root of the trouble lay deeper. It was to be found in a religious tradition, of which the Yin Yang and Five Agents theory was but one theological restatement. We shall resume this point in the last part of this paper.

II. The impact of the West

In the course of her long history, China has witnessed the rise and fall of many dynasties. She has endured protracted alien domination. Yet, until the late nineteenth century she had never doubted her faith in Confucianism; generations of emperors, regardless of their extraction, paid homage to Confucius, professing him to be "the teacher of all teachers." It is therefore all the more surprising to learn that she repudiated her millenary tradition a few decades after her contact with modern Europe. Hence, questions have been raised: What was the secret that enabled Confucianism to dominate the Chinese society over more than two thousand years? How was it that the Confucianist society corroded irreparably as soon as it came into contact with Western civilization? An observation of the Earl of Macartney may help us to seize the nature of these questions. Macartney sent on an embassy to the court of Ch'ien-lung in 1793, was received by the latter as a tribute bearer from a far-away country, for China was then at the height of its might. But, even in such circumstances, he made the following pertinent comment: "The Empire of China is an old, crazy, first rate Man of War ... She may, perhaps, not sink outright; she may drift some time as a wreck, and will then be dashed to pieces on the shore; but she can never be rebuilt on the old bottom ..." [21] It would be interesting to examine the basis on which Macartney made this prediction.

-----

[21] Quoted according to *East Asia*, p. 77, note.

216

However, to those who have seen the poverty of the masses of Chinese people and have understood the way in which they were kept alive and bound together, Marcartney was no prophet.

Indeed, China is an agrarian country with over 75 percent of her population engaged in farming but only 20 percent of her land suitable for agriculture. In the traditional period farms were family enterprises. The land, the house, and the tools were regarded as family property. Upon the death of the parents, the inheritance was divided among all the sons. Thus, over the centuries, available lands were reduced to small units. It is estimated that "prior to the Communist period farms averaged about 3,5 acres per farm-household or 0,7 acre per each member of a five-member household." [22] This means that the average Chinese farmer produced merely enough to provide bare necessities of life. He was defenseless against recurring natural calamities and destitute of any prospect of making significant improvement in his economic conditions. Thus, uncertain of its very subsistence the Chinese peasantry formed an amorphous mass. It was, to use an expression of Sun Yat-sen, the Father of the Republic of China, "a bowl of scattering sand."

The cohesion and consistence of the Chinese society was due to the gentry, a special social group originating in the third century B. C. Prior to that date, Chinese society was sharply divided. On the one hand, no commoners ever had any part in government. On the other hand, all nobles shared real political power. But this system, known as feudalism in Chinese history, gave way to absolute monarchism when Ch'in Shih Huang-ti had conquered all China in 211 B. C. Under the new system political power became concentrated in the person of one man, the emperor, who was assisted by officials chosen no longer from his kin but among the commoners. Thus, bureacracy was introduced in China. This in turn gave rise to that particular group that is the gentry. [23]

---

[22] *China: Its People, Its Society, Its Culture* (edited by Hsiao Hsia, *Survey of World Cultures*, London, 1959, p. 337.

[23] Fei Hsiao-tung, "The Role of the Gentry," in: *Chinese Society under Communism: A Reader* (edited by William T. Liu, New York, 1967), pp. 47-57.

The gentry was the cement of Chinese society. It gathered the peasant mass and fashioned them into a viable body with the threefold function it exercised among them. This was at once economic, administrative and educational in nature. Indeed, the members of the gentry were mostly landowners. In this capacity they not only leased the lands to the peasants who tilled them but also were responsible for the construction and maintenance of the necessary waterworks. In many instances they had to provide their husbandmen with indispensable farm implements, seeds, even food and medication as well. On similar occasions usury inevitably occurred. But knowing the misery that plagued the majority of Chinese farmers, we can not complain. We must recognize that, undesirable as it was, usury was a part of the productive system in traditional China.

The administrative role of the gentry was more conspicuous. It was exercised at two different levels. At a higher level, it provided candidates for officialdom. It thus assisted the emperor in the government of the whole country. At a lower level, the gentry, being the natural leaders of the local communities, were normally consultants to the local magistrate. It was indeed in recognition of their cooperation in this regard that the imperial law granted them certain privileges.

But the importance of the gentry rested ultimately upon the fact that it was the class of the literati. To realize the significance of this observation we must keep in mind that the traditional religion of China has no order of priests. The Buddhist bonzes and Taoist shamans have never been recognized by the Chinese as something comparable to the Christian monks in medieval Europe. It was rather the literati who fulfilled in traditional China the function that the monks once fulfilled in Christian Europe. Like the latter, they were bearers of the tradition and educators of the younger generations.

Nothing indicated better the nature of Chinese society than ancestral worship. By this word " ancestral worship," I do not mean those ceremonies which individual families held in honor of their forefathers. Such rites were found even in peasant households. Though more genuine in religious effervescence, they were actually less expressive of the Confucian values. The ancestral worship in the proper sense was one in which a whole clan took part. It was indeed the clan, not the individual families, that was the natural community of that worship.[24]

The clan worship involved the possession of an ancestral hall, some ritual land, and perhaps also an ancestral graveyard. It needed necessarily gentry participation: a fact which had serious social implications. The sociologist Fei Hsiao-t'ung states:

> A piece of land is usually contributed to the clan organization by a member who is a governmental official, the pretext being that the products of the land may cover the expenses necessary in the keeping up of the ancestors' tombs and regular sacrifices. But, in fact, this common property is a common security with which the position of the clan may be maintained in the wider power structure of the community. It finances the education of the young members so that they may be able to enter the scholar class and attain high official position and protect the interest of their kinsmen. [25].

Such a disposition made possible the education of the sons of the poor clansmen and offered opportunity to the brightest of them to pursue higher studies and to become eventually mandarins. Thus, not only did ancestral worship sanction the union of the clan and integrate the gentry and the peasantry, the two otherwise quite disparate social classes; but it also fostered social mobility and was responsible for the fact that, while their counter-part in Japan found it ridiculous to ape the life of the Samurai, the Chinese peasants looked forward to living in a manner comparable to that of the gentry. That was how the code of Confucian morals, which belonged properly to the gentry alone, came to be accepted by the peasantry as well. [26]

[24] Hsiao Kung-chuan, *The Role of the Clan and Kinship Family, Ibid.,* pp. 33-46.
[25] *Ibid.,* p. 38.
[26] It is an opinion of Marion J. Levy, Jr., the author of *The Family Revolution in China,* New York, 1963.

Thus, we arrive at two important conclusions. First, a particular feature of Chinese society was the mutual dependence and close relation between the gentry and the peasantry. Second, this mutual dependence and close co-operation constituted, so to speak, the socio-economic basis of Confucianism. In the light of these conclusions, the two questions raised above find ready solutions. During the imperial period the numerous political upheavals caused no substantial change in the mode of production. They did not disturb the usual relation between the gentry and the peasantry. They left intact the socio-economic basis of Confucianism. It was because of the persistence of this basis that Confucianism was able to survive the whole imperial period. But the situation changed with the introduction of Western industrialism. We shall see how this disrupted China's traditional economy, and, by doing so, corroded the Confucian society.

Western industrialism disrupted China's traditional economy in two ways. On the one hand, it made obsolete her mode of production. Take, for example, the textile industry. For centuries the Chinese had engaged in this kind of work. In most parts of China, hand looms belonged to every household. " Man tills while woman weaves " was a stereotyped description of daily life in a Chinese village. Given the scanty land tenure of the average Chinese farmer, domestic handicraft industry was indeed of vital importance to the family budget. Failure in that branch of family undertaking meant in most cases the ruin of the families concerned. This was what happened to the Chinese domestic textile industry under the impact of Western industrialism.

It should be recalled that China opened to foreign trade under the " unequal treaty system ". In 1882, the Treaty of Nanking, besides ceding Hong Kong to Britain, opened five ports to British residence and trade. In 1860, a second treaty settlement opened further the whole of China to foreign trade. An immediate effect of this disposition was the sudden increase of imports of British cotton goods. It is true that in the first decades that followed, the growth was limited to those of cotton yarn. " This was because machine-spinning of yarn was some 80 times as productive as hand-spinning, while machine-weaving of cloth was only about 4 times as fast as hand-weaving. Thus the cheaper cotton yarn from abroad crippled the native Chinese spinning industry, while weaving still continued for many years on hand looms in peasant households as before." [27] But after 1890, even hand looms fell out of use.

On the other hand, spurred on by the increasing imports of industrial products, China, too, set about industrialising herself. As early as 1878, Li Hung-chang (1823-1901) began to sponsor a Chinese textile mill to compete with foreign imports. His Shanghai Cotton Cloth Mill suffered an initial set back. But "beginning in 1890, some 4000 factory workers were soon turning out excellent cloth and yarn, and 25 per cent was paid on shares in 1893, when the mill unfortunately burned down." [28] In 1899, Chang Chien (1853-1926) launched his Ta-sheng Cotton Spinning Mill, which continued to dominate the Chinese textile industry up to the Communist period. Meantime the British and the Japanese also established their Cotton Cloth Mills in the treaty ports. These and similar enterprises offered opportunities for employment and opened up alternatives to the deteriorating peasant life.

But in both ways the advent of industrialism disturbed the established order of Chinese society. It is true that most pioneers in Chinese industrialisation stemmed from the gentry. Chang Chien, for example, was the top scholar of the empire (*chuang-yüan*) in 1894. Though he adopted Western technical advice and production method, he handled his labor force in a Confucian manner. He was " paternally concerned with their joys and sorrows alike as well as their living quarters and education." [29] Moreover, as a good Confucianist, he dedicated himself particularly to the development of his hometown, Nantung:

> Prospering, he built three more mills and branched out into cotton-growing, steamship transport, and consumer industries — flour, oil, and salt production —

---

[27] *East Asia,* p. 346.
[28] *Ibid.,* p. 358.
[29] *Ibid.,* p. 628.

and also became a philanthropist, eventually making Nantung a model district with schools and technical colleges, roads, parks, homes for the orphaned and aged, even a new jail. [30]

But though men like Chang Chien might have kept the Confucian virtues, their enterprises had a disruptive effect on Confucian society. First of all, they themselves had made the transit from scholar-gentry to entrepreneur. They might have interest, personally, in education and government. But their status in society was determined principally by their ability to manage their industrial undertakings. Their fellow townsmen still showed great respect for them as they used to respect the gentry; but they could no longer expect from them what they used to expect from the latter. They felt somehow that the traditional relationship between the gentry and the peasantry no longer held.

Besides, men and women employed in the newly founded factories also received new status in their families. The change was particularly significant in the case of women, who traditionally held a subordinate position with regard to men. In this connexion it is interesting to read an observation which Fei Hsiao-tung has made in his *Peasant Life in China: A Field Study of Country Life in the Yangtze Valley*:

> Wage-earning is now regarded as a privilege because it makes an immediate contribution to the domestic budget. Those who have no adult daughters begin to regret it. The woman's position in society has undergone a gradual change. For instance, a girl who was working in the village factory actually cursed her husband because he forgot to send her an umbrella when it rained. It is interesting because this little incident indicates changes in the relation between husband and wife. According to the traditional conception, the husband is not supposed to serve his wife, at least he cannot do so in public. Moreover, the husband cannot accept his wife's curse without any protest or counter-curse. [31]

---

[30] *Ibid.*, p. 628.
[31] London, 1962, p. 233.

The following is an extreme case, cited by the same author, but it illustrates very well the effects of industrialisation on kinship relations:

A girl left her husband about one year after she had married. She stayed in a factory in Wuhsi and fell in love with a workman in the same factory. They were both discharged by the factory when the illegal union was discovered. Having lived together for two months, but being pressed for money, they separated. The girl returned to the village and was greatly disgraced. Her parents-in-law refused to admit her, but afterwards accepted her because they planned to arrange a remarriage for her in order that they could get a sum of money for compensation. Later, in view of her earning capacity in the silk factory in the village, her parents-in-law cancelled their plan and treated her as usual. Her husband took a passive attitude towards the entire affair.[32]

Once the established order had been upset, traditional morals were called into question. In the example cited above an adulterous woman was re-established in her conjugal state. At first sight the reason for the condonation seems to have been purely economic in nature. But the fact that such a woman could survive her disgrace and find opportunity of earning money supposed a significant change in the morals of the country. It was, indeed, the changing morals of the country that led the leaders of the May Fourth Movement to see in Confucianism a major obstacle to development of the country.

III. THE PROBLEMS OF DEVELOPMENT

If the Treaty of Nanking opened China to Western influence, it was the Treaty of Shimonoseki, which concluded the First Sino-Japanese War in 1895, that spurred her on toward effective modernization. Indeed, it has been reported that at the latter convention an informal conversation took

---

[32] *Ibid.*, p. 234.

place between the two signatories. Itō Hirobumi (1841-1909), who represented the victorious party, is said to have rebuked Li Hung-chang for his failure in carrying out necessary reform in China. "Ten years ago at Tientsin," he said, "I talked with you about reform. Why is it that up to now not a single thing has been changed or reformed?" To this Li replied grudgingly: "Affairs in my country have been so confined by tradition."[33] To us, today, the answer seems banal. Everywhere in the world, tradition resists change. How could it be invoked, then, to excuse the delay of necessary reform in China? Yet to both Itō, and Li himself the statement was quite meaningful. It revealed a real obstacle to the modernization of China.

To understand the nature of the obstacle it is necessary to examine what had happened before 1895. Ever since her contact with modern Europe China had decided to strengthen herself through adopting Western technology. At first, the adoption was limited to the manufacture of European weapons. Later, it was extended to acquiring Western knowledge in general. The program was then stated under the motto, *chung-hsueh wei t'i; hsi-hsueh wei yung,* which means "to maintain Chinese studies to consolidate the substance of the society and to introduce Western studies to improve its manifold functions."[34] "The substance of the society" means nothing but the Confucian tradition. Hence it appears that what moved China to set about adopting Western civilization was precisely her zeal to defend herself as a cultural unit. The contradiction of such a program was later illustrated by the satirist Lu Hsün (1881-1936) in the following fictitious conversation:

> A: We must really strengthen ourselves through adopting Western civilization. Otherwise we shall be wiped out by Western powers.
> B: It is a pity. We shall have to abandon our cultural heritage.

---

[33] *East Asia,* p. 383.
[34] Ssu-yu Teng, John K. Fairbank, *China's response to the West: A documentary survey 1839-1923,* Cambridge, Mass., 1961, pp. 50, 164, 183.

A: What is the use of keeping our cultural heritage when there will be no Chinese in the world?

B: What is the use of having Chinese in the world if they no longer behave like Chinese? [35]

In the conversation cited above, both A and B recognize the need of adopting Western civilization. B hesitates, however, to take practical steps. He fears that, by doing so, he might cease to be a Chinese. A, on the contrary, has decided to throw overboard the whole lump of " cultural heritage ". His sole preoccupations to secure China's survival in the world of competing nations. Both A and B are Chinese. But the latter is a traditionalist, while the former is a nationalist. What the Treaty of Shimonoseki did precisely was to turn a small but significant portion of Chinese from traditionalists into nationalists. In doing so, it put into Chinese society a catalyst needed for starting the desired cultural reform.

It was not long before the effects appeared. In 1911, the Chinese cast off the Manchu domination and dispensed themselves all together from imperial government. A republic was established instead. In 1919, students in Peking demonstrated against the government's foreign policy. The incident occured on May 4. But what was originally a local and patriotic movement, soon spread out through the whole country and turned into a vast campaign for intellectual and social revolutions. [36] Because of the close association of nationalistic aspiration and revolutionary fervor, the May Fourth movement is of special interest to us. We must, therefore, seek to discover what the Movement saw as the principal problems of China's development.

According to Ch'en Tu-hsiu (1879-1942), a leader of the movement, the aim of the May Fourth Movement was to " advocate Mr. D. and Mr. S. " Mr. D. and Mr. S. were two nicknames, given to democracy and science. These were generally believed to be the quintessence of Western civiliza-

---

[35] *Jo Feng* (*Hot Wind*) in: *Lu Hsün Ch'üan chi* (The Complete Works of Lu Hsün, 1938).

[36] Chow Tse-tsung, *The May Fourth Movement*, Cambridge, Mass., 1960, pp. 84-268.

tion. In the opinion of Ch'en, they were incompatible with Chinese tradition. Hence he held that in order to develop China it was necessary to liberate her from the burden of her past. He declared this point of view in an article, intended to celebrate the third anniversary of the publication of the monthly *New Youth* and to defend it against its critics:

> They accused this magazine on the grounds that it intended to destroy Confucianism, the code of ritual, the " national quintessence, " chastity of women, traditional ethics, traditional arts, traditional religion, and ancient literature, as well as old-fashioned politics.
>
> All of these charges are conceded. But we plead not guilty. We have commited the alleged crimes only because we supported the two gentlemen, Mr. Democracy and Mr. Science. In order to advocate Mr. Democracy, we are obliged to oppose Confucianism, the codes of rituals, chastity of women, traditional ethics, and old-fashioned politics; in order to advocate Mr. Science, we have to oppose traditional arts and traditional religion; and in order to advocate both Mr. Democracy and Mr. Science we are compelled to oppose the cult of the "national quintessence" and ancient literature. Let us then ponder dispassionately: has this magazine committeed any crimes other than advocating Mr. Democracy and Mr. Science? If not, please do not solely reprove this magazine; the only way for you to be heroic and to solve the problem fundamentally is to oppose the two gentlemen, Mr. Democracy and Mr. Science. [37]

Though Ch'en and his collaborators spoke ostensibly of Mr. D. and Mr. S., it is not clear whether they all meant the same thing. However one thing is certain. They all agree that the two gentlemen would not have anything to do with Confucianism. This means they were more conscious of the negative effects of democracy and science than of their positive contents. In this sense, Prof. Benjamin I. Schwartz is right in seeing in Ch'en's conception of democracy a fruit of Manchester liberalism and in giving to it the following explanation:

---

[37] *Ibid.,* p. 59.

What then was Ch'en's conception of democracy? Essentially it was the concept of Manchester liberalism. By removing the fetters which tradition had placed on the individual, by granting him the liberty to pursue his enlightened self-interest, and by securing this liberty in law, democracy had set free the energies of the individual. [38]

Similarly his interpretation of Ch'en's conception of the role of science is very pertinent:

Ch'en's conception of the role of science reminds one above all of the Russian nihilists. Like them, he saw in science a weapon, a corrosive to be used in dissolving traditional society. [39]

In the heat of the intellectual and social revolutions, some authors imputed hideous crimes to Confucianism and used abusive language in this regard. Wu Yü, for example, called Confucianism a "Man-eating institution." [40] Lu Hsün gave the following description of the Confucian teaching: "I looked at a book of Chinese history. On every page are written such words as 'righteousness' and 'moral virtues'. After reading carefully for half the night, I found other words in between the columns; everywhere in the book are the two words 'man-eating'." [41] But, by and large, the chief grievance against Confucianism was, indeed, that it suffocated individual personality with the ethics of three major and six minor relationships. In Confucianism, so it was claimed, a man was not so much himself as "a son of his father." Such a conception, Ch'en argued, was inconsistent with modern living. Here, indeed, we recognize the first problem of development, namely the crisis of traditional morals.

It is interesting to note that the leaders of the May Fourth Movement, on the whole, were more Confucian than

[38] *Chinese Communism and the Rise of Mao*, Cambridge, Mass., 1961, p. 9.
[39] *Ibid.*, p. 9.
[40] Chow Tse-tsung, *op. cit.*, pp. 303-305.
[41] *Ibid.*, p. 308.

they would themselves admit. It is true they opposed Confucianism. But they did so on a Confucianist ground. If they advocated democracy it was not so much because they recognized the inalienable rights of individual persons but because they considered it more conducive to the economic development of the society. If they promoted science it was not so much because they appreciated its dynamic role in conquering nature as because they took it as a weapon against "superstitions." Their frame of mind was typically Confucian. It was moralistic. It believed that the transformation of the world began with the conversion of individual minds. No wonder, then, they did not bother about defining the nature of the incompatibility which they thought to exist between Chinese and Western civilizations.

The unfinished task was taken up by Liang Shu-ming, one of the very few intellectuals who dared defend Confucianism in those days. Like most of his contemporaries, Liang saw in democracy and science the common properties of Western civilizations. But he complained that the new intellectuals, while repeating it over and over again, had never asked themselves how it was that the West had invented these two wonderful things, or why China had not been able to produce them. He himself attempted to answer this question in a series of lectures which he delivered at Peking University and elsewhere in 1920 and 1921 on the subject "Eastern and Western Civilizations and Their Philosophies." The solution he proposed was based on his conception of civilization and types of civilization. [42]

Liang had not been abroad. He was above all a Buddhist scholar. His analysis of Eastern and Western civilizations owed much of its insight to the subtlety of Buddhist philosophy, particularly the Wei-ssu school (Yogācāra school). For the sake of convenience, I shall reduce his argument to a small catechism:

— What is civilization?
— It is the way of life of a people.
— What is life?

---

[42] *Ibid.*, pp. 329-332.

— It is infinite will with its incessant satisfactions and frustrations.
— How does it happen that peoples show so many contrasts in their ways of life?
— Because life has split into various courses and has accordingly developed itself in contrasting patterns.

In Liang's opinion, the will, the root of all civilizations, had split mainly into three different courses according to the three fundamental attitudes of man towards life, namely: conflict, compromise, and surrender. He described these courses in the following terms:

FIRST COURSE: to go forward to seek satisfaction.
SECOND COURSE: to modify one's desire, to regulate it, to follow the golden mean.
THIRD COURSE: to go backward.

Liang argued that Western civilizations with "democracy and science" as their common properties had taken the first course, while China had followed the second course, and India the third. It is immaterial to us whether Liang gave the right definition of civilization, or whether he estimated correctly the relative values of the three courses of civilization. What is important is to note that he saw in China's attitude toward life the ultimate cause of its failure to produce democracy and science. It is in this observation that we recognize the second problem of development, namely the crisis of traditional religion.

Another sign of the unreformed Confucianist mentality on the part of the leaders of the May Fourth Movement was their proneness to accept global solutions. Hu Shiih (1891-1962) was a fortunate exception. Being a disciple of John Dewey, he took a pragmatic point of view on the question of modernization of China. In an article titled "More Study of Problems, Less Talk of Isms," he denounced the futility, and even the danger, of advocating high-toned, all-embracing isms. The problems of China, he argued, could not be solved all at once, but must be tackled individually. [43] The article caused a furor

---

[43] *Ibid.*, pp. 218-222.

among many intellectuals, specially those of Marxists tendency. To them, indeed, "all problems were linked together in all-embracing structures, and all-embracing isms were groups of ideas with similar character. Isms were needed both as standards for the judgement of situations and problems, and as instruments for the solution of such linked problems." [44]

But even the pragmatist Hu Shih did not long resist the general enthusiasm. Soon, as if he had grown impatient with introducing a "pragmatist point of view" and a "genetic method" he imported outright scientism, believing it incumbent upon him to spread and popularize it. His ten points on what he called a "scientific philosophy of life" aroused such indignation of Christian missionaries that they ridiculed them as "Hu Shih's decalogue." [45] They read as follows:

1. On the basis of knowledge of astronomy and physics, one should appreciate the infinity of space.

2. On the basis of knowledge of geology and paleontology, one should know the infinity of time.

3. On the basis of all the sciences, one should be aware that the universe and all things in it move and change according to natural laws—in the Chinese sense of the term, "being so of themselves"—and do not depend on a so-called supernatural Ruler or Creator.

4. On the basis of knowledge of the biological sciences, one should realize the waste and ruthlessness of the struggle for existence in the biological realm, hence the indefectibility of the hypothesis that there is a benevolent ruler.

5. On the basis of the sciences of biology, physiology, and psychology, one should be aware that man is but another form of animal and is differentiated from other animals only in degree (of development) and not in kind (of species).

6. On the basis of the biological sciences and the sciences of anthropology, genetics, and sociology, one should understand the historical evolution of living organism and human society, and the causes for such an evolution.

---

[44] *Ibid.*, p. 218.
[45] D. W. Kwok, *Scientism in Chinese Thought 1900-1950,* New Haven, 1965, p. 105.

7. On the basis of the sciences of biology and psychology, one should learn that all psychological phenomena have causes.

8. On the basis of the sciences of biology and sociology one should know that ethics and religion are always in evolution, and that the causes for this evolution can all be located by scientific methods.

9. On the basis of the new knowledge of physics and chemistry, one finds out that matter is not dead, but live, not static, but dynamic.

10. On the basis of knowledge of biology and sociology, one should realize that the individual—the Smaller Self—is susceptible to death, but humanity as a whole—the larger Self—is undying and immortal; that religion, the highest religion, is "to live for the sake of the whole species and posterity," and that those religions which seek heaven and the Pure Land for after death are religions of the most selfish kind. [46]

Not unlike his Marxist opponents, Hu Shih, too, was an iconoclast who fabricated idols. A similar case implies certain inconsistence. But the inconsistence in question is understandable. In the history of philosophy there has been an argument against scepticism. It consists in pointing out the inconsistency of doubting the power of mind with a doubting mind. Taken in the abstract the argument does seem convincing. But, as a matter of fact, no sceptic has ever doubted mind as such with a mind as such. A mind as such does not think. What he objects to is a mind imbued with a certain complex of principles, and what prompts him to object is a mind imbued with another complex of principles. That is why scepticism is usually a symptom of drastic cultural change. In China, it appeared in the fourth century B. C., on the eve of the foundation of the Chinese empire. It reappeared in the third and fourth centuries A. D. after the fall and disintegration of the Han empire. In the May Fourth period scepticism did not come to the fore. Instead it was the fervor of importing Isms and the uncritical acceptance of new faiths that characterized the new intellectuals of the time. But whether it is a case of scepticism, or it is

---

[46] *Ibid.*, pp. 155-156.

a case of dogmaticism, the significance of the phenomenon is the same. It is a sign of the break down of a tradition and of the search for a new faith. Thus, the case of Hu Shih discloses the third problem of development. This has to do with ideology. It calls for a theology of secularization.

* * *

Thus, in reviewing the Chinese case, we have identified three prominent aspects of development that call for theological consideration. They reveal three important effects of development, namely 1° the crisis of traditional morals, 2° the crisis of traditional religion, and 3° the search for a new ideology. Before bringing the matter to the attention of our theologians, we must add two observations. One of them regards the method we have adopted. It must be noted that we have arrived at our conclusions chiefly through reading the intellectual history of modern China. The first two parts of the paper, which deal with the burden of the past and the impact of the West, are meant rather to provide historical background. Even the May Fourth Movement is mentioned mainly as social and political setting. Moreover, our reading of the history is not complete. We have deliberately omitted the chapter that describes the various attempts to re-evaluate and to restore to a certain extent the tradition of ancient China. Knowing as we do the importance of the revival of traditional religions in many parts of Asia and Africa today, we do not fail to recognize here a real lacuna in our exposition. [47] We acknowledge our limitation.

However, despite its obvious shortcomings, the method we have adopted is not only valid but also particularly suitable for our purpose. Indeed, development is a cultural phenomenon. It is as much a product of human activities as a result of socio-economic forces. It may be studied, therefore, either by examining the minds that move the human activities, or by analysing the objective conditions that give rise to the

---

[47] Vittorio Lanternari, *The Religions of the oppressed: A study of Modern Messianic Cults* (A Mentor Book) 1965.

socio-economic forces. We have chosen the first approach. It may be objected that, by doing so, we have committed ourselves to the fancy of some intellectuals. These men might have misjudged the objective conditions or they might have formed a wrong idea of development. The objections would hold if we sought to learn from them what the problems of development are and how they are to be solved. But this is not the purpose of this paper. As we have explained, we seek only to determine those problems of development that call for theological consideration. To us, it does not matter what Ch'en Tu-hsiu or Hu Shih said against "Confucius and Co." The fact that they did so, and in doing so aroused loud echoes from various parts of China is sufficient indication that the traditional morals of China had been brought to a crisis. Similarly, the different opinions concerning the traditional religion and imported Isms are in themselves of little importance to us. Their significance consists solely in disclosing the religious crisis and the search of a new ideology, which had resulted from China's contact with the industrial West. In other words, if we have relied on the intellectuals of the May Fourth period it was not so much because they were critical spectators, but because they were passionate actors in the drama of China's development.

The second observation warns against a common bias. During the May Fourth period some missionaries thought of taking advantage of the corrosion of Chinese society. In their zeal for souls, they did not hesitate to aggravate China's moral and religious crisis by importing a new morality and new religion. Their manoeuvre was simple. They declared; "Chinese morals suppress the rights of individuals; Christianity defends them. Chinese religion encourages superstitions; Christianity condemns them. Chinese religion is a barbarian religion; Christianity is the religion of civilized people." Given the intellectual climate of the time, the argument was readily accepted. Both Ch'en Tu-hsiu and Hu Shih agreed that Christianity is superior to the Chinese religion, though they did not become Christians. The same argument turns up today under a new guise. All non-Christian religions, so it is claimed, are based on revelations that took place in Nature. They supposed a circular notion of time. They are incompatible with the modern scientific view of the world. Christianity alone is based on a revelation that took place in history. It gave rise to the linear notion of time. It is the only religion of the modern "secular city." The argument sounds reassuring. It is tempting. But it supposes a certain bias on the part of those who accept it. Indeed, it takes for granted the opposition between development and religion. It allies Christianity with the stronger party, in this case, development, and dissociates it at once from the family of world religions. Thus it deliberately closes its eyes to the values the latter obviously possess and announces proudly the superiority of Christianity. But if we examine closely the arguments it provides we find them lame. When the missionaries then condemned Chinese religion in favor of Christianity they actually contrasted Chinese realities with Christian ideals. When certain theologians claim modernity exclusively for Christianity, they actually compare pagan religious practices with secularized Christian theology. In the one and the other case, it is a hidden ambiguity that constitutes the secret of their success. Since neither partiality nor confusion is helpful in formulating a sound theology of development, we must take precautions against them.

Thus, we discourage any hasty comparison between Christianity and the Chinese religion. But we invite the reading of the Chinese history in the light of the Christian faith. This means that we intend to confront China's determination for development with God's redemptive purpose. In doing so, we introduce an eschatological dimension into an historical narrative and translate the descriptions of particular events into statements of relevant theological issues. We shall do so point by point.

(1) The crisis of traditional morals: During the May Fourth period the Confucianist morality was called in question. The chief charge against it was the fact that it was particularistic and, consequently, hindered economic development. It is interesting to recall that a similar accusation had been brought against Confucianism by the philosopher Mo Ti (about 479-381 B. C.), and that a refutation had been attempted by the Confucianist Men Ko (about 372-285 B. C.).

234

Though this is a very old case it does throw light on the present question. Therefore, let us dwell a while upon it.

Mo Ti charged Confucianism with particularism because it recommended the practice of differentiated love for one's kin, for one's neighbours, and for all creatures. He preached instead universal love. He based his argument on "self-interest." Thus he stated: "Virtue means self-interest, for one who loves virtue loves all men. He works necessarily to benefit them." [48] The statement is abrupt. To seize its meaning we must complete it with an additional note, namely "if everyone works to benefit others everyone benefits." Men Ko admitted the accusation, but he pleaded not guilty. He explained that a morality, such as the one proposed by Mo Ti, was not practical. It would only foment contention and breed disorder. [49] He contended that virtue did not mean self-interest, but conformity. It is what agrees with the existing social order. Since Chinese society was particularistic, love, too, must be differentiated. He could not imagine a man who did not love his kin as capable of loving his neighbours. He, too, acknowledged the need of loving all men, but he insisted that it must be done in accordance with the moral order. Thus, he stated the law of universal love in terms of particularistic moral principles: "Loving my parents, I love the parents of all other men; loving my children, I love the children of all other men." [50]

Men Ko was a traditionalist. He defended the established order. He held on to the traditional morals, and valued any measures of social reform in the light of such moral principles. Mo Ti, on the other hand, was a revolutionist. He discovered the need of loving all men through observing contemporary events, namely the continual conflict. He adopted the concept of "self-interest" as a rationale of universal love. What he preached was not, properly speaking, a moral precept. It was rather an ideal. It would have become a moral precept if it had exercised such an influence on the Chinese society that it reformed its structure and made

---

[48] Fung Yu-lang, *History of Chinese Philosophy* (translated by Derk Bodde), Princeton, 1952, vol. 1, pp. 84-87.
[49] *Ibid.*, p. 143.
[50] *The I Ching*, vol. 1, p. 287.

the love of any man as normal love of one's kin. Was Men Ko right, or was Mo Ti right, in that particular case of universal love? The answer depended on the possibility of transforming the particularistic society of China into a universalistic one. And the fact is that, till the downfall of imperial China, Chinese society had remained solidly particularistic.

But when a similar case occurred during the May Fourth period the situation of China had changed. Owing to the introduction of Western industrialism the traditional family system began to disintegrate. On the one hand, individuals could no longer depend on their families for the security of their existence. On the other, they could earn their living independently from their kin. Then it was that a more universalitic social order became a real alternative, and Confucianist morals were finally brought to a serious crisis.

Viewed under this aspect, development is a desirable thing. It is true that, in itself, a particularistic moral code is as acceptable as a universalistic one to the Christian faith, which demands the love of all men; for though the latter prompts a definite motivation it does not impose any particular way of realizing it. From the point of view of the Christian faith, as long as we love our neighbours it does not matter whether we love them as heads of their families or as our fellow citizens. Under certain circumstances the former is even preferable. For example, in the traditional society of China, in which the sense of citizenship had not been developed, it may be reasonably supposed that one loved his neighbour as the head of a family. Since he loved the head of his own family, he understood the need of loving the heads of other people's families. In this sense, the love of all men was a part of his moral code. On the contrary, the love of his neighbours as fellow citizens seemed so abstract to him that it made no appeal to his moral conscience. Since we believe that it is better to love one's neighbours in some capacity than not to love them at all, we will not deny to a particularistic morality its positive values. Nor do we hesitate to recognize in the Chinese family system

236

with its particularistic moral code a natural sacrament of supernatural salvation.

However, it is not wise to close our eyes to the short-comings of a moral system when people living under it have shown it their aversion. To say the truth, the allegations made against Confucianism during the May Fourth period were derived more from the abuse than from the observance of the Confucianist moral code. Nevertheless, the abuses in question were by no means accidental. They resulted from the very nature of Confucianist society. Indeed, in Confucianist society one did love his neighbours, but he loved them not as someone of his own kind, but as strangers. He was, therefore, prone to nepotism, an arch-enemy of economic development which demands above all impersonal and rationalized management. Further, in Confucianist society the worth of an individual was measured by his ability to secure the survival of his family and clan. Under such conditions, the position of a woman was weak, and concubinage and infanticide were usually tolerated. Now, it was the merit of Western industrialism to have offered to the Chinese an alternative way of living in which such abuses might be more easily avoided. This was because it introduced a more rationalized mode of production. By doing so, it knocked down the barriers between families within which people in traditional China used to confine their existence. Thus, it gave rise to a more universalistic social order and laid the foundation for a more universalistic morality.

This is how we are led to believe in a Christian significance of development. We see in it a providence of God whose will it is to unite all peoples in Christ. Consequently, we hold that men who work for the development of the underdeveloped nations, work in fact for the kingdom of God. But if our consideration is sensible it raises some difficult questions. These are: 1° What is the relation between the Christian faith and the particular morality of a given society? 2° What is the role of the Christian faith in shaping the structure of a given society and in inspiring it to a more universalistic morality? 3° What is the relation between the Christian faith and so-called Christian morality?

(2) The crisis of traditional religions: The Chinese religion was a diffused religion. It had no dogma, no priesthood, no institutions of its own. It existed in the society of men and was undistinguishable from it. Thus, the emperor of China, being a sovereign of this world, was hailed Son of Heaven. Similarly, the Yin Yang and Five Agents theory, which purported to legitimize his dominion and define his role in the cosmos, revealed at once the Providence of Heaven and made it relevant to the history of the Chinese people. If the Chinese religion is rightly said to be a wordly religion, the Chinese view of the world was essentially religious. Indeed, in traditional China, society and religion were one and the same thing.

Because of the fusion and confusion between society and religion, the collapse of a social order necessarily called forth a religious crisis. This happened in the twelfth century B. C., when king Wu of Chou overthrew the Shang dynasty and substituted a government by a federation of several tribal communities for the former one which was essentially a clan organization. This happened again during the period of " warring states " (5-3 centuries B. C.) that followed the downfall of the Chou order. This happened time after time on several similar occasions. But the case during the May Fourth period was an unique one. We shall examine it under the following three aspects.

As we know, the God of the Chinese is called *T'ien,* meaning Heaven. He is a sky god. In most parts of the world sky gods had long faded away. If Heaven alone had withstood the wear of time he must have possessed a secret. The secret was quite simple. He had adopted a powerful son in the person of the Chinese emperor. It was indeed the stability of the Chinese empire that had kept him alive in the minds of men and active in the affairs of this world. But when imperial China came to an end in 1911 his fate was also doomed. Deprived at last of his usual pedestal, he too lost touch with the earthly existences. Consequently, he came to be ignored by men and pushed out of their world.

238

No sooner had Heaven been put out of their way than the Chinese found faults with the laws he had left. As a matter of fact, these laws had derived properly from the particular structure of an ancient Chinese society. Hence, he was not their author in the strict sense of the word. But he had given them his sanction. He had declared by means of the Yin Yang and Five Agents theory that the three major and six minor relationships in the traditional society of China were the laws of Nature, and that those who violated them would incur his punishments. In doing so, he had, so to speak, compromised his authority with a human institution which is of temporary nature. It is therefore not surprising to learn that during the May Fourth period, when Confucian morals were finally called in question, Heaven too was found wanting both in wisdom and in justice. I have alluded to such slogans as " down with Confucius and co. " and Confucianism is " a man-eating institution. " These slogans were meant, indeed, to protest not only against Confucianism but also against the God of the Confucianists.

However, neither the retirement of God nor the obsolescence of his laws enables us to assess the damage which Western industrialism inflicted upon the traditional religion of China. Neither of them demonstrated the particular nature of the religious crisis under consideration. To realize the gravity of the present case, we must therefore turn to a third aspect, namely the obscurity of the messages of God. Because of its grave importance we shall consider this last aspect at length.

We must first determine the channel or channels through which God speaks to men. Today it is a commonplace to say that God speaks to men either through natural phenomena or through historical events. For example, in the Judeo-Christian traditions, greater emphasis is put on historical events, though natural phenomena were by no means altogether neglected. Even the New Testament mentions an earthquake at the death of Jesus. In the Chinese religion the two channels of information about God are noticeable in two names of God, namely *Ti* and *T'ien*, or God-on-High and Heaven. The meanings of the two words should not bother us here. What is important is to note the fact that they are associated with two religious traditions. In one of them, let us call it *Ti*-tradition, God is said "to come forth in the sign of *chen*," [51] *Chen*, meaning arousing, stands for thunder. [52] But the thunder in question is spring thunder, for it is explicitly stated:

> Thunder brings success.
> Thunder comes — oh, oh
> Laughing words — ha, ha
> Thunder terrifies for a hundred miles,
> And he does not let fall the sacrificial spoon and chalice.[53]

The last verse hints at the spring sacrifices to one's ancestors and to the Spirit of Soil. A hymn bearing the title "the coming of God-on-High" and sung on the occasion of the suburban sacrifice in spring suggests the same interpretation. Here indeed God-on-High is praised as the Spirit of Spring:

> As the spring bursts forth,
> It stirs the roots of plants.
> Its unction extends to all,
> Touching even insects and worms.

> For as the spring thunder sounds,
> Plants regain their vigour;
> Torpid insects lend their ears.
> And nature thus revived
> Goes on to fulfil its fate.

> Everyone is now happy
> Even children and babies.
> All living beings enjoy themselves,
> Thanks to the benediction of spring. [54]

In brief, according to the *Ti*-tradition, God reveals himself in Nature which renews itself periodically in spring. This is indeed the belief that underlies the Chinese ancestral worship as well as the Taoist mysticism.

---

[51] *Ibid.*, p. 286.
[52] *Ibid.*, p. 210.
[53] *Ibid.*, vol. 2, p. 297.
[54] *Numen*, 16 (1969), p. 113.

In the other tradition God is named *T'ien*. *T'ien*, meaning Heaven, manifests himself also in a natural phenomenon. Thus, *Hao-T'ien*, sky free from cloud, indicates that God is luminous, and *Min-T'ien*, sky covered with cloud, signifies that God is either merciful or just. Cloud, indeed, refers to both rain and thunderbolt. [55] But, as suggested by the two epithets, Heaven is endowed with moral qualities. He is apt to preside over human society. He is expected to interfere in the business of men. Unlike God-on-High, who comes forth in the sign of arousing and, consequently, is honored as the lord of Nature, Heaven is represented above all as the lord of men and of history.

This means that, according to the *T'ien*-tradition, God speaks to men not only through natural phenomena but also through historical events. Men Ko, the great Confucian philosopher, attested this belief in a twofold consideration. On the one hand, he declared:

> Heaven sees according as my people see;
> Heaven hears according as my people hear. [56]

On the other hand, he contended that practically it was from his people that a prince learned to know the will of God. In the one way as the other he took human beings to be media of communication between God and men. [57] The same belief was professed by the Yin Yang and Five Agents school under the statement "*T'ien-jen ho-i.*" I have interpreted the statement as follows: "perfect correspondence between what happens in Nature and what happens to men." But the literal translation must be this: "union or communion between *T'ien* and *jen.*" Here *T'ien* stands for both Heaven and Nature; *jen* for both men and culture. The expression makes sense only if one accepts the supposition that culture, consequently history, is—as Nature also— a channel of information about God.

---

[55] Bruno Schindler, *The Development of the Chinese Conception of Supreme Beings,* (Hirth Anniversary volume, Asia Major: Introductory volume), pp. 299-300 note.

[56] *The Chinese Classics.* vol. 2, p. 357.

[57] *Ibid.,* p. 166.

Thus, in traditional China, Heaven was believed not only to guarantee the dynastic succession and to secure the moral order, but also to stand in constant touch with the life of the Chinese. The numerous religious crises which took place in the course of her long history led generally to the metamorphosis of Chinese religion though not to its death. But the latest case was unique. Then, indeed, under the impact of "science" and "democracy" Nature came to be disenchanted also before the eyes of the Chinese. Society too was secularized at last. As a result, both natural phenomena and historical events lost their luminosity. They turned opaque and impervious to the message of God. This time the Chinese religion is not likely to evade its death.

The above consideration raises in our mind two questions, one as to the place of Chinese religion in the history of salvation and the other as to the role of development in the evangelization of China. These are theological questions. They are to be left to the theologians to answer. However, I venture to offer the following suggestions. Concerning the first question two points seem to be established: 1° The Chinese religion is a provisional institution. It has existed. It is coming to the end of its existence. 2° The Chinese religion has been a providential means for the salvation of the Chinese. It has been a "pedagogue," a slave who guided the son of his master on his way to salvation. Concerning the second question two further points may be proposed for discussion: 3° Development opens the Chinese society to pluralism, thus making possible the preaching of the Gospel. 4° Development delivers the Chinese from the dominion of the "elements" of the world which, while revealing to them the divine message, still kept it in captivity.

However, we must temper immediately our optimism. Despite its positive value, development does not lead automatically to christianization. A stumbling-block stands on its way, and it has been the lot of China to have stumbled upon it.

(3) The search for an ideology! The stumbling-block is ideology, for which the Chinese seem to have had a weakness. Not only did they invent the theory of the Mandate of Heaven, but they added to it the principle of "perfect

correspondence between what happens in nature and what happens to men. " They seem to be unable to free themselves from the idea of the *Tao* which they believed to be that highest principle which is at once the object of perfect knowledge and the norm of practical action. Indeed, if one reads through the dynastic histories of China he will find hardly any contenders for the throne who did not claim the exclusive possession of the *Tao*. Given such a weakness, it is not surprising to learn that as soon as the tradition had declined, a frenzied enthusiasm for foreign Isms broke out in China. It is true that the turmoil soon quieted down, but the ground was prepared for the Communists to seed and reap their harvest.

The story of the success of Communist ideology is in itself a worthy object of consideration. First of all, two facts are worth noting. Li Ta-chao (1888-1927), who formed the first Marxist study groups in Pekin in 1918 and found the Chinese Communist Party in 1921, declared his conversion to Communism in 1920 in an article entitled " The Value of Historical Materialism in Modern Historical Science. "[58] And the first sign of Marxist influence in the Chinese literature is the controversy on the history of the evolution of Chinese society.[59] These are significant facts. They reveal the secret of Communist appeal to an underdeveloped nation. Indeed, in China as in other parts of the world, poverty has never been a virtue. Rather it is seen as a sign of inferiority not only in economic condition but also in intellectual and physical capacity. Often it is taken as a proof of lack of virtue. Thus, at one time, the Chinese intellectuals did not hesitate to accept " Darwinism" and to take seriously underdevelopment as evidence of the inferiority of the Chinese race with regard to the Western peoples. Lu Hsün (1881-1936), who had studied some medicine in Japan, was the most ardent but ironical proponent of this view.[60] Whatever truth there is in this

---

[58] Benjamin I. Schwartz, *op. cit.*, p. 24.

[59] Kuo Chan-po, *Chin wu-shih-nien Chung-kuo ssu-hsiang-shih* (An intellectual History of China in the Last Fifty Years, Jen-wen shu-tien, Peiping, 1935), pp. 332-346.

[60] C. T. Hsia, *A History of Modern Chinese Ficion 1915-1957*, New York, 1961, pp. 37-38.

interpretation it is certainly not a pleasant one to the Chinese. Now Communism provides another version. Basing itself on historical materialism, it rejects any opinion that encourages fatalism. It argues therefore that since it is men, not nature, that determine the course of history, the cause of China's underdevelopment must not be sought in the inferiority of the Chinese race, but in the imperfection of the Chinese society. The advantage of the latter explanation is obvious. Apart from heightening the spirits of the Chinese, it rouses them to work positively for the future of the nation.

But, if Communism appealed to some Chinese intellectuals through historical materialism, to the mass of the people it was the Leninist theory of imperialism that was most tempting. This is easily understandable. On the one hand, the Leninist theory is rather simple. It supposes a naïve view according to which the world is divided into two fronts. " On the one side was the concert of Capitalist-imperialist power. On the other, the Soviet State of workers and peasants, which represented the interest of the toilers as well as all the oppressed nations and colonies." [61]   On the other hand, the Chinese had at least some reasons for believing in this theory. While the Allies acted in concert at Versailles in support of Japanese imperialism the newly founded Soviet Union placed itself squarely on the side of China in its Karakhan proposal, in which it renounced " all territory obtained through aggressive means by the former Russian imperial government in China " and " all special privileges formerly obtained by Russia in China. " [62]   The effect of the Leninist propaganda was very visible in the literature of the latter part of the Mary Fourth period. A novel of Mao Tun (1896-), *The Twilight,* was a case to the point. The novel, written in 1933, was a piece of naturalistic fiction, purporting to be a chronicle of contemporary China. The hero of the novel was called Wu Sun-fu. He was a powerful industrialist with a strong faith in national capitalism. But in spite of his intelligence and diligence he

---

[61] Benjamin I. Schwartz, *op. cit.,* p. 21.
[62] *Ibid.,* p. 215, note 44.

244

went bankrupt, beaten in a speculation on the stock market by Chao Po-t'ao, a sensualist, and financier amply backed by foreign capital. C. T. Hsia, the author of A History of Modern Chinese Fiction, assesses the character of Wu and appraises its meaning in the following terms:

> On one level, Wu is the conventional tragic hero defeated by overpowering fate or circumstance, a familiar figure in the naturalistic fiction of Zola, Norris, and Dreiser. But on another level, as a man fired with the zeal to industrialize China by use of native capital, Wu is a pathetic, blind Oedipus, unredeemed even after his decline and fall because he has never heard or heeded the Marxian oracle. His personal tragedy is embedded in his larger failure to perceive certain historical forces, whose eventual assertion alone is the guarantee of China's salvation. Insofar as rampant feudalism and imperialism foredoom any attempt to develop national capital, Wu's grandiose gesture is utterly futile in his unawareness of the necessity for a complete overhaul of Chinese economy and politics. [63]

In brief, if historical materialism provides China with an expedient explanation of its underdevelopment, the Leninist theory of imperialism lends it a convenient excuse for the slowness of its development.

Recent events in China reveal a third advantage of Communist ideology with respect to the development of an underdeveloped nation. To illustrate this point, let us quote some passages from a publication of the liberation army which tells the edifying story of "president Mao's good combatant," named Wang Chieh. The passages in questions are headed by the title: "A Letter from his Fiancée".

> No sooner had the small group of soldiers arrived at the appointed place than Wang Chieh received a letter from his fiancée, who reminded him of his adult age and urged him to leave the army to marry her. His sister too wrote to him, insisting on the same demand and adding the reason that after his marriage their sick mother would have some one to tend her.

---

[63] C. T. Hsia, op. cit., p. 157.

At first, Wang Chieh had some hesitation. But soon he realized that he had been selfish. He said to himself: How can I convince my fiancée and my folks, if I myself do not free my mind of such personal calculations. Thereupon, he set about studiing the articles "The Role of the Chinese Communist Party in the Wars of National Independence" and "On the virtue of a Communist Party Member," until he came to a better understanding that, whatever the circumstances were, a Communist never puts his personal interests above other things. He believed that though he was not a Communist Party Member he ought to act like one all the same. Then, he exhorted himself: Today, the imperialists are still conducting aggressive wars against Vietnam; how can I, a revolutionary combatant, lay down my arms and go back home? Having thus cleared his mind of impure thoughts he began to write to his fiancée and his folks. He instructed them on the actual situation of the world. He explained to them the disposition of the government concerning late marriage. He bade his fiancée to spare her youth and to spend it fruitfully on reforming her thought, on working, and on studying. In the same letter, he told his fiancée the progressive deeds of a certain Kung Chiung-chien who had insisted on postponing his marriage for eight years in order to improve the lot of backward villages.

Two months later, his fiancée came. She stayed for two days. Then she went away. The incident piqued his camarades: What had happened? They asked among themselves. Was it some conflict on the matter of marriage? This was unlikely, for she went away apparently in high spirits. The explanation is that, with the help of Wang Chieh, the fiancée had made rapid progress. Not only had she consented to late marriage, but she had come to consult him about a generous decision. She was prepared to leave her home province, Shantung, for inner Mongolia where his family lived. There she would take care of his sick mother and younger sisters and brothers. Meantime she would dedicate herself to work for the development of that region. [64]

[64] *Wang Chieh ti ku-shih* (The Story of Wang Chieh, Peking, 1965), pp. 62-63.

An ideology is not a religion. It is rather an ersatz of religion. In this capacity, an ideology shares with a genuine faith two important characteristics . Both transcend experimental knowledge. Both appeal to feeling. Because of these common qualities both ideology and religion have the power to induce men to ignore their present sufferings and to venture on ambitious tasks. Ideology, as well as religion, inspires, therefore, sacrifice and heroism. In the story of Wang Chieh and his fiancée we have learned indeed how, like Protestantism, the Communist ideology can serve the cause of development.

Yet, despite its obvious advantages, the Communist ideology harms in fact the cause of development, for it frustrates the fruit of development. Development, we have said, has the effect of broadening the community in which we live. It knocks down gradually the barriers between families and families, nations and nations, races and races. It accustoms us to see in other men our fellow men, no longer members of rival families, of rival nations, and of rival races. It leads us to humanism, of which the Church should be an eminent sign. Communism divides, instead, society into two classes and the world into two fronts. It ignores individual men, seeing in them only representatives of their respective classes. Communism resists therefore the will of God who wants to unite all men in Christ. Again, development has the effect of introducing tolerance and pluralism in society and of delivering men from the captivity of the elements of the world. Communism imposes, instead, " the dictatorship of the people, " arresting thus the providential growth of the moral and religious conscience of mankind.

To meet the challenge of ideology and to avert the obstacles it sets to the realization of God's saving plan, a theology of development is urgently needed. Though it is the office of theologians to propose such a theology, I venture to offer some suggestions. These may be stated in the following three points: 1° Without doing injustice to the moral and religious systems of a traditional society, a theology of development should bring into light the function of development in fostering the growth of the moral and religious conscience of the society concerned. 2° Without diminishing in any way the mission of the Church in evangelizing all people, a theology of development should foster genuine humanism, discouraging discrimination of any kind. 3° Without minimizing the intrinsic values of the earthly reality, a theology of development should establish the meaning of evangelical perfection, putting thus in proper perspective the problems of development within the framework of the meditation on the history of salvation.

PAOLO TUFARI, s. j.

THE CHURCH BETWEEN IDEOLOGY AND UTOPIA

Several fluid situations with contradictory trends characterize the present moment in the life of the Church. The endeavour to produce a Christian vision of that complex phenomenon generally known as social development is one of these. This effort has given rise to a vast literature encompassing papal encyclicals, conciliar statements, papers prepared by « experts » for episcopal conferences and interfaith meetings. In addition there are the manifestos of innumerable spontaneous groups. To top it all there is a growing tide of published essays, all seeking to define new tasks for Christians in the light of biblical precepts applied to economic data.

To gather such widely varying material under the common heading of "theology of development" is undoubtedly a gross oversimplification. But it is not altogether arbitrary since the whole is unified by a basic thread. For common to all this writing is the concern to elaborate in a Christian perspective a doctrine capable of inspiring that social action which is needed if the poor nations of the world are ever to surmount their present state of deprivation.

The fact of this common concern does more than justify gathering the disparate products of this effort under the single label of theology of development. It also makes meaningful the disparity itself, by demonstrating that theology of development, far from being the product of any one particular group (much less the brainchild of a single thinker) is the product of different currents of thought, and in this only shares in that plurality of theologies that characterizes the historical moment of the Church's life. [1]

By "Church" we here mean the collectivity of Christian denominations. For, the emergence of theology of development as a movement is not confined to any single one of them. We do not hereby imply that this theology represents the actual beliefs and aspirations of all individual members. The point is rather that this theology presents itself as interpreter of beliefs and aspirations which *should* animate all believers in the Church of Christ. In this sense theology of development is not simply a movement *in* but *of* the Church. Some, it should be noted in passing, reject the designation of "theology" for a doctrine which in their view is nothing more than philosophical anthropology that derives from values prevailing in the cultural tradition of western Christianity.

Theology of development gives rise to both *normative and positive questions*.

The normative questions concern the legitimacy, either of a particular interpretation or of the general claim to interpret social problems in the name of religious beliefs.

When the point at issue is a particular "theological" view, then the legitimacy of such a derivation of view will depend on the one hand on one's use of Christian sources, and on the other on one's capacity to grasp the social problem which is to be given an interpretation in the light of faith.

Today this normative question concerns less the validity of any particular interpretation and much more the right of any religious institution to issue pronouncements on matters that are secular and subject to opinion. Once the question is posed this way, we move beyond requirements of proper hermeneutics and adequate social knowledge to a still more fundamental question in the movement of theology of development, that is whether the Church should pronounce on the meaning and function of human institutions. [2]

---

[1] The bibliography at the end of this volume — an abridged version of a much more extended list of titles to the published in another form — constitutes a significant indicator of the growing attention paid to the subject.

[2] For a recent discussion of this cf. André Manaranche,

Whatever views one may have about this last question, we shall set it apart. For, in fact, a theology of development is something which exists and seeks to make human institutions develop in the best way possible. Accordingly we can suspend judgment on its legitimacy.

This ἐποχή permits that we move beyond the normative to study theology of development positively, that is, in the same way as any other cultural phenomenon whose proximate origin and historical consequences are empirically observable. This shift concerns only the method of approaching our object and not the object itself. The reason is that even from an empirical point of view, *theology of development is understood as a normative system designed to exert positive influence on the existing social order.* This theology is a "fact" — something which exists and operates; but it is also in process and unfinished since it provides presently only an ideal anticipation of the future and therefore does not necessarily portray what the true course of events must look like. [3]

Ideology and Utopia Contrasted

Theology of development (to pursue our positive approach) should be listed among those "unreal ideas" in which "the order of life is enmeshed" according to Mannheim's classical approach to Ideology and Utopia. He argues:

Y-a-t-il une éthique sociale chrétienne?, Paris: Seuil, 1969. The author maintains his own thesis, but is quite accurate in expounding others' point of view, including those that deny to the Church the very capability of arriving at an unbiased comprehension of social phenomena.

[3] This chapter focuses on the effort to give a theological meaning to the process of human development. The same phenomenon could be considered from the point of view of the impact which contemporary social problems may have on the *development of theology.* Needless to say, the two points of view are logically complementary and historically interdependent. It is only for a question of method that we keep them separate, setting apart the problems concerning the development of theology. Cf. *supra* the article of Alszeghy-Flick, esp. iv. "Contingent data in the theology of development" (pp. 116-118).

"For the sociologist, « existence » is that which is « concretely effective », i.e. a functioning social order, which does not exist only in the imagination of certain individuals but according to which people really act. [...] But every « actually operating » order of life is at the same time enmeshed by conceptions which are to be designated as « transcendent » or « unreal », because their contents can never be realized in the societies in which they exist, and because one could not live and act according to them within the limits of the existing social order. In a word, all those ideas which do not fit into the current order are « situationally transcendent » or unreal". [4]

To speak of a doctrine as *unreal* is not disparaging, at least in the present context. Rather, the qualification points only to those tensions which emerge in society owing to the gap between a real situation and its ideal representation. In point of fact, social institutions and civilizations themselves continue to evolve wherever men are aware of the inconsistency between fact and principle, the experienced and the desirable, between φύσις and νόμος. [5] From this point

---

[4] Karl Mannheim, *Ideologie und Utopie*, Bonn, 1929. Engl. transl., *Ideology and Utopia. An Introduction to the Sociology of Knowledge*, New York: Harcourt, 1955, pp. 194-195.

[5] Anthropologists see in the incest-taboo the very first cultural expression of mankind: cf. Claude Lévi-Strauss, *Les structures élémentaires de la parenté*, Paris: Mouton, 1967, ch. I, "Nature et culture" (pp. 3-13). A full awareness of the opposition emerges among the Greeks: cf. Mario Untersteiner, *I Sofisti*, Torino: Einaudi, 1949, ch. 11 « Prodico. Storia dell'umanità: da 'physis' a 'nomos'. Conquista dell'etica e della civiltà" (pp. 252-273). On the psychological mechanisms and cultural consequences of human dissatisfaction see Freud's enlightening essay *Das Unbehagen in der Kultur*, Wien: Internationaler Psychoanalytischer Verlag. 1930. "It is said that each one of us behaves in some respect like the paranoic, substituting a wish-fulfilment for some aspect of the world which is unbearable to him, and carrying this delusion through into reality. When a large number of people make this attempt together and try to obtain assurance of happiness and protection from suffering by a delusional transformation of reality it acquires special significance. The religions of humanity, too, must be classified as mass-delusions of this kind. Needless to say, no one who shares a delusion recognizes it as

of view, the theology of development can be considered a particular instance of the general process whereby knowledge and human organizations grow through mutual interaction. Actually, the occasion, if not the reason, for the emergence of this theological movement is to be found in a growing awareness that Christian ideals were not as compatible with social reality as they should and could be. Hence, the renewed efforts to induce men to live up to ideals that transcend "the actually operating order of life."

A doctrine, unreal in this sense, falls between what might be called pure aesthetics and rational social planning, possessing something of both, yet realizing neither in full. As a matter of fact, it may be questioned whether any system of thought, including scientific, manages to keep free of this polarity. [6]

Hence it is necessary to sharpen our understanding of the distinction between ideology and utopia. According to Mannheim:

"Ideas which correspond to the concretely existing and *de facto* order are designated as « adequate » and situationally congruous. These are relatively rare and only

---

such." (engl. transl., *Civilization and Its Discontents,* London: Hogarth Press, 1957, p. 36). Freud seems concerned less with the *origin* and more with the *consequences* of cultural evolution. See his conclusive paragraph: "The fateful question of the human species seems to me whether and to what extent the cultural process developed in it will succeed in mastering the derangements of communal life caused by the human instinct of aggression and self-destruction. In this connection, perhaps the phase through which we are at this moment passing deserves special interest. Men have brought their powers of subduing the forces of nature to such a pitch that by using them they could now very easily exterminate one another to the last man. They know this — hence arises a great part of their current unrest, their dejection, their mood of apprehension. And now it may be expected that the other of the two 'heavenly forces,' eternal Eros, will put forth his strength so as to maintain himself alongside of his equally immortal adversary." (*ib.,* p. 143-144; note that the essay was published in 1930).

[6] See "Ages of Utopia," "Freedom and Predicability," "Intuitive Forecasting by Experts." "Inventing the Future," in François Hetman, *The Language of Forecasting,* Paris: SEDEIS, 1969.

a state of mind that has been sociologically fully clarified operates with situationally congruous ideas and motives. Contrasted with situationally congruous ideas and adequate ideas are the two main categories of ideas which transcend the situation — ideologies and utopias.

Ideologies are the situationally transcendent ideas which never succeed *de facto* in the realization of their projected contents. [...]

Utopias, too, transcend the social situation, for they too orient conduct towards elements which the situation, in so far as it is realized at the time, does not contain. But they are not ideologies, i.e. they are not ideologies in the measure and in so far as they succeed through counteractivity in transforming the existing historical reality into one more in accord with their own conceptions." [7]

One might take exception to the coherence of Mannheim's definition or to the correspondence between words defining and things defined. Nor would materials for a discussion of the kind be wanting, seeing that the terms have received a remarkable variety of meanings and applications, beginning with More's *Utopia* (1515) and Marx-Engels' *Deutsche Ideologie* (1846). [8]

The discussion, historical and linguistic, that surrounds this topic we here set aside. Mannheim was quoted only to serve as point of reference for a methodological discussion

---

[7] Mannheim, *cit.*, pp. 195-196.

[8] The literature on the subject is immense, all the more so as the topic lies at the intersection of several disciplines, such as history, literary criticism, political and social sciences, cultural anthropology, clinical psychology. For a first orientation in the field of sociology, cf. Norman Birnbaum, *The Sociological Study of Ideology, 1940-1960*, Oxford: Blackwell, 1962; *Bibliographie de la sociologie de la connaissance*, in *Cahiers Internat. de Sociologie*, XXXII (1962), 135-176. Manuel, Frank E. (Ed.), *Utopias and Utopian Thought*, Boston: Houghton Mifflin, 1966; Apter, David E. (Ed.), *Ideology and Discontent*, New York: Free Press, 1964; Servier, Jean, *Histoire de l'utopie*, Paris: Gallimard, 1967. For a more direct reference to religious problems and the Church cf. the "Documentation" on *Utopia* in *Concilium* [engl. ed.], I. 5 (1969), 74-81.

of how to study that cultural phenomenon which is theology of development.

Mannheim's alternatives — to succeed or to fail in transforming historical reality — as a criterion for distinguishing between utopia and ideology is so altogether neat that it seems to provide an unexceptionable criterion. In fact, his poles mask ambiguities in the very concept of "transforming society", let alone the technical difficulty of determining how and to what extent "the existing historical reality" has in fact been transformed.

Does the criterion refer to changes actually realized or to the subjective intention of realizing them? This is not altogether clear. Certain terms like existence, social order, ideas, goals and purposes often overlap — and there is always the additional problem of whose they are; those of the leaders in the promotion of a certain conception of life, or of the followers or of both.

To illustrate from Mannheim:

> "The term utopian, as here used, may be applied to any process of thought which receives its impetus, not from the direct force of *social reality,* but from concepts such as *symbols,* fantasies, dreams, *ideas* and the like; which in the most comprehensive sense of that term are non-existent. Viewed from the standpoint of sociology, such mental constructs may in general assume two forms: they are 'ideological' if they serve the *purpose* of glossing over or stabilizing the existing social reality; 'utopian' if they *inspire* collective activity which aims to change such *reality* to conform with their *goals,* which transcend reality." [9]

In reality, it is difficult to disentangle the subjective from the objective components of social interaction; in point of fact, full understanding of any process of change requires that account be taken of the intentions of those who participate in that process as well as of the actual consequences of their participation. But from a methodological point of

[9] Karl Mannheim, *Utopia,* in E.R.A. Seligman (Ed.), *Encyclopedia of the Social Sciences,* New York: MacMillan, 1935, vol. XV, p. 201 (italics supplied).

255

view, it is preferable to keep these aspects distinct. We shall therefore treat separately the will to transform existing reality, and the capacity of realizing the proposed transformations.

The Will to Transform Reality

Is theology of development truly utopian, or is it "ideological", that is serving "the purpose of glossing over or stabilizing the existing social reality?" Those writing theologically about human progress declare their intention of setting in motion processes of innovation that may go so far as to embrace the so-called revolutionary hypothesis.

But verbal declarations, as everyone knows, sometimes conceal (and scarcely ever reveal) one's full intention. Hence arises the need of considering *implicit assumptions* lying beyond the formal declarations. Implicit assumptions may be defined as feelings, needs, convictions and aspirations which, while not entering formally into programmatic declarations, actually influence both their theoretical formulation and the procedures for accomplishing them. [10]

What is at issue is not the disclosure of unconscious motives or secret reasons of particular persons. For our approach is neither ethical nor psychoanalytical. In what follows, we draw attention to certain *general conditions of life which presumably affect the type of people who appear to be most active in promoting theology of development.*

Take first the social status of these. Is it reasonable to expect that there will be an effective will "to transform

---

[10] Many theories of human behaviour rest on a two-level approach. These range from the classical opposition between infra- and overstructure, conscious and unconscious, drives and rationalizations to the more recent analyses of implicit-explicit culture in anthropology (Kluckhohn) or occupations versus preoccupations in group psychotherapy (Foulkes, Bion). In sociology, special attention has been paid to the distinction and interdependence of rational versus non-logical action, beginning with Pareto's theory on residues and derivations. Cf. Firmin Oulés, "Applications, limites et enseignements de la théorie des 'residus' et des 'dérivations' dans le monde d'aujourd'hui" *Cahiers Vilfredo Pareto*, 5 (1965) pp. 269-316.

the existing order of life" on the part of people who have as a rule achieved their professional competence within a well-established cultural tradition; who speak in the name of an officially recognized institution — the Church; and who may hold prestigious posts in organizations requiring financial support for their activities whether national or international? Can this transforming be hoped for from people whose profession and programs are, if not dependent on, certainly facilitated by the continued functioning of the very structures which must, according to their verbal declarations, be transformed if a new and more equitable social order is to be realized?

Our question should not surprise. It is only an application of that more general sociological problem of whether a substantial process of change can ever be initiated within a system, by its very representatives, where "system" signifies allocation of economic resources, hierarchy of power and theoretical legitimation of both. [11]

---

[11] One thing is to adapt an institution to new historical circumstances, another is to adopt a critical attitude with regard to the very principles which supposedly legitimatize the very existence of that institution. In the first case, reforms are encouraged to maintain the system functioning while in the other people are called to reform their belief in the function of the system as such. The latter seems possible only when people see undermined the economic basis of everyday existence along with the disruption of the normal criteria of one's social identification. All this implies a kind of basic "conversion" on a large scale and consequently the emergence of a new "spirit" under the impact of a new powerful myth. In this perspective one understands that most movements developed within the Church constitute an effort of adaptation rather than of radical innovation. In any case efforts like these are due for the most part to groups and people not connected with the established hierarchy. Cf. G. B. Ladner, *The Idea of Reform. Its Impact on Christian Thought and Action in the Age of the Fathers,* Cambridge, Mass.: Harvard University Press, 1959. As to the difficulty of seeing a substantial process of change initiated by the very representatives of the system, recall that in the Catholic Church the ascent to leading positions — whether administrative or cultural — depends largely on a nomination from above. As in any system based on co-optation, the newly co-opted members tend to be those who offer the greatest guarantee of adherence to the norms and goals of the establishment. As a

Next we raise a question that emerges from the historical circumstances in which theology of development has taken shape. The "verbal declaration" would have it that this theological movement stems from the Church's awareness that she can and must take a stand in support of the masses striving to attain the benefits which thus far only the few have gained through cultural, social and welfare organization. The fact of critical disparity of income between poor lands and rich lands is everywhere recognized. The Church's concern over this disparity can surely not be denied. At the same time, it is also a fact that the Church finds herself growingly estranged from the world of cultural and social organization which seeks to humanize life. For this reason surveys are multiplied to search out a more meaningful role for priests in a secularized society, while other artistic and anthropological enquiries seek to make old rites more meaningful for modern man.

Theology of development has grown up in association with these factors. Is the association merely casual, or is it also to some extent causal? Some will inevitably be inclined to presume that (at the level of implicit assumptions) the theological endeavor is intended not only to help men overcome alienation from the benefits of culture but also to help the Church surmount her own cultural alienation from men. Support for this hypothesis is found in the introduction into the vocabulary of this theology of words and expressions already made fashionable in certain philosophical circles and political movements. Consider, for instance, the search for appealing titles and new designations, with the result that to an already inflated list of "theologies" that include those of "leisure" and of "urban behavior," of "technocratic structures" and "human transplants," of "tourism" and of "sex," we now add "theology" of liberation, of revolution, of violence. These are just few examples drawn from a picturesque list of titles published by catholic theological reviews in the last two years. One could take exception to the very idea

---

result, the hierarchy reproduces rather than reform its body, the newly appointed members being made *ad imaginem et similitudinem* of those who need replacement.

of theologizing about the most disparate aspects of human existence. But apart from this normative question, the point here is that the very choice of words and topics seems to make plausible the hypothesis that theology of development seeks to make itself interesting to a society which in different ways shows no interest in Churchly pronouncements. [12] Surely, the hint is slight, but the hypothesis is worth of being tested, since it is intimately connected with the basic query as to whether theology of development really intends to transform the existing order or is rather an ideology meant "to serve the purpose of glossing over or stabilizing the existing social reality." Should such a hypothesis be confirmed, then theology of development could be rightly considered a particular instance of that process by which *well established institutions tend to transform the symbols of their presence according to changing circumstances in order to preserve unchanged their acquired ascendancy.*

An analysis of these two conditions — social status

---

[12] Once the possibility in accepted of having a theology of something pertaining to the realm of social experience, the door is opened to theologies of everything, seeing that there are indefinite ways of defining objects and areas of empirical knowledge. See R. Aron, *Introduction à la philosophie de l'histoire*, Paris: Gallimard, 1948 [engl. transl., *Philosophy of History*, Boston: Beacon Press, 1961], esp. sect. II, part 2 "Intellectual Universes and the Plurality of Systems of Interpretation — The Dissolution of the Object;" P. L. Berger and T. Luckmann, *The Social Construction of Reality*, Garden City, N. Y.: Doubleday, 1966, esp. ch. III on the process of restructuring reality. Recall Max Weber's discussion on the assumed neutrality of the social sciences, especially as regards the *wertbeziehung* whereby the subject delimits the knowable reality according to his values, interests and existential condition. Note the analogy between the process of selection and emphasis in social knowledge, and the mechanisms of ego-defense described by Anna Freud when she points out the subject's tendency to remove and/or isolate in his consciousness those informations which affect the very roots of self-identity. On the connection between the emergence of new historical circumstances and the development of Church doctrine see K. v. Bismark - W. Dirks, *Christlicher Glaube und Ideologie*, Stuttgart-Mainz, 1964; R. L. Camp. *The Papal Ideology of Social Reform. A Study in Historical Development - 1878-1967*, Leiden: Brill, 1969.

and historical context — might on rigorous inquiry reveal a certain inconsistency between verbal declarations and implicit assumptions in the case of theology of development. Apriori, this cannot be excluded. What, however, can be excluded apriori, and must, is the assumption that such inconsistency is always a sign of illicit motivation or of vested interests. For it remains altogether possible that people, while influenced by their existential conditions, choose nevertheless to work for values of their faith rather than for their private interests. To deny this possibility is to fall into a social determinism as dogmatic as it is pseudo-scientific.

Let it be recognized, then, that among promoters of theology of development it is possible to find a basic ideological orientation (at the level of implicit assumptions) together with typically utopian traits (insofar as regards consciously-pursued goals). How people manage to operate effectively when they are caught in such inconsistency between immediate self-interests and fundamental religious values is another matter. [13] Still, perhaps we can count as one utopian trait of theology of development this conscious determination to pursue goals and ideals under conditions that many consider either impossible or unacceptable.

---

[13] Much has been written about social constraints on human knowledge and motivations, beginning with Bacon's *idola* or Halbwach's *cadres sociaux de la mémoire,* up to the most recent developments of the so-called *stimulus-response* theory in social psychology. Relatively less attention has been paid to man's capability of developing a value-orientation of his own, functionally autonomous as regards his social origin and primary drives. Cf. Martin Scheerer, "Cognitive Theory," in G. Lindzey (Ed.), *Handbook of Social Psychology,* Cambridge, Mass.: Addison-Wesley, 1954, I, pp. 91-137 [esp. pp. 118-123]. The two aspects are inter-dependent, but not in the least identical, as emerges from Leon Festinger's studies on *cognitive dissonance* [*Conflict, Decision, and Dissonance,* Stanford, Calif.: Stanford Univ. Press, 1964] as well as from contemporary researches in the area of *creative behavior.* Cf. R. Mooney and T. Razik (Eds.), *Explorations in Creativity,* New York: Harper & Row, 1967; J. W. Jr., "Social Psychological Characteristics of Innovators" in *Amer. Sociolog. Review,* 34 (1969), 73-82. As to the relations between group creativity and condition of anomie, see F. Perroux, "Aliénation et création collective," in *Cahiers de l'Institut de Science Économique Appliquée,* 20 (1964), 5-108.

The Capacity to Transform Reality

For theology to qualify as utopian, besides the proclamation of its message, it must possess the objective capacity to "transform *de facto* the existing reality into one more in accord with its own conceptions."

The principle is clear, but in fact raises difficult problems concerning the analysis of social causality. In our case the question appears even more intricate, because the phenomenon under consideration affects people in widely different cultural contexts, let alone the fact that the whole process is still developing. We must, accordingly, limit ourselves to altogether tentative considerations about implications of present efforts to "orient conduct towards elements which the situation, insofar as it is realized at the time, does not contain."

In the first place, the power of a utopia lies less in the intrinsic reason the message contains than in the feeling of commitment that the message is capable of arousing. To transform reality the utopian message must "orient conduct" in a way that evokes both ethos and pathos so as to provoke action on the part of the many to the benefit of all.

Has theology of development such power of evocation and provocation? One is prone to doubt it, considering the abstractness of certain theological papers; consider in addition those carefully balanced official pronouncements which speak about the urgent need for courageous action without conveying either a sense of urgency or courage to act. In view of these considerations, the doubt appears reasonable, but surely more empirical study is needed before we transform our plausible hypothesis into a definite assertion.

At any rate this is nor the only nor is it the most relevant way of considering the question. In fact, one must always bear in mind that no judgment is valid that considers only results without weighing costs. The heart of the matter, therefore, concerns not so much the capacity of achieving certain effects as the hazards involved in such an achievement.

Let us consider one case in particular, namely, the risk that theology of development may arrive at stressing its own thesis at the cost of other Christian values and alternative

261

orientations. The risk does not seem merely hypothetical. In point of fact, one cannot escape the impression that writings on theology of development tend to ignore or at least to play down a number of relevant aspects which do not fit into the simplified scheme of a Church deeply concerned with social progress in the present world. A scheme like this makes difficult the insertion of certain aspects which are typical and proper to the Christian calling. By way of illustration, let us mention: renunciation of visible goods in favor of hope in the world to come; the call to a contemplative style of life alien to any utilitarian view of time, nature and knowledge; the supreme importance of the individual as individual, attainable only through the personal bonds of long-lived friendship.[14] In a word, all that is ultimate rather than instrumental, understandable but not explainable, supremely important and yet not directly useful; in St. Thomas' terms, the act of *frui* over and above the actions of *uti*.

This list is neither systematic nor exhaustive. It was drawn up on the basis of preliminary observations which a more accurate analysis might confirm, modify or even prove basically incorrect. But there is one thing which needs neither confirmation nor proof. This is that the values just listed are so essential to the Christian calling that their loss

---

[14] "Christ had no patience with the dull lifeless mechanical systems that treat people as if they were things, and so treat everybody alike; for him there were no laws: there were exceptions merely, as if anybody, or anything, for that matter, was like aught else in the world: [...] In opposition to [the Philistines'] tithing of each separate day into the fixed routine of prescribed duties, as they tithe mint and rue, he preached the enormous importance of living completely for the moment. Those whom he saved for their sins are saved simply for beautiful moments in their lives [...] All that Christ says to us by the way of a little warning is that every moment should be beautiful, that the soul should always be ready for the coming of the bridegroom, always waiting for the voice of the lover, Philistinism being simply that side of man's nature that is not illuminated by the imagination ». Oscar Wilde, *De Profundis*. For a discussion on the relation between the spontaneity of everyday experience and the search for an ultimate meaning in life, see G. Lukacs, *Ästhetik I. Die Eigenart des Ästhetischen,* Neuwied-Berlin: Luchterhand,, 1963, ch. XVI, iii ["daily life, private person and religious need].

would undermine the very foundation of the Church's self-identity.[15]

Of course, the same can be said of doctrines which simplify the Christian message in the opposite direction — the so-called vertical dimension. However, at the present moment the latter is a more remote possibility, given the unpopularity of any teaching which does not extol "terrestrial realities."

Our line of enquiry may lead one to conclude that theology of development suffers from a built-in contradiction. On the one hand, to be effective, it has to present a simplified message in terms of social needs and needed social action. On the other, this very simplification entails the risk of rendering meaningless the ultimate foundation on which the "theology" rests. Should such a price be paid, no one would

---

[15] One notices at the present a rather general awareness of the risk that too great an emphasis on social development may obscure the Christian ideal of voluntary poverty or the full meaning of eschatology. But other aspects equally characteristic of Christianity seem more exposed to lack of consideration. We think in particular of those forms of knowledge and self-surrender which — for want of appropriate terms — people vulgarly call non-rational. On the relevance of these forms in Christian history, see for instance Hans Urs von Balthasar, "Revelation and the Beatiful," in *Word and Revelation. Essays in Theology I*, New York: Herder & Herder, 1964, pp. 121-163 [orig. *Verbum Caro. Skizzen zur Theologie I*, Einsiedeln: Johannes Verlag, 1960]; T. Spidlík - F. Vandenbroucke, "Fous pour le Christ," in *Dictionnaire de Spiritualité*, Paris: Beauchesne, 1964, V, 752-770.

It is revealing to compare these writings with the line of thought followed by those who find fault with the utopian optimism. "Anti-utopian writers deplore the idea of a harmonious society characterized by perpetual peace, the satisfaction of human wants, and a nearly effortless virtue. It would not be correct to say that anti-utopianism is a doctrine; rather it is an aggregate of ideas, sentiments, feelings, and prejudices directed at various aspects of the idea of a utopian society. The roots of anti-utopianism are to be found in the writings of Dostoevski and Nietzsche. Dostoevski's *Notes from the Underground* and passages in his novels *The Possessed* and *The Idiot* display a number of anti-utopian sentiments. The life of risk, of uncertainty, of suffering, of inexplicable will, and of spirituality is championed at the expense of the utopian life, which is seen as stultifying." George Kateb, "Utopianism," in *The International Encyclopedia of the Social Sciences*, New York: MacMillan, 1968, vol. XI, p. 270.

claim that theology of development — however appealing and influential — was succeeding "in transforming reality into one more in accord with *its own* conceptions."

The contradiction exists and must be solved in concrete situations which demand choice and action. For at a purely theoretical level there is no particular difficulty in recognizing that Christianity cannot be reduced to any unilateral understanding of the individual and his society, of time and eternity, reason and mystery. And always a theoretical analysis can expound these polarities simultaneously showing their complementarity. The real difficulty arises when judgment must be made in concrete situations as to which of these polarities should receive preference and where appropriate action should be taken in order to direct the course of events towards the preferred direction.[16]

Therefore theology of development — like any other doctrine meant to orient conduct and determine action — has to take side in favor of what at the present appears more urgent. This implies unbalancing the theoretical equilibrium of the complementary polarities proper to the Christian message so as to arrive at an operative interpretation of specific, impelling human problems. But this should never be at the cost of elevating such warranted interpretations into universally valid absolutes, lest the totality of the Christian mystery as well as the pluralism of personal callings should be misconceived.

---

[16] There is a certain vogue — especially on the part of official documents — of defining the Christian stand towards social problems as an intermediate position between capitalism and communism. An attitude defined in terms of concern for avoiding extremes, properly speaking signifies escape from acting. Action, in fact, implies of necessity a preferential choice, hence a responsible particularization of one's several potentialities in favor of what is judged *hic et nunc* both preferable and possible. For a historical instance of a definition between extremes, recall the group of Schleiermacher's disciples known as "the theologians of the happy mean" in opposition to other disciples, the "orthodox," on the one hand, and the "liberals," on the other. For a contemporary case of prudent equidistance, consider the pronouncements issued here and there by the hierarchy as regards church and polics in the so-called Third-World. Brazil or Southeast Asia offer a case in point.

The capacity to be selective without becoming unilateral is a crucial test of any form of knowledge which aims at giving a significant representation of a complex situation. The test is all the more severe in the case of those movements of thought which — for being utopian — aim "to inspire collective activity" in order "to change such reality to conform with their goals which transcend reality."

Should the theology of development manifest *de facto* such capacity, it could properly be judged utopian; and this not on the basis of any *a-priori* value-judgment nor in view of any sociological definition, but on the basis of the historical evidence which shows that seldom or ever has "the existing order of reality" been transformed by a doctrine that was radical but not demagogic, mindful of social necessitie without being utilitarian, centered on the absolute respect for the individual, and yet not aristocratic.

A Problem of Communication

The objective of theology of development can be stated as that of making meaningful in the present historical context the fundamental message discoverable in the original sources of Christianity.

The validity of such an endeavor might be measured several ways. A purely theoretical measure would be that of logical consistency between the general premises of Christian belief and the particular conclusions for development drawn from them. Another might be the degree of consensus among "experts" possessing the time and knowledge required to elaborate a systematic theology of social development.

Granted the merit of both methods of measuring neither suffices if our focus is on theology of development as *a cultural phenomenon designed "to inspire collective activity"* so as to "succeed through counter-activity in transforming the existing historical reality." From this standpoint, neither logical consistency nor the internal cohesion of a relatively small *Intelligentsia* are particularly relevant.[17]

---

[17] In between the individual thinker and the collectivity at large one has to consider that "the characteristic and primal

From a sociological point of view, theology of development implies first and above all a process of social communication that should affect people and institutions of several countries. In fact, only on this condition can theology of development fulfil the function of inspiring collective activity in favor of far-reaching changes.

As any similar process, this, too, can be viewed from the standpoint of either those seeking to communicate or of those for whom the communication is intended. The distinction is of rather methodological interest, since, in reality, the process involves a constant interaction that makes it difficult

bearer of an ideology is an *ideological primary group* (what Herman Schmalebanch called a *Bund*). The bond which unites the members of the ideological primary group to each other is the attachment to each other as sharers in the ideological system of beliefs; the members perceive each other as being in possession of, or being possessed by, the sacredness inherent in the acceptance of the ideology. Personal, primordial, and civil qualities are attenuated or suppressed in favour of the quality of 'ideological possession.'" [...] "In reality, of course, the ideological quality never completely supplants all other qualities, and the fully developed ideological primary group is never completely realized. Thus, the ideological primary group is subject to recurrent strains inherent within the ideology as an intellectual system, but also because the other qualities become, in various measures for many of the members of the group, significant qualities, on the bases of which supplementary and often alternative and contradictory attachments are formed." Edward Shils, "Ideology — Concept and Function," in *The International Encyclopedia of the Social Sciences,* New York: MacMillan, 1968, vol. VII, p. 70. This definition is applicable to ideologies in the strict sense of the word as well as to utopias. In either case, the definition describes an *ideal type,* i. e., a simplified model in terms of which one can isolate, analyse and evaluate concrete historical occurrences. In this framework and with reference to contemporary Catholicism, a good case in point is offered by the proposals which an international group of leading theologians has made public in order to reorganise the Roman Congregation in charge of ascertaining the orthodoxy of theological writings. According to the proposed reorganization, the task of evaluating kind and degree of orthodoxy should be given to an internationally selected group of "experts," such as those who took the initiative of proposing the reorganization. Thirty-eight theologians subscribed this *Déclaration,* published in *Concilium* [French ed.], 41 (1969), no pagination.

to separate communication from reception (except for the rare case of an absolute passivity on the part of one or other). Not so rare, on the other hand, are cases where interaction takes place, but with the result of a widening gulf between communicator and receiver for the simple reason that the meaning intended by one is not that understood by the other.

Such bifurcation of meaning may occur at any level of social communication from the equivocations in a person-to-person interview to the boomerang-effect of mass propaganda, not to mention the many forms of misunderstandings that complicate everyday life of the best intentioned people.[18] For the study of all such cases it is particularly useful to stress the *methodological distinction between the meaning communicated to someone and the meaning taken by the receiver of the communication.*

Applying this to ideology and utopia, it can happen that a doctrinal call to action may receive full support but for reasons having little to do with the real intentions of those who authored the doctrine, and, on that basis, called for action. Or th eopposite may happen. Support is refused simply because the message has been received through media or institutions not conducive to its proper comprehension. Might this be the fate of a theology of development also?

The possibility cannot be denied, and there is some reason for believing that this actually happens in fact.

Let us consider first the case that the message is accepted but not for the reasons proposed by the message communicators. Presumably, those who elaborate a theology of development know that Christian concern for social problems

---

[18] As to the three inter-acting variables in social communication — symbols, feelings and personal qualities — cf. respectively G. H. Mead, "Thought, Communication and the Significant Symbol," in *Mind, Self and Society,* Chicago: The University of Chigago Press, 1934, pp. 68-75; R. Tagiuri, J. S. Bruner and R. R. Blake, "On the Relation Between Feelings and Perception of Feelings Among Members of Small Groups," in E. E. Maccoby, Th. M. Newcomb and E. L. Hartley (Eds.), *Readings in Social Psychology,* New York: Henry Holt, 1958, pp. 110-116; Arthur R. Cohen, *Attitude Change and Social Influence,* New York-London: Basic Books, 1964, ch. 2: "Characteristics of the Communicator," pp. 23-36.

can convey "theological" meaning only in so far as it is derived from, and related back to, an orientation of faith transcending all particular situations delimited in terms of time, space, social institutions and visible achievements. Accordingly, one rightly presumes that in interpreting any particular historical situation in the light of ultimate Christian principles, they will not attribute absolute value to their particular interpretation. The question, then reduces itself to this other, can we suppose that this understanding is shared also by the collectivity hearing the message? Perhaps, but not necessarily so.

To begin, a bifurcation of meaning may occur owing to the *difficulty in communicating the full process of thought whereby one has arrived from general premises of faith to the taking of an active stand in view of solving a concrete problem.* Promoters of a theology of development will have gone through that process in its entirety. Receivers of this message, from their side, are prone to understand the solution better than the premises, seeing that urgent social needs are much more felt since the call to immediate action is much more appealing than its ultimate derivation from faith.

In addition, one must take into account the *difficulty of presenting a particular interpretation of a general value-system without inducing the idea that other interpretations are either impossible or invalid.* Within the circle of experts it may be well understood that there is not just one but several "theologies" (just as there are numerous ways of defining "development", in terms of economic production, social mobility, cultural ascendance, psychological liberation and so forth). However, in the communication of the message to the general public, it is easily possible for the less sophisticated recipients to lose sight of this theological pluralism, and to attach unquestionable validity to the views of one or other "theologian." The probability of this happening is increasing now that the area of theological concern tends to become ever wider without the public being able to determine what really qualifies a "theologian" to enter this area. And it is even more probable that people will dedicate themselves to leaders whose call carries no suggestions that there may be other interpretations or alternative courses of action. The reason is that "ideological leaders, so it seems, are subject to excessive fears which they can master only by reshaping the thoughts of their contemporaries; while those contemporaries are always glad to have their thoughts shaped by those who se desperately care to do so."[19]   This may be the reason; sure enough there are several known writers and lecturers who are more forceful than others in stating what "the Christian" is called to do in the modern world according to "the spirit" of the Vatican II, where "the Christian" stands for a good half billion of people and the Vatican II refers to number of documents containing in embryo a plurality of theologies enmeshed in a far from-coherent series of callings to action.[20]

---

[19] Erik H. Erikson, *Young Man Luther. A Study in Psychoanalysis and History,* New York: W. W. Norton, 1958, p. 110. To this add the empirical evidence drawn from studies on mass communication: "Communication research has been almost perennially concerned with the question of whether persuasion is more effective when it presents only one side of an argument or when it also cites opposing arguments. [...] In general, the investigators found that presentation of "both sides" was more effective in converting the highly educated, but that one-sidedness was more effective in converting the poorly educated. One-sidedness also proved generally more effective among men originally favoring the advocated view, i. e., as a technique of reinforcement." Joseph T. Klapper, *The Effects of Mass Communication,* New York: Free Press, 1965, p. 113.

[20] Undue attributions and false identifications are likely to occur in any social system where there is no clear distinction between the authority *ascribed* to one's office and the ascendancy *acquired* through one's own competence. The sociological discussion on ascription and achievement, role and self has contributed to clarify the basic terms of the question. See R. Linton, *The Study of Man,* New York: Appleton-Century, 1936, esp. ch. VIII; *The Cultural Background of Personality,* New York: Appleton-Century, 1945, esp. ch. III. As to contemporary Christianity, the problem appears particularly prominent among the Catholics in as much as these tend to identify a priest's personal views on theological matters (competence) with the whole Church that he represents in virtue of a sacred ordination (office). An improper identification of the kind sets at hazard both the personal integrity of the individual priest and the maintenance of Church integration.   The problem presents many analogies with the much debated question concerning the position of the "intellectuals" who act at the same time as individual scholars and members

Bifurcation of meaning may, of course, work in the opposite way. It is the case when people show unwillingness to accept the message proposed, not because of its intrinsic content but because of the distorting influence of the circumstances in which the communication takes place. We move from the premise that it is very difficult to make a communication meaningful *when the message does not fit into the prevailing framework of signs and symbols of everyday experience.* The message of theology of development is surely that of freedom and equality for every human person (with all that this involves in terms of radical redistribution of wealth, mobility in the community's power structure and responsible participation at every level in the decision-making process, whether in labor organizations, political structures or cultural institutions.)

But this noble message is presented in the framework of a hierarchically-organized church which in many respects is identified with signs and symbols scarcely consonant with the message. It suffices to think of the signs of power embodied in solemn monuments and sumptuous edifices destined to worship, ecclesiastical administration, preparation of future priests, life of religious communities. To these material signs must be added the many kinds of symbols which, in one way or another, both express and reinforce the conception of an inviolable scale of prestige based on a system of co-optation from on high of sacral type. These signs and symbols have been diffused geographically and radicated in the historical tradition of Christianity. They speak of the Church, not in verbal formulas, but in a

---

of established institutions such as universities or political parties. See, for instance, P. Goodman, "The Freedom to be Academic," in M. R. Stein, A. J. Vidich and D. M. White (Eds.), *Identity and Anxiety,* New York: Free Press, 1960, pp. 351-366. So far, current research on church and ministry does not seem to have paid much attention to this particular aspect. Cf. R. J. Menges and J. E. Dittes, *Psychological Studies of Clergymen. Abstracts of Research,* New York: Nelson, 1965; *Le Clergé dans l'Eglise et la Société.* Actes de la IX Conférence Internationale de Sociologie Religieuse. (Montréal, 1967), Rome: Conf. Int. Soc. Rel., 1967; *The Ministry and Life of Priests Today,* a series of articles and debates in *Concilium* [Engl. ed.], III, 5 (1969).

"silent language," all the more persuasive as it is the more pervasive. The verbalized message of theology of development — freedom, equality, service, democracy — thus often finds itself in contrast with this silent language. Hence arises the doubt whether people will be able to believe in what they hear in explicit formulas when it comes enveloped in a whole frame of reference that gives the real and yet contradictory image of the institutional church.[21]

This doubt becomes all the more plausible if we consider it in the light of the well-known sociological generalization: People will not be effectively moved to strive after benefits not hitherto enjoyed unless they see that such are both desirable and attainable. What then becomes essential is to make *visible* this possibility. But this is virtually impossible where the entire surroundings offer neither concrete sign nor symbolic representation pointing in the desired direction.[22]

---

[21] Consider that while the Church preaches to the world the moral obligation of making every effort for fighting poverty and achieving equality, there are underveloped countries in which moneyed dioceses keep investing large sums in ecclesiastical enterprises; or in which Religious Congregations meet with serious internal strains for lack of integration between foreign and native members of their Congregation. In situations like this, appeals to political leaders and world financiers recalling them to their social responsibilities lose weight and credibility. One might advance the hypothesis that the amount of appeals to the outside world increases with the difficulties met in realizing certain ideals inside the church. The hypothesis reminds us of that mechanism of scapegoating which consists in placing the blame for one's frustration on persons and circumstances which have nothing to do with the real source of frustration. In point of fact, sociological evidence seems to confirm that such a mechanism is not extraneous to the development of certain ideological trends, whether political or religious. Cf. Shils, *cit.*, p. 81. To be sure, *verbal alienation* becomes the salient trait of a social group when this proves to be either incapable of or unwilling to make one, single and delimited choice away from the infinite realm of wishful thinking.

[22] One might recall here the marxist criticism against the *utopian* socialists who — in line with the 18th century "Philosophes" — deemed it possible to transform society by simply representing abstract ideals of an ideal society. Cf. Friedrich Engels, *Die Entwicklung des Sozialismus von der Utopie zur Wis-*

In the above instances of bifurcation (whether resulting from inadequate knowledge or misplaced trust) the lack of comprehension on either side of the communication process implies no moral blame against any person in particular. For, in such cases, the misunderstanding need not be explained in terms of ill-will. It depends mainly on the general social and cultural conditions in which the communication takes place.

From this one sees the obstacles that "theology of development" may encounter when it leaves its academic world and tries to transform its doctrine into a force of inspiration destined to help the collectivity change the very structures in which it lives and communicates. But bad as are the foregoing consequences of misinterpretation, there is a still worse one. *This would be to achieve certain objective results, not in spite of, but owing to the bifurcation of meaning.* Such achievement would imply several things. First, that people have uncritically accepted a practical solution without understanding its ultimate justification. Secondly, that they have been content with marginal reforms within the established framework of signs and symbols of the old system. Finally, that they have given a kind of fideistic support to a particular, contingent, and perhaps questionable interpretation of Christianity.

In a word, this would imply that the *finis operantis* has been subordinated to the *finis operis;* which is only another way of saying that people have been made objects and not subjects of the processes of change. That the changes may have been for the better in economic or other terms, may be so. But betterment at such a price is not a goal for any doctrine which insists on distinguishing religious motivation from social action, and with respect to the latter puts a supreme value on a "conscientization" that makes men capable of liberating themselves.

---

senschaft. For a critical analysis of fictional communities, see Negley, Glenn and Patrick, J. Max (Eds.), *The Quest for Utopia,* New York: Schuman, 1952.

272

In view of these considerations, we are led to reconsider the criterion which defines as utopian those ideas that "succeed in transforming the existing historical reality into one more in accord with their own conception." The reconsideration may lead us to conclude that — at least in so far as Christianity is concerned — the measure of utopianism is to be found not so much in mere capacity of transforming reality, as in the ideal conception which guides the transformation of reality, less in facts transformed and much more in the way facts are transformed.

But if one accepts these two criteria, one has to accept also the difficulties inherent in each one of them. In fact, whether considering the term or the process of social reform from the Christian point of view, we see emerging an underlying contradiction between the objectives pursued by the theology of development and the religious premises on which those objectives are grounded. In view of this, one might be tempted to conclude that a theological movement of this kind is caught in a dilemma: either to become a truly utopian force but at the price of losing its religious meaning, or to lose true influence on the existing social order in view of keeping sound the Christian spirit.

Should this be so, then one could still qualify theology of development as utopian, but in the ordinary and not quite complimentary sense of an implausible flight of fancy. But a qualification in this sense lies on the threshold of sophistry, for it calls impossible the improbable. Such an identification runs against any logic, including that of a strictly statistical analysis applied to measurements and prediction of social occurrences. [23] As to our case in par-

---

[23] "Tendency statements and chance-statements have one notable feature in common; they each leave open a way of dealing with exceptions. A law of the straightforward empirical type must be rejected if we find any single instance in which it does not hold. In a chance-statement this consequence is avoided by exceptions being admitted in the statement itself. In a tendency statement the consequence is also avoided, but in another way, by the exceptions being accounted for by interfering conditions. The form of a law is thus retained, while

ticular, some considerations are in point to show that the dilemma between religious beliefs and social efficacy is real but not inescapable.

For one thing, our discussion has laid the emphasis on certain case-limits somehow or other involved in today's theology of development. From a methodological point of view, this sort of *reductio ad absurdum* is expedient inasmuch as it leads to detection of latent forces and paradoxes not ascertainable through an analysis focused upon the "normal" manifestations of the phenomenon under study. At the same time a procedure like that should not lead to the absurdity of reducing that very phenomenon to its paradoxical results. [24]

Besides, boomerang trends and paradoxical results are likely to come out of any reform movement, however revolutionary in its origin, including those which disclaim all kinds of religious concern. Sure enough, a belief-system that dislocates man's final end to a point beyond the limits of experience might deserve the epithet of "opium of the people" in so far as it diverts attention from urgent social changes required *hic et nunc* in the name of human dignity, indeed of sheer survival for many. Be that as it may, it is equally possible that social utopias designed for the realization of

---

at the same time it is recognized that there are circumstances under which the law does not hold. For this reason it is always possible to replace any chance-statement by a corresponding statement about a tendency. [...] So easy is it to make this transition that the phrases 'usually happens' and 'tends to happen' are often used almost interchangeably. The extra implication when we say that something tends to happen is that exceptions could be accounted for in some way or another." Quentin Gibson, *The Logic of Social Enquiry,* London: Routleddge & Kegan, 1960, p. 141.

[24] A qualitative evaluation of the potential forces which could either disrupt or reform society requires paying attention more to the *dispersion* than to the *central tendency* with regard to the usual values and patterns of behavior. The van of cultural movements — whether in the area of aesthetics or literature, politics or ethics — may introduce into society a new style which, unusual as it is at the present, will become widespread in the near future. Dynamics of this kind — including the rise of utopian trends — do not fit in the classical « règles rélatives à la distinction du normal et du pathologique » (E. Durkheim, *Les Règles de la Méthode Sociologique,* Paris: Alcan, 1895, ch. III).

exclusively temporal reforms may — even while they succeed in bringing about sought-after changes — rationalize or absolutize these to the point of dismissing the possibility that further reforms may be called for. Having transformed the external situation, the utopia tends to transform itself into an ideology, i. e. into an apparatus designed to "control those situationally transcendent ideas and interests which are not realizable within the bounds of the present order, and thereby to render them socially impotent, so that such ideas would be confined to a world beyond history and society, where they could not affect the *status quo*." [25] In political terms, this means that a successful revolution sooner or later may turn itself into dictatorship. The case is neither hypothetical nor rare. [26]

That being so, the mere fact of being "socially potent" cannot be the final criterion for distinguishing ideologies from utopias; for if the seed of an "opium of the people" is present in a purely extramundane view of life, it is equally inherent in doctrines that elevate a specific social program to an absolute. Paradoxical as it may seem, those very conceptions which keep men mindful of "goals not-realizable within the bounds of the present order" can turn to be a source of continuous reforms of the present order precisely inasmuch as they hold that no historical situation, however equitable, ever matches the potentialities of human history. [27]

---

[25] Mannheim, *cit.*, p. 193.

[26] See Barrington Moore, jr., *Social Origins of Dictatorship and Democracy,* Boston: Beacon Press, 1966, esp. the Epilogue on reactionary and revolutionary ideologies. Lest one is trapped into a sociological formalism — as lucid as sterile — the point in question is not so much that of defining in the abstract types of mental constructs, but that of analyzing the concrete forces and circumstances which tend to transform one type into its opposite. Certainly an analysis of this kind — especially on a comparative level — would be facilitated by a stricter formalization of the terminology, but this is not the case. Consider, for instance, that Sorel opposes *myth* to *utopia,* calling myth what in Mannheim's terms is a utopia. Cf. Georges Sorel, *Réflexions sur la violence,* Paris: Rivière, ⁵1921, pp. 46-50 [Introduction, iv].

[27] "For us man is characterized above all by his going beyond a situation, and by what he succeeds in making of what he has been made — even if he never recognizes himself in his objectifica-

One is tempted to add that — when compared with other "transcendent conceptions" — Christianity has an even greater chance to become a source of continuous reforms, owing to its own way of relating time and eternity. "By sketching a comparison with the positions of three other major *Weltanschauungen* [... and] by ignoring complexities, one might arrange representatives of these faiths in a graded series as follows: the Hindu, for whom ultimately history is not significant; the Christian, for whom it is significant but not decisive; the Muslim, for whom it is decisive but not final; the Marxist, for whom it is all in all." [28] In this sense, Christianity is utopian inasmuch as it inspirits men to improve more and more the present order of life, perfection being a tendency, never a condition of human history.

To be sure, the call to Christian perfection is nothing new in the Church. New is the growing emphasis on bringing the Church to the world. Thus at present it looks improbable that people understand the appeal to perfection in the self-centered manner traditional to the flight from the world. In point of fact, the *fuga mundi* has hardly ever been a mass-phenomenon in Christianity, maybe not even at the legendary times of the "Desert Fathers;" at all events, it is not so in our times, now that the Church is moving away from isolation for the sake of realizing within secular institu-

---

tion. This going beyond we find at the very root of the human — in *need*. [...] The most rudimentary behavior must be determined both in relation to the real and present factors which condition it and in relation to a certain object, which it is trying to bring into being. This is what we call *the project*. Starting with the project, we define a double simultaneous relationship. In relation to the given, the *praxis* is negativity; but what is always involved is the negation of a negation. In relation to the object aimed at, *praxis* is positivity, but this positivity opens onto the 'non-existent,' to what *has not yet been*. [...] Thus knowing is a moment of *praxis*, even its most fundamental one; but this knowing does not partake of an absolute Knowledge." J. P. Sartre, *The Problem of Method*, London: Methuen, 1963, pp. 91-92 [orig. *Question de Méthode*, prefatory essay in *Critique de la Raison Dialectique*, I, Paris: Gallimard, 1960].

[28] Wilfred Cantwell Smith, *Islam in Modern History*, Princeton: Princeton University Press, 1957, p. 21.

tions the Christian ideal of brotherly love. [29] Theology of development signifies this move.

These considerations warrant the conclusion that the dilemma between social efficacy and religious ideals is not inescapable; on this account, theology of development *can* be utopian, in the afore-defined sense of the word.

Admittedly, a conclusion such as that affirms a possibility, at best a tendency, not a necessary result. In point of fact, it is more exact to conclude that there are certain conditions which — *if verified* — will lead the theology of development to transform *de facto* the present course of social history into one more in accord with Christian belief.

Some of these conditions came out of our discussion, whether as regards the position of those who promote this theological movement or in connection with the communication between the promoters and the collectivity at large. There is no need here to resume that discussion nor do we need to stress once again the relevance of those conditions which — being beset with difficulties — constitute a crucial test for gauging the utopian character of today's theology of development. At the same time, a consideration seems in point, namely, that our discussion has not been dealing with separate phenomena but with different aspects of the very same problem. Consequently, one should not speak

---

[29] "One of the oldest brief summaries of the Desert rule is the answer of an old man questioned as to what manner of man a monk should be: 'So far as in me is, alone to alone (*solus ad solum*). 'Except', — said the Abbot Allois, 'a man shall say in his heart, I alone and God are in this world, he shall not find peace'." Helen Waddell, *The Desert Fathers,* London: Constable, 1954, p. 18. Compare with John XXIII's appeal to the "Catholics [so that] they can meet and come to an understanding both with Christians separated from this Apostolic See, and also with human being who are not enlightened by faith in Jesus Christ, but who are endowed with the light of reason and with a natural and operative honesty. [...] Meetings and agreements, in the various sectors of daily life, between believers and those who do not believe or believe insufficiently because they adhere to error, can be occasions for discovering truth and paying homage to it." Encyclical Letter *Pacem in Terris,* V. (Vatican Polyglot Press, 1963, pp. 40-41).

of several conditions which the theology of development has
to fulfil if it aims at overcoming the alternative between
social efficacy and religious ideals; properly speaking, there
is only one basic condition observable from different angles.
On the whole, the condition is that of establishing a meaningful connection between action in the world and hope in
a transcendent condition of life, between a non-utilitarian
view of one's existence and an operative undertaking in
support of what appears useful and possible for the benefit
of many.

The Mediating Function of Conscience

There are different ways of making this connection meaningful. It can be solemnly put in writing or proclaimed in
speech; this may help in defining a belief-system, but will not
affect actual history. To become effective, a principle has
to be converted into a motivating force of conduct. In turn,
a conversion like this postulates that the individual's
conscience mediate between the general principles of a creed
and the concrete historical circumstances in which he is
called to operate, understanding by circumstances the external
situation and the subject's dispositions as well. [30]

One should have no great difficulty in recognizing the
legitimacy of this mediating function. The original sources
of Christianity give evidence of it, as do ever so many
studies — whether exegetic or philosophical — which prove
that the Christian understanding of freedom is irreconciliable
with any form of social life based on uniformity of thought
and control of ideas. [31]

---

[30] "Conscience" is used here in the general sense of "the
more-or-less integrated functioning of a person's system of moral
values in the approval or disapproval of his own acts or proposed
acts." H. B. English and A. C. English, *A Comprehensive Dictionary of Psychological and Psychoanalytical Terms,* New York:
Longmans, 1958, p. 111.

[31] See, for instance, Helmut Gollwitzer, *Die marxistiche Religionskritik und der christliche Glaube,* in *Marxismusstudien,* Vierte
Folge, Tübingen: Mohr, 1962, pp. 1-143 (esp. VI, 2: "Die Übe-
ranstrengung der Utopie durch Messianismus, Individuum und
Gemeinschaft).

Granted that from a Christian point of view the mediating function of conscience is a desirable *ideal*, it remains to be seen which are the actual implications of this ideal, should a concrete effort be made so as to render the desirable *real*.[32]

For all one knows, these implications are manifold; let us consider just a few aspects, and even that tentatively.

To begin with, a system that sets store by the mediating function of conscience cannot enforce the execution of a program upon people who understand neither the premise nor the scope of that program. On the face of it, the principle appears so evident that it makes one wonder whether it even calls for a reminder. In point of fact, the evidence

---

[32] We need not to rehearse the old debate concerning "the order of effectiveness of the real and ideal factors" (see K. Mannheim, "Sociology of Knowledge from the Standpoint of Modern Phenomenology," in *Essays on the Sociology of Knowledge*, London: Routledge & Kegan, 1952, p. 159). At any rate, one cannot infer the characteristics of a real situation from the mere knowledge of its ideal definition. This elementary norm of method is not as obvious as it seems. Consider how many writings depict the way in which "Christians" or "Marxists" operate in society, as if the everyday life of those people were completely consistent with their respective Credo or Manifesto. In view of such a recurrent fallacy, what Malinowski wrote some fifty years ago remains up to date: "The manner in which ethnological information about beliefs is usually formulated is somewhat like this: 'The natives believe in the existence of seven souls'; or else, 'In this tribe we find that the evil spirit kills people in the bush,' etc. Yet such statements are undoubtedly false, or at the best incomplete, because no 'natives' (in the plural) have ever any belief or any idea; each one has his own ideas and his own beliefs. Moreover, the beliefs and ideas exist not only in the conscious and formulated opinions of the members of a community. They are embodied in social institutions and expressed by native behavior, from both of which they must be, so to speak, extricated. [...] To test this sociological principle on civilized instances; when we say that the "Roman Catholics believe in the infallibility of the Pope", we are correct only in so far as we mean that this is the orthodox belief, enjoined on all members of that church. The Roman Catholic Polish peasant knows as much about this dogma as about the Infinitesimal Calculus." B. Malinowski, *Baloma: the Spirits of the Dead in The Trobriand Islands,* viii "Some Statements concerning the Sociology of Belief," in *Magic, Science and Religion. And other Essays,* Garden City, N.Y.: Doubleday, 1954, pp. 240, 273.

reminds us of the many difficulties in carrying that principle out. Suffice it to recall that not infrequently theological documents on social development — including some in the front ranks of progressivism — seem more intent on *programming for* than *programming with* the very people who are waiting for promotion to active roles in society. [33]

At all events, the mediation of conscience implies much more than avoiding the sheer enforcement of a pre-established program. It requires in addition the avoidance of holding forth *inspired norms* of behavior, so as to be content with the announcement of *inspiring principles* of conduct. This means placing the whole emphasis on *why* there is need for social action, leaving to the individuals the choice and specification of *what* kind of action is needed. This statement, too, is made with ease; still to put it in practice involves perplexing questions.

Some of these questions are matters of principle, others, of fact, the two overlapping each other. As to the question of fact, there exist at present social problems and situations which call for radical solutions without further delay. And it is a fact, too, that the official Church often finds itself in a position to exert influence on public opinion so as to induce the public powers — whether political or economic — to take steps in favor of a given solution. That being so, the question arises whether the Church representatives may on principle confine themselves to proclaiming a general

---

[33] The tendency to *programming for* other people could be assessed through an appropriate content analysis of the several documents which somehow or other concern the theology of development, especially of those documents that aim at being operative. In particular it might be revealing to *analyze the language* of those writings with regard to the frequency of (a) verbs in the *active* voice - Help, Instruct, Liberate, and neologisms such as Alphabetize, Conscientizate and the like; - (b) the *universal* terms used to indicate the object of those verbs - People, Men, Mankind, The Poor, The Oppressed; - (c) the *imperative* form of auxiliary verbs or adverbs - Must, Will, Absolutely, Urgently, Completely. On the general usage of such a method, cf R. C. North, O. R. Holsti, M. G. Zaninovich and D. A. Zinnes, *Content Analysis,* Evanston, Ill.: Northwestern University Press, 1963, esp. pp. 131-145 on the theoretical and technical problems involved in "Dictionary Construction."

280

value-orientation, instead of entering into the specific terms of a crucial social problem and supporting a side in a disputed situation.

The question is not in the least academic. One has only to recall issues such as racial discrimination, armed intervention by powerful countries in foreign affairs, the absolutely uneven distribution of wealth in so many nations, the arbitrary limitation of civil liberties on the part of police-states. Under similar circumstances, the refusal to take sides might appear — and may actually be — an escape from responsibilities on the part of those who hold responsible positions in the Church, all the more so when anomalies of this sort occur in those countries where ecclesiastical institutions are revered, not to say privileged.

We can take for granted that an anomalous situation might call for an extraordinary intervention. But it is not in this sense that we speak of the recourse to the mediating function of conscience. As a matter of fact, this recourse neither presupposes an exceptional event nor manifests itself in a single formal statement. It is rather *a question of style,* understanding by this term an ordinary, consistent and re-current pattern which should characterize both the theoretical declarations and the concrete activities of those who seek to relate theological premises to contemporary social prob-lems. For all we know, it is precisely in virtue of such a style than the Church can more than ever succeed "through counteractivity in transforming the existing historical reality into one more in accord with its own conceptions." [34]

In fact, a systematic recourse to the mediation of con-science implies the rejection of any kind of authoritarianism, especially of that form, subtle and dispotic at the same time,

---

[34] The notion of style has been developed especially in the area of linguistics, but it finds several applications in sociological analysis as well. It is noteworthy that, usage apart, the term is prevalently associated with the idea of a *choice* between alternative ways of doing things and of a *deviation* from the norm. See A. Levavasseur, "Style et stylistique," in *Linguistique. Guide Alphabetique sous la direction d'André Martinet,* Paris: Denoël, 1969, p. 358; E. H. Gombrich, "Style," in *International Encyclopedia of the Social Sciences,* New York: Macmillan, 1968, vol. XV, esp. p. 353.

which consists in urging a definite line of conduct in the name of absolute morals or alleged divine commands Clearly enough, we do not speak of a rejection coming from subjects who, having long been dominated, eventually arrive at rebelling against that kind of dominance. On the contrary, we speak of a Church which — while being still in a position to exert a dominance like that, *voluntarily* abandons this position, leaving to the individuals' conscience the task of defining the more appropriate course of social action. [35]

When this rejection is really voluntary, i. e. when it stems neither from tactics nor from defeat, then we can rightly speak of a "counter-activity" on the part of the Church. In other words, we see emerging a style that runs against the usual pattern prevailing in all forms of established power. The general tendency, in fact, is to confirm, extend and reinforce one's sphere of influence, so much so that it becomes almost unthinkable the case of a powerful institution voluntarily proclaiming its own incompetence to direct the course of events.

From the beginning of our discussion we have left to one side questions concerning the limits of the Church's competence in social matters, and we do not intend to take up now a normative question of this sort. However, without leaving the level of facts, it seems safe to say that these limits tend to expand rather than to contract. This appears from the ever more rapid increase in theological writings, conventions, discourses and interventions of the kind which aim to state, more or less authoritatively, the responsibilities

---

[35] A case in point is offered by the 3rd National Congress of the Italian Moralists (Padova, 1970), where an attempt was made at reconsidering certain traditional aspects of the Church doctrine in the light of recent historical acquisitions, whether in the area of theological inquiry or social analysis. Especially relevant to our problem is José Diez-Alegría, "La lettura del magistero pontificio in materia sociale alla luce del suo sviluppo storico," *ib.*, pp. 211-255. The author analyzes two points in particular, private property and social revolution. In publishing the Acts — *Magistero e Morale,* Bologna: Dehoniane, 1970 — the Editors had to omit "at the command of the Superior Ecclesiastical Authority" (p. 390) the final document which had been approved by the Convention and already made public through the press.

of Christians in the world and of the world with respect to Christian principles. This proliferation of pronouncements is attributable in part to pressure from without, including political leaders and chiefs of international organizations who see in the official church a potential ally, endowed with a prestige not easily found elsewhere. But it seems we must recognize as well a tendency within the Church itself, revealing a desire to regain that "lay" area whose autonomy the Council affirmed so clearly. Regardless of the intentions of those who do it, the will to theologize on social problems could in fact give rise to a new form of "clericalism" or, if you wish, a resurgent "Constantinianism." By these terms we mean the emergence of a privileged group claiming to exercise control over profane culture and institutions. The paradoxical thing — or is it? — is to discover, within this current, people who were most outspoken in putting an end to clerical power and Constantinian era. [36]

---

[36] Concerning "clericalism," the issue is not so much whether there are priests or laymen to take the lead in bringing the Church to the world, but whether a given group — however composed — may claim a special title to instruct others as to the more appropriate "religious" way of acting in the sphere of profane activities. As to the so-called Constantinian era, clearly enough the term does not define a historical period but an attitude on the part of the ecclesiastical hierarchy as regards secular areas such as politics, economics, science. As historical periods change it might well be that the *degree* of this attitude changes, but not of necessity its *kind*. We think of expressions such as "the Church blesses," "the Church looks with complaisance," "the Church approves," "the Church encourages," and the like; expressions of this sort — when they recur in recent documents — make one doubt that if a change took place, this has been a move from arrogance to benevolence, but not in the direction of a definite autonomy between the realm of faith and the world of political or scientific affairs. In this connection it does not seem entirely out of place to insist on the futility of a style meant to enlighten Mankind: "Esta costumbre de hablar a la Humanidad, que es la forma más sublime y, por lo tanto, más despreciable de la demagogía, fue adoptada hacia 1750 por intelectuales descarriados, ignorantes de sus proprios límites y que siendo por su oficio, los hombre del decir, del *logos,* han usado de él sin respeto ni precauciones, sin darse cuenta de que la palabra es un sacramento de muy delicada administración."

If this is the situation, it is understandable that *vindication of the mediating function of conscience, on all levels, may represent the emergence of a new style.* And it is understandable that bucking the current in this way means conforming to the evangelical *vos autem non sic.* In fact, however one interprets it exegetically, this precept ever vindicates the irreducible opposition between the worldly logic of power and the Christian conception of life. [37]

But in what way are we to understand similar "counter-activity" as succeeding "in transforming the existing historical reality?" This transformation may occur in two ways, different but complementary, which we shall only mention.

It may come about first of all through *symbolic causality.* Voluntarily abandoning a prestige position in social affairs, the institutional Church would offer society a symbolic representation of a renewed way of living. A representation such as this would constitute an example both real and transcendent — real because concretized in a historical situation and by means of a notable modification in its current vogue; transcendent because superior to the style of activity prevalent in any institution founded on the basis of power and social control. Naturally, for an example to have transformative power it is not enough that it be real and transcendent; it must also evoke latent aspirations found in the society within which and for which the paradigm is proposed. Otherwise there would be no question of a symbol, even less of a transforming process. For the present, we do believe that an open acceptance of the mediation of conscience in the afore-defined sense of the term, answers real aspirations which are widespread but largely unexpressed. Confirmation of this view can be found in many areas, for instance in the so-called "new morality" with its abandonment of abstractly defined norms in favor of subjective evaluations of human activity, or, to quote a different area of social concern, in the most recent development among labor unions,

---

J. Ortega y Gasset, *La Rebelión de las masas, Prologo para franceses* (1927), Madrid: Revista de Occidente, 1962, p. 7.

[37] Cf Josef Schmid, *Das Evangelium nach Matthäus,* Regensburg: Pustet, 1959, pp. 154-160 ("Das theologische Problem der Bergpredigt).

which appear at present less intent on obtaining specific economic advantages for the workers than on motivating the workers themselves to take part in decision procedures. [38]

Symbolic causality is the manner in which utopian movements have sought, with more or less success, to transform "the existing historical reality." Indeed this seems to be a characteristic trait shared by movements of this sort which are otherwise quite disparate. [39] For present purposes, however, we deem it useful to stress a difference which often is not sufficiently attended to: it is one thing to offer a model *to* society, and another to provide a model *of* society. In both cases we may speak of symbolic causality, but when a utopian movement presents itself as a model *of* society, the final term is already fixed and the transformation can consist only in the reproduction on a larger scale of what is already realized in the narrower group of reformers. But this is not the case of the Church, namely, it is not so as far as the Church wishes to affirm the mediating function of conscience. Precisely in virtue of such an affirmation, the institutional Church can offer a model *to* society, but not a model *of* society. The reason is that the mediation of conscience implies of necessity leaving ever more room for the responsible initiative of the individual Christians, and as a consequence, a progressive reduction of the visibile borders of the ecclesiastical institutions. [40]

---

[38] Cf Joseph Fletcher, "What's in a Rule: A Situationist's View," in G. H. Outke and P. Ramsey (Eds.), *Norm and Context in Christian Ethics,* New York: Scribners' Sons, 1968, pp. 325-349.

[39] Cf H. Desroche, *Socialismes et sociologie religieuse,* Paris: Cujas, 1965, esp. pp. 117-142 "Messianismes et Utopies. Notes sur les origines du Socialisme occidentale." For a comparative analysis between utopian movements in "primitive" or industrialized societies, see S. L. Thrupp, *Millennial Dreams in Action*: *Essays in Comparative Study,* The Hague: Mouton, 1962; M. I. Pereira de Queiroz, *Réforme et Révolution dans les sociétés traditionnelles*: *histoire et ethnologie des mouvements messianiques,* Paris: Anthropos, 1968.

[40] "We assume that the more closed the system, the more will the world be seen as threatening, the greater will be the belief in absolute authority. [...] On the other hand, the world is seen to be a more friendly place by the relatively open person. He should thus be more free and more impervious to irrelevant

Thus we come to the second manner in which a reasserted mediation of conscience can succed in transforming "the existing historical reality." Here there is no longer question of symbolic causality, but of *creative action originating from individuals,* i. e. from those persons to whom the Church's message will be addressed not as an appeal to do this or that, but as an invitation to discover, nay to invent, what should be done. This line of thought brings us into an area which is largely unexplored, since sociological research, even if it has not completely ignored creative processes, has long given incomparably more attention to social continuity, in the framework of an "over-socialized view" of human conduct. [41] Perhaps, though, it would be more accurate to say that we find ourselves in an area which cannot be explored, for the simple reason that no one can postulate the direction and spread creative action will take, especially when, as in our case, it involves not a limited group, but all those who will continue to see — or begin to find — in the Church a source of inspiration and a call to personal initiative on behalf of others.

In this perspective, social development tends to become by definition unpredictable. We can thus understand a remark made about the "significance of Utopia for Theology," namely, that "the question is not whether Christianity *has* a future but whether it *makes* one. [...] The Christian cannot dispose of the future because this future is more than what

---

pressures. For him, the power of authority is still there, but depends upon the authority's cognitive correctness, accuracy, and consistency with other information he has about the world. [...] The more open the belief system, the less should beliefs held in common be a criterion for evaluating others, and the more should others be positively valued, regardless of their belief." Milton Rokeach (Ed.), *The Open and Closed Mind. Investigations into the Nature of Belief Systems and Personality Systems,* New York: Basic Books, 1960, pp. 62-63.

[41] In his *Wissenssoziologie,* Max Scheler drew a distinction between the *ars inveniendi* and the *ars demonstrandi;* modern psychologists contrast a *problem oriented* vs a *solution oriented* type of personality. In any case, eagerness for inventing a new solution to a complex problem can give origin to unpredictable results which in turn will bring about new stimuli to invention. This process requires that thought and action develop in unbroken

he can make of it with other people. He experiences it always as something provisional." [42]

But remarks such as this — like so many others which occur in normative discourses — risks the familiar mistake of turning a merely ideal orientation into a statement of fact. No one can safely affirm that "the Christian always *experiences* history as something provisional." The historical fact is rather that Christians or, better, those who more formally call themselves such, have time and again met with the objective difficulty in realizing history concretely and at the same time surpassing it, in applying and yet not confining the unlimited creative powers of the human spirit.

It was this difficulty that we wished to express, considering the church as standing in *between* ideology and utopia. Indeed, the ultimate meaning of Christian history is to be found in the recurrent oscillation between the two poles. Either "moment" of this oscillation prepares, accelerates, maybe distorts the other. Properly speaking, one should speax of a spiral which at every moment runs the danger of either flying off at a tangent or turning into a circular movement, sterile and monotonous. Paradoxically as it may seem, the significance of a theology of development focused on the mediation of conscience may be that of fostering the dis-adaptation of the ecclesiastical institutions from culture and society so as to lead the Christians towards a personal, free and imaginative renewal of human existence.

Theology of development is a particular occurrence of a recurrent process. Truly, it does not exhaust Christian history, yet it does take a particular significance at present, since it can either solidify the past into ideology or pave the way to an utopian transformation of the Church.

Which of these directions will prevail is a question that requires testing. This might well be a proper matter for future sociological concern. But much more than sociological analysis is at stake. For ultimately *the issue is whether Christianity can make history without becoming history.*

---

succession. On this last point see W. Sombart, *Der proletarische Sozialismus*, Jena, 1924, p. 140.

[42] *Documentation Concilium*: *Utopia*, in *Concilium* [Engl. ed.], I, 5 (1969), p. 79.

THEOLOGY AND DEVELOPMENT

A Systematic Bibliography
compiled by GERHARD BAUER

This bibliography claims only to be a basic tool for future study and research. It comprises an international list of books and the most significant articles on the particular topics. Because of the limits imposed by the size of the volume, encyclopedia articles are in general presupposed, historical sources are not included and (with few exceptions, especially in the field of historical works) the list contains publications of the past ten years only.

That the bibliography be organized in systematic fashion was clearly in the user's interest. But this necessarily involved a certain amount of overlapping. The main problem is due to the fact that it is virtually impossible to achieve completeness in the specialized fields of the economist, the sociologist and the philosopher, for example, as in Parts II and III. On the other hand it would represent a serious misunderstanding of the vast problem of a "theology of development" to neglect such pre-theological disciplines. The reader of this bibliography will undoubtedly perceive the dilemma.

Again because of physical limitations, no consideration was given to certain far from unimportant topics, such as spirituality of world, of work, the special task of the layman, or the problem of intraecclesiastical development. For the same reason, section V, 1 (biblical data) was not elaborated beyond the presentation of some themes; the corresponding literature is readily available in biblical reference works. Finally, the reader is referred to the select and annotated bibliography on theology of development, which will be published this year by the Committee on Society, Development and Peace of the World Council of Churches and the Pontifical Commission Justice and Peace (Sodepax), Geneva.

PLAN OF THE BIBLIOGRAPHY

I. GENERAL WORKS OF REFERENCE

II. ECONOMIC AND SOCIAL DATA

    1. RELIGION AND CHURCH IN TECHNOLOGICAL SOCIETY

    2. WORLD SITUATION ON SOCIO-ECONOMIC LEVEL
    (Development and Underdevelopment)

    3. CRITICAL ANALYSIS
       a. *Analysis, Aspects, Theories of Socio-Economic
         Development*
       b. *Development Planning*
       c. *Education and Development*

    4. CONCRETE AID
       a. *General Data, U. N., Governments, Volunteers*
       b. *The Churches' Aid*
       c. *Critical Analysis of the Actual Motivation*

III. PROGRESS AND DEVELOPMENT IN THE HISTORY OF
IDEAS

    1. GENERAL STUDIES

    2. MARXISM AND DEVELOPMENT
       a. *Marxist Concept of Development*
       b. *Critics, Marxist-Christian Dialogue*

    3. DEVELOPMENT IN PRESENT-DAY THINKING

IV. THE HUMAN ASPECT OF DEVELOPMENT

    1. MANKIND IN EVOLUTION
    2. CONCERN FOR MAN IN DEVELOPMENT
    3. ETHICAL QUESTIONS

V. SOURCES FOR A "THEOLOGY OF DEVELOPMENT"

    1. BIBLICAL DATA
    2. HISTORY OF CHRISTIAN THOUGHT
    3. CHRISTIAN CONCERN FOR DEVELOPMENT
    4. DECLARATIONS OF THE CHURCHES
       a. *Papal Encyclicals and Vatican II*
         aa. Mater et Magistra
         bb. Pacem in Terris

LIST OF ABBREVIATIONS

Bibl.	*Bibliography*
Christ. soc.	*Christianisme social*
Chron. Soc. Fr.	*Chronique sociale de France*
Concilium	*(quoted according to the english edition)*
Dév. et Civ.	*Développement et Civilisations*
Disk. Theol. Rev.	*Diskussion zur Theologie der Revolution, hg. von E. Feil und R. Weth, München-Mainz: Kaiser-Grünewald, 1969*
Doc. Cath.	*La Documentation Catholique*
Econ. et Hum.	*Économie et Humanisme*
Eph. Theol. Lov.	*Ephemerides Theologicae Lovanienses*
Ecum. Rev.	*The Ecumenical Review*
Ev. Komm.	*Evangelische Kommentare*
Ev. Theol.	*Evangelische Theologie*
Handb. d. Past.	*Handbuch der Pastoraltheologie, hg. v. Fr. X. Arnold u. a., Freiburg: Herder, 1964 ss*
Int. Dialog Z.	*Internationale Dialog Zeitschrift*
Int. Rev. Miss.	*International Review of Mission*
Just. Monde	*Justice dans le Monde*
Mü. Th. Z.	*Münchner Theologische Zeitschrift*
N. Rev. Th.	*Nouvelle Revue Théologique*
PUF	*Presses Universitaires de France*
Rev. Bibl.	*Revue Biblique*
Rev. Ecl. Bras.	*Revista Eclesiástica Brasileira*
Rev. Sc. Phil. Theol.	*Revue des Sciences Philosophiques et Théologiques*
Z. ev. Ethik	*Zeitschrift für Evangelische Ethik*
Z. f. Miss. u. Rel. wiss.	*Zeitschrift für Missionswissenschaft und Religionswissenschaft*
Z. Theol. Kirche	*Zeitschrift für Theologie und Kirche*

I. GENERAL WORKS OF REFERENCE

Barason, J., *Technology of Underdeveloped Areas.* An Annotated Bibliography, Oxford: Pergamon Pr., 1967.

Bernard, J., *The Nature of Conflict.* Studies on the Sociological Aspects of International Tensions, Paris: UNESCO, 1957 (Compreh. Bibliography).

Brode, J., *The Process of Modernization.* An Annotated Bibliography on the Sociocultural Aspects of Development, London: Harvard Univ. Pr. and Oxford Univ. Pr., 1969.

Carrier, H. - Pin, E. - Fasola-Bologna, A., *Sociology of Christianity.* International Bibliography, Supplement 1962-66, Rome: Gregorian Univ. Press, 1968.

Entwicklungsländer—Studien. Bibliographie der Entwicklungslänlerforschung. Bonn: Deutsche Stiftung für Entwicklungsländer, 1966 ss.

Entwicklungspolitik, Handbuch und Lexikon, hg. v. H. v. Besters und E. E. Boersch, Stuttg.-Berlin-Mainz: Kreuz-Grünewald, 1966.

L'Idea dello sviluppo nella letteratura degli ultimi 20 anni. Bibliografia ragionata. Milano: Etas-Kompass, 1966.

Knop, E. - Aparico, K., *Current Sociocultural Change Literature.* An Annotated Classification of Selected Interdisciplinary Sources, Grand Forks: Univ. North Dakota, 1967.

Literatur über Entwicklungsländer, (Schriftenreihe des Forschungsinstituts der Friedrich Ebert Stiftung), Hannover: Verlag für Literatur und Zeitgeschehen, 1961 ss, (english, french, german, russian).

Martinez Arango, D., *Reseña de bibliografías en sociología general y aplicada,* Roma: Gregorian Univ. Press, 1969.

Metz, R. - Schlick, J., *Répertoire bibliographique des institutions chrétienne,* Strasbourg: C.E.R.D.I.C. (Palais Univ.), vol. 3, 1968-70.

Society transformation and Church in Latin America. A Bibliography, in: *Cif-reports* 3 (July, 18, 1964) 1-6.

Thomas, B., *International Migration and Economic Development.* A Trend Report and Bibliography, Paris: UNESCO, 1961.

Utz, A.-F., *Grundsatzfragen des öffentlichen Lebens.* Bibliographie (Darstellung und Kritik). Recht, Gesellschaft, Wirtschaft, Staat. Unter Mitwirkung von W. Büchi u. a., Freiburg: Herder, 1960 ss. From vol. 3 on under the title: *Bibliographie der Sozialethik* Bd. 1).

Wish, J. R., *Economic Development in Latin America.* An Annotated Bibliography, New York: Praeger, 1965.

II. ECONOMIC AND SOCIAL DATA

1. RELIGION AND CHURCH IN TECHNOLOGICAL SOCIETY

Adolfs, R., *La tombe de Dieu — L'Église a-t-elle encore un avenir?*, Mulhouse: Ed. Salvator, 1967, (orig. dutch).

Ausgewählte internationale Bibliographie zur neuen Religionssoziologie, in: *Kölner Zeitschrift für Soziologie und Sozialpsychologie*, 6 (1962), 264-289.

Bahrdt, H. P., *Die moderne Grosstadt*. Soziologische Überlegungen zum Städtebau, Hamburg: Rowohlt, 1961.

Berger, P. L., *A Rumor of Angels* — Modern Society and the Rediscovery of the Supernatural, New York: Doubleday & Co., 1969.

—, *The Sacred Canapy* — Elements of a Sociological Theory of Religion, New York: Doubleday & Co., 1967.

—, *The Social Reality of Religion*, London: Faber & Faber, 1967.

Brockmöller, K., *Industriekultur und Religion*, Frankfurt: Knecht, 1964 (french: Civilisation industrielle et religion, Paris, Éd. Desclée et Cie, 1968).

Carrier, H., *Psychosociologie de l'appartenance religieuse,,* Roma, Gregorian Univ. Pr., 1960.

Caster, M. van, *Signes du temps et rédemption*, II. — *Les signes de notre temps*, Bruxelles: La Pensée cath., 1967.

Chenu, M. D., *I segni dei tempi*, in: S. Quadri, *La chiesa nel mondo contemporaneo*, Torino: Borla, 1966, 85-102.

Daujat, J., *Le christianisme et l'homme contemporain*, Paris: Mame, 1962.

Dewart, L., *The Future of Belief. Theism in a World Come of Age*, New York: Herder, 1966.

Edwards, D. L., *Religion and Change*, London: Hodder & Stoughton, 1969.

Évolution du christianisme, (Recherches internationales à la lumière du marxisme, 49), Paris: Éd. de la Nouv. Critique, 1965.

Färber, K., (ed.), *Krise der Kirche — Chance des Glaubens*. Die « kleine Herde » heute und morgen, Frankfurt: Knecht, 1968.

Foi et technique, XIIIᵉ assemblée plenière de Pax Romana, Mouvement international des intellectuels catholiques, Louvain, juillet-1959, Paris: Plon, 1960.

Freyer, H., *Über das Dominantwerden technischer Kategorien in der Lebenswelt der industriellen Gesellschaft*, Mainz - Wiesbaden: Steiner in Komm., 1961.

—, *Theorie des gegenwärtigen Zeitalters*, Stuttgart: Deutsche Verl. Anstalt, 1958.

Glock, C. Y. - Stark, R., *Religion and Society in Tension,* Chicago: Rand Mc Nally & Co., 1965.

Goddijn, W. - H. P. M., *Kirche als Institution.* Einführung in die Religionssoziologie, Mainz: Grünewald, 1963.

Görres, A., *Pathologie des katholischen Christentums,* in: *Handb. d. Past.* II 1, Freiburg: Herder, 1966, 277-343.

Greinacher, N., *Soziologische Aspekte des Selbstvollzuges der Kirche,* in: *Handb. d. Past.* I, Freiburg: Herder, 1964, 413-448.

—, *Die Kirche in der städtischen Gesellschaft,* Mainz: Grünewald, 1966.

—, *Soziologie der Pfarrei,* in: *Handb. d. Past.,* Freiburg: Herder, 1968, 111-139.

Höffner, J., *Industrielle Revolution und religiöse Krise.* Schwund und Wandel des religiösen Verhaltens in der modernen Gesellschaft, Köln: Westdeutscher Verl., 1961.

Hoefnagels, H., *L'Église et la société prométhéenne.* Problèmes de sociologie religieuse, Paris: Desclée de Brouwer, 1966. (germ.: Kirche in veränderter Welt. Religionssoziologische Gedanken, Essen: Driewer, 1964).

Hoekendijk, J. C., *The Church Inside-Out.* (ed. by L. H. Hoedemaker and P. Tijmes), Philadelphia: Westminster Press, 1966, (orig. dutch-german transl.: *Die Zukunft der Kirche und die Kirche der Zukunft,* Stuttgart: Kreuz Verl., 1964).

Houtart, F., *Les aspects sociologiques des « signes du temps »,* in: *L'Église dans le monde de ce temps,* II, Paris: Mame, 1967, 171-204.

Houtart, F. - Remy, J., *Église et société en mutation,* Tours: Mame, 1969.

Kirche in der Stadt. Bd. II: *Probleme, Experimente, Imperative,* (Beiträge des österreichischen Seelsorgeinstituts, Wien: Herder, 1968.

Kraft und Ohnmacht. Kirche und Glauben in der Erfahrung unserer Zeit, (hg. von. M. von Galli - M. Plate, Karl Färber zum 75. Geb.) Frankfurt: Knecht, 1963.

Marty, M. S. - Lee, R., *Religion and Social Conflict,* New York: Oxford Univ. Press, 1964.

Matthes, J., *Die Emigration der Kirche aus der Gesellschaft,* Hamburg: Furche, 1964.

—, *Religion und Gesellschaft.* Einführung in die Religionssoziologie, Hamburg: Rowohlt, 1967.

Metz, J. B., *Die Zukunft des Glaubens in einer hominisierten Welt,* in: J. B. Metz, *Zur Theologie der Welt,* Mainz-München: Grünewald-Kaiser, 1968, 51-71.

Oppen, D. von, *Das personale Zeitalter.* Formen und Grundlagen gesellschaftlichen Lebens im 20. Jahrhundert, Stuttgart-Gelnhausen: Verlagsgemeinschaft Burckhardthaus u. Kreuz Verl., 1960.

—, *Der sachliche Mensch*. Frömmigkeit am Ende des 20. Jahrhunderts, Stuttgart: Kreuz, 1968.

Ostermann, H., *Grosstadt zwischen Abfall und Bekehrung*, Graz: Styria, 1964.

Pol, W. H. van de, *Das Ende des konventionellen Christentums*, Freiburg: Herder, 1968[3], (orig. dutch).

Rahner, K., *Der Mensch von heute und die Religion*, in: *Schriften* VI, Einsiedeln: Benziger, 1965, 13 33.

—, *Über den Dialog in der pluralistischen Gesellschaft*, ib., 46-58.

—, *Konziliare Lehre der Kirche und künftige Wirklichkeit*», ib., 479-498.

—, *Der Auftrag der Kirche in der bleibend säkularen Welt*, in: *Handb. d. Past.*, Freiburg: Herder, 1966, 35-46.

—, *Theologische Deutung der Gegenwartsituation als Situation der Kirche*, in: *Handb. d. Past.* II-1, Freiburg: Herder, 1966, 233-256.

—, *Das Verhältnis der Kirche zur Gegenwartsituation im allgemeinen*, in: *Handb. d. Past.* II-2, Freiburg: Herder, 1966, 19-45.

Rahner K. - Greinacher, N., *Die Gegenwart der Kirche*. Theologische Analyse der Gegenwart als Situation des Selbsvollzugs der Kirche, in: *Handb. d. Past.* II-1, Freiburg: Herder, 1966, 178-276.

—, *Religion und Kirche in der modernen Gesellschaft*», ib., 222-233.

Richardson, A., *Religion in Contemporary Debate*, London: SCM, 1966, (*Le procès de la religion*, Paris: Casterman 1967).

Rickman, H. P., *Living with Technology*, London: Hodder, 1967.

Ringeling, H., *Christen im technischen und sozialen Umbruch unserer Zeit*, in: *Ökum. Rundschau* 16 (1967), 9-32.

Robinson, J. A. T., *The New Reformation?*, Philadelphia: Westminster Press, 1965.

Routereau, R. G., *Conscience religieuse et mentalité technique*, Paris: Desclée, 1963.

Scarpati, R., *Hope or Hindrance?* The Church of the Future, New York: Sheed & Ward, 1967.

Schasching, J., *Kirche und industrielle Gesellschaft*, Wien: Herder, 1960.

—, *Das Verhältnis der Kirche zur sozialen Dynamik der Gegenwart*, in: *Handb. d. Past.* II-2, Freiburg: Herder, 1966, 314-366.

Schreuder, O., *Kirche im Vorort*. Soziologische Erkundung einer Pfarrei, Freiburg: Herder, 1962.

Soziologie der Kirchengemeinde, (hg. von D. Goldschmidt, F. Greiner, H. Schelsky) Stuttgart: Enke, 1960. (Bibl. pp. 239-253).

Strohm, Th., *Kirche und demokratischer Sozialismus.* Studien zur Theorie und Praxis politischer Kommunikation, München: Kaiser, 1968.

Taylor, R., *Christians in an Industrial Society,* London: SCM, 1961.

Unamuno, M. De, *La agonía del cristianismo,* Barcelona: Ed. A. M. R., 1966.

Walters, G., (ed.) *Religion in a Technological Society,* Bristol: Bath U. P., 1968.

Winter, G., *The Suburban Captivity of the Churches.* And the Prospects of their Renewal to Serve the Whole Life of the Emerging Metropolis. An Analysis of Protestant Responsibility in the Expanding Metropolis, New York: Doubleday & Co., 1961.

2. WORLD SITUATION ON SOCIO-ECONOMIC LEVEL
(Development and Underdevelopment)

Austruy, J., *Le scandale du développement,,* Paris: Rivière, 1965.

Barnes, Sir W. G., *Europe and the Developing World,* London, PEP Chatham Ho., 1967.

Batschelder, A. B., *The Economics of Poverty,* London: Wiley, 1967.

Bishop, J., *Latin America and Revolution,* London: Sheed & Ward, 1965.

Bosc, R. J. M., *Le tiers monde dans la politique internationale,* Paris: Aubier-Montaigne, 1968.

Castro, J. de, *Le livre noir de la faim,* Paris: Ouvrières, 1961.

Cépède, M. - Gounelle, H., *La faim,* Paris: PUF, 1967.

Cépède, M. - Houtart, F. - Grond, L., *Nourrir les hommes,* Bruxelles: éd. du CEP, 1963.

Coste, R., *Violence et révolution dans le monde contemporain,* in: *N. Rev. Th.* 91 (1969), 65-84.

Couvreur, G., *La pauvreté des sociétés du penurie à la société d'abondance,* Paris: Fayard, 1964 (span. transl.: *La pobreza de las sociedades de penuria a la sociedad de abundancia,* Santiago de Chile - Barcelona: Ed. Pomaire, 1966).

Debray, R., *Révolution dans la révolution?* et autres essais, Paris: Maspero, 1967.

Delavignette, R., *Christianisme et colonialisme,* Paris: Fayard, 1960.

Drogat, N., *Face à la faim,* Paris: Spes, 1961.

F. A. O., *La situation mondiale de l'alimentation et de l'agriculture,* Paris: Pedona, 1966.

Fritsch, B., (ed.), *Entwicklungsländer*, Köln-Berlin: Neue Wiss. Bibliothek, 1968.

Furtado, C., *Développement et sous-développement*, Paris: PUF, 1966.

Gendarme, R., *La pauvreté des nations*, Paris: Éd. Cujas, 1963.

Helder Camara, D., *Terzo mondo defraudato*, Milano: E.M.I., 1968.

Houtard, F., *El cambio social en América Latina*, Bruxelles: FERES, 1964.

Humphreys, R. A., *Tradition and Revolt in Latin America* and other essays, London: Weidenfels and Nicolson, 1969.

Klanfer, J., *Le sous-développement humain*, Paris: Ouvrières, 1967.

Jacobs, P., - Saul Landau, *The New Radicals*. A Report with Documents, Harmondsworth: Penguin, 1967.

Lacoste, Y., *Géographie du sous-développement*, Paris: PUF, 1965.

Lenica, J., - Sauvy, A., *Population Explosion. Abundance*. New York: Dell publ., 1962.

Lloyd, P. C., *Africa in Social Change*, Harmondsworth: Penguin, 1967.

McCormack, A. G., *The Population Explosion and World Hunger*, London: Burns & Oates, 1963.

Meynaud, J., *La révolte paysanne*, Paris: Payot, 1963.

Migeon, H., *Structures et concentrations*. Le monde en révolution. Paris: Éd. d'Organisation, 1967.

Moussa, P., *Les nations prolétaires*, Paris: PUF, 1960 [2].

Myrdal, G., *Asian Drama*. An Inquiry into the Poverty of Nations, 3 vol, New York: Pantheon Press, 1968.

Paraf, P., *Le racisme dans le monde*, Paris: Payot, 1967.

Pearson, L. B., *Partners in Development*. Report of the Commission on International Development, New York: Praeger, 1969.

Reale, M., *Das Selbstverständnis des heutigen Menschen aus der Sicht eines unterentwickelten Landes*, in: R. Schwarz, (ed.), *Menschliche Existenz und moderne Welt*, v. II, Berlin: de Gruyter, 1967, 180-188.

Sauvy, A., *Le « Tiers-Monde ». Sous-développement et développement*, Paris: PUF, 1961 (réédition augmentée).

Silvert, K. H., *The Conflict Society*. Reaction and Revolution in Latin America, New York: Am. Un. Field Staff, 1966.

Silvert, K. H., *The Conflict Society*. Reaction and Revolution, in: *Concilium* vol. 5, II (1966), 18-27.

Le Tiers Monde, l'Occident et l'Église (par B. Atangana, G. de Bernis ...) Paris: Cerf, 1967.

La Violence dans le monde actuel, (par Michel Amiot, Jean Dupuy ...) Bruges: Desclée de Brouwer, 1968.

3. CRITICAL ANALYSIS.

a. *Analysis, Aspects, Theories of Socio-Economic Development.*

Adorno, Th. W., *Über Statik und Dynamik als soziologische Kategorien,* in: M. Horkheimer - Th. W. Adorno, *Sociologica* II, Frankfurt: Europ. Verlagsanstalt, 1962, 223-240.

Arendt, H., *On Revolution,* New York: Viking Press, 1963 (Bibl.).

Albertini, J. M., *Les mécanismes du sous-développement,* (avec la collaboration de M. Auvolat et F. Lerouge), Paris: Éd. Brière, 1968 ³. (Bibl.).

Barrère, A., *Le développement à l'échelle mondiale,* (Leçon d'ouverture de la 54ᵉ semaine sociale de France), in: *Doc. Cath.* no. 150 (3 sept. 1967) col. 1488-1503.

Behrendt, R. F., *Soziale Strategie für Entwicklungsländer.* Entwurf einer Entwicklungssoziologie, Frankfurt: Fischer, 1965.

Beltrão, P. C., *Sociología do desenvolvimento,* Rio de Janeiro: Ed. Globo, 1965.

Bhagwati, J., *L'Économie des pays sous-développés,* Paris: Hachette, 1966. (orig. engl / transl. italian).

Blanc, E., *Problèmes internationaux* (Bibliographie), in: *Econ. et Hum.* n. 167 (1966), 80-88.

Borel, P., *Les trois révolutions du développement,* Paris: Ouvrières, 1968.

British Sociological Association, *The Development of Industrial Societies,* New York: Humanities Press, 1966.

Clark, C., *Population, Growth, and Land Use,* London: Macmillan, 1968.

Congrès Mondial de Sociologie: *The Sociology of Development.* (Fifth World Congress of Sociology), Washington, D. C., 1962.

Coste, R., *Dynamique de la paix,* Paris: Desclée & Cie, 1965.

Desarrollo de la comunidad. Teoría y práctica, Mesa redonda Banco-Interamericano de Desarrollo, Mexico, 1966.

Desroche, H., *Coopération et développement,* Paris: PUF, Tome I.: *Mouvements coopératifs et stratégie du développement,* 1964, Tome II: *Mouvements coopératifs et typologie du développement.*

—, *Sociologie religieuse et Sociologie du développement,* in: H. Desroche, *Sociologie religieuse,* Paris: PUF, 1968, 150-173.

Development and Society. The Dynamics of Economie Change, (ed. by D. E. Novack and R. Lekachman), New York: St. Martin's Press, 1964.

Developments and Trends in the World Cooperative Movement, (Meeting of panel of experts on co-operation, Geneva, 1962), Genève: Internat. Labour Off., 1962.

De Vries, E., *Man in Rapid Change,* New York: Doubleday, 1961.
De Vries, E. - Echaverría, J. M., *Social Aspects of Economic Development,* Tournai: Desclée, 1963.
Dreitzel, H. P., (ed.) *Sozialer Wandel.* Zivilisation und Fortschritt als Kategorien der soziologischen Theorie, Neuwied-Berlin: Luchterhand, 1967.
Eisenstadt, S. N., *Essays on Sociological Aspects of Political and Economic Development,* The Hague: Mouton & Co., 1961.
Eisermann, G., (ed.), *Soziologie der Entwicklungshilfe,* Stuttgart: Kohlhammer, 1968.
Etzioni, A., *Studies in Social Change,* London: Holt, 1967.
F.A.O., *La sociologie facteur de progrès,* Paris: Pedona, 1966.
Gaeng, P. - Reiche, R., *Modelle der kolonialen Revolution.* Beschreibungen und Dokumente, Frankfurt: Suhrkamp, 1967.
Gannage, E., *Économie du développement,* Paris: PUF, 1962.
—, *Développement économique,* Paris: PUF, 1963.
—, *Institutions et développement,* Paris: PUF, 1966.
Geiger, T., *Statik und Dynamik.* Eine dynamische Analyse der sozialen Mobilität. Typologie und Mechanik der gesellschaftlichen Fluktuation, in: *Arbeiten zur Soziologie,* hg. von P. Trappe, Neuwied: Luchterhand, 1962, 97-150.
Horowitz, I. L., *Three Worlds of Development.* The Theory and Practice of International Stratification., New York: Oxf. Univ. Press, 1966 (chapter IV: *Toward a General Theory of Development and Revolution).*
Hunt. C. L., *Social Aspects of Economic Development,* New York: McGraw-Hill, 1966.
International Trade Theory in a Developing World, ed. by Harrod, Roy, and Hague, D. C., New York: St. Martin's Press, (1963) 1966[2].
Internat. Social Council: *Economic Development and its Social Implications,* Paris: PUF, 1962.
Kindleberger, C. P., *Economic Development,* New York: McGraw-Hill, 1964[2].
Kautsky, J., *Political Change in Underdeveloped Countries.* Nationalism and Communism, New York-London, John Wiley & Sons Inc., 1962.
Janssen, L. H., *Chronique: Le développement économique,* in: *Just. Monde* 7 (1965-66) 366-396.
Johnson, H. G., *The World Economy at the Crossroads.* A survey of current problems of money, trade and economic development, Oxford: Clarendon, 1965.
—, *Economic Policies Towards Less Developed Countries,* London: George Allen and Unwin Ltd., 1967.

Lacharrière, G. de, *Commerce extérieur et sous-développement,* Paris: PUF, 1964.

Lacoste, Y. - Ibn Khaldoun, *Naissance de l'histoire passé du tiers-monde,* Paris: Maspero, 1969[2].

Lebret, L. J., *Dynamique concrète du développement,* (by) Paul Borel etc., Paris: Ouvrières, 1961, (réédition mise à jour 1967).

Lewis, W. A., *The Theory of Economic Growth,* London: George Allen and Unwin, 1963, (transl. french, span., ital.).

Meier, G. M., *Leading Issues in Development Economics,* New York: Oxford Univ. Press, 1964.

Meynaud, O., *Social Change and Economic Development,* Paris: UNESCO, 1963.

Munby, D., (ed.) *Economic Growth in a World Perspective,* (Vol. III., Church and Society Conference, 1966), New York: Association Press, 1966, (transl. french: *Le développement économique dans une perspective mondiale,* Genève: Labor et Fides, 1966).

Myint, H., *The Economics of the Developing Countries,* London: Hutchinson, 1964.

Myrdal, G., *Economic Theory and Underdeveloped Regions,* London: Duckworth Ltd., 1957.

Oglesby, C. - Shaull, R., *Containment and Change,* New York-London: Macmillan, 1967.

Ohlin, G., *Population Control and Economic Development,* Paris: Development Centre Studies, 1967.

Olmedo, R., *Theorien zur Situation Lateinamerikas,* in: *Int. Dialog. Z.* 2 (1969), 173-186.

Papcke, S. G., *Ausgewählte Bibliographie zur politischen Soziologie des Krieges und Revolution,* in: Bahr, H. - E. (ed.), *Weltfrieden und Revolution,* Hamburg: Rowohlt, 1968, 73-78.

Parsons, I., *Structure and Process in Modern Societies,* New York: Glencoe, 1960.

Perroux, F., *L'Économie des jeunes nations.* Industrialisation et groupements de nations, Paris: PUF, 1962.

Pfeffer, K. H., *Welt im Umbruch.* Gesellschaftliche und geistliche Probleme in den Entwicklungsländern, Gütersloh: G. Mohn Verl., 1966.

Prebisch, R., *Dinâmica do desenvolvimento latino-americano,* Sâo Paulo: Ed. Fundo de Cultura, 1964, (span. tr.).

Ramos-Regidor, J., *Sviluppo dei popoli e rivoluzione,* in: *Aggiornamenti sociali* 19 (1968), 495-518. 575-602.

Restless Nations. A Study of World Tensions and Development.

(by) M. S. Diseshin, C. D. Deshmukh, Roscoe Drummond ...),
New York: Dodd, Mead & Co., 1962.

Riga, P., *Modernization and Revolutionary Change,* in: *World
Justice* 7 (1965-66) 335-367.

Rostow, W. W., *The Stages of Economic Growth.* A Non-Com-
munist Manifest, Cambridge: Univ. Press, 1960.

Sauvy, A., *Malthus et les deux Marx.* Le problème de la faim et
de la guerre dans le monde, Paris: Denoël, 1963.

Smolik, J., *Revolutionary Violence and the Dictatorship of Consumption,* Genève: John Knox House, 1967.

Stone, L., *Theories of Revolution,* in: *World Politics* (Jan. 1966),
159-176.

United Nations, (Population Division), *World Population Trends,*
(Working Paper Number 17), New York: U.N., Oct. 1967.

b. *Development Planning.*

Cottier, G. M. M., *Régulation des naissances et développement dé-
mographique,* Paris: Desclée de Brouwer, 1969.

Desroche, H., *Planification et volontariat dans les développements
coopératifs,* Paris, La Haye: Mouton & Co., 1963.

Development through Food. A Strategy for Surplus Utilization.
Roma, F.A.O., 1964².

Development of the Emerging Countries. An Agenda for Research.
Washington: Bookings Institution, 1962.

Family Planning and Population Programs. A Review of World
Developments. (by B. Barelson, R. K. Anderson, O. Harkavy,
J. Maier, W. P. Mauldin, S. J. Segal), Chicago-London: Chicago
Univ. Press, 1966.

Gannage, E., *Planification et développement économique,* Paris:
PUF, 1963.

Hallowell, J. (ed.), *Development for What?* (by A. Allot, G. McLead
Bryan ...), Durham: Duke Univ. Press, 1964.

Heinrichs, J., *Hunger und Zukunft.* Aspekte des Welternährungs-
problems, Göttingen: Vandenhoeck & Ruprecht, 1969.

Hirschman, A. O., *The Strategy of Development,* New Haven,
Connecticut: Yale Univ. Press, 1962, (transl. span. and french:
Stratégie du développement économique, Paris: Ouvrières,
1964).

Hyman, H. - Levine, G. - Wright, G., *Inducing Social Change in
Developing Communities,* Genève: U. N. Research Inst. for
Soc. Dev., 1966.

Kaiser, J. H., *Exposé einer pragmatischen Theorie der Planung,*
in: J. H. Kaiser, (ed.), *Planung, I. Recht und Politik der*

Plannung in Wirtschaft und Gesellschaft, Baden-Baden: Nomos Verlagsgesellschaft, 1965.

Lestapis, S. de, *Internationale Zusammenarbeit auf dem Gebiet der Bevölkerungspolitik,* in: *Oeconomia Humana,* Köln: Bachem, 1968, 401-421.

Lewis, W. A., *Development Planning.* The Essentials of Economic Policy, London: Allen & Unwin, 1968, (French tr.).

Perroux, F., *Les techniques quantitatives de la planification,* Paris: PUF, 1965.

The Population Crisis. Implications and Plans for Action, Bloomington: Indiana Univ. Press, 1965.

Prebish, R., *Towards a New Trade Policy for Development,* (Report to the Secretary-General of the U. N. Conference on Trade and Development), New York: U. N. 1964.

Raes, J., *L'intégration économique des nations, panacée pour la paix du monde?,* in: *Just. Monde* IX (1967/68), 357-387.

Spicer, E., *Human Problems in Technological Change.* A casebook, New York: Russell Sage Foundation, 1952.

Tinbergen, J., *Shaping the World Economy,* Suggestions for an International Economic Policy, New York: Twentieth Cent. Fund, 1962.

—, *Development Planning,* New York: McGraw-Mill, 1967.

—, *Wanted: A World Development Plan,* in: *Internat. Organisation,* XXII (1968) 417-431.

United Nations, *World Population Conference, 1965,* (Belgrade, 30 Aug. to 10 Sept., 1965), vol. I. Summary Report, New York: U. N. (Deptm. of Econ. and Soc. Affairs), 1966.

—, *Report on the First Interregional Seminar on Development Planning,* Ankara, Turkey, 6-17 Sept., 1965, New York: U. N., 1967.

World Economic Review and Forecast, New York: Grosset & Dunlap, 1965.

c. *Education and Development.*

Bosc, R., *L'éducateur face à la vie internationale.* Principes, méthodes, exemples, Paris: Centurion, 1962.

Gillespie, H. M., *Education and Progress,* London: Evan Brothers Ltd., 1966.

Harbison, F.-Myers, *Human Resources, Education, and Economic Growth,* New York: McGraw-Hill, 1964.

—, *Education, Manpower and Economic Growth.* Strategies of Human Resource Development, New York: McGraw-Hill, 1964.

Philips, H. M., *Education and Development,* in: *Economic and Social Aspects of Educational Planning,* Paris: UNESCO, 1964, 15-58.

4. CONCRETE AID

a. *General Data, U. N., Governments, Volunteers.*

Antweiler, A., *Entwicklungshilfe.* Versuch einer Theorie, Trier: Paulinus Verl., 1962.

Arnold, H. J. P., *Aid for Development.* A Political and Economic Study, Chesterspring: Dufour, 1966.

Development Guide. A Directory on non-commercial Organizations in Britain providing facilities for developing countries, London: Overseas Development Institute, 1963.

Effective Aid, London: Overseas Development Institute, 1967.

Handbuch der Entwicklungshilfe, ed. by Havemann - Kraus, 3 vol., Baden-Baden: Nomos Verlagsgesellschaft, 1960 ss.

The Haslemere Declaration. A Radical Analysis of the Relationships between the Rich World and the Poor World, published by the Haslemere Declaration group c/o 515 Liverpool Road, London N. 7, (1968) 1969[4].

Labin, S., *Communisme et pays sous-développés,* in: *Rev. de Droit .nter., de Sc. Pipl. et Pol.,* (janv.-mars 1967), 26-37.

Maxwell, J. F., *Direct Private Investment in the Developing Countries and Fairer Distribution of Wealth among Nations,* in: *World Justice* IX (1967/68) 447-487.

Montgomery, J. D., *Foreign Aid in International Politics,* London: Prentice Hall, 1967.

Müller, O., *Über Kalkutta nach Paris?* Strategie und Aktivität des Ostblocks in den Entwicklungsländern, Hannover: Verl. f. Literatur und Zeitgeschehen, 1964.

OECD/ICVA Directory, *Development Aid of Non-Governmental Non-Profit Organizations,* Paris: OECD, 1967.

United Nations, *The United Nations Development Decade.* Proposals for Action. Report of the Secretary-General, New York: U. N., (Deptm. for Ec. and Soc. Aff.), 1962.

Ward, B., *The U. N. and the Decade of Development,* in: *World Justice* VII (1965/66), 309-335.

b. *The Churches' Aid.*
(Cf: Christian Concern for Development).

Considine, J., *The Missionary's Role in Socio-Economic Betterment,* Westminster: Newman Press, 1960.

Dickinson, R., *Do Church-sponsored Projects Assist Development?*,
in: *Social Compass* 16 (1969), 63-76.

Drogat, N., *Le chrétien et l'aide aux pays sous-dévéloppés*. Documents et données statistiques, Paris: Centurion, 1962.

Glendenning, F. J., *Servant of the Servant Church*. A Discussion
Guide about Christian Aid, London: Christian Aid, 1965.

Kerkhofs, J., *Church Aid for Developing Countries*, in: *Concilium*
vol. 3, I (1965), 25-31.

Osner, K., *Kirchen und Entwicklungshilfe*. Ziele, Leistungen und
Arbeitsweise kirchlicher Organisationen in Deutschland, (Bun-
desministerium für wirtschaftliche Zusammenarbeit), Kevelaer:
Butzon und Bercker, 1967.

Overseas Aid-priorities for the Churches, London: Christian Aid,
1967.

Schall, J. V., *Christian Political Approaches to Population Problems*,
in: *World Justice* 8 (1966-1967), 301-323.

c. *Critical Analysis of the Actual Motivations.*

Broekmeijer, M. W. J. M., *Fiction and Truth about the Decade of
Development*, Leijden: Sijthoff, 1966.

Clark, C., *Growthmanship. A Study in the Methodology of Investment*, London: Institute of Econ. Aff., 1961[2].

Larson, D. J., *The Puritan Ethic in U. S. Foreign Policy*, London:
Van Nostrand, 1967.

Lefringhausen, K. (ed.), *Gerechtigkeit und Solidarität*. 87 Empfeh-
lungen zum Wirtschaftsverhalten der EWG gegenüber den
Entwicklungsländern; eine Europäische Denkschrift, Gütersloh: Mohn, 1969.

Motivations and Methods in Development and Foreign Aid, (ed.
by T. Geiger and L. Solomon, World Conference of the
Society for International Development), New York: Oceana
Publ., 1966.

Ricoeur, P., *Prévision économique et choix éthique*, in: *Esprit*
34 (1966), 178-193.

Schmauch, J., *Herrschen oder Helfen?* Kritische Überlegungen zur
Entwicklungshilfe, Freiburg: Rombach, 1967.

United Nations, *1965 Report on the Social Situation, with Special
Reference to Popular Participation and Motivation for Development*, New York, U. N., 1966.

III. PROGRESS AND DEVELOPMENT IN THE HISTORY OF IDEAS

1. GENERAL STUDIES *

Becker, C. I., *The Heavenly City of the XVIIIth Century Philoso-phers,* New Haven: Yale Univ. Press, 1932 (span: *La ciudad de Dios del Siglo XVIII,* Mexico, Fondo de Cultura Económi-ca, 1943).

Bury, J. B., *The Idea of Progress.* An Inquiry into its Origin and Growth, London, 1920, New York, 1932², Constable & Co., Dover Publ., 1955; (ital.: *Storia dell'Idea di progresso,* Milano: Feltrinelli, 1964).

Cohn, N., *Das Ringen um das Tausendjährige Reich.* Revolutio-närer Messianismus im Mittelalter und sein Fortleben in den modernen, totalitären Bewegungen, Bern-München: Francke, 1961.

Dawson, Ch., *Progress and Religion.* An Historical Inquiry, New York: Longmans, Green & Co., 1929, (Bibl. pp. 251-254).

Desroche, H., *Messianismes et utopies.* Notes sur les origines du socialisme occidental, Paris: C.R.C., 1960.

Freyer, H., *Die politische Insel.* Eine Geschichte der Utopien von Platon bis zur Gegenwart, Leipzig: Bibliogr. Inst., 1936.

Loewith, K., *Meaning in History.* The Theological Implications of the Philosophy of History, Chicago: Chicago Univ. Press, 1949, (germ., span., dutch and ital. transl.).

Maier, H., *Revolution und Kirche.* Studien zur Frühgeschichte der christlichen Demokratie (1789-1850), Freiburg: Rombach, 1965².

Picht, G., *Der Sinn der Unterscheidung von Theorie und Praxis in der griechischen Philosophie,* in: *Z. ev. Ethik* VIII (1964), 321-342.

Sampson, R. V., *Progress in the Age of Reason.* The Seventeenth Century to the Present Day, London: Heinemann, 1956.

Utopia, (Documentation Concilium), in: *Concilium* vol. 1, V (1969), 74-81.

2. MARXISM AND DEVELOPMENT

a. *Marxist Concept of Development*

(Marxist and Neo-Marxist Authors: *)

*Adorno, Th. W., *Dialektik der Aufklärung.* Philosophische Frag-mente, Amsterdam: Querido Verl. N. V., (1947) 1955.

---

* (For a more complete bibliography on the history of the idea of progress, see above pp. 80-83.

—, *Prismen, Kulturkritik und Gesellschaft*, Frankfurt: Suhrkamp, 1955 (München dtv., 1963).

—, *Negative Dialektik*, Frankfurt: Suhrkamp, 1966².

—, *Fortschritt*, in: *Argumentationen*, Festschrift f. J. König (hg. v. H. Delius u. G. Patzig), Göttingen: Vandenhoeck & Ruprecht, 1964, 1-19.

*Benjamin, W., *Zur Kritik der Gewalt und andere Aufsätze*, Frankfurt: Suhrkamp, 1965.

*Bloch, E., *Das Prinzip Hoffnung* (in fünf Teilen) (1938-47), 2 vol., Frankfurt: Suhrkamp. 1959, especially:
Weltveränderung oder die Elf Thesen von Marx über Feuerbach, ib. 288-334.
Freiheit und Ordnung. Abriss der Sozialutopien, ib., 547-729.
Wille und Natur, die technischen Utopien, ib. 729-817.
Wachsender Menscheinsatz ins religiöse Geheimnis, in Astralmythos, Exodus, Reich; Atheismus und die Utopie des Reiches, ib. 1392-1550.
Karl Marx und die Menschlichkeit; Stoff der Hoffnung, ib. 1602-28.

—, *Philosophische Grundfragen. Zur Ontologie des Noch-Nicht-Seins*, Frankfurt: Suhrkamp, 1961.

—, *Naturrecht und menschliche Würde*, Frankfurt: Suhrkamp, 1961.

—, *Tübinger Einleitung in die Philosophie*, 2 vol., Frankfurt: Suhrkamp (1963-1964), 1965-67², especially:
Über die Bedeutung der Utopie, ibd. I, 124-133.
Differenzierungen im Begriff Fortschritt, ib. I, 160-203.

—, *Thomas Münzer als Theologe der Revolution*, Frankfurt: Suhrkamp, 1962.

—, *Geist der Utopie* (Bearbeitete Neuauflage der erweiterten Fassung von 1923), Frankfurt: Suhrkamp, 1964.

*Borgeanu, C., *Sur l'actualité de l'idée de progrès*, in: *Actes du XIVème Congrès International de Philosophie*, Vienne du 2 au 9 Sept. 1968, Wien: Herder, 1969, IV, 584-590.

Delekat, F., *Zum Geschichtsverständnis im Marxismus*, in: *Hören und Handeln*, Festschrift für Ernst Wolf, hg, v. H. Gollwitzer u. H. Traub, München: Kaiser, 1962, 52-63.

Dumont, R.-Mazoyer, M., *Développement et socialismes*, Paris: Seuil, 1969.

Fetscher, I., *Developments in the Marxist Critics of Religion*, in: *Concilium* vol. 6, II (1966), 57-68.

*Garaudy, R., *Création et liberté*, in: *Christianisme social* 3-4, 75 (1967), 211-233.

*Glezerman, G., *The Laws of Social Development*, Moscow, ca. 1965 (orig. russ: Moskva: Gospolitizdat, 1960).

*Habermas, J., *Strukturwandel der Öffentlichkeit*. Untersuchungen zu einer Kategorie der bürgerlichen Gesellschaft, Neuwied: Luchterhand, 1962.

—, *Theorie und Praxis*. Sozialphilosopische Studien, Neuwied: Luchterhand, 1963 (hg. W. Hennies und R. Schnur).

—, *Technik und Wissenschaft als « Ideologie »*, Frankfurt: Suhrkamp, 1968.

*Klaus, G., *Kybernetik und Gesellschaft*, Berlin: Dt. Verl. der Wiss., 1964.

*Klaus, G. - Schulze, H., *Sinn, Gesetz und Fortschritt in der Geschichte*, Berlin: Dietz Verl., 1967.

Kolarz, W., (ed.), *Books on Communism. A Bibliography*, (New Enlarged Edition), London: Ampersand Ltd., (1959) 1963².

Marcuse, H., *Reason and Revolution*. Hegel and the Rise of Social Theory, New York: The Humanities Press, 1954².

—, *One-Dimensional Man*. Studies in the Ideology of Advanced Industrial Society, Boston: Beacon Press, 1964.

—, *Das Ende der Utopie*, Berlin: Peter von Maikowski, 1967.

Le Marxisme et l'Asie, 1853-1964. Textes traduits et présentés par Stuart Schram et Hélène Carrère d'Encausse, Paris: Colin, 1965.

Die marxistisch-leninistische Philosophie und die technische Revolution. Materialien des philosophischen Kongresses vom 22. - 24. 4. 1965 in Berlin, in *Deutsche Zeitschrift f. Philosophie*, Sonderheft 1965.

*Müller, W., *Gesellschaft und Fortschritt*. Eine philosophische Untersuchung, Berlin: Dt. Verl. der Wiss., 1966.

Mumby, L. M. - Wangermann, E., *Marxism and History*. A Bibliography of English Language Works, London: Lawrence & W., 1967.

Skoda, F., *Die sowjetrussiche philosophische Religionskritik heute*, (Quaestiones disputatae, 36), Freiburg: Herder, 1968, (Bibl. pp. 155-160).

Soubise, L., *L'aliénation politique chez les néo-marxistes*, in: Projet 1967, 389-408.

*Suchý, J., *Die Gewalt in der Aneignung der Zukunft*. Zur Problematik des moralischen Wertes der Gewalt, in:*Akten des XIV. Internat. Kongr. f. Philos.*, Wien, 2.-9. Sept. 1968, Wien: Herder, 1969, IV, 65-70.

b. *Critics. Marxist-Christian Dialogue.*

Bent, A. J. van der, *The Christian Marxist Dialogue. An Annotated Bibliography,* 1959-1969, Genève: World Council of Churches, 1969.

Diez, P. - Herrero-Velarde, R., *Revolución marxista y progreso cristiano,* Barcelona: Nova Terra, 1969².

Farner, K., *Theologie des Kommunismus?* Frankfurt: Stimme Verl., 1969 (especially vol. III: *Die grosse Hoffnung.* Kurze Geschichte der Utopie, der Paradieserwartung, der Reich-Gottes Idee und des Kommunismus).

Girardi, G.,*Marxismo e cristianesimo,* Assisi: Citadella, 1969⁴ (translations in 7 languages).

—, *Credenti e non credenti per un mondo nuovo,* Firenze: Vallecchi, 1969 (french transl.: *Dialogue et révolution,* Paris: Cerf, 1969).

Klugmann, J. (ed.), *What Kind of Revolution?* A Christian-Communist Dialogue, London: Panther, 1968.

Krieger, E., *Das Prinzip Hoffnung. Auseinandersetzung mit Ernst Bloch,* in: E. Krieger, *Grenzwege.* Das Konkrete in Reflexion und Geschichte von Hegel bis Bloch, Freiburg: Alber, 1968, 9-36.

Kurakov, J. G., *Science, Technology and Communism. Some Questions of Development,* London: Pergamon Press, 1966. (orig. russ.).

Marsch, W. - D., *Hoffen worauf?* Auseinandersetzung mit Ernst Bloch, Hamburg: Furche, 1963.

Marxistisches und christliches Weltverständnis, (von B. Bosnjak, W. Dantine, J. Y. Calvez), Freiburg: Herder, 1966.

Mury, G., *Un marxiste devant Gaudium et Spes.* De la contradiction à l'espérance, in: *L'Église dans le monde de ce temps,* III, Paris: Mame, 1967, 133-154.

Rahner, K., *Marxistische Utopie und christliche Zukunft des Menschen,* in: *Schriften,* Einsiedeln: Benziger, vol. VI, 1965, 77-88.

Sowjetssystem und demokratische Gesellschaft. Eine vergleichende Enzyklopädie in 5 Bänden, (hg. von C. D. Kerning ...), Freiburg: Herder, 1966.

3. DEVELOPMENT IN PRESENT-DAY THINKING.

Behrendet, R. F., *Zwischen Anarchie und neuen Ordnungen*. Soziologische Versuche, Freiburg: Rombach, 1967.

Bissiere, R. - Vacherot, J., *Science, seule espérance? Marx? Teilhard?*, Paris: Ouvrières, 1967.

Boehler, E., *Die Zukunft als Problem des modernen Menschen*, Freiburg: Rombach, 1966.

Buber, M., *Paths in Utopie*, London: Routledge & Kegan Paul, 1949.

Burck, E., (ed.), *Die Idee des Fortschritts*. Neun Vorträge über Wege und Grenzen des Fortschrittsglaubens, München: C. H. Beck, 1963.

Delfgaauw, B., *Geschichte als Fortschritt*, Köln: Bachem, 3 vol., 1962-66 (orig. dutch).

Eliade, M., *Le mythe de l'éternelle retour. Archétypes et répetition*, Paris: Gallimard, 1949.

Fiedler, F. - Müller, W., *Zukunftsdenken im Kampf der Ideologien — eine Kritik der Futurologie*, in: *Deutsche Zeitschr. f. Philosophie*, 15 (1967), 253-272.

Florez, C., *Dialéctica, historia y progreso*, Salamanca: Sigueme, 1968.

Freyer, H., *Theorie des gegenwärtigen Zeitalters*, Stuttgart: Deutsche Verl.Anstalt, 1958.

Guardini, R., *Das Ende der Neuzeit*. Ein Versuch zur Orientierung, Basel: Hess, 1950 (engl.: *The End of the Wodern World*, A Search for Orientation, London: Sheed & Ward, 1957.)

Hengstenberg, H. E., *Moderner Fortschrittsglaube und Geschichtlichkeit*. Ein Beitrag zur Gegenwartsanalyse, in: R. Schwarz, (ed.), *Menschliche Existenz und moderne Welt*, Berlin: De Gruyter, 1967, 462-497.

Jöhr, W. A., *Der Fortschrittsglaube und die Idee der Rückkehr in den Sozialwissenschaften*, Tübingen: Mohr, 1964.

Kimmerle, H., *Die Zukunftsbedeutung der Hoffnung*. Auseinandersetzung mit Ernst Blochs 'Prinzip Hoffnung' aus philosophischer und theologischen Sicht, Bonn: Bouvier, 1966.

Lebret, L. J. - Delprat, R. - Debruyères, M. F., *Développement-Révolution solidaire*, Paris: Ouvrières, 1967.

Löwith, K., *Das Verhängnis des Fortschritts*, in: *Die Philosophie und die Frage nach dem Fortschritt*, ed. H. Kuhn-F.Wiedmann, München: Pustet, 1964, 15-29.

McLean, G., *Philosophy and the Future of Man*, (Proceedings of the American Catholic Philosophical Association, 42), Washington: Cath. Univ. of America, 1968.

Mannheim, K., *Mensch und Gesellschaft im Zeitalter der Umbaus,* Darmstadt: Wissenschaftliche Buchgesellschaft, 1958.

Marcel, G., *Homo Viator.* Prolégomènes a une métaphysique de l'espérance, Paris: Aubier-Ed. Montaigne, 1944.

—, *Un changement d'espérance.* A la rencontre du Réarmement moral, Paris: Plon, 1958.

Melsen, A. G., M. van, *Naturwissenschaft und Technik.* Eine Philosophische Besinnung, Köln: Bachem, 1964.

Molnar, Th., *Utopia. The Perennial Heresy,* New York: Sheed & Ward, 1967.

Petit-Pont, M., *Structures traditionelles et développement,* Paris: Ed. Eyrolles, 1968.

Die Philosophie und die Frage nach dem Fortschritt, hg. von H. Kuhn u. F. Wiedmann, (Verhandlungen des 7. Deutschen Kongressus für Philosophie, Münster 1962), München: Pustet, 1964.

Picht, G., *Prognose-Utopie-Planung.* Die Situation des Menschen in der Zukunft der technischen Welt, Stuttgart: Klett, 1967.

—, *Mut zur Utopie.* Die grossen Zukunftsaufgaben, (Zwölf Vorträge - Sendereihe des Süddeutschen Rundfunks), München: R. Piper & Co., 1969.

Plessner, H., *Diesseits der Utopie. Beiträge zur Kultursoziologie,* Düsseldorf: Diederichs, 1966.

Le prix du progrès, in: *Chron. soc. Fr.* 75 (1967) 2-129.

Schlechta, K., (ed.) *Der Mensch und seine Zukunft,* (Darmstädter Gespräch 1966), Darmstadt: Neue Darmstädter Verl., 1967.

Teilhard de Chardin, P., *Le phénoméne humain,* Paris: Seuil, 1955.

—, *Les fondements et le fond de l'idée d'évolution* (1926), in: *Oeuvres III,* Paris: Seuil, 1957, 163-197.

—, *Le milieu divin,* Paris: Seuil, 1957.

—, *Note sur le progrès* (1920), in: *Oeuvres V,* Paris: Seuil, 1959, 21-37.

—, *Hérédité sociale et progrès* (1921), ib. 39-53.

—, *Réflexions sur le progrès* (1941), ib. 83-106.

—, *La foi en la paix* (1947), ib. 189-197.

—, *Esquisse d'un Univers personnel* (1936), in: *Oeuvres VI,* Paris: Seuil, 1962, 67-114.

—, *La centrologie* (1944), in: *Oeuvres VII,* Paris: Seuil, 1963, 103-134.

—, *Sience et Christ* (1921), in: *Oeuvres IX,* Paris: Seuil, 1965, 45-62.

—, *Catholicisme et science* (1946), ib. 235-241.

—, *Recherche, travail et adoration* (1955), ib. 281-289.

—, *Comment je crois* (19344)4, in: *Oeuvres X,* Paris: Seuil, 1969, 115-152.

cf. Crespy, G., *La pensée théologique de Teilhard de Chardin*, Paris: Éd. Univers., 1961.

Cuenot, C., *Pierre Teilhard de Chardin*. Les grandes étapes de son évolution, Paris: Plon, 1958.

Geiger, M., *Zukunft und Geschichte in der Weltschau Teilhard de Chardins*, in: Fangmeier, J.-Geiger, M., *Geschichte und Zukunft*. Zwei Studien zu Oscar Cullmanns 65. Geburtsstag Zürich: EVZ, 1966.

Lubac, H. de, *La pensée religieuse du Père Teilhard de Chardin*, Paris: Aubier, 1962.

Mermord, D., *La morale chez Teilhard*, Paris: Éd. Univers., 1967.

Polgar, L., *Internationale Teilhardbibliographie 1955-1966*, Freiburg: Alber, 1965.

Toynbee, A. J., *Perspektiven der Welt von morgen*, in: *Menschliche Existenz und moderne Welt*, II, Berlin: de Gruyter, 1967, 473-485.

Tüchel, K., *Die Technik als Problem der Gegenwartsphilosophie*, in: *Neue Zeitschrift für Syst. Theol. und Religionsphilosophie* 8 (1966) 265-288.

Wittram, R., *Zukunft in der Geschichte*. Zu Grenzfragen der Geschichtswissenschaft und Theologie, Göttingen: Vandenhoeck & Ruprecht, 1966.

IV. THE HUMAN ASPECT OF DEVELOPMENT

1. MANKIND IN EVOLUTION
(cf. Teilhard de Chardin, III[3])

Armagnac, C. d', *Épistemologie et philosophie de l'évolution*, in: *Archives de Philosophie* 23 (1960), 153-163.

Bartsch, H., *Über die biologische Zukunft des Menschen*, in: R. Schwarz, (ed.), *Menschliche Existenz und moderne Welt*, I, Berlin: de Gruyter, 1967, 656-669.

Bröker, W., *Der Sinn der Evolution*, Düsseldorf: Patmos, 1967.

—, *Aspects of Development*, in: *Concilium* vol. 6, III (1967), 5-13.

Büchel, W., *Entwicklung und Entropie*, in: *Stimmen der Zeit* 170 (1961-62), 186-199.

—, *Mensch und Automat*. Literatur zur Kybernetik, in: *Stimmen der Zeit* 184 (1969) 113-120.

Cottier, J L., *La technocratie, nouveau pouvoir*, Paris: Cerf, 1959.

Cube, F. von, *Was ist Kybernetik?* Grundbegriffe, Methoden, Anwendungen, Bremen: Schünemann, 1967[2].

Erisman, Th. H., *Zwischen Technik und Psychologie.* Grundpro-
bleme der Kybernetik, Berlin: Springer, 1968.
Die Frage nach dem Sinn der Evolution, (Reihe Weltgespräch, 9),
mit Beiträgen von W. Heitler, H. Zoller, H. Mohr, O. Loretz,
Freiburg: Herder, 1969.
Frisch, J., *Die Krise der menschlichen Evolution,* Mainz: Grüne-
wald, 1969.
Haas, A., (ed.), *Das stammesgeschichtliche Werden der Organismen
und des Menschen,* Bd. I, Deutung und Bedeutung der Abstam-
mangslehre, Freiburg: Herder, 1959.
—, *Die Entwicklung des Menschen,* Aschaffenburg: Pattloch, 1961.
—, *Der Mensch, Sinn der Entwicklung,* Kevelaer: Butzon u. Ber-
cker, 1963.
A History of Technology, (ed. by Ch. Singer, E. J. Holmyard ...),
Oxford: Clarendon, 5 vol., 1954 ss.
Heiler, F., *Die religiöse Einheit der Menschheit,* in: R. Schwarz,
(ed.), *Menschliche Existenz und moderne Welt,* Berlin: de
Gruyter, 1967, 578-593.
Iwao Munakata, P. F., *Socialization towards Humanity* (IPRA Stu-
dies in Peace research. Proceedings of the International Peace
Research Ass. Inaugural Conf.). Assen: Van Gorcum, 1966.
Kybernetik und die Philosophie der Technik, in: *Akten des XIV.
Internat. Kongr. f. Philosophie,* 2.-9. Sept. 1968 in Wien, Wien:
Herder, 1968, vol. II, 477-614.
Lederberg, J., *Experimentelle Genetik und menschliche Evolution,*
in: R. Schwarz, (ed.), *Menschliche Existenz und moderne Welt,*
I, Berlin: de Gruyter, 1967, 670-88.
Marcic, R., *Seinsrecht als Einheitsgrund des Menschengeschlechtes,*
ib. II, 486-540.
Melsen, A. van, *Scientific Aspects of Mankind's Future,* vol. I, Den
Haag: Inst. of Soc. Studies, 1962.
Mukerjee, R., *The Oneness of Mankind,* London: Macmillan, 1966.
—, *The Community of Communities,* Bombay: Manaktala, 1966.
Mynarek, H., *Der Mensch-Sinnziel der Weltentwicklung.* Entwurf
eines christlichen Menschenbildes auf dem Hintergrund eines
dynamisch-evolutionären Kosmos unter besonderer Berück-
sichtigung von Ideen K. Schells und Teilhard de Chardins,
München-Paderborn-Wien: Schöningh, 1967.
Nogar, R. J., *Science de l'évolution, données scientifiques et pensée
chrétienne,* Paris: Castermann, 1965.
Overhage, P., *Die Evolution des Lebendigen. Das Phänomen,* (Quaest.
disp. 20-21), Freiburg: Herder, 1963.
—, *Die Evolution des Lebendigen. Die Kausalität,* (Quaest. disp.
26-27), Freiburg: Herder, 1965.

Schilling, K., *Philosophie der Technik*. Die geistige Entwicklung der Menschheit von den Anfängen bis zur Gegenwart, Herford: Maximilian Verl., 1968.

Schulz, G., *Technische Revolution und Strukturwandel in der Industrie*, Berlin: Dietz, 1966.

Steinbuch, K., *Automat und Mensch*. Kybernetische Tatsachen und Hypothesen, Berlin: Springer, 1965[3].

L'uomo e la città. Atti del Convegno di urbanisti, Assisi 5-10 ottobre 1966, a cura di Pina Ciampani, Assisi: Cittad. Ed., 1967.

Wiener, N., *Kybernetik*. Regelung und Nachrichtenübertragung in Lebewesen und Maschine, Hamburg: Rowohlt, 1968.

2. CONCERN FOR MAN IN DEVELOPMENT

Bacht, H., *Die Selbstzerstörung des Menschen im Spiegel des modernen Zukunftsromans*, in: H. Bacht, (ed.), *Weltnähe oder Weltdistanz*, Frankfurt: Knecht, 1966.

Biser, E., *Gewinn im Verlust*. Zum Strukturwandel im technischen Zeitalter, in: J. B. Metz, (ed.), *Weltverständnis im Glauben*, Mainz: Grünewald, 1966[2], 24-44.

Civilisation technique et humanisme. Colloque de l'Académie Internationale de philosophie des sciences, (Bibliothèque des archives de philosophie, 6), Paris: Beauchesne, 1968.

Coste, R., *Morale internationale. L'humanité à la recherche de son âme*, Paris: Desclée, 1964.

Ellul, J., *The Technological Evolution*. Its Moral and Political Consequences, in: *Concilium* vol. 6, III (1966), 47-51.

Gehlen, A., *Die Seele im technischen Zeitalter*. Hamburg: Rowohlt, 1960.

Heistermann, W., *Mensch und Maschine*. Die Bedeutung der Kybernetik für das Verständnis des Menschen, in: R. Schwarz, (ed.), *Menschliche Existenz und moderne Welt*, I, Berlin: de Gruyter, 1967, 783-802.

Hiller, E., *Humanismus und Technik*, Düsseldorf: Patmos, 1966.

Johann, R. O., *Building the Human*, New York: Herder, 1968.

Klineberg, O., *Die menschliche Dimension in den internationalen Beziehungen*, Berlin-Stuttgart: Huber, 1966.

Marcel, G., *Les hommes contre l'humain*, Paris: La Colombe, 1951.

—, *The Existential Background of Human Dignity*, (William James Lectures 1961-1962) Cambridge, USA: Harvard Univ. Press, 1964.

Maritain, J., *Les conditions spirituelles du progrès et de la paix*: Rencontres des cultures à l'UNESCO sous le signe du Concile Oec. Vat. II, Paris: Mame, 1966.

Martin, A. von, *Humanität als Problem der Gegenwart*, in: R. Schwarz, (ed.), *Menschliche Existenz und moderne Welt*, I, Berlin: de Gruyter, 1967, 33-62.

Michel, E., *Der Prozess " Gesellschaft contra Person "*. Soziologische Wandlungen im nachgoetheschen Zeitalter, Stuttgart: Klett, 1959.

Mynarek, H., *Der Mensch-das Wesen der Zukunft*. Glaube und Unglaube in anthropologischer Perspektive, Paderborn: Schöningh, 1968.

Le progrès scientifique et technique et la condition de l'homme, Paris: PUF, 1960.

Rahner, K., *Christlicher Humanismus*, in: *Schriften*, vol. VIII, Einsiedeln: Benziger, 1967, 239-259.

—, *Das Christentum und der "Neue Mensch"*, ib. vol. V, 1964, 159-179.

—, *Würde und Freiheit des Menschen*, ib. vol. II, 1964[7], 247-277.

Riscoperta dell'uomo. Documentazione IDO-C, Milano: Mondadori, 1967.

Schelsky, H., *Der Mensch in der wissenschaftlichen Zivilisation*, Köln-Opladen: Westdeutscher Verlag, 1961.

Schwarz, R., (ed.), *Menschliche Existenz und moderne Welt*. Ein internationales Symposion zum Selbstverständnis des heutigen Menschen, hg. und mitverfasst v. Richard Schwarz, Teil I und II, Berlin: Walter de Gruyter & Co., 1967.

Tellegen, F., *The Responsible Development of Technology*, in: *Concilium* vol 5, V (1969), 31-37.

Verantwortung für den Menschen. Beiträge zur gesellschaftlichen Problematik der Gegenwart, hg. v. F. Karrenberg und J. Beckmann, Stuttgart: Kreuz, (1957) 1962.

Westphalen, F. A., *Humanisierung der Wirtschaft*, in: *Die Neue Ordnung* 21 (1967), 81-94.

3. ETHICAL QUESTIONS

Aukrust, T., *Die Freiheit des Menschen und der manipulierte Mensch*, in: *Glaube und Gesellschaft*, Beiträge zur Sozialethik heute, Stuttgart: Kreuz, 1966, 26-41.

Dubarle, D., *Does Man's Manner of Determining his Own Destiny Constitute a Threat to his Humanity?*, in: *Concilium* vol. 6, III (1967), 41-46.

Experiments with Man (World Council Studies, No. 6), Geneva: World Council of Churches, 1969.

Internationales Colloquium über Menschenrechte. International Round-table discussion on Human Rights. Colloque Internationale sur les Droits de l'homme, Berlin, 3-8 Okt. 1966, Berlin: Deutsche Gesellschaft für die Vereinten Nationen, 1968.

Kautzky, R., *Scientific Progress and Ethical Problems in Modern Medicine*, in: *Concilium* vol. 5, V (1969), 38-45.

Löbsack, Th., *Die unheimlichen Möglichkeiten der manipulierten Seele*, Düsseldorf: Econ, 1967.

Lotz, J. B., *Möglichkeiten und Grenzen der Manipulierbarkeit des Menschen*, in: *Zivilisation und menschliche Zukunft*, (Studien und Berichte der Kath. Akademie in Bayern, vol. 35), Würzburg: Echter, 1966, 123-151.

Overhage, P., *Experiment Menschheit*. Steuerung der menschlichen Evolution, Frankfurt: Knecht, 1967.

Pappworth, M. H., *Menschen als Versuchskaninchen*. Experiment und Gewissen, Rüschlikon-Zürich: Albert Müller, 1968.

Paupert, J. M., (ed.), *Contrôle des naissances et théologie*. Le dossier de Rome, Paris: Seuil, 1967.

Rahner, K., *Experiment Mensch*. Theologisches über die Selbstmanipulation, in: *Schriften*, vol. VIII, Einsiedeln: Benziger, 1967, 260-85.

—, *Zum Problem der genetischen Manipulation*, ib. pp. 286-321.

Rauh, F., *Zur moraltheologischen Beurteilung einer biologischen Manipulation des Menschen*, in: *Mü. Th. Z.* 19 (1968), 81-91.

Rostand, J., *Inquiétudes d'un biologiste*, Paris: Stock, 1968.

Theobald, R., *Droits de l'homme à l'âge de la cybernation*, in: *Econ. et Hum.* n. 173, XXVI (1967) 29-37.

V. SOURCES FOR A "THEOLOGY OF DEVELOPMENT"

1. BIBLICAL DATA

See in biblical reference works and in the current biblical bibliographies the following themes:

Biblical conception of history, liberation (Exodus), estimation of land, work, technique ..., Sabbatical Year, promise of the Land, Messianic promises (peace ...) and hope, social sensibility (prophets), poverty (the Servant of Yahweh), christian charity, Kingdom of God, eschatological vision of the Kosmos.

2. HISTORY OF CHRISTIAN THOUGHT

Alessio, F., *La Filosofia e le "Artes Mechanicae" nel secolo XII*, in: *Studi Medievali* 6 (1965), 71-161.

Alszeghy, Z., *Ein Verkündiger der Welt predigt Weltverachtung.*
Zum Verständnis der "Vanitas-mundi" - Literatur des Mittel-
alters, in: *Geist und Leben* 35 (1962), 197-207.
—, *Fuite du monde (fuga mundi),* in: *Dict. de Spir., Asc. et Myst.,*
Paris: Beauchesne, 1964, col. 1575-1606.
Auer, A., *Christsein im Beruf.* Grundsätzliches und Geschichtliches
zum christlichen Berufsethos, Düsseldorf: Patmos, 1966.
Balthasar, H. U. von, *Kosmische Liturgie.* Das Weltbild Maximus
des Bekenners, Einsiedeln: Johannes-Verl., 1961², (french:
Paris: Aubier, 1947).
Bianchi, U., *Il dualismo religioso.* Saggio storico ed etnologico,
Roma: L'Erma, 1958.
Biehler, A., *Gottes Gebot und der Hunger der Welt.* Calvin, Prophet
des industriellen Zeitalters. Grundlage und Methode der So-
zialethik Calvins, Zürich: EVZ, 1966.
Bornkamm, H., *Luthers Lehre von den zwei Reichen im Zu-
sammenhang seiner Theologie,* Gütersloh: Bertelsmann, 1958.
Bultmann, R., *Le christianisme primitif dans le cadre des religions
antiques,* Paris: Payot, 1950.
Bultot, R., *Christianisme et valeurs humaines,* Louvain: Nauwelaerts,
1963.
Décarraux, J., *Les moines et la civilisation en Occident,* Paris:
Arthaud, 1962.
Delavignette, R., *Christianisme et colonialisme,* Paris: Fayard, 1960.
Dempf, A., *Sacrum Imperium. Geschichts- und Staatsphilosophie
des Mittelalters und der politischen Renaissance,* München:
Oldenbourg, 1929.
—, *La concepción del mundo en la edad media,* Madrid: Greda,
1958.
Diez-Alegria, J. M., *La perfection de la charité et l'activité écono-
mique et social,* in: *Sainteté et vie dans le siècle* (Laïcat et
sainteté II), Roma: Herder, 1965, p. 225-254.
Dittburner, H., *A Theology of Temporal Realities: Explanation
of St. Jerome,* Roma: Gregorian Univ. Press, 1966.
Dodd, C. H., *Gospel and Law. The Relation of Faith and Ethics
in Early Christianity,* New York: Columbia Univ. Press, 1957.
Gandillac, M. de, *Place et signification de la technique dans
le monde médiéval,* in: *Tecnica e casistica,* Padova: Cedam,
1964, 265 ss.
Grégoire, R., *Introduction à une étude théologique du "mépris
du monde",* in: *Studia Monastica* 8 (1966), 313-328.
Gribomont, J., *Le renoncement au monde dans l'idéal ascéthique
de Saint Basile,* in: *Irénikon* 31 (1958), 282-307. 460-475.

317

Höffner, J., *Christentum und Menschenwürde.* Das Anliegen der spanischen Kolonialethik im goldenen Zeitalter, Trier, Paulinus Verl., 1947, (2. verb. Auflage 1968: *Kolonialismus und Evangelium*; span.: *La ética colonial española del siglo de oro.* Cristianismo y dignidad humana, Madrid: Ed. de cultura hispànica, 1957).

Krumwiede, H. W., *Glaube und Geschichte in der Theologie Luthers.* Zur Entstehung des geschichtlichen Denkens in Deutschland, Göttingen: Vandenhoeck und Ruprecht, 1952. (Bibl. pp. 117-120).

Ladner, G. B., *The Idea of Reform.* His Impact on Christian Thought and Action in the Age of the Fathers, Cambridge: Harvard Univ. Press, 1959.

Lagarde, G. de, *La naissance de l'esprit laïque au déclin du Moyen Age,* Louvain-Paris: Nauwelaerts, 1956-58[2].

Lammers, W., (ed.), *Geschichtsdenken und Geschichtsbild im Mittelalter,* Darmstadt: Wissensch. Buchgesellschaft, 1961.

Lubac, H. de., *Augustinisme et théologie moderne,* Paris: Aubier, 1965.

Luneau, A., *L'histoire du salut chez les Pères de l'Eglise.* La doctrine des âges du monde, Paris: Beauchesne, 1964.

Marrou, H. I., *The Resurrection and St. Augustine's Theology of Human Values,* Villanova: Univ. Press, 1965.

Milburn, R. L. P., *Early Christian Interpretations of History,* London: Adam and Karl Black, 1954.

Möllerfeld, J., *Nichtigkeit der Welt? Zu Leib, Geist und Welt in frühscholastischer Sicht* (Literaturbericht), in: *Geist und Leben* 35 (1962), 66-73.

Orbe, A., *La Unción del Verbo,* Roma: Gregorian Univ. Press, 1961.

Rahner, K., *Die ignatianische Mystik der Weltfreudigkeit,* in: *Schriften,* Einsiedeln: Benziger, 1964, vol. III, 329-348.

Ranke-Heinemann, U., *Das Verhältnis des frühen Mönchtums zur Welt,* in: *Mü. Th. Z.* 7 (1956) 289-295.

Repo, E., *Der "Weg" als Selbstbezeichnung des Urchristentums.* Eine traditionsgeschichtliche und semasiologische Untersuchung, Helsinki: Suomalainen Tiedeakatemia, 1964.

Schrey, H. H., *Reich Gottes und Welt.* Die Lehre Luthers von den zwei Reichen, Darmstadt: Wiss. Buchgesellschaft, 1969.

Sierra Bravo, R., *Doctrina social y económica de los Padres de la Iglesia,* Colección general de documentos y textos, Madrid: Ed. Compi, 1967.

Spoerl, J., *Das Alte und das Neue im Mittelalter.* Studien zum

Problem des mittelalterlichen Fortschrittsbewusstseins, in: *Hist. Jahrbuch der Görresgesellschaft*, 50 (1930), 297-341, 498-524.

Stammler, W., *Frau Welt: eine mittelalterliche Allegorie,* Freiburg: Univ. Verl., 1959.

Tscholl, *Augustinus' Aufmerksamkeit am Makrokosmos,* in: *Augustiniana* 15 (1965), 389-413.

Vandenbroucke, F., *Moines: pourquoi?* Théologie critique du monachisme, Paris: Lethielleux, 1967.

Wachtel, A., *Beiträge zur Geschichtstheologie des Aurelius Augustinus,* (Bonner Histor. Forschungen, 17) Bonn: Rohrscheid, 1960.

3. CHRISTIAN CONCERN FOR DEVELOPMENT

Abrecht, P., *The Churches and Rapid Social Change,* London: SCM, 1961.

Acebal Montfort, L., *Upsal, un symptôme?* Signification théologique de la contestation des jeunes, in: *N. Rev. Th.* 91 (1969), 47-64.

América Hoy. Acción de Dios y responsabilidad del hombre, Montevideo: ISAL, 1966.

Beaver, P., *Christian Responsibility in the Emerging World Economic Situation, Industrialization and World Mission,* Chicago: Univ. of Chicago Press, 1958.

Bosc, R., *La société internationale et l'Église,* 2 vol., Paris: Spes, 1961-68.

Chaigne, H., *Bogotá et la révolution nécessaire,* in: *Frères du Monde* 57 (1969), 31-62.

CELAM, *Presentia activa de la Iglesia en el Desarrollo y en la Integración de América Latina,* Bogotá: Departemento de Acción Social, 1967.

Le Développement, la Justice et la Paix, (54ᵉ semaine soc. de France), Lyon: Chron. Soc. Fr., 1967.

Dewart, L., *Christianity and Revolution.* The Lesson of Cuba, New York: Herder & Herder, 1963.

Dickinson, R., *Line and Plummet.* The Churches and Development, Geneva: World Council of Churches, 1968 (transl.: french, germ., span.).

Domenach, J. M. - Montvalon, R. de, *Une Eglise en marche,* Paris: Desclée de Brouwer, 1964.

Duquoc, Chr., *L'Église et le progrès,* Paris: Cerf, 1964.

Eastman, A. Th., *Christian Responsibility in One World,* New York: Seabury Pr., 1965.

Fagley, R. M., *The Population Explosion and Christian Respon-sibility,* New York: Oxford Univ. Press, 1960.

Forero, J. M., *Camilo Torres,* Bogotá: Ed. Kelly, 1960.

Gheerbrant, A., *L'Église rebelle d'Amérique latine,* Paris: Seuil, 1969.

Gollwitzer, H., *Die reichen Christen und der arme Lazarus.* Die Konsequenzen von Uppsala, München: Kaiser, 1968².

Gozzer, G., *Religione e rivoluzione in America Latina,* Milano: Bompiani, 1968.

Guissard, L., *Catholicisme et progrès social,* Paris: Fayard, 1959.

Guzman Campos, G., *Cattolicesimo e rivoluzione in America Latina.* Vita di Camillo Torres, Bari: Laterza, 1968 (french transl.: *Camilo Torres, le curé-guérillero,* Paris: Castermann, 1968).

Habegger, N., *Camilo Torres, el cura guerillero,* Buenos Aires, 1967, (transl. ital.: *Camilo Torres, prete e guerillero,* Firenze: Cultura Ed. 1968).

Helder Camara, D., *Evangelização e Humanização num mundo em desenvolvimiento,* in: *Rev. Ecl. Brasil.* 25 (1965), 269 ss.

Houtart, Fr., *L'Église latino-américaine à l'heure du Concile,* Fribourg: Feres, 1963 (engl. and span. tr.).

—, *The Challenge to Change,* The Church Confronts the Future, New York: Sheed & Ward, 1964.

—, *L'Église à l'heure de l'Amérique latine,* Tournai: Casterman, 1965, (tr. engl. and span.).

—, *The Eleventh Hour: Explosion of a Church,* (ed. by Mary Anne Chouteau with an introduction by H. Cox), London: Burns & Oates, 1968.

Kirchen als Träger der Revolution. Ein politisches Handlungsmo-dell am Beispiel der USA, von H.-J. Benedict und H.-E. Bahr, Hamburg: Furche, 1968.

Jarlot, G., *La Iglesia ante el progreso social y político,* Barcelona: Peninsula, 1967.

Lambert, B., *Le Chrétien dans un monde en marche vers l'unité,* in: *Doc. Cath.,* (6-20 août) 1967, 1401-1426.

Lebret, L. J., *Dynamique concrète du développement* (Développe-ment et civilisations), Paris: Ed. Ouvrières, 1961.

—, *Développement, révolution solidaire,* Paris: Ed. Ouvrières, 1967.

Lüning, H., *Camilo Torres, Priester, Guerillero.* Darstellung, Analyse und Dokumentation, Hamburg: Furche, 1969.

McCormack, A. G., (ed.), *Christian Responsibility and World Poverty.* A Symposium, London: Burns & Oates, 1963.

Osner. K. - Koch, U., *Entwicklung — der neue Name für Friede.* Auf dem Weg zu einer Weltsozialpolitik, in: *Stimmen der Zeit* 182 (1968) 167-180.

Plädoyer für die Dritte Welt. Eine Erklärung von 15 kathol. Bischöfen der Dritten Welt, in: *Herderkorrespondenz* 21 (1967), p. 511; (french in: *Témoignage Chrétien* no. 1208 [31. 8. 1967] 13-16).

Reissig, H. F., *Man's New Home. A Christian Approach to Changing World Problems,* Philadelphia: United Church Press, 1964.

Rian, E., (ed.), *Christianity and World Revolution,* New York: Harper & Row, 1963.

Riga, P. J., *The Church and Revolution.* Some Reflections on the Relationship of the Church to the Modern World, Milwaukee: The Bruce Publ. Co., 1967.

Rogers, E., *Poverty on a Small Planet.* A Christian looks at living standards, New York: Macmillan, 1965.

Schooyans, M., *Chrétientᴳ en contestation. L'Amérique latine,* Paris: Cerf, 1969.

Schweitzer, W., *Christen im raschen sozialen Umbruch heute.* Eine theologische Skizze, (Beiheft zur Oekum. Rundschau, Nr. 2), Stuttgart: Ev. Miss. Verl., 1966.

—, *Christians in Changing Societies,* London: Lutterworth, 1967.

Thomas, M. M., *Asien und seine Christen in der Revolution,* München: Kaiser, 1968.

Torres, C., *Camilo Torres* (Sondeos 5), Cuernavaca: CIDOC, 1966 (french transl.: *Ecrits et Paroles,* Paris: Seuil, 1968).

—, *Camilo Torres.* Biografia, Plataforma, Mensajes, Medellìn: Ed. Carpel-Antorcha (transl. germ.: *Revolution als Aufgabe der Christen,* Mainz: Grünewald, 1969).

4. DECLARATIONS OF THE CHURCHES

a. *Papal Encyclicals and Vatican II.*

aa. Mater et Magistra (Johannes XXIII, 15. 5. 1961), Acta Apost. Sedis, LIII (1961), 401-464.

Arató, P., *Bibliographia de Encyclica Mater et Magistra,* in: *Archivum Hist. Pontificiae*: 1 (1963) 652-656 - 2 (1964) 525-527 - 3 (1965) 536-538 - 4 (1966) 566 - 5 (1967) 593-594 - 6 (1968) 670-671 - 7 (1969) 722.

Abaitua, C. - Alberdi, R. - Setien, J. M., *Exigencias cristianas en el desarrollo económico-social.* Comentarios a la encíclica " Mater et Magistra ", Madrid: Ed. Studium, 1962.

Calvez, J.-Y., *Église et société économique. L'enseignement social de Jean XXIII,* Paris: Aubier, 1963.

Cronin, J. F., *Christianity and Social Progress.* A Commentary on Mater et Magistra, Baltimore: Helicon, 1965.

L'Enciclica "Mater et Magistra". Linee generali e problemi particolari. A cura di Th. Mulder ed H. Carrier, (Studia socialia 7), Roma: Gregorian Univ. Press, 1963.

Jean XXIII, *Encyclique Mater et Magistra*. Trad. sur le texte latin officiel. Commentaire et index analytique par l'Action Populaire. Préface du Card. Richaud, Paris: Spes, 1963.

Loewenstein, F., *Mater et Magistra. Gedanken zur Sozialenzyklika Papst Johannes XXIII*, Text und Kommentar, Mannheim: Peschhaus, 1962.

Masse, B. L., (ed.), *The Church and Social Progress*. Background Readings for Pope John's Mater et Magistra, Milwaukee: Bruce, 1966.

bb. PACEM IN TERRIS (Johannes XXIII, 11. 4. 1963), Acta Apost. Sedis, LV (1963), 257-304.

Arató, P., *Bibliographia de Encyclica Pacem in terris*, in: *Archivum Hist. Pontificiae*, 2 (1964) 527-532 — 3 (1965) 538-539 — 4 (1966) 566-567 — 5 (1967) 594 — 6 (1968) 670-671 — 7 (1969) 722.

Aguilar Navarro, M. - Aranguren J. L. L., *Comentarios civiles a la Enciclica Pacem in Terris*, Madrid: Taurus, 1963.

Hünermann, J., *Kommentar zur Friedensenzyklika Pacem in Terris*, Essen: Wirgen, 1963.

Instituto Social Leon XIII, *Comentarios a la « Pacem in Terris »*, Madrid: B. A. C., 1963.

Jean XXIII, *Encyclique Pacem in Terris*. Commentaire et Index analytique par l'Action Populaire, Paris: Spes, 1963.

PACEM IN TERRIS, *Lettera enciclica di Giovanni XXIII*, testo e commenti, (vari autori), Milano: Relazioni sociali, 1963.

Moine, A., *Après « Pacem in terris »*. Chrétiens et communistes, Paris: Éd. sociales, 1965.

Riga, P., *Peace on Earth*. A Commentary on Pope John's Encyclical, New York: Herder, 1964.

Utz, A. F., (ed.) *Die Friedensenzyklika Papst Johannes XXIII Pacem in Terris, Über den Frieden ...*, Kommentar von A. F. Utz, Freiburg: Herder, 1963.

cc. GAUDIUM ET SPES (Vat. II. Constitutio pastoralis de Ecclesia in mundo huius temporis, 7. 12. 1965), Acta Apost. Sedis, LVIII (1966) 1025-1120.

Arató, P., *Bibliographia de Constitutione Gaudium et Spes*, in: *Archivum Hist. Pontificiae*, 3 (1965) 560 — 4 (1966) 594-595 — 5 (1967) 623-628 — 6 (1968) 689-692 — 7 (1969) 734-735.

Brugarola, M., *El Concilio y la vida económico-social,* Santander: Sal Terrae, 1966.

La Chiesa e la Cultura, (S. Salerno, R. Sigmond, E. Franceschini, H. de Riedmatten, Ch. Moeller, M. Pellegrino, P. Arrupe), Napoli: Ed. Domenicane Italiane, 1967.

La Chiesa nel mondo contemporaneo. Costituzione pastorale del Concilio Vaticano II. Introduzione e commento a cura di S. Quadri, Torino: Borla, 1966.

La Chiesa nel mondo di oggi. Studi e commenti intorno alla Costituzione pastorale « Gaudium et Spes ». Opera collettiva diretta da G. Baraúna, Firenze: Vallecchi, 1967².

Commentary on the documents of Vatican II, vol. 5, Pastoral Constitution on the Church in the Modern World, London-New York: Burns & Oates - Herder and Herder, 1969.

Constitution Pastorale « Gaudium et Spes »: L'Eglise dans le monde de ce temps, ... Introduction, notes et index analytique par l'Action Populaire, Paris: Spes, 1966.

La Costituzione Pastorale sulla Chiesa nel Mondo Contemporaneo. Introduzione storicodottrinale, testo latino e traduzione italiana, esposizione e commento, Torino: Leumann, Elle Di Ci, 1966.

L'Église dans le monde de ce temps. Constitution « Gaudium et Spes ». Commentaires de schéma XIII, Paris: Mame, 1967.

L'Église dans le monde (N. A. Nissiotis, Ph. Maury, P. A. Liégé), Paris: Mame, 1967.

Estudios sobre la Constitución « Gaudium et Spes », Bilbao: Mensajero, 1967.

Hanssler, B., *Glaube und Kultur,* (Kommentarreihe zur Pastoralkonstitution des II. Vat. Konzils: Über die Kirche in der Welt von heute, Bd. 6), Köln: Bachem, 1968.

Houtart, Fr., *L'Église et le monde. A propos du schéma 13,* Paris: Cerf, 1964.

La Iglesia en el mundo de hoy. Estudios y comentarios a la Constitutión « Gaudium et Spes » del Concilio Vat. II. Obra colectiva dirigida por G. Baraúna, (Ed. esp. por J. De Abarzuza), Madrid: Studium, 1967.

Die Kirche in der Welt von heute. Eine Einführung in die Pastoralkonstitution Gaudium et Spes mit Beiträgen von F. Hengsbach, A. Guggenberger ..., Würzburg: Arena, 1966.

Das Konzil zur Wirtschaftsgesellschaft. Lateinischer und deutscher Text nach der Pastoralkonstitution über die Kirche in der Welt dieser Zeit. Mit Erläuterungen von W. Weber, W. Schreiber, A. Rauscher, Münster: Regensberg, 1966.

Oeconomia Humana, Wirtschaft und Gesellschaft auf dem II. Vat. Konzil. Eine Veröffentlichung der Internationalen Stiftung Humanum, Köln: Bachem, 1968.

Riga, P. J., *The Church Made Relevant*. A Commentary on the Pastoral Constitution of Vatican II, Notre Dame, Ind.: Fides, 1967.

Turner, D., *The Church in the World*. Essays on the Second Vatican Council's Pastorale Constitution on the Church in the World today with Texts of Church teaching on Social Questions, Dublin: Scepter P., 1968.

dd. POPULORUM PROGRESSIO (Paulus VI., 26.3.1967), Acta Apost. Sedis, LIX (1967), 257-299.

Arató, P., *Bibliographia de Encyclica « Populorum Progressio »*, in: *Archivum Hist. Pontificiae*, 6 (1968) 698-700 — 7 (1969) — 741.

Aubert, J.-M., *Populorum Progressio, le développement des peuples*. L'Église face à la croissance du monde. Texte ... Essai de théologie du développement. Commenté ... bibliographie ... index analytique, par J.-M. Aubert, Paris: Fleurus, 1968.

Bigorda, J. - Marti, C., *Pablo VI. Progreso de los pueblos*. Texto y comentarios, Barcelona: Nova terra, 1967.

Bopp. J., *Populorum Progressio. Aufbruch der Kirche?* Stuttgart: Kohlhammer, 1968.

Calvez, J.-Y. *Église et développement*, in: *Gregorianum* 49 (1968), 623-636.

Ceriani, G. - Gheddo, P. - Melzi, C., *Commento all'enciclica « Populorum Progressio » sullo sviluppo dei popoli*, Milano: Massimo, 1967.

Garcia, M., *Teología y Sociología del desarrollo*. Comentario a la "Populorum Progressio". Ed. dirigada por M. Garcia, Madrid: Razón y Fe, 1968.

Krauss, H., (ed.), *Über den Fortschritt der Völker*. Die Entwicklungsenzyklika Papst Paul VI. Populorum Progressio. Mit einem Kommentar von H. Krauss. Freiburg: Herder, 1967.

Lateinamerikanische Reaktionen auf "Populorum Progressio", in: *Herderkorrespondenz* 21 (1967), 410-413.

La pace e lo sviluppo dei popoli nella "Populorum Progressio", Vicenza: Centro Studi N. Rezzara, 1968.

Paul VI., *Encyclique Populorum Progressio sur le développement des peuples*. Introduction et commentaire par l'Action Populaire, Paris: Spes, 1967.

—, *Le développement des peuples, Populorum progressio*. Introduction de Vincent Cosmao, directeur général adjoint de l'IRFED, Paris: Centurion, 1967.

Quadri, S. - Levi, V. - Morero, V., *"Populorum Progressio"*. Testo, commento e documentazione con indice analitico-ragionato, Roma: Ed. Paoline, 1967.

ee. GENERAL WORKS

Alszeghy, Z., *Development in the Doctrinal Formulations of the Church concerning the Theory of Evolution,* in: *Concilium* vol. 6, III (1967), 14-17.

Baum, G., *The Magisterium in a Changing Church,* ib. vol. 1, III (1967), 34-42.

Bigo, P., *La doctrine Sociale de l'Église,* Paris: PUF, 1965 (span. transl.: Barcelona: Inst. Cat. Est. Soc., 1967).

Calvez, J.-Y. - Perrin, J., *L'Église et société économique.* L'enseignement social des Papes de Léon XIII à Pie XII, Paris: Aubier, 1961².

Hörmann, K., *Peace and Modern War in the Judgement of the Church,* Gless Rock (N. J.): Newman Press, 1966.

McDonagh, E., *The Declaration on Religious Freedom of Vatican Council II,* London: Darton L & T, 1967.

Montvalon, R. de, *Trois encycliques sociales:* Mater et Magistra, Pacem in Terris, Populorum Progressio, Paris: Seuil, 1967.

Murray, J. C., *The Declaration of Religious Freedom,* in: *Concilium* vol. 5, II (1966), 3-10.

Rauscher, A. - Lio, E., *Die Bestimmung der Erdengüter für alle Menschen im Lichte der christlichen Soziallehre,* in: *Oeconomia Humana,* Köln: Bachem, 1969, 187 ss.

Riga, P., *John XXIII and the City of Man,* Westminster: Newman Press, 1966.

Schillebeeckx, E., *The Magisterium and the World of Politics,* in: *Concilium* vol. 6, IV (1968), 12-21.

b. *World Council of Churches:*

cf. A. J. van der Bent - P. Beffa, *Index to Ecumenical Statements and World Council of Churches Reports, 1948-1967,* Geneva: World Council of Churches, 1968 (engl., fr., germ.).

aa. OFFICIAL REPORTS AND STATEMENTS.

General Assemblies:

AMSTERDAM, 1948, *The First Assembly of the World Council of Churches,* held at Amsterdam, August 22nd to September 4th, 1948, Edited by W. A. Visser't Hooft, London: SCM Press, 1949 (cf. pp. 65 & 75, developing nations).

EVANSTON, 1954, *The Evanston Report.* The second Assembly of the World Council of Churches, 1954, London: SCM Press. 1955. (cf. pp. 123-126, 138, 147, developing nations and development aid).

New Delhi, 1961, *The New Delhi Report.* The Third Assembly of the WCC, 1961, London: SCM Press, 1962 (cf. pp. 100, 106-107, 112-113,273-276, development, aid ...).

Uppsala, 1968, *The Uppsala Report on the Fourth Assembly of the WCC. 1968, Geneva:* WCC, 1968, (cf. sections III & IV)

Other Reports and Statements:

Church and Society, *The Common Christian Responsibility toward Areas of Rapid Social Change.* 2nd statement, Geneva: WCC, Dept. on Church and Soc., 1956.

Thessalonica, 1959, *Dilemmas and Opportunities.* Christian Action in Rapid Social Change. Report of an International Ecumenical Study Conference, Thessalonica, Greece, July 25 - August 2, 1959, Geneva: WCC, Dept. on Church and Soc., 1959.

Geneva, 1966, *World Conference on Church and Society, Geneva, July 12-26, 1966.* The Official Report. Geneva: WCC, 1967, (cf. especially pp. 70, 75-76, 82, 84-90, 138, 151, 210, on development aid, and pp. 66-67, 101-106, 115-116, 140-143, 199-200, on revolution).

Bangkok, 1964, *The Christian Community within the Human Community.* Containing statements from the Bangkok Assembly of the East Asia Conference Febr. 25th - March 5, Bangalore, India, 1964, (cf. pp. 18, 40-42 on development).

Division of World Mission and Evangelism, *The Healing Church.* The Tübingen Consultation, 1964, Geneva: WCC, 1965.

Division of Studies, *The Arnoldshain Report, 1956.* A Regional Conference on the Responsible Society in National and International Affairs, Geneva: WCC, 1956, (cf. pp. 14-16, 19-20, on rapid social change).

Department on Church and Society, *Statements of the World Council of Churches on Social Question.* With a Preface on the Development of Ecumenical Social Thinking, Geneva: WCC, 1956.

Department on Church and Society, *Ecumenical Statements on Race Relations.* Development of Ecumenical Thought on Race Relations, 1937-1964, Geneva: WCC, 1965.

Secretariat on Religious Freedom, *Main Ecumenical Statements on Principles concerning Religious Freedom,* Geneva: WCC, Division of Studies, Secretariat on Rel. Freedom, 1965 (Mimeographed).

Interchurch Aid, *Digest of the 1966 World Consultation on Interchurch Aid at Sawanick, Great Britain,* Geneva: WCC, Dicarws, 1966, (cf. section I, p. 102-107 on development Aid).

The Commission of the Churches in International Affairs, *(Annual) Reports 1947-1967,* Geneva: WCC, 1947-1968.

bb. OTHER PUBLICATIONS

The Challenge of Development. The Montreal Conference. A Sequel to the Beirut Conference of April 21-27, 1968; Montreal, Canada, May 9-12, 1969, sponsored by the Committee on Society, Development and Peace (Sodepax), Geneva: Sodepax, 1969.

Die Kirche als Faktor einer kommenden Weltgemeinschaft, Auswahlband der Vorbereitungsbände z. Weltkonferenz f. Kirche u. Gesellsch. (Ök. Rat. der Kirche), Stuttgart: Kreuz, 1966.

Krüger, H., (ed.) *Kirche zwischen Gott und Welt,* Vorträge von Uppsala, (Beiheft Nr. 9-10 der Ökum. Rundschau), Stuttgart: Ev. Miss. Verl., 1969.

Justice in a Developing World. Studies pointing to the Lutheran World Federation Assembly in 1970, Geneva: World Council of Churches, 1968.

Mosley, J. B., *Christians in the Technical and Social Revolutions of Our Time.* Suggestions for Study and Action, Cincinnati, Ohio: Forward Movement Publications, 1966.

Ramsey, P., *Who speaks for the Church?* A Critique of the 1966 Conference on Church and Society, Nashville: Abingdon, 1967.

Reactions to Uppsala. Letters of Criticism and Advise, in: *Study Encounter* IV (1968), 199-218.

Theological Issues of Church and Society. Statement of the Zagorsk Consultation, held at St. Sergius Monastery, Zagorsk, USSR, March 17-23, 1968, in: *Study Encounter* 4 (1968), 70-81.

Uppsala speaks, Section Reports of the Fourth Assembly of the World Council of Churches, Geneva: WCC, 1968.

Wilkens, E. (ed.), *Die Zukunft der Kirche und die Zukunft der Welt.* Die Synode der EKD 1968 zur Weltverantwortung der Kirche in einem revolutionären Zeitalter. Im Auftrage der Synode herausgegebeen v. E. Wilkens, München: Kaiser 1969.

World Development, Challenge to the Churches. The Conference for World Development in Beirut, Lebanon, 21 to 27 April, 1968, Geneva: Committee on Society, Development and Peace, 1968.

World Poverty and British Responsibility. A Report commended by the British Council of Churches, London: SCM Press, (1966) 1967[2].

VI. TOWARDS A THEOLOGY OF DEVELOPMENT
AND PROGRESS

1. METHODOLOGY

a. *Christianity and the Critics of Ideology.*

Albert, H., *Traktat über kritische Vernunft,* Tübingen: Mohr, 1968.
Marion, J., *Was ist Ideologie?.* Studie zu Begriff und Problematik, Bonn: Bouvier, 1964.
Bell, D., *The End of Ideology.* On the Exhaustion of Political Ideas in the Fifties, (1960). Revised ed. New York: Free Press of Glencoe, 1965.
Christlicher Glaube und Ideologie, hg. v. K. v. Bismarck und W. Dirks, Stuttg.-Berlin-Mainz: Kreuz-Grünewald, 1964.
Egenter, R. - Matussek, P., *Ideologie, Glaube und Gewissen.* Diskussion an der Grenze zwischen Moraltheologie und Psychotherapie, München-Zürich: Droemer-Knaur, 1965.
Flechtheim, O. K., *Utopie, Gegenutopie und Futurologie,* in: O. K. Flechtheim, *Eine Welt oder keine?* Beitrag zur Politik, Politologie und Philosophie, Frankfurt: Europ. Verlagsanst., 1964, 31-47.
Höfich, E., *Ideologien in der Kirche,* in: *Frankfurter Hefte* 20 (1965), 637-646.
Kelsen, H., *Aufsätze zur Ideologiekritik,* hg. v. E. Topitsch, Neuwied: Luchterhand, 1964.
Die Kirche und die Herrschaft der Ideologien, in: *Handb. d. Past.,* II/2, Freiburg: Herder, 1966, 109-202.
Knoll, A. M., *Katholische Gesellschaftslehre.* Zwischen Glaube und Wissenschaft, Wien: Europaverlag, 1966.
Lehmann, K., *Wesen und Struktur der Ideologien,* in: *Handb. d. Past.,* II/2, Freiburg: Herder, 1966, 115-148.
Lenk, K., (ed.) *Ideologie,* Neuwied: Luchterhand, 1964².
Lochman, J. M., *Ideologie und Toleranz,* in: *Z. ev. Ethik* 21 (1966), 284-294.
Mannheim, K., *Ideologie und Utopie,* Frankfurt: G. Schulte-Bulmke, 1952³.
Meynaud, J., *Destin des idéologies,* Lausanne: Maynard, 1961.
Rahner, K., *Ideologie und Christentum,* in: *Schriften,* vol. VI, Einsiedeln: Benziger, 1965, 59-76.
Santoni, R., (ed.), *Religious Language and the Problem of Religious Knowledge,* Bloomington & London: Indiana Univ. Press, 1968.
Schlette, H. R., *Aporetik-Kriteriologie-Philosophische Ideologie-Kritik,* in: H. R. Schlette, *Die Zukunft der Philosophie,* Olten: Walter, 1968, 184-202.

—, *The Problem of Ideology and Christian Belief* (Bulletin), in: *Concilium* vol. 6, I (1965), 56-67.

Splett, J., *Ideologie und Toleranz.* Die Wahrheitsfrage in der pluralistischen Gesellschaft, in: J. B. Metz, *Weltverständnis im Glauben*, Mainz: Grünewald, 1966², 269-286.

Zeltner, H., *Ideologie und Wahrheit.* Zur Kritik der politischen Vernunft, Stuttgart-Bad Constatt: Frommann, 1966.

cf. II, 2, a. b. (Marxism) and II, 3 (Utopia).

b. *Is there a Theology of Development?*

Alfaro, J., *Progresso umano e rivelazione divina*, in: J. Alfaro, *Teologia del progresso umano*, Assisi: Cittadella Editrice, 1969, 96-98.

Borovoj, V., *Rôle de la théologie dans les révolutions sociales de notre temps*, in: *Christ. Social* (janv.-fevr.), 1967, 31-37.

Burke, T. P., (ed.), *Künftige Aufgaben der Theologie*, München: Hueber, 1967.

Flick, M., *Riflessioni metodologiche per una teologia del progresso*, in: *Gregorianum* 50 (1969), 19-32.

Gremillion, J., *La Chiesa nel mondo contemporaneo. Un appello alla teologia*, in: J. Miller, (ed.), *La Chiesa dopo il Vaticano II*, Brescia: Morcelliana, 1967, 653-686.

Land, Ph., *What is Development?* Questions Raised for Theological Reflexion, in: *Gregorianum* 50 (1969), 33-62.

Laurentin, R., *Y-a-t-il une théologie du développement?* in: R. Laurentin, *Développement et Salut*, Paris: Seuil, 1969, 72-79.

Ratzinger, J., *Heilsgeschichte und Eschatologie.* Zur Frage nach dem Ansatz des theologischen Denkens, in: *Theologie im Wandel*, (Festschrift Tübingen), München-Freiburg: Erich Wewel Verl., 1967, 68-89.

Schultz, H. J., (ed.), *Tendenzen der Theologie im 20. Jahrhundert.* Eine Geschichte in Portraits, Stuttgart: Kreuz Verl., 1966.

Seckler, M., *Der Fortschrittsgedanke in der Theologie*, in: *Theologie im Wandel*, (Festschrift Tübingen), München-Freiburg: Erich Wewel Verl, 1967, 41-67.

Serrand, A. F., *Évolution technique et théologies*, Paris: Cerf, 1965.

La Théologie du renouveau, Texte intégral des travaux présentés au congrès international de Toronto, Montreal-Paris: Fides-Cerf, 1968, 2 vol.

Cf. the papers and proceedings of an ecumenical consultation on the methodology of a theology of development, held at Cartigny, Geneva in November 1969, Geneva: Sodepax, 1970.

2. THEOLOGICAL CONCEPTIONS

a. Anthropological Perspective

Alfaro, J., *Riflessione antropologica*, in: J. Alfaro, *Teologia del progresso umano*, Assisi: Citt. Ed., 1969, 38-69.

Alszeghy, Z., *L'immagine di Dio nella storia della salvezza*, in: *La costituzione past. sulla Chiesa nel mondo contemporaneo ...*, Torino: Elle Di Ci, 1966[2], 425-441.

Flick, M., *L'attività umana nell'universo*, in: S. Quadri, (ed.), *La Chiesa nel mondo contemporaneo*, Torino: Borla, 1966, 581-631.

Manaranche, A., *L'homme dans son univers*, Paris: Éd. Ouvrières, 1966.

Rahner, K., *Die Einheit von Geist und Materie im christlichen Glaubensverständnis*, in: *Schriften*, vol. VI, Einsiedeln: Benziger, 1965, 185-214.

—, *Grundentwurf einer theologischen Anthropologie*, in: *Handb. d. Past.*, vol. II/1, Freiburg: Herder, 1966, 20-38.

—, *Grundsätzliches zur Einheit von Schöpfungs- und Erlösungswirklichkeit*, in: *Handb. d. Past.*, vol. II/2, Freiburg: Herder, 1966, 208-228.

—, *Theologie und Anthropologie*, in: *Schriften*, vol. VIII, Einsiedeln: Benziger, 1967, 43-65.

Ratzinger, J., *Gratia praesupponit naturam.* Erwägungen über Sinn und Grenze eines theologischen Axioms, in: *Einsicht und Glaube* (hg. von J. Ratzinger u. H. Fries), Freiburg: Herder, 1962, 135-149.

Schillebeeckx, E., *L'homme et son monde corporel*, in: E. Schillebeeckx, *Le Monde et l'Église*, Bruxelles: édit. du CEP, 1967, 266-300.

Stoeckle, B., *Ich glaube an die Schöpfung*, Einsiedeln: Benziger, 1966.

Wolf, E., *Christliche Freiheit für die "freie Welt"*, in: *Existenz und Ordnung*, hg. von Th. Würtenberger, W. Maihofer u. A. Hollerbach, (Festschrift für Erik Wolf z. 60. Geb.), Frankfurt: Klostermann, 1962, 15-35.

b. Christological Perspective:

Alfaro, J., *Fondamenti cristologici del progresso umano*, in: J. Alfaro, *Teologia del progresso umano*, Assisi: Citt. Ed., 1969, 70-95.

Auer, A., *Weltoffener Christ.* Grundsätzliches und Geschichtliches zur Laienfrömmigkeit, Düsseldorf: Patmos (1960) 1966[4], (engl. tr.: *Open to the World*, Baltimore: Helicon).

Besret, B., *Incarnation ou eschatologie?* Contribution à l'histoire du vocabulaire religieux contemporain, 1935-1955, Paris: Cerf, 1966.

Colombo, G., *Escatologismo ed incarnazionismo: le due posizioni,* in: *Scuola Cattolica* 87 (1959), 344-376, 401-424.

Mersch, E., *Le Christ, l'homme et l'univers.* Prolégomènes à la théologie du Corps Mystique, Paris: Desclée de Brouwer, 1962.

Metz, J. B., *Weltverständnis im Glauben.* Christliche Orientierung in der Weltlichkeit der Welt heute, in: J. B. Metz, *Zur Theologie der Welt,* Mainz: Grünewald, 1968, 11-45.

Teilhard De Chardin, P., cf. III, 3.

c. *Eschatological Perspective.*

Balthasar, H. U. von, *Eschatologie,* in: J. Feiner - J. Trütsch - Fr. Böckle, (eds.), *Fragen der Theologie heute,* Einsiedeln: Benziger, 1957, 403-421.

Boros, L., *Mystery of Death,* New York: Herder & Herder, 1969, (germ. orig.: *Mysterium mortis.* Der Mensch in der letzten Entscheidung, Olten: Walter-Verl., 1962).

—, *Aus Der Hoffnung leben.* Zukunftserwartung in christlicem Dasein, Olten: Walter, 1968[2].

Bosc. J., *L'office royal du Seigneur Jésus-Christ,* Genève: Labor et Fides, 1957.

Bultmann, R., *History and Eschatology.* The Gifford Lectures 1955, Edinburgh: Univ. Press, 1957.

Duquoc, Ch., *Eschatologie et réalités terrestres,* in: *Lumière et Vie* 9 (1960), 4-22.

Eschatology: special issue of *Concilium,* vol. 1, V (1969), 1-82.

Flanagan, D., *Eschatology and the Assumption,* in: *Concilium* vol. 1, V (1969), 68-73.

Kirchhoff, H. (ed.), *Kaufet die Zeit aus.* Beiträge zur christlichen Eschatologie, (Festgabe für Th. Kampmann), Paderborn: Schöningh, 1959.

Koerner, J., *Eschatologie und Geschichte.* Eine Untersuchung des Begriffes des Eschatologischen in der Theologie Rudolf Bultmanns, Hamburg: Herbert Reich, 1957.

Metz, J. B., *Kirche und Welt im eschatologischen Horizont,* in: J. B. Metz, *Zur Theologie der Welt,* Mainz-München, Grünewald-Kaiser, 1968, 75-86.

Moltmann, J., *Das Ende der Geschichte,* in: J. Moltmann, *Perspektiven der Theologie,* Kaiser-Grünewald, München-Mainz, 1968, 232-250.

Müller-Goldkuhle, P., *Post-Biblical Developments in Eschatological Thought*, in: *Concilium* vol. 1, V (1969), 13-21.

Mussner, F. - Boros, L. - Kolping, A., *Le Christ devant nous*. Études sur l'éschatologie chrétienne, Paris: Desclée, 1967.

Rahner, K., *Kirche und Parusie Christi*, in: *Schiften*, vol. 6, Einsiedeln: Benziger, 1965, 348-367.

—, *Theologische Prinzipien der Hermeneutik eschatologischer Aussagen*, in: *Schriften*, vol. IV, Einsiedeln: Benziger, 1964, 401-428.

—, *Über die theologische Problematik der « Neuen Erde »*, in: *Schriften*, vol. VIII, Einsiedeln: Benziger, 1967, 580-592.

—, *Immanente und transzendente Vollendung der Welt*, ib., 593-609.

Scheffczyk, L., *Die Wiederkunft Christi in ihrer Heilsbedeutung für die Menschheit und den Kosmos*, in: J. B. Metz, (ed.), *Weltverständnis im Glauben*, Mainz: Grünewald 1966[2], 161-183.

Schillebeeckx, E., *Some Thoughts on the Interpretation of Eschatology*, in: *Concilium* vol. 1, V (1969), 22-29.

Schlier, H., *Das Ende der Zeit*, in: *Geist und Leben* 40 (1967), 203-217.

Unter der Herrschaft Christi. Vorträge von K. G. Steck u. a. gehalten a. d. Tagung der Gesellschaft f. Ev. Theol. im Oktober 1960 in Berlin-Spandau, München: Kaiser, 1961.

Wenz, H., *Die Ankunft unseres Herrn am Ende der Welt*. Zur Überwindung des Individualismus und des blossen Aktualismus in der Eschatologie R. Bultmanns und H. Brauns, Stuttgart: Calwer, 1965.

Wilder, A. N., *Kerygma, Eschatology, and Social Ethics*, Philadelphia: Fortress Press, 1966.

Winter, G., *The New Creation as Metropolis*. A Design for the Church's Task in an Urban World, New York-London: Macmillan, 1963.

3. THEOLOGICAL ANSWERS

a. *Theology of Terrestrial Realities.*

aa. THEOLOGY OF WORLD

Auer, A., *Gestaltwandel des christlichen Weltverständnisses*, in: *Gott in Welt* (Festschrift für K. Rahner z. 60. Geburtstag, hg. v. J. B. Metz u. a.), Freiburg: Herder, I, 1964, 333-365.

Brugarola, M., *Sociología y teología de la técnica*, Madrid: BAC, 1967.

Chenu, M. D., *Théologie de la matière*, Paris: Cerf, 1968.

Der Christ und die Technik, in: *Anima* 15 (1960), 97-192 (special issue).

Comblin, J., *Vers une théologie de l'action*, Bruxelles: Éd. Pensée cath., 1964.

Daubercies, P., *La condition charnelle*. Recherches positives pour la théologie d'une réalité terrestre, Tournai: Desclée, 1959.

Gonzales Ruiz, J. M., *El cristianismo no es un humanismo*. Apuntes para una teología del mundo, Madrid: Ed. Peninsula, 1966.

—, *Povertà evangelica e promozione umana*, Assisi: Cittadella Ed., 1967.

Grand'Maison, J., *Le sacré dans la consécration du monde*, Montréal: Univ. Press, 1965.

Maritain, J., *Religion et culture*, Paris: Desclée de Brouwer, 1968.

Metz, J. B., (ed.), *Weltverständnis im Glauben*, Mainz: Grünewald, 1966.

—, *Zur Theologie der Welt*, Mainz-München: Grünewald-Kaiser, 1968.

Michalson, C., *Wordly Theology*. The Hermeneutical Focus of an Historical Faith, New York: Scribner, 1967.

Morcillo, C., *El hombre cristiano ante la técnica*, Madrid: Euroamérica, 1962.

Pieper, J., *Zustimmung zur Welt*. Eine Theorie des Festes, München: Kösel, 1963.

Schillebeeckx, E., *Foi chrétienne et attente terrestre*, in: E. Schillebeeckx, *L'Église dans le monde de ce temps*, Tours: Mame, 1967, 117-160.

Schoonenberg, P., *God's World in the Making*, Pittsburgh: Duquesne Univ. Pr., 1964.

Thils, G., *Théologie des réalitées terrestres*, Louvain: Desclée de Brouwer, 2 vol., 1946-1949.

bb. THEOLOGY OF WORK

Auer, A., *Auf dem Wege zu einer Theologie der Arbeit*, in: *Theologie im Wandel*, (Festschrift Tübingen), München-Freiburg: Wewel, 1967, 543-564.

Bahrdt, H. P., *Entmythologisierung der Arbeit*, in: *Z. ev. Ethik* 9 (1965), 35-47.

Chenu, M. D., *Pour une théologie du travail*, Paris: Seuil, 1955.

Lartigolle, J., *Vocation chrétienne du travailleur moderne*. Essai sur la théologie du travail, Paris: Lethielleux, 1964.

The Meaning of Work, Geneva: World Council of Churches, Study Department, 1950.

Rondet, H., *Eléments pour une théologie du travail*, in: *N. Rev. Th.* 77 (1955), 27-48, 123-143.

Todd, J. M., *Work: Christian Thought and Practice*, London: Darton, Longman & Todd, 1960.

Truhlar, C. Vl., *Labor christianus. Initiatio in theologiam spiritualem systematicam de labore*, Roma: Herder, 1961.

cc. Secularisation as a Theological Problem.

Analyse et critique de la théologie de la sécularisation, Tournai-ⅼParis: Castermann, 1969.

Callahan, D. J. (ed.), *The Secular City Debate*, New York: Macmillan, 1966.

Cox, H., *The Secular City*. Secularization and Urbanization in Theological Perspective, New York: Macmillan (London: SCM), 1965.

Dantine, W., *Säkularisierung*. Versuch zur theologischen Bewältigung eines geschichtlichen Prozesses, in: *Wort und Wahrheit* 22 (1967), 657-674.

Delekat, F., *Über den Begriff der Säkularisation*, Heidelberg: Quelle und Meyer, 1958.

Geffré, C., *The Tension between Desacralization and Spirituality*, in: *Concilium* vol. 9, II (1966), 57-66.

Loen, A. E., *Secularization. Science without God?* Philadelphia: Westminster Pr., 1967, (orig. germ.).

Lübbe, H., *Säkularisierung*. Geschichte eines ideenpolitischen Begriffs, Freiburg: K. Alber, 1965.

Mascall, E. L., *Le sécularisme et la théologie*, in: *La théologie du renouveau*, Paris: Cerf, 1968, vol. I., 265-276.

—, *The Secularization of Christianity*. An Analysis and a Critique, London: Darton, Longman and Todd, 1965.

Murgoitio, J., (ed.), *Problemi morali della « teologia della secolarizzazione ».* Bibliografia, Roma: Gregorian Univ. Press, 1968-69.

Ouwerkerk, C. van, *Secularism and Christian Ethics*. Some Types and Symptomes, in: *Concilium* vol. 5, III (1967), 47-67.

Rahner, K., *Theologische Reflexionen zum Problem der Säkularisation*, in: *Schriften*, Einsiedeln: Benziger, vol. VIII, 1967, 637-666.

Rendtorff. T., *Säkularisierung als theologisches Problem*, in: *Neue Zeitschrift f. Syst. Theol.* 4 (1962), 318-339.

Rich, A., *Die Weltlichkeit des Glaubens*. Diakonie in Horizont der Säkularisierung, Zürich-Stuttgart: Zwingli, 1966.

Richard, R., *Secularization Theology*, New York: Herder, 1967.

Schlette, H. R., *Valutazione teologica della secolarizzazione*, in: *Processo alla religione* (IDOC 9) Milano: Mondadori, 1968, 41-61.

Schillebeeckx, E., *Säkularisierung und christlicher Gottesglaube,* in: F. Schillebeeckx, *Gott - Die Zukunft des Menschen,* Mainz: Grünewald, 1969, 49-79.

Schürmann, H., *Réflexions en marge du problème de la « désacralisation »* in: *Paroisse et Liturgie* 49 (1968), 401-432.

Thils, G., *Christianisme sans religion?,* Paris: Castermann, 1968.

Tihon, P., *La foi chrétienne et l'Église face au monde en voie de sécularisation,* Bulletin, in: *N. Rev. Th.,* 90 (1968), 307-330, 91 (1969) 316-329, 92 (1970) 206-221.

Vahanian, G., *Theology and the End of the Age of Religion,* in: *Concilium* vol. 6 II (1966), 51-56.

Wehrhahn, H., *Das Vorschreiten der Säkularisierung,* Bonn: Bouvier, 1969.

b. *Theology of History.*

aa. PHILOSOPHY AND THEOLOGY OF HISTORY.

Balthasar, H. U. von, *Theologie der Geschichte.* Ein Grundriss, Einsiedeln: Johannesverl., 1959³, (span. and ital. tr.).

Berkhof, H., *Christ the Meaning of History,* London: SCM Press, 1966.

Branden, S.G.F., *History, Time, and Deity.* A Historical and Comparative Study of the Conception of Time in Religious Thought and Practice (Bibl. pp. 211-226), Manchester: Univ. Pr., 1965.

Chifflot, Th. G., *Approches d'une théologie de l'histoire,* Paris: Cerf, 1960.

Cullmann, O., *Le salut dans l'histoire.* L'existence chrétienne selon le Nouveau Testament, Neuchâtel: Delachaux, 1966.

Danielou, J., *The Lord of History.* Reflections on the Inner Meaning of History, London: Longmans, 1958.

Darlapp, A., *Fundamentale Theologie der Heilsgeschichte,* in: *Mysterium Salutis,* hg. v. J. Feiner u. M. Löhrer, Einsiedeln: Benziger, vol. I, 1965, 3-158.

Dawson, Ch., *The Dynamics of World History* (ed. by J. J. Mulloy), New York: New Amer. Libr., 1962.

Geffré, C. J., *Bulletin de théologie dogmatique: Théologie de l'histoire,* in: *Rev. Sc. Phil. Theol.* 47 (1963), 130-135.

Heimann, E., *Theologie der Geschichte.* Ein Versuch, Stuttgart: Kreuz, 1966.

Kümmel, W. G., *Heilsgeschehen und Geschichte.* Gesammelte Aufsätze 1933-1964, Marburg: Elwert, 1965.

Marrou, H. I., *The Meaning of History,* Baltimore: Helicon, 1966.

—, *Théologie de l'histoire,* Paris: Seuil, 1968.

Moltmann, J., *Die Wahrnehmung der Geschichte in der christlichen Sozialethik*, in: J. Moltmann, *Perspektiven der Theologie*, München-Mainz: Kaiser-Grünewald, 1968, 149-173.

Mouroux, J., *Le mystère du temps*. Approche théologique, Paris: Aubier, 1962.

Niebuhr, R., *The Self and The Drama of History*, New York: Scribner, 1955.

—, *Faith and History*. A Comparison of Christian and Modern Views of History, New York: Scribner, 1949.

Offenbarung als Geschichte. (Programmheft von W. Pannenberg, R. Rendtorff, U. Wilckens, T. Rendtorff), Göttingen: Vandenhoeck & Ruprecht, 1961.

Rahner, K., *Weltgeschichte und Heilsgeschichte*, in: *Schriften*, vol. V, Einsiedeln: Benziger, 1964[2], 115-135.

Schlette, H. R., *Epiphanie als Geschichte*. Ein Versuch, München: Kösel. 1966.

Thielicke, H., *Geschichte und Existenz*. Grundlegung einer Evangelischen Geschichtstheologie, Gütersloh: G. Mohn, 1964.

Tillich, P., *Systematic Theology*, vol. III: *Life and the Spirit*. History and the Kingdom of God, Chicago: Univ. Pr., 1963.

bb. THEOLOGY OF HOPE.

Fangmeier, J. - Geiger, M., *Geschichte und Zukunft*. Zwei Studien zu Oscar Cullmanns 6. Geburtstag, Zürich: EVZ, 1967.

Leeuwen, A. Th. van, *Prophecy in a Technocratic Era*, New York: Scribner, 1968.

Margull, H. J., *Hope in Action*, Philadelphia: Muhlenberg Pr., 1962.

Marsch, W. - D., (ed.), *Diskussion über die «Theologie der Hoffnung»*, München: Kaiser, 1967.

Mascall, A. L., *Theology and the Future*, London: Darton, Longman & Todd, 1968.

Metz, J. B., *Gott vor uns*. Statt eines theologischen Arguments, in: S. Unseld, (ed.), *Ernst Bloch zu ehren*, Beiträge zu seinem Werk, Frankfurt: Suhrkamp, 1965, 227-241.

Moltmann, J., *Theologie der Hoffnung*. Untersuchungen zur Begründung und zu dem Konsequenzen einer christlichen Eschatologie, München: Kaiser, (1964) 1968[7] (*Theology of Hope*. On the Ground and the Implications of a Christian Eschatology, London: SCM. 1967).

—, *Perspektiven der Theologie*. Gesammelte Aufsätze, München-Mainz, Kaiser-Grünewald, 1968.

—, *Exegese und Eschatologie der Geschichte*, ib. 57-92.

—, *Antwort auf die Kritik der Theologie der Hoffnung,* in: W.-D. Marsch, (ed.), *Diskussion über die Theologie der Hoffnung,* München: Kaiser, 1967, 201-238.

—, *Die Kategorie NOVUM in der christlichen Theologie,* in: S. Unseld, (ed.), *Ernst Bloch zu ehren,* Beiträge zu Seinem Werk, Frankfurt: Suhrkamp, 1965, 243-264.

Pieper, J., *Hoffnung und Geschichte.* Fünf Salzburger Vorlesungen, München: Kösel, 1967.

Rahner, K., *Fragment aus einer theologischen Besinnung auf den Begriff der Zukunft,* in: *Schriften,* Einsiedeln: Benziger, vol. VIII, 1967, 555-560.

—, *Zur Theologie der Hoffnung,* ib. pp. 561-579.

Sauter, G., *Zukunft und Verheissung.* Das Problem der Zukunft in der gegenwärtigen theologischen und philosophischen Diskussion, Zürich-Stuttgart: Zwingli-Verl., 1965.

—, *Angewandte Eschatologie.* Überlegungen zu Jürgen Moltmanns « Theologie der Hoffnung », in: *Pastoraltheologie* 55 (1966), 384-402.

Schillebeeckx, E., *Gott - Die Zukunft des Menschen,* Mainz: Grünewald, 1969.

—, *Das Neue Gottesbild.* Säkularisierung und Zukunft des Menschen auf Erden, ib. 142-174.

Schutz, R., *Dynamique du provisoire,* Taizé: Les Presses de Taizé, 1965.

Valsardien, P., *La révolution totale, en tout.* Vers l'homme future et le christianisme cosmique, Gedalge: A. West & Cie, 1968.

c. *Toward a Theology of Development*

aa. « THEOLOGY OF MISSION » AND DEVELOPMENT

Armendariz, L. M., *Impaciencia misionaria y esperanza cristiana,* Bilbao: Ed. Mensajero, 1968.

Congar, Y. M., *Vaste monde, ma paroisse.* Vérité et dimensions du salut, Paris: Témoignage Chrét., 1966⁴.

Congrès mondial sur l'évangelisation. Un seul monde, un seul évangile, un seul dévoir, Genève: Labor et Fides, 1967.

De Groot, A., *The Missions after Vatican II,* in: *Concilium* vol. 6. IV (1968), 82-90.

Krusche, M., *Missio - Präsenz oder Bekehrung?* in: *Kerigma und Dogma,* 14 (1968), 119-140.

Land, Ph., *Populorum Progressio, Mission and Development,* in: *Int. Rev. Miss.* 58 (1969), 400-407.

Lebret, L., - Camara, H. P. - Anawati-Nebreda, *Nuovi orizzonti del dialogo missionario,* Brescia: Queriniana, 1968.

Maurier, H., *Religion et Développement.* Traditions africaines et catechèses, Tours: Mame, 1965.

Mission and Development, in: *Int. Rev. Miss.* 58 (1969, Oct.) (Special issue), 373-483.

Mission in the Modern World. The Islington Conference Papers 1968, London: Patmos Pr., 1968.

Repenser la Mission. Rapports et compte rendu de la 35ᵉ semaine de Missiologie Louvain, 1965, Louvain: éd. du Muséum Lessianum, 1965.

Richardson, W. J. (ed.), *Revolution in Missionary Thinking.* A Symposium, Mary Knoll: Mary Knoll, 1966.

Rossel, J., *Mission dans une société dynamique,* Genève: Labor et Fides, 1967.

Wiedenmann, L., *Mission und Eschatologie.* Eine Analyse der neueren deutschen evangelischen Missionstheologie, Paderborn: Bonifatiusdruckerei, 1965.

bb. THEOLOGY OF REVOLUTION.
(Bibl. cf.: *Disk. Theol. Rev.,* p. 365-373).

Bahr, H. - E. (ed.), *Weltfrieden und Revolution.* Neun politisch-theologische Analysen, Hamburg: Rowohlt, 1968.

J. CAMERON, *Obedience to Political Authority,* in: Todd, J. M. (ed.), *Problems of Authority.* The papers read at an Anglo-French symposion ..., Baltimore-London: HeliconPress, Darton Longman & Todd, 1962, 199-214.

Castro, E., *Conversion and Social Transformation,* in: J. C. Bennet (ed.), *Christian Social Ethics in a Changing World,* New York - London: Association Pr. - SCM, 1966, 348-366.

Cox, H., *God's Revolution and Man's Responsibility,* Valley Forge (USA): Judson Press, 1965.

Daim, W., *Christentum und Revolution,* München: Manz, 1967.

Diez-Alegria, J. M., *Cristianesimo e rivoluzione,* in: *Cristianesimo senza Cristo?,* Assisi: Cittadella, 1968, 65-103.

Diskussion zur « Theologie der Revolution », hg. v. E. Feil und R. Weth, München-Mainz: Kaiser-Grünewald, 1969 (Bibl. 365-373).

Évangile et révolution. Au coeur de notre crise spirituelle, (par M. J. Le Guillou, Clément, J. Bosc), Paris: Centurion, 1968.

Fragoso, A., *Évangile et révolution sociale,* Paris: Cerf, 1969.

Graham, B., *Conversion — A Personal Revolution,* in: *Ecum. Rev.* 19 (1967), 271-284.

Grässer, E., *Die falsch programmierte Theologie.* Kritische Anmerkungen zu ihrer gegenwartigen Situation, in: *Ev. Komm.* 1 (1968) 694-699.

338

Helder Camara, D., *La violence: option unique?* in: *Informations cath. internat.* n. 312, 15 mai, 1968, 4-7.

Honecker, M., *Zwischen Planung und Revolution.* Theologische Sozialethik vor der Verantwortung der Zukunft, in: *Ev. Komm.* 1 (1968), 571-579.

Lehmann, P. L., *Christliche Theologie in einer Welt der Revolution,* in: *Disk. Theol. Rev.* 174-204.

Lotz, M., *Der Begriff der Revolution in der ökumenischen Diskussion,* in: *Disk. Theol. Rev.* 17-28.

Marcuse, H., *Ethik und Revolution,* in: H. Marcuse, *Kultur und Gesellschaft 2,* Frankfurt: Suhrkamp, 1965, 130-146.

Meinhold, P., *Römer 13. Obrigkeit, Widerstand, Revolution, Krieg.* Stuttgart: Kreuz, 1960.

Middleton, N., *The Language of the Christian Revolution,* London: Sheed & Ward, 1968.

Moltmann, J., *Die Revolution der Freiheit,* in: J. Moltmann, *Perspektiven der Theologie,* München-Mainz: Kaiser-Grünewald, 1968, 189-211.

—, *Gott in der Revolution.* Thesen vorgetragen auf der Weltstudentenkonferenz in Turku, Juli 1968, in: *Ev. Komm.* 1 (1968), 565-571.

O'Brien, W. V., *Guerre juste et juste révolution, 1968,* in: *Just. Monde* IX (1967/68), 334-356.

Pinto de Oliveira, C. J., *Evangelho e revolução social,* Sâo Paulo: Libraria duas cidades, 1962.

Rasker, A. J. / Machovec, M. *Theologie und Revolution.* Ein westöstlicher Dialog, Hamburg: H. Reich, 1969.

A la recherche d'une théologie de la violence, Paris: Cerf, 1968.

Revolución violenta? (por C. L. Restrepo, P. Bigo ...), Bogotá: Ed. Campesino, 1965.

Revolution und Theologie. Das Neue in unserem Zeitalter. Ein Symposion, in: *Frankfurter Hefte* 23 (1967), 616-630.

Ringeling, H., *Politische Theologie und totale Revolution,* in: *Luth. Monatshefte* 7 (1968), 490-497.

Rock, M., *Widerstand gegen die Staatsgewalt.* Sozialethische Erörterung, Münster: Regensberg, 1966.

—, *Christ und Revolution.* Widerstandsrecht-Widerstandspflicht, Augsburg: Winfried Werk, 1968.

Shaull, R., *Revolutionary Change in Theological Perspective,* in: J. C. Bennet (ed.), *Christian Social Ethics in a Changing World,* New York-London: Association - SCM Pr., 1966, 23-43.

—, *Revolution: Heritage and Contemporary Option,* in: C. Oglesby - R. Shaull, *Containment and Change,* New York: Macmillan, 1967, part. II.

—, *Die Kirche und die Revolutionen*: *gegensätzliche Ansichten*, in: *Ev. Theol.* 27 (1967), 646-663.

Sölle, D., *Gott und die Revolution*, in: *Almanach I für Literatur und Theologie*, hg. v. D. Sölle u. a., Wuppertal: Hammer, Bd. I, 1967, 126-136.

Zur Theologie der Revolution, in: *Ev. Theol.* n. 12, 27 (1967), 629-685 (special issue).

Theology *and Revolution*, ed. by Marty, M. E. - Peermann, D. New York, 1969.

Tödt, H. E. - Rendtorff, T., *Theologie der Revolution*. Analysen und Materialien, Frankfurt: Suhrkamp, 1969³.

Tödt, H. E., *Theologie der Revolution*. Revolution als sozialethisches Konzept und seine theologischen Grenzen, in: *Oekum. Rundschau* 17 (1968), 1-22.

Vaccari, G., (ed.), *Teologia della Rivoluzione*. I testi inediti della rivolta sociale e politica della Chiesa Latinoamericana, Milano: Feltrinelli, 1969.

Vangelo, Violenza, Rivoluzione (IDOC, Documenti Nuovi, 10), (by) M. Fr. Blanco, P. L. Geschiere, Milano: Mondadori, 1969.

La Violence. Semaine des Intellectuels catholiques, 1-7 févr. 1967, Paris: Desclée de Brouwer, 1967.

La Violence, in: *Lumière et Vie* n. 91, XVIII (1969), (special issue).

Walther, Chr., *Christenheit im Angriff*. Zur Theologie der Revolution, Gütersloh: G. Mohn, 1969.

Wendland, H. D., *Die Kirche in der revolutionären Gesellschaft*, Gütersloh: G. Mohn, 1967.

Weymann-Weyhe, W., *Ins Angesicht widerstehen*. Darf ein Christ revolutionär sein? Olten: Walter, 1969.

Weth, R., « *Theologie der Revolution* » *im Horizont von Rechtfertigung und Reich*, in: *Disk. Theol. Rev.*, 82-109.

Windass, G. St., *Le christianisme et la violence*. Étude sociologique et historique de l'attitude du christianisme à l'égard de la guerre, Paris: Cerf, 1966. (*Christianity versus Violence*, London: Sheed & Ward, 1964).

cc. THEOLOGY OF PEACE

Berkenings, H. J., *Der Frieden als Aufgabe*, in: *Ev. Theol.* 25 (1965), 485-512.

Bosc, R. J. M., *Sociologie de la paix*, Paris: Spes, 1965.

Comblin, J., *Théologie de la paix*, Paris: Éd. Univ. 2 vol., 1960-1963.

Ebert, Th., *Gewaltfreier Aufstand*. Alternative zum Bürgerkrieg, Freiburg: Rombach, 1969.

Église, guerre et Paixe, in: *Chron. Soc. Fr.* 75 (1967), n. 3, 2-96.

Etzioni, A., *The Hard Way to Peace,* New York: Collier Books, 1962.

Gollwitzer, H., *Forderungen der Freiheit.* Aufsätze und Reden zur politischen Ethik, München: Kaiser, 1962.

Goss-Mayr, H., *Die Macht der Gewaltlosen.* Der Christ und die Revolution am Beispiel Brasiliens, Graz: Styria, 1968.

—, (ed.), *Revolution ohne Gewalt?* Christen aus Ost und West im Gespräch, Wien: Sensen Verl., 1968.

Häring, B., *La contestazione dei non violenti,* Brescia: Morcelliana, 1969.

Howe, G. - Tödt, H. E., *Frieden im wissenschaftlich technischen Zeitalter.* ökumenische Theologie und Zivilisation, Stuttgart: Kreuz, 1966.

Krippendorf, E. (ed.), *Friedensforschung,* Köln: Kiepenheuer & Witsch, 1968. (Bibl.).

Lindner, R., *Gewaltfreiheit im sozialen Konflikt,* in: *Z. ev. Ethik* 13 (1969), 89-109.

Muller, J. M., *L'évangile de la non-violence,* Paris: Fayard, 1969.

Peace through Revolution (Documentation), in: *Concilium* vol. 5 IV (1968), 75-87.

Rahner, K., *Der Friede Gottes und der Friede der Welt,* in: *Schriften,* Einsiedeln: Benziger, vol. VIII, 1967, 689-707.

Regamey, P. R. - Jolif, J. Y., *Face à la violence. Pour un statut des objecteurs de conscience,* Paris: Cerf, 1962.

Riga, P., *La Mission de la Paix,* in: *Just. Monde* IX (1967/68), 309-327.

Schmid, R., (ed.), *Aggression und Revolution.* Zumutungen des Friedens, (mit Beiträgen von R. Denker, M. Opočenský, A. van der Ziel), Stuttgart: Kohlhammer, 1968.

Schmidt, H. P., *Das biblische Zeugnis vom Frieden und die politische Verantwortung für den Frieden,* in: *Vom Frieden,* Beiträge von R. Bergius u. a., (Hannoversche Beiträge zur politischen Bildung, Bd. 4). Hannover: Jänecke, 1967, 181-208.

Schutz, R. L., *Violence des pacifiques,* Taizé: Les Presses de Taizé, 1968.

Shermon, I. S., *World Peace through Common Sense,* Poughkeepsen: The Author, 1966.

Streit um den Frieden, hg. v. W. Beck und R. Schmid, Mainz-München, Grünewald-Kaiser, 1967.

Westow, Th., *The Argument about Pacifism.* A Critical Survey of Studies in English, in: *Concilium* vol. 5, II (1966), 56-63.

Comblin, J., *Théologie de la ville,* Paris: Éd. Univ. 1968.

Coste, R., *Évangile et politique,* Paris: Aubier-Montaigne, 1968. (Bibl.).

De Clercq, B. J., *Religion, idéologie et politique,* Tournai: Castermann, 1968.

Dewart, L., *The Church and Political Conservativism,* in: *Concilium* vol. 6, IV (1968), 52-57.

Ebert, Th. - Benedict, H.-J., *Macht von unten.* Bürgerrechtsbewegung, ausserparlamentarische Opposition, Kirchenreform. Hamburg: Furche, 1969.

Gerlaud, M. - J. - Ranquet, J. G. *Église et politique,* Paris: Ouvrières, 1961.

Ermecke, G., *Christliche Politik - Utopie oder Aufgabe,* Köln: Bachem, 1966.

Faith and the World of Politics, in: *Concilium* vol. 6, IV (1968), 1-91 (special issue).

Gollwitzer, H., *Die christliche Gemeinde in der politischen Welt,* in: H. Gollwitzer, *Forderungen der Freiheit,* München: Kaiser, 1962, 3-60.

Gonzalez-Ruiz, J. M., *The Public Character of the Christian Message and of Contemporary Society,* in: *Concilium* vol. 6, IV (1967), 29-33.

Heckel, R., *Le chrétien et le pouvoir.* Légitimité, résistance, insurrection, Paris: Centurion, 1962.

Hörl, R. (ed.), *Die Politik und das Heil.* Über die öffentliche Verantwortung des Christen, Mainz: Grünewald, 1968.

Jullien, J., *Le chrétien et la politique,* Paris: Desclée & Cie, 1963.

Jung, H. G., *Befreiende Herrschaft.* Die politische Verkündigung der Herrschaft Christi, München: Kaiser, 1965. (Dissertation).

Kirche und Staat, (Festschrift für H. Kunst z. 60. Geb.), hg. v. K. Alan und W. Schneemelcher, Berlin: De Gruyter, 1967.

Maier, H., *Politische Theologie? Einwände eines Laien,* in: *Stimmen der Zeit* 183 (1969), 73-91.

Metz, J. B., *Kirche und Welt im Lichte einer « politischen Theologie »,* in: J. B. Metz, *Zur Theologie der Welt,* Mainz-München: Grünewald-Kaiser, 1968, 99-116 (french transl.: *Les rapports entre l'Église et le monde à la lumière d'une théologie politique,* in: *La théologie du renouveau,* t. II, Paris: Cerf, 1968, 33-47).

—, *« Politische Theologie » in der Diskussion,* in: *Stimmen der Zeit* 184 (184 (1969), 289-308.

Moltmann, J., *Existenzgeschichte und Weltgeschichte.* Auf dem Wege zu einer politischen Hermeneutik des Evangeliums, in:

J. Moltmann, *Perspektiven der Theologie*, München-Mainz, Kaiser-Grünewald, 1968, 128-146.

Pannenberg, W., *Die politische Dimension des Evangeliums*, in: R. Hörl, (ed.), *Die Politik und das Heil*, Mainz: Grünewald, 1968, 16-20.

Paupert, J. M., *Pour une politique évangélique*, Toulouse: Privat, 1965.

Peterson, E., *Der Monotheismus als politisches Problem*. Ein Beitrag zur Geschichte der politischen Theologie im Imperium Romanum, Leipzig: Hegner, 1935.

Peukert, H., (ed.), *Diskussion zur « Politischen Theologie »*, Mainz-München: Grünewald-Kaiser, 1969.

Rahner, K., *Theologie der Macht*, in: *Schriften*, vol. IV, Einsiedeln: Benzinger, 1964⁴, 485-508.

Rich, A., *Glaube in politischer Entscheidung*. Beiträge zur Ethik des Politischen, Zürich-Stuttg.: Zwingli, 1962.

Schlette, H. R., *Religion ist Privatsache*. Ein Beitrag zur politischen Theologie, in: *Orientierung* 33 (1969), 17-20.

Schmidt, H., *Politics and Christology*: The Historical Background, in: *Concilium* vol. 6, IV (1968), 39-45.

Schmitt, C., *Politische Theologie. Vier Kapitel zur Lehre von der Souveränität*, München: Duncker, 1934, (Leipzig, 1922).

—, *Estudios políticos. La época de la neutralidad — Teología política — El concepto de la política*, Madrid: Fax, 1941.

Schmölz, F. M., *Chance und Dilemma der politischen Ethik*, Köln: Bachem, 1966.

Die sogenannte Politisierung der Kirche. Beiträge zur Sache von H. - E. Bahr, u. a., Hamburg: Furche, 1968.

Strohm, Th., *Kirche und demokratischer Sozialismus*. Studien zur Theorie und Praxis politischer Kommunikation, München: Kaiser, 1968.

Tillich, P., *Love, Power and Justice*. Ontological Analyses and Ethical Applications, New York: Oxford Univ. Pr., 1960.

Tödt, H. E., *Theologie der Gesellschaft oder theologische Sozialethik?*, in: *Z. ev. Ethik* V (1961), 211-241.

Tucci, R., *Les aspects civils et politiques de renouveau de l'Église*, in: *La théologie du renouveau*, Paris: Cerf, 1968, vol. II, 155-164.

Was will die politische Theologie?, in: *Herderkorrespondenz* 22 (1968), 345-349.

ee. THEOLOGY OF DEVELOPMENT AND PROGRESS
(cf.: VI, 1, b).

Alfaro, J., *Hacia una teologia de progreso humano*, Barcelona: Herder, 1968, (*Teologia del progresso umano*, Assisi: Cittadella Ed., 1969).

Armendariz, L. M., *Apunte para una teologia del progreso*, in: *Fomento Social* 76 (1964), 345-362.

Aubert, J. M., *Pour une théologie du développement*. Introduction à la lecture de l'encyclique, in: *Populorum Progressio, Le développement des peuples*, Paris: Fleurus, 1968, 13-19.

Beckmann, K. M., *Ökumenische Theologie der Strukturveränderungen*, in: *Die Mitarbeit* 17 (1968), 113-125.

Bibliographie: Kirche und Entwicklungsländer, in: *Z. ev. Ethik* 14 (1970) 121-127.

Comblin, J., *Theologia do desenvolimiento*, Belo Horizonte: Movimento Familiar Cristao, 1968.

Cox, H., *Evolutionary Progress and Christian Promise*, in: *Concilium* vol. 6, III (1967), 18-23.

Cragg, K. « *The Tempter said ...* » *Reflections on Christian Theology and Development*, in: *Int. Rev. Miss.* 58 (1969), 379-389.

Development and Salvation, in: *Clergy Rev.* 54 (1969), 497-576 (special issue).

Fromm, E., *The Revolution of Hope*. Toward a Humanised Technology, New York: Harper & Row, 1968.

Houtart, Fr. - Vetrano, V. O., *Hacia una teologia del desarrollo*. Algunas reflexiones, Buenos Aires: Latino Americanos Libros, 1967.

Lachenmann, H., *Entwicklung und Endzeit*. Möglichkeiten und Grenzen einer zukünftigen Entwicklung des Menschen und der Menschheit in christlicher Sicht, Hamburg: Fr. Wittig, 1967.

Lanquetin, A., *Développement de l'homme et progrès de la foi*, Paris: Éd. S. O. S., 1968.

Laurent, P. H., *Vision chrétienne du développement*, in: *Rev. d'Action Pop.* 152 (1961), 1043-1063.

Laurentin, R., *Développement et Salut*, Paris: Seuil, 1969.

Lebret, L. J., *Pour une éthique du développement*, in: *Econ. et Hum.* 22 (1963) no. 148, 1-11.

—, *Verantwortlich für die Welt*. Der Aufstieg der Menschheit und die Christen, Graz: Styria, 1963.

Metz, J. B., *Christliche Verantwortung für die Zukunftsplanung in einer weltlichen Welt*, in: J. B. Metz, *Zur Theologie der Welt*, Mainz-München: Grünewald - Kaiser, 1968, 132-146.

Pellegrini, V., *La teologia del desarrollo*, in: *CIAS* XVI, 167 (Oct., 1967), 7-10.

Richards, M., *Toward a Theology of Development*, in: *Clergy Rev.* 544 (1969), 510-518.

Schell, H., *Der Katholizismus als Prinzip des Fortschritts*, Würzburg: Göbels, 1897.

Shriver, D. W.,*Towards a Theology of Social Change*, New York: Jewish Theol. Seminary, 1967.

Van Baelen, L., *Morale du développement*, Lyon: Mappus, 1967.

Warendorp, E., *Katholizismus als Fortschrittsprinzip?*, Bamberg: Handelsdruckerei, 1897.

Walther, Chr., *Theologie und planende Vernunft*, in:*Oekum. Rundschau* 17 (1968), 353-363.

Weber, W., *Der technisch-wirtschaftliche Fortschritt und das Heil des Menschen*, in: *Oeconomia Humana*, Köln: Bachem, 1968, 80-101.

4. CHRISTIAN ETHICS IN A CHANGING WORLD

Barry, F. R., *Christian Ethics and Secular Society*, London: Hodder & Stoughton, 1966.

Bennet, J. C., (ed.), *Christian Social Ethics in a Changing World*, (Vol. I, Church and Society Conference, 1966), New York-London: Association SCM Press., 1966.

Cox, H., *On not Leaving it to the Snake*, New York-London: Macmillan-SCM, 1968.

Curran, Sh. E., (ed.), *Absolutes in Moral Theology?*, Washington: Corpus-Books, 1968.

Diez-Alegría, J. M., *Actitudes cristianas ante los problemas sociales*, Barcelona: Estela, 1967.

Dunphy, W., (ed.), *The New Morality*. Continuity and Discontinuity, New York: Herder & Herder, 1967.

Eisenstadt, S. N., (ed.), *The Protestant Ethic and Modernization*. A Comparative View, New York-London: Basic Books, 1968.

Fletscher, J., *Situation Ethics*. The New Morality, Philadelphia: Westminster Pr., 1966.

—, *The Situation Ethics Debate*, Philadelphia: Westminster Pr., 1968.

Fuchs, J., *Secolarismo e morale cristiana*. Morale umana umanistica cristiana, Assisi: Cittad. Ed., 1968.

—, *De progressu humano. Considerationes morales*, in: *Periodica de re morali, canonica, liturgica* 58 (1969), 613-639.

Glaube und Gesellschaft. Beiträge zur Sozialethik heute, hg. von der theol. Abteilung und dem Sekretariat für soz. Verantwortung in der Abteilung Weltdienst des Luth. Weltbundes (Beiheft zur Lutherischen Rundschau), Stuttgart: Kreuz, 1966.

Gründel, J.,*Wandelbares und Unwandelbares in der Moraltheologie*, Düsseldorf: Patmos, 1967.

Hochgrebe, V., (ed.), *Christliche Verantwortung*. Eine ökumenische Bestandsaufnahme zeitgemässer Ethik, Würzburg: Arena, 1968.

Hoefnagels, H., *Erneuerung der Moral*. Soziologische Erwägungen zu einigen Tendenzen im modernen Denken, in:*Wort und Wahrheit* 21 (1966), 178-190.

Lehmann, P. L., *Ethics in a Christian Context*, New York: Harper & Row, 1963.

Manaranche, A., *Y-a-t-il une étique sociale chrétienne?*, Paris: Seuil, 1969.

Marsch, W.-D., *Christliche Ethik in der technischen Welt*, Berlin: Wichern Verlag, 1968.

Melsen, A. van, *Natural Law and Evolution*, in: *Concilium* vol. 6, III (1967), 24-29.

Milhaven, J. G. - Casey, D. J. *Introduction to the Theological Background of the New Morality*, in: *Theol. Studies* n. 2, 28 (1967), 213-244.

Norm and Context in Christian Ethics, ed. by G. H. Outka and P. Ramsey, New York: Scribner, 1968.

Obenhaus, V., *Ethics for an Industrial Age*. A Christian Inquiry, London: Wiley, 1967.

Ouwerkerk, C. A. J. van, *Gospel Morality and Human Compromise*, in: *Concilium* vol. 5, I (1965), 5-12.

Rahner, K., *Das Dynamische in der Kirche*, (Quaestio disputata, 5) Freiburg: Herder, 1965.

—, *Prinzipien und Imperative*, ib. 14-37.

Trilhaas, W., *Zwingt uns die veränderte Sozialstruktur zu einem neuen Konzept der christlichen Ethik?*, in: *Die Mitarbeit* 14 (1965), 44-54.

Verghese, P., *Righteousness and the Coming Kingdom*, in:*Ecum. Rev.* 19 (1967), 417-427.

Walgrave, J. H., *Is Morality Static or Dynamic?* in: *Concilium* vol. 5, I (1965), 13-22.

Wendland, H.-D., *Der Begriff der « verantwortlichen » Gesellschaft in seiner Bedeutung für die Sozialethik der Ökumene*, in: *Z. ev. Ethik* 9 (1965), 1-16.

Winter, G., *Elements of a Social Ethic*. Scientific and Ethical Perspectives on Social Process, New York: Macmillan, 1966.